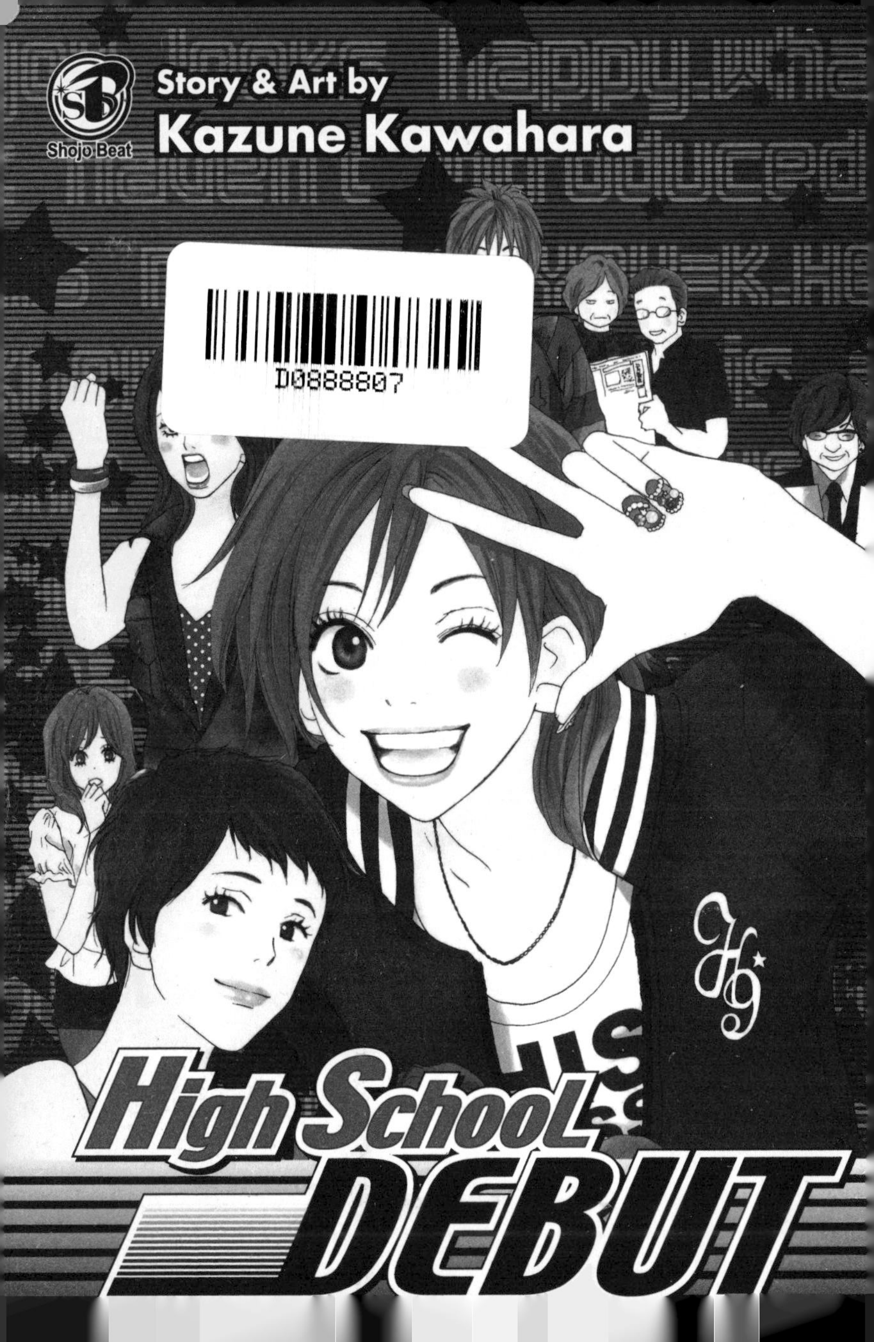
Shojo Beat
Story & Art by
Kazune Kawahara
High School
DEBUT

High School DEBUT

★★ Contents

Story Thus Far...

High school student Haruna used to spend all her time playing softball in junior high, but now she wants to give her all to finding true love instead! While her "love coach" Yoh is training her on how to be popular with guys, the two of them start dating.

It's the summer of Haruna's second year, and Yoh is preparing to take his university entrance exams. At the prep classes he's taking, he meets a strange girl who immediately accuses him of thinking that all girls like him. Later, she learns that Haruna is Yoh's girlfriend and starts being mean to her!

This strange girl turns out to be the sister of Akito Jyoho, a boy that Haruna helped out during the entrance ceremony. According to Akito, his sister has always had a complex about her looks ever since she was little. Akito warns Haruna that his sister is planning something weird, so Haruna sneaks into the prep school. All of a sudden, she sees Yoh smiling at Akito's sister...!

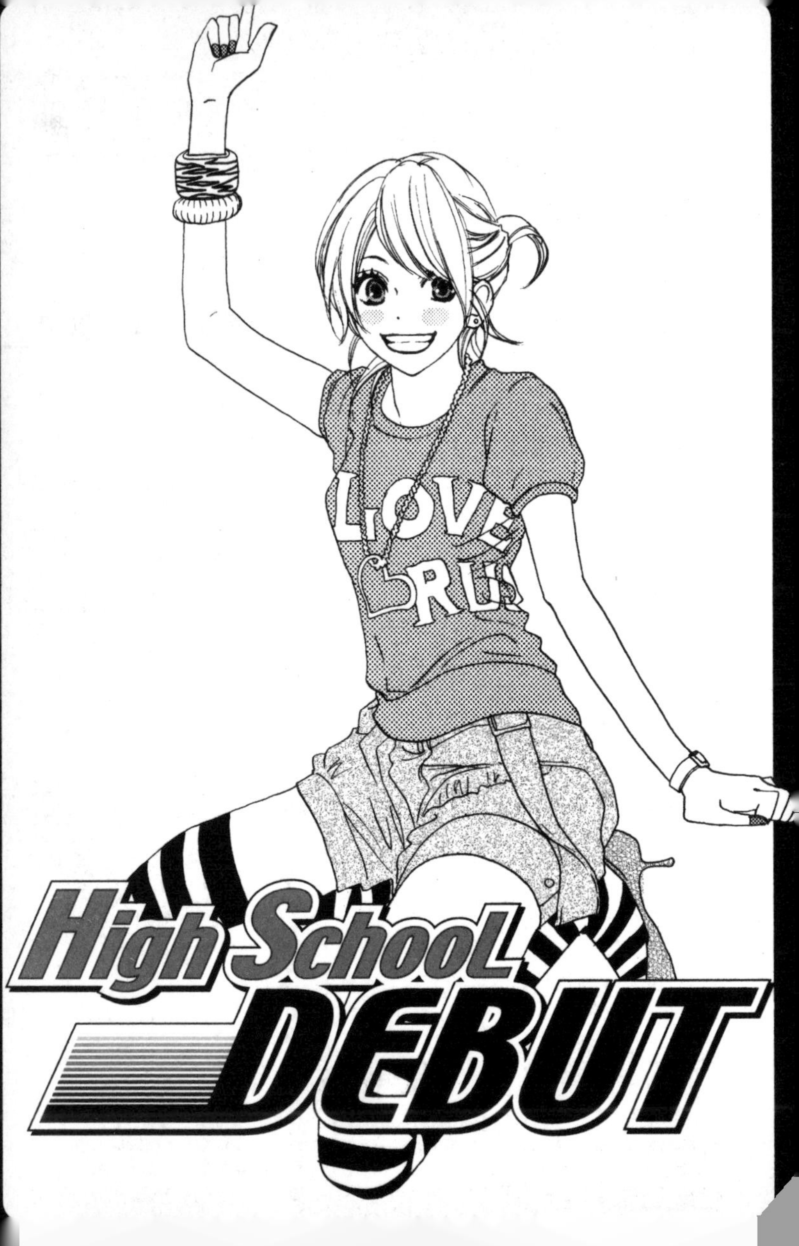
LOVE
High School
DEBUT

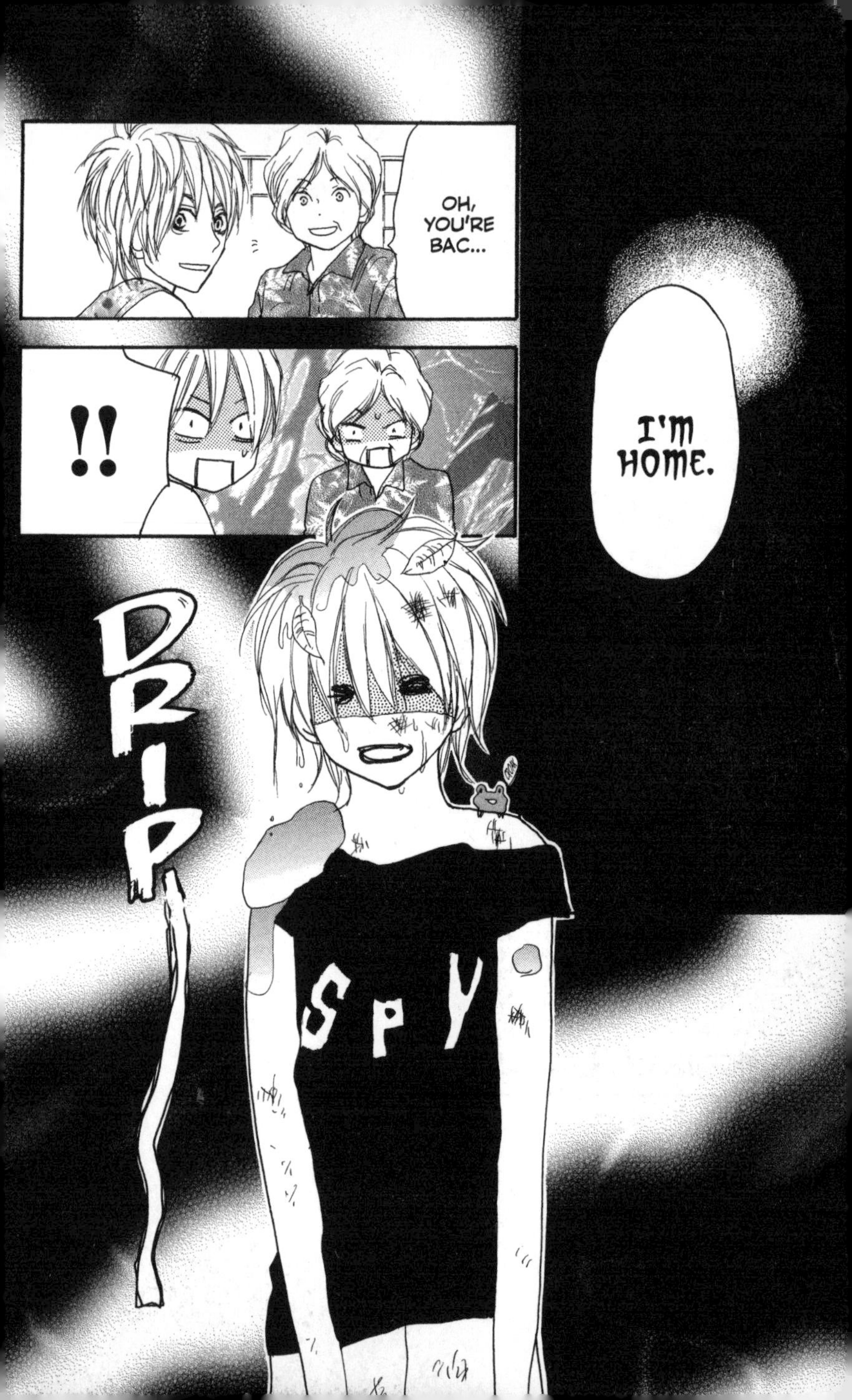
OH, YOU'RE BAC...
!!
I'M HOME.
DRIP

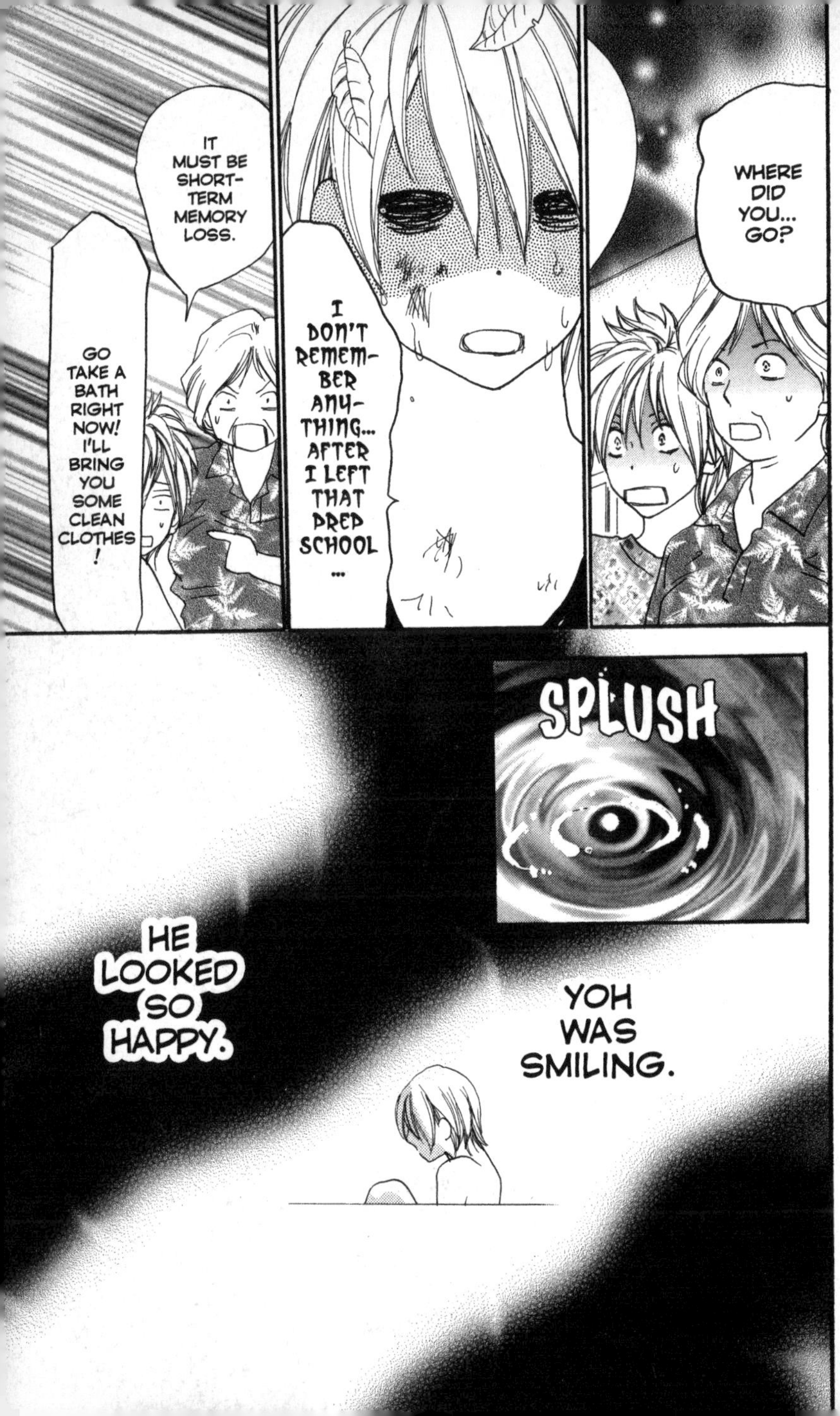
WHERE DID YOU... GO?
I DON'T REMEMBER ANYTHING... AFTER I LEFT THAT PREP SCHOOL...
IT MUST BE SHORT-TERM MEMORY LOSS.
GO TAKE A BATH RIGHT NOW! I'LL BRING YOU SOME CLEAN CLOTHES!
SPLUSH
YOH WAS SMILING.
HE LOOKED SO HAPPY.

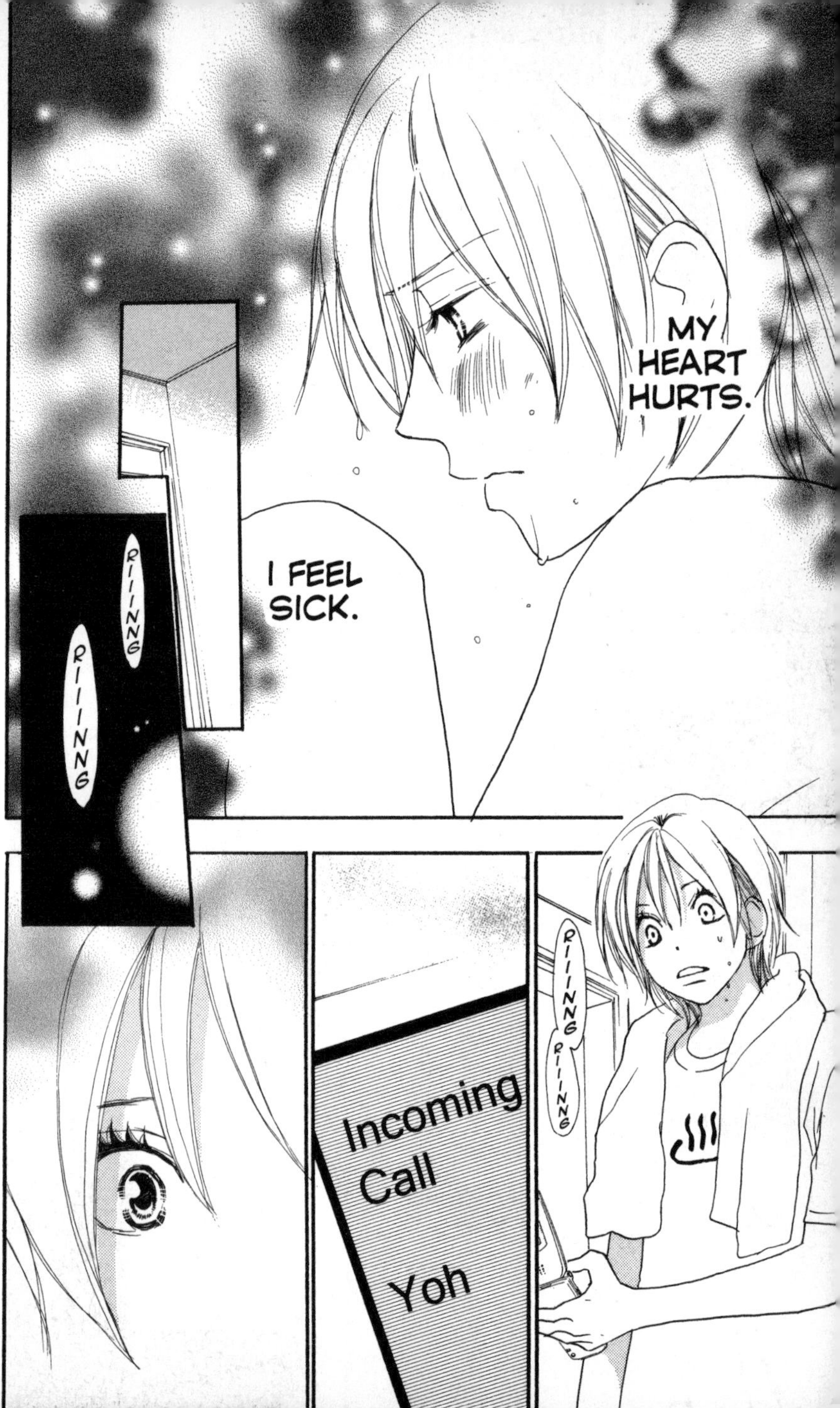
MY HEART HURTS.
I FEEL SICK.
RIIIINNG
RIIIINNG
RIIIINNG
RIIIINNG
Incoming Call
Yoh

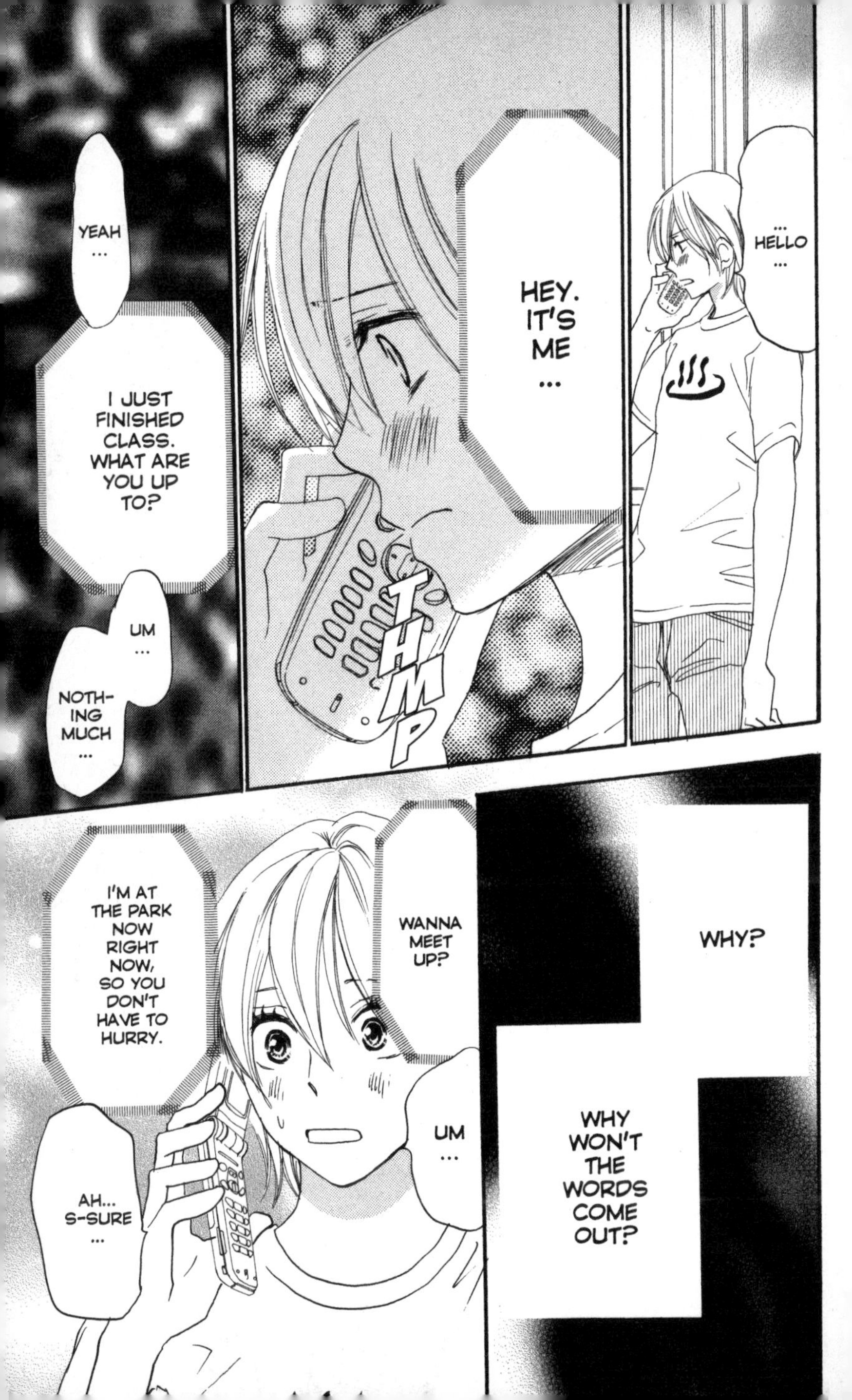
... HELLO ...
HEY. IT'S ME ...
THMP
YEAH ...
I JUST FINISHED CLASS. WHAT ARE YOU UP TO?
UM ...
NOTH-ING MUCH ...
WHY?
WHY WON'T THE WORDS COME OUT?
WANNA MEET UP?
UM ...
I'M AT THE PARK NOW RIGHT NOW, SO YOU DON'T HAVE TO HURRY.
AH... S-SURE ...

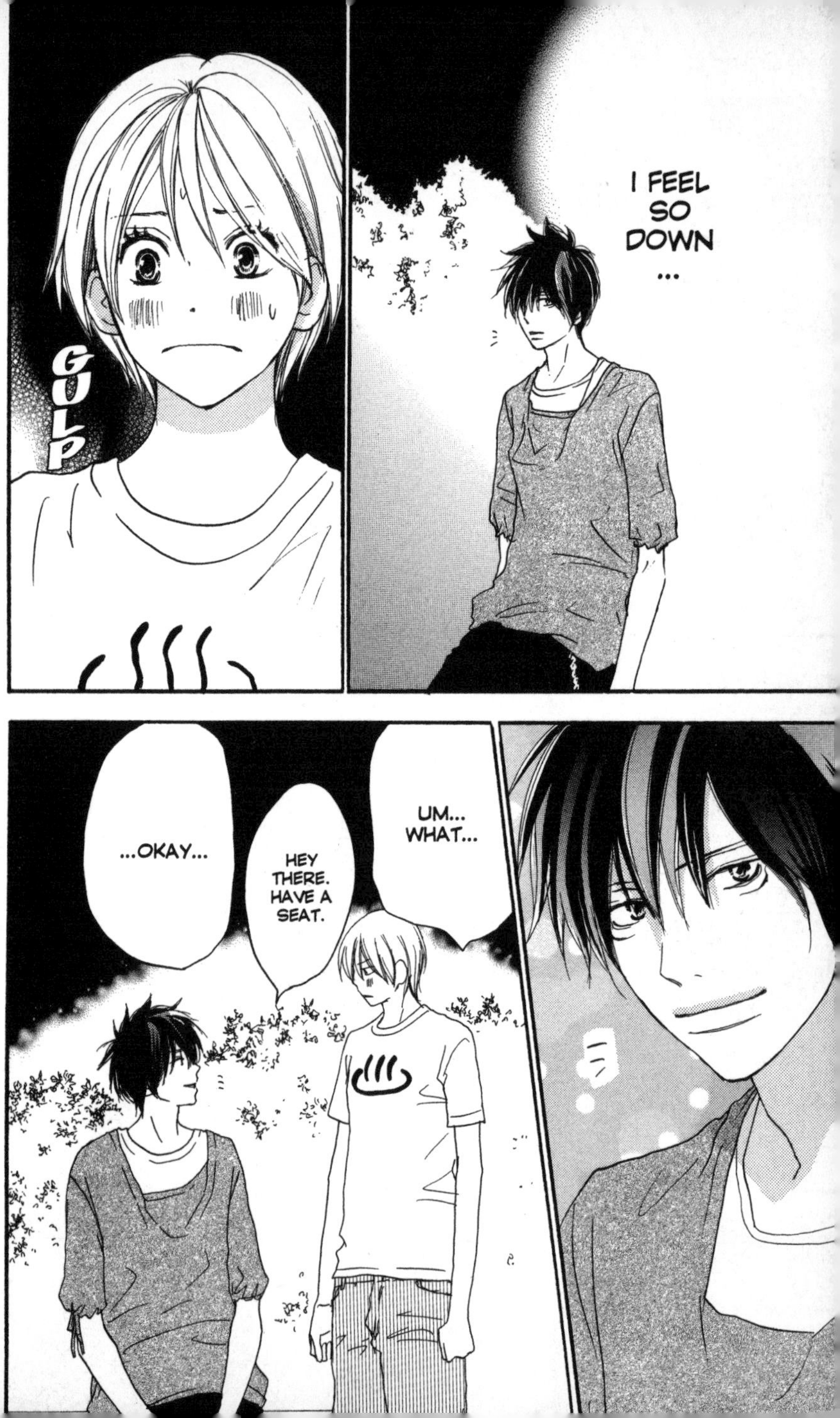
I FEEL SO DOWN ...
GULP
UM... WHAT...
HEY THERE. HAVE A SEAT.
...OKAY...

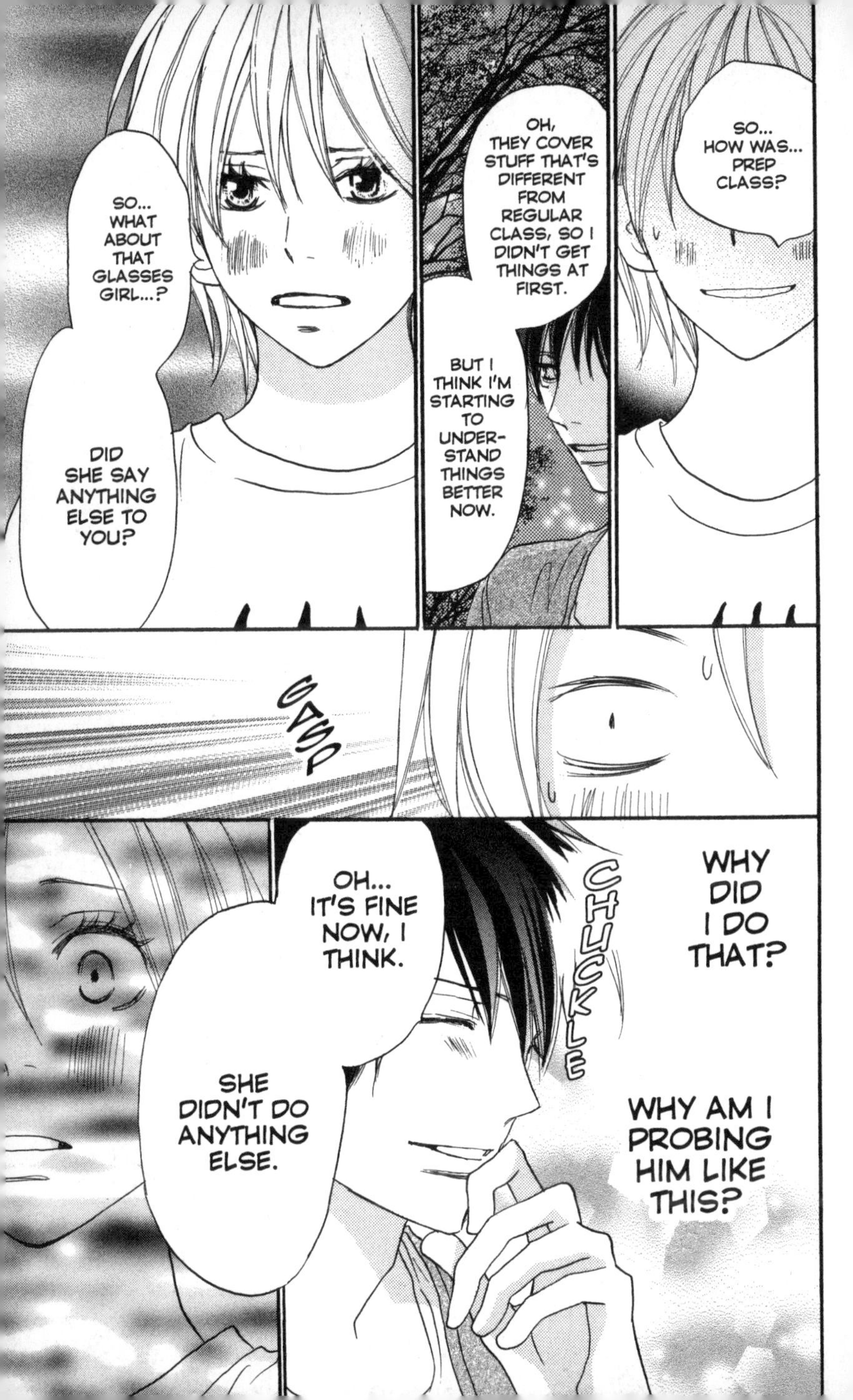
SO... HOW WAS... PREP CLASS?
OH, THEY COVER STUFF THAT'S DIFFERENT FROM REGULAR CLASS, SO I DIDN'T GET THINGS AT FIRST.
BUT I THINK I'M STARTING TO UNDER-STAND THINGS BETTER NOW.
SO... WHAT ABOUT THAT GLASSES GIRL...?
DID SHE SAY ANYTHING ELSE TO YOU?
GASP
WHY DID I DO THAT?
CHUCKLE
OH... IT'S FINE NOW, I THINK.
WHY AM I PROBING HIM LIKE THIS?
SHE DIDN'T DO ANYTHING ELSE.

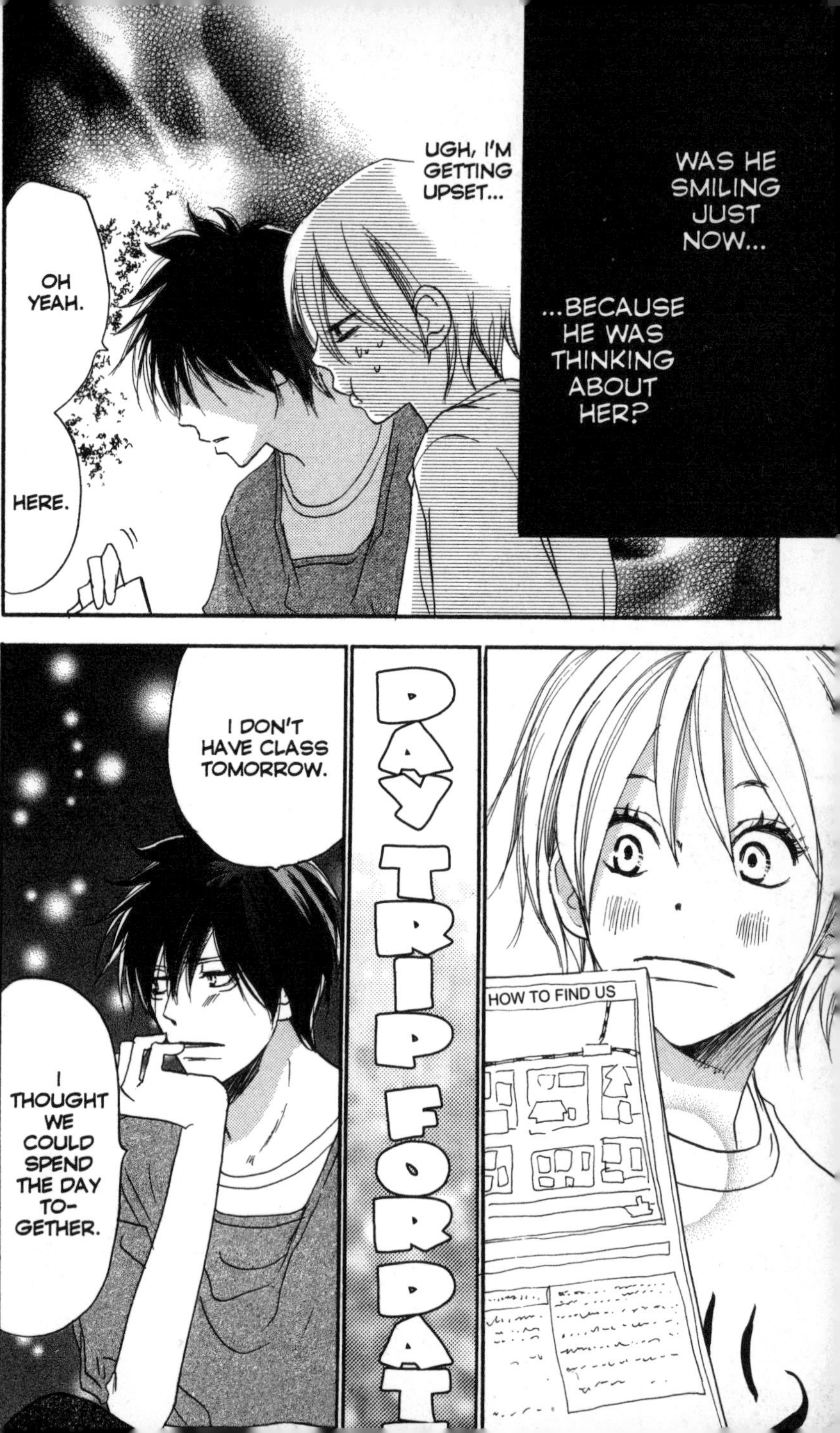
WAS HE SMILING JUST NOW...
...BECAUSE HE WAS THINKING ABOUT HER?
UGH, I'M GETTING UPSET...
OH YEAH.
HERE.
HOW TO FIND US
DAY TRIP FOR DAT
I DON'T HAVE CLASS TOMORROW.
I THOUGHT WE COULD SPEND THE DAY TO-GETHER.

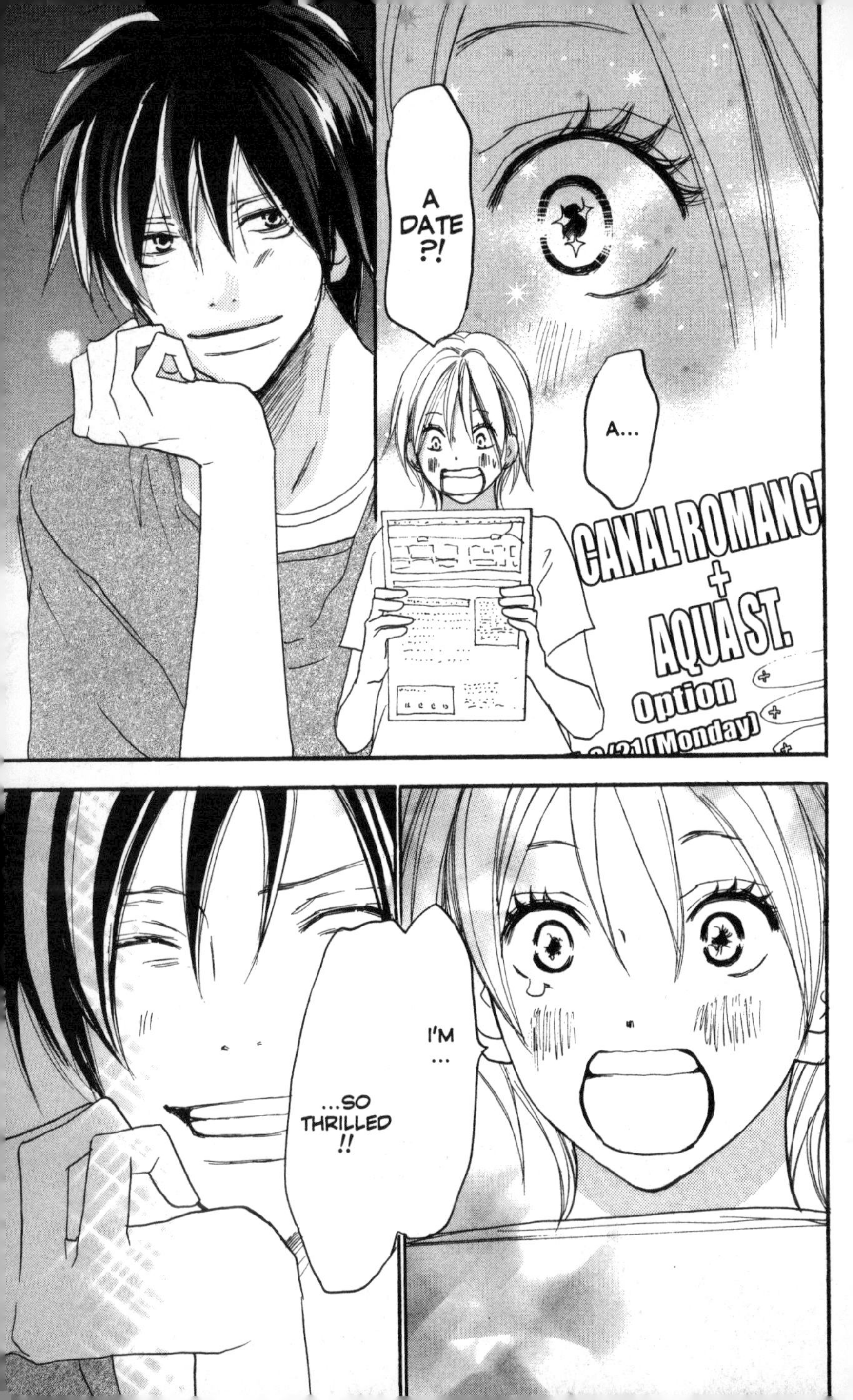
A DATE ?!
A...
CANAL ROMANC
+
AQUA ST.
Option
/21 (Monday)
I'M ...
...SO THRILLED !!

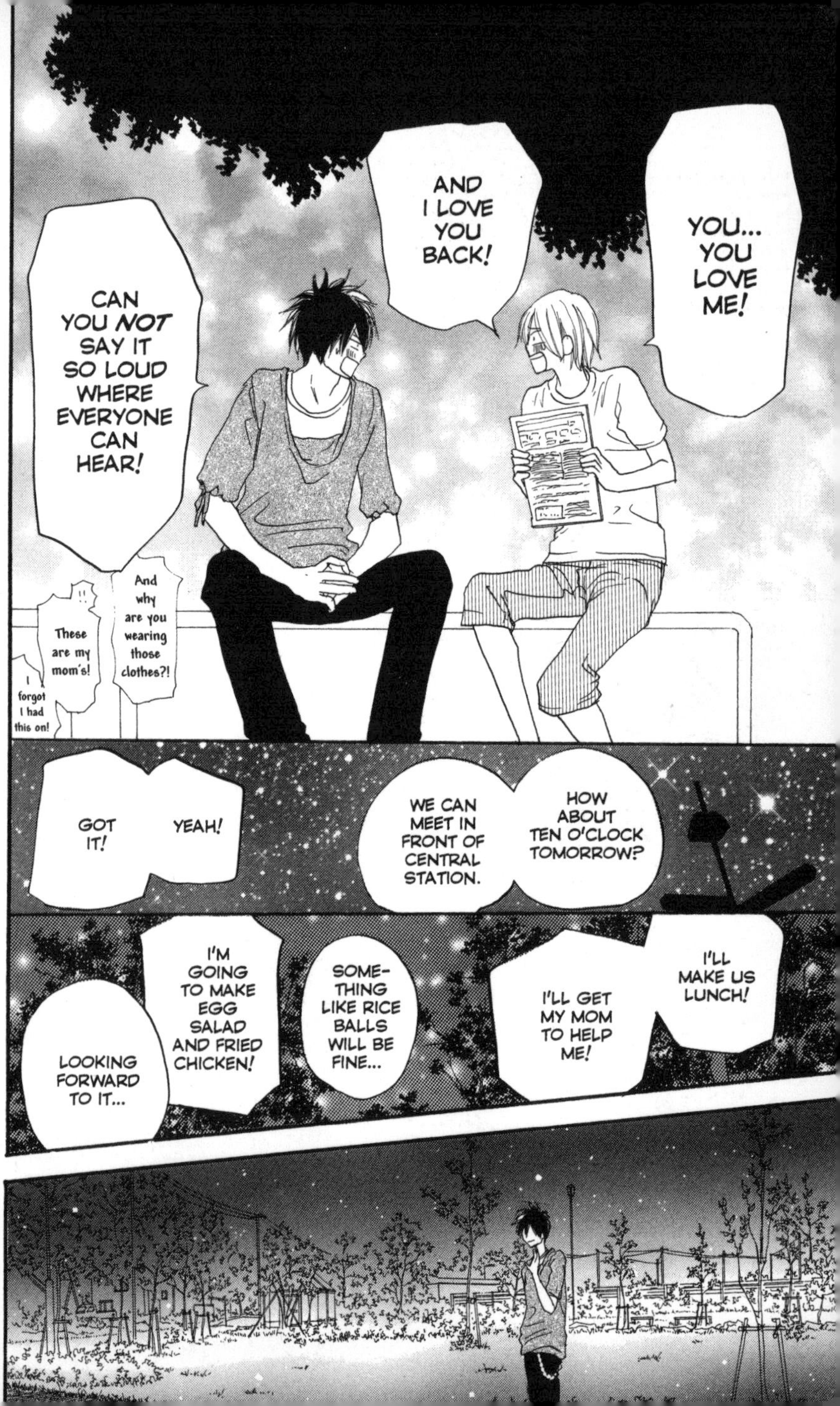
YOU... YOU LOVE ME!
AND I LOVE YOU BACK!
CAN YOU *NOT* SAY IT SO LOUD WHERE EVERYONE CAN HEAR!
And why are you wearing those clothes?!
These are my mom's!
I forgot I had this on!
HOW ABOUT TEN O'CLOCK TOMORROW?
WE CAN MEET IN FRONT OF CENTRAL STATION.
YEAH!
GOT IT!
I'LL MAKE US LUNCH!
I'LL GET MY MOM TO HELP ME!
SOME-THING LIKE RICE BALLS WILL BE FINE...
I'M GOING TO MAKE EGG SALAD AND FRIED CHICKEN!
LOOKING FORWARD TO IT...

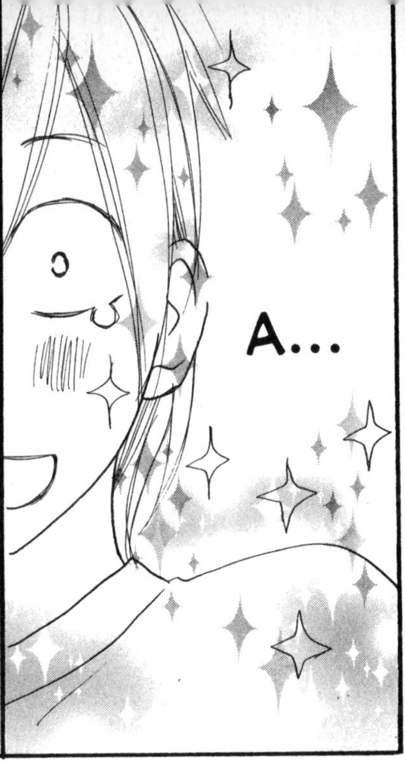
A...

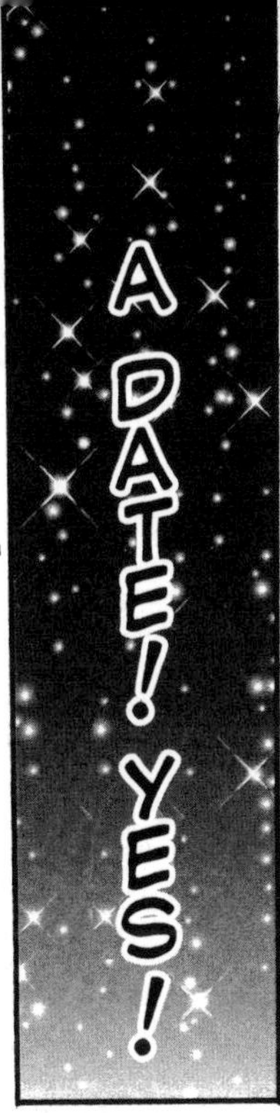
A DATE! YES!

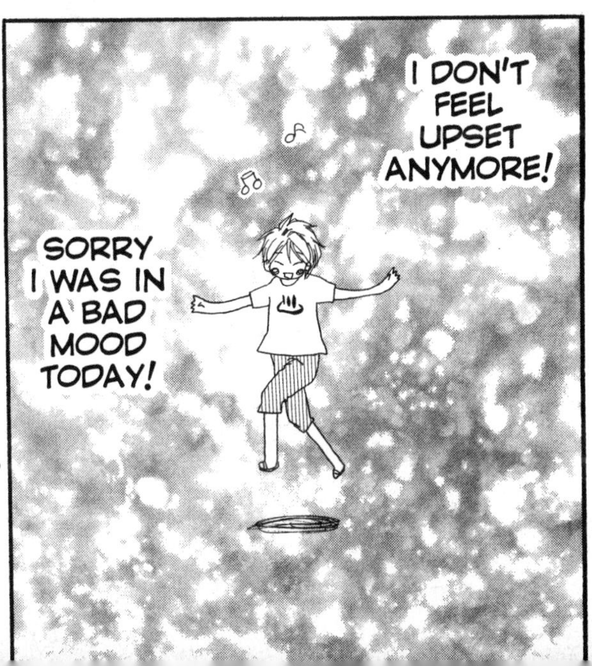
I DON'T FEEL UPSET ANYMORE!
SORRY I WAS IN A BAD MOOD TODAY!

1

I went to New Zealand with my friend and my kid. I don't even speak English! I haven't even traveled much in Japan! However, we didn't go with a tour group because we have a friend in Christchurch. I got off the first plane in a relaxed manner, but...

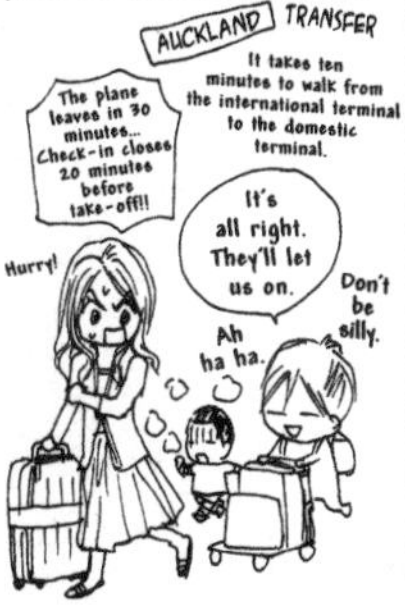
AUCKLAND TRANSFER
It takes ten minutes to walk from the international terminal to the domestic terminal.
The plane leaves in 30 minutes... Check-in closes 20 minutes before take-off!!
It's all right. They'll let us on.
Hurry!
Don't be silly.
Ah ha ha.

We were late for our connecting flight and got scolded.

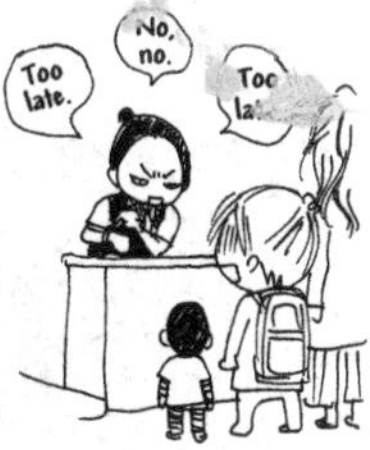
Too late.
No, no.

Some of the nice New Zealanders tried to talk to us.

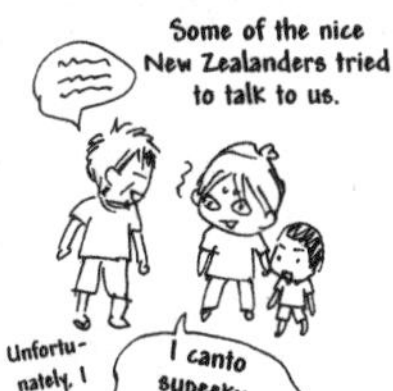
I canto supeeku Engulishu!!
Unfortunately, I couldn't say much back.

I couldn't get the pronunciation right. No one could understand me. I really wanted to speak English, so I bought an English training game for my Nintendo DS when I got home.

I'm still not doing that well, but I hope I improve soon.

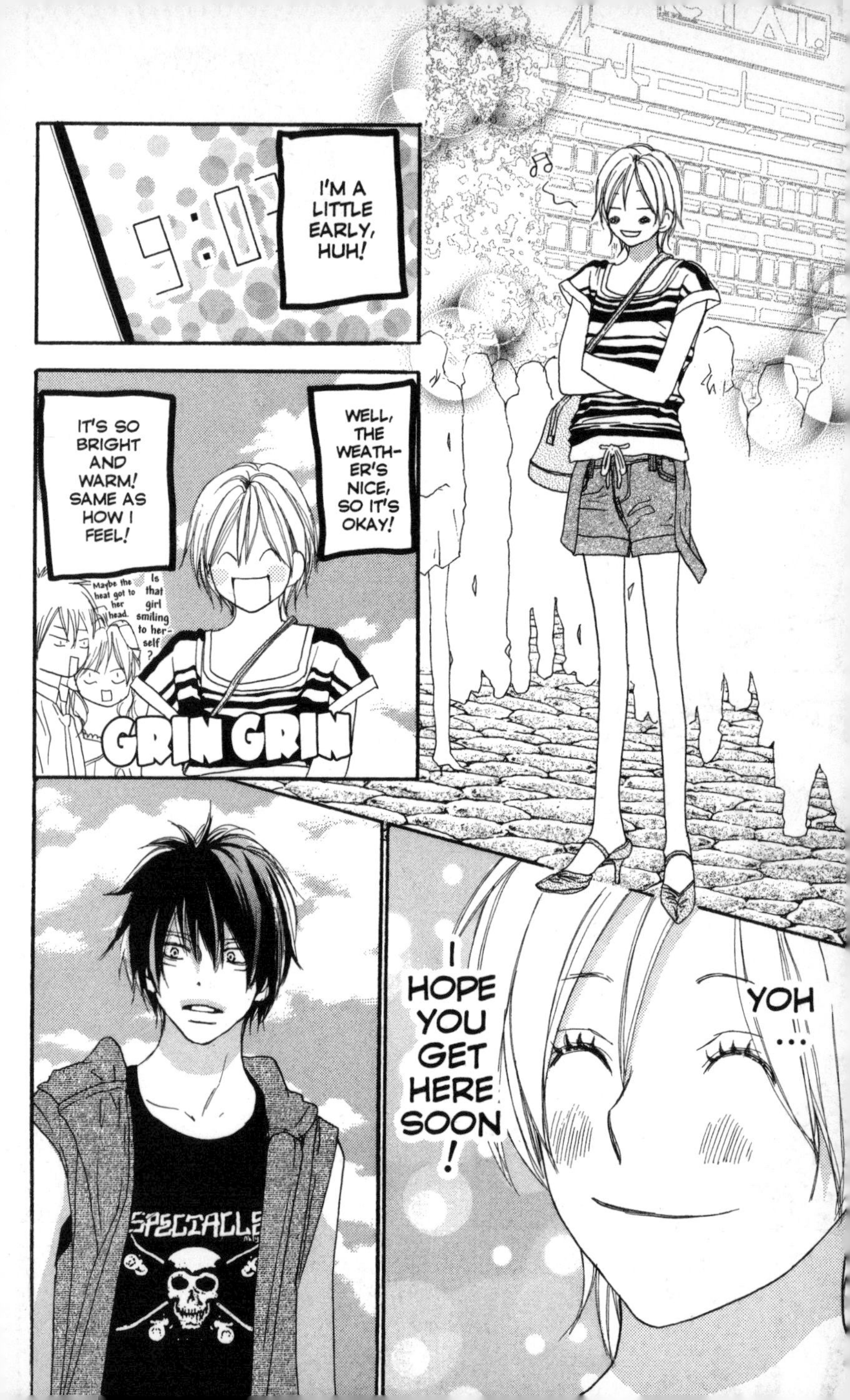
I'M A LITTLE EARLY, HUH!
WELL, THE WEATHER'S NICE, SO IT'S OKAY!
IT'S SO BRIGHT AND WARM! SAME AS HOW I FEEL!
Is that girl smiling to herself?
Maybe the heat got to her head.
GRIN GRIN
YOH...
I HOPE YOU GET HERE SOON!

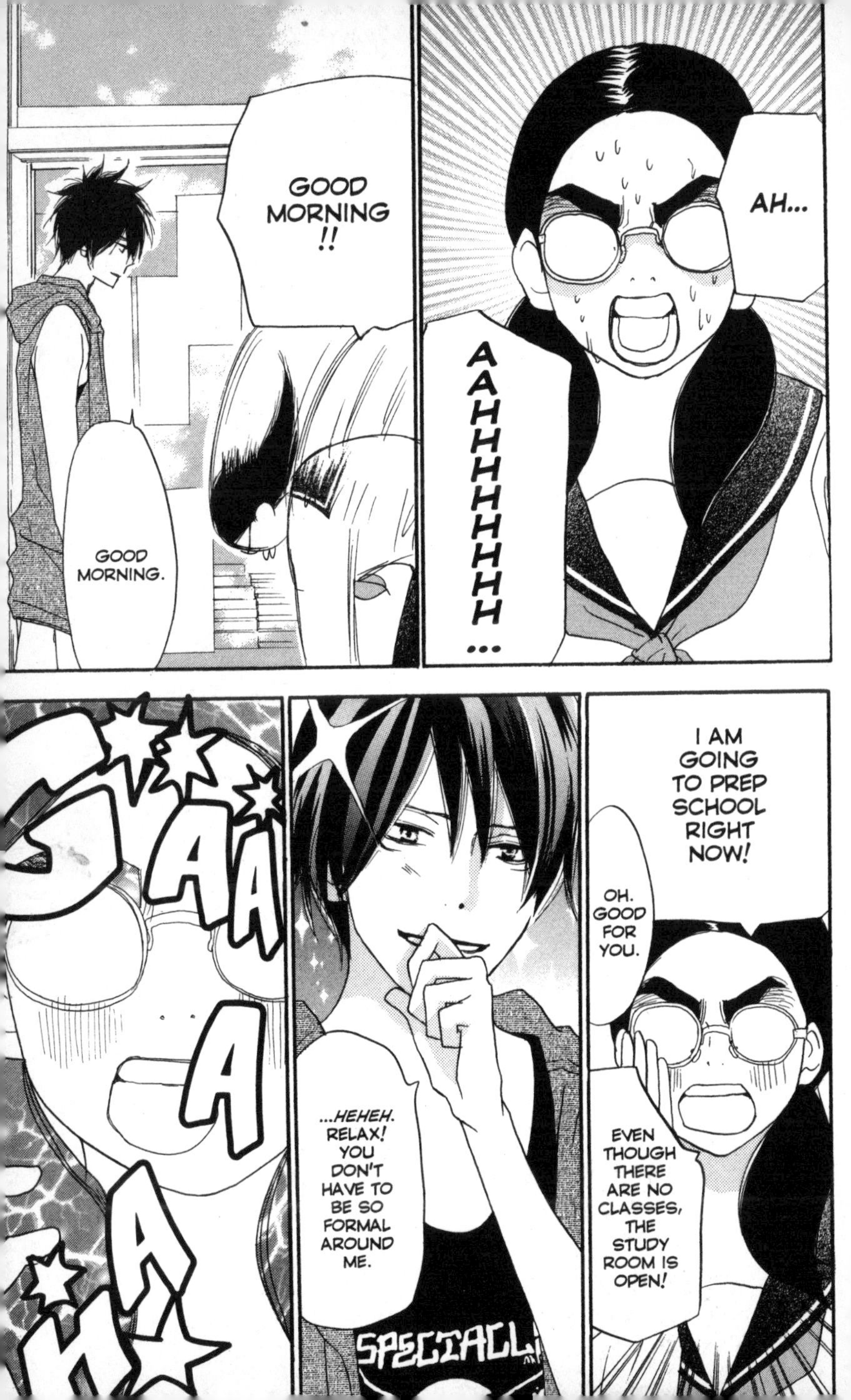
AH...
AAHHHHHHHH...
GOOD MORNING!!
GOOD MORNING.
I AM GOING TO PREP SCHOOL RIGHT NOW!
OH. GOOD FOR YOU.
EVEN THOUGH THERE ARE NO CLASSES, THE STUDY ROOM IS OPEN!
...HEHEH. RELAX! YOU DON'T HAVE TO BE SO FORMAL AROUND ME.

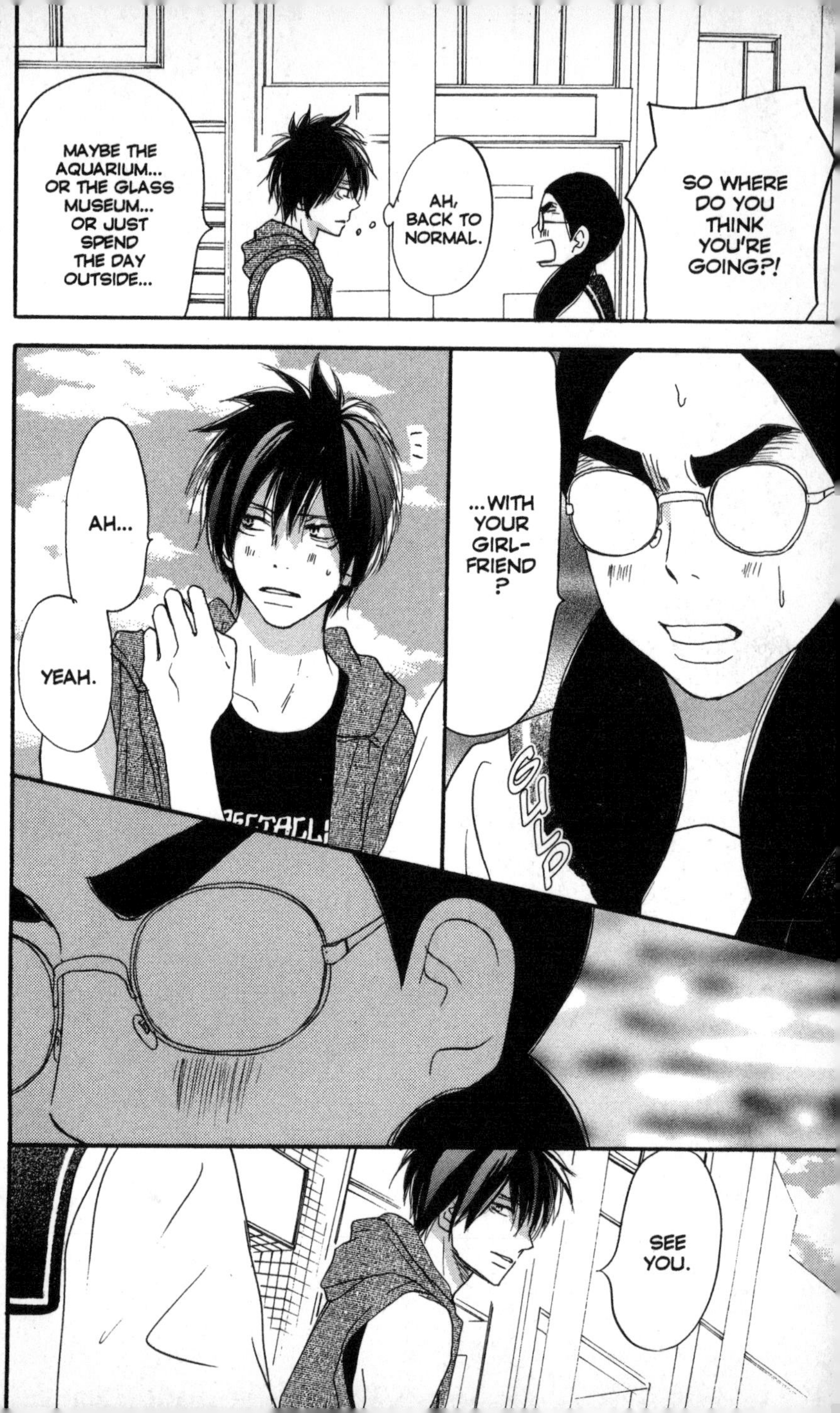
SO WHERE DO YOU THINK YOU'RE GOING?!
AH, BACK TO NORMAL.
MAYBE THE AQUARIUM... OR THE GLASS MUSEUM... OR JUST SPEND THE DAY OUTSIDE...
...WITH YOUR GIRL-FRIEND?
GULP
AH...
YEAH.
SEE YOU.

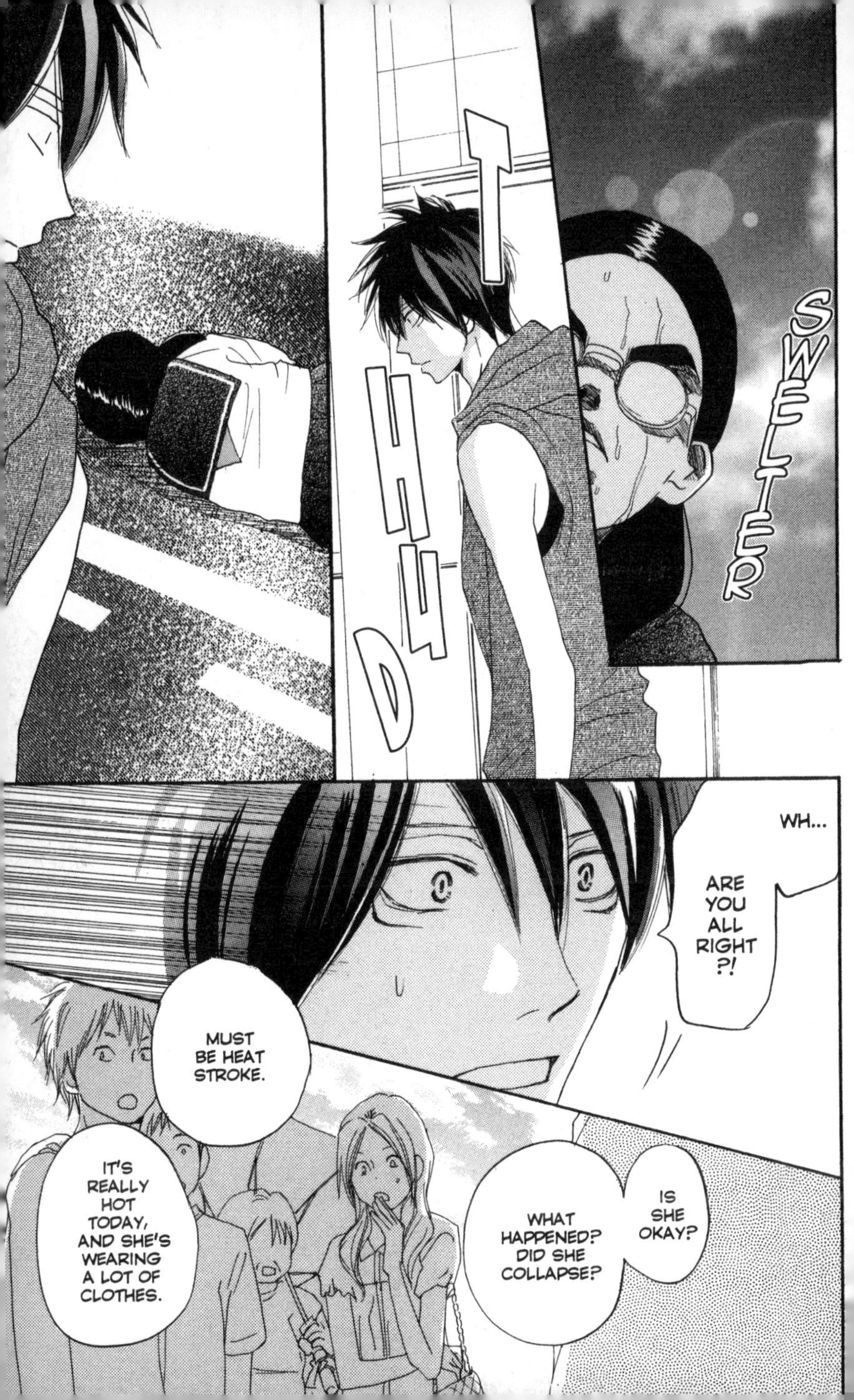
SWELTER
THUD
WH...
ARE YOU ALL RIGHT?!
IS SHE OKAY?
WHAT HAPPENED? DID SHE COLLAPSE?
MUST BE HEAT STROKE.
IT'S REALLY HOT TODAY, AND SHE'S WEARING A LOT OF CLOTHES.

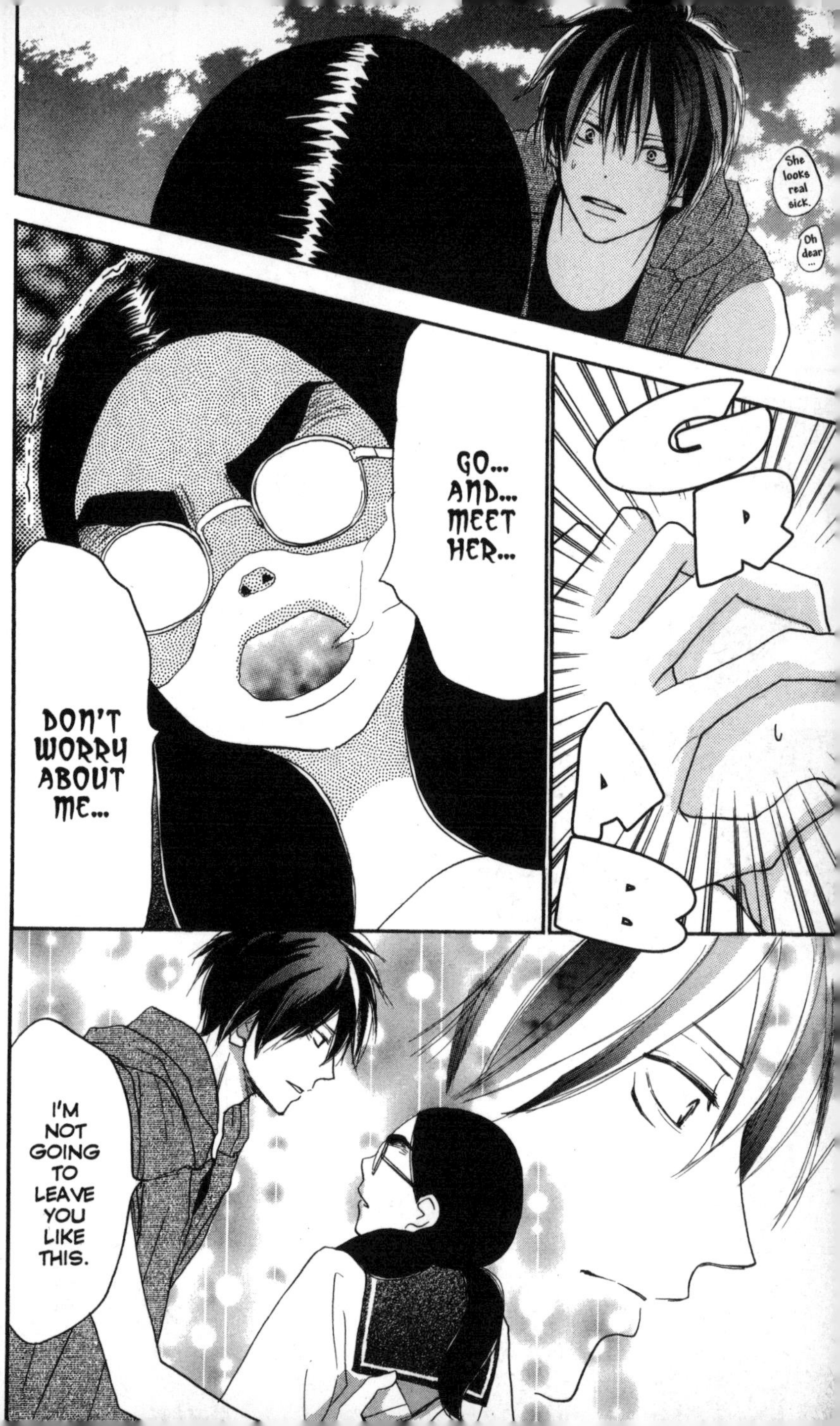
She looks real sick.
Oh dear ...
GRAB
GO... AND... MEET HER...
DON'T WORRY ABOUT ME...
I'M NOT GOING TO LEAVE YOU LIKE THIS.

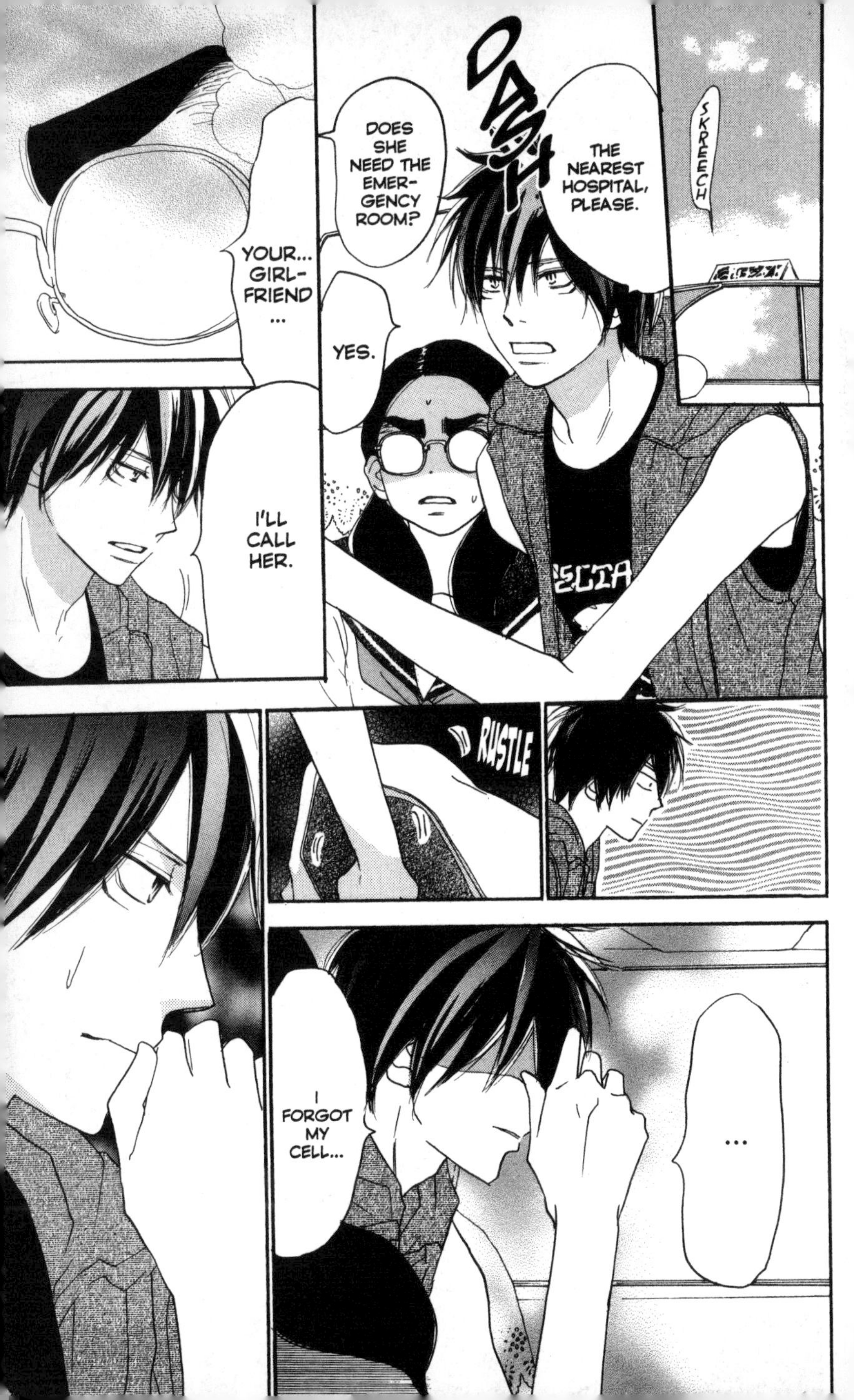
SKREECH
DASH
THE NEAREST HOSPITAL, PLEASE.
DOES SHE NEED THE EMERGENCY ROOM?
YES.
YOUR... GIRLFRIEND ...
I'LL CALL HER.
RUSTLE
...
I FORGOT MY CELL...

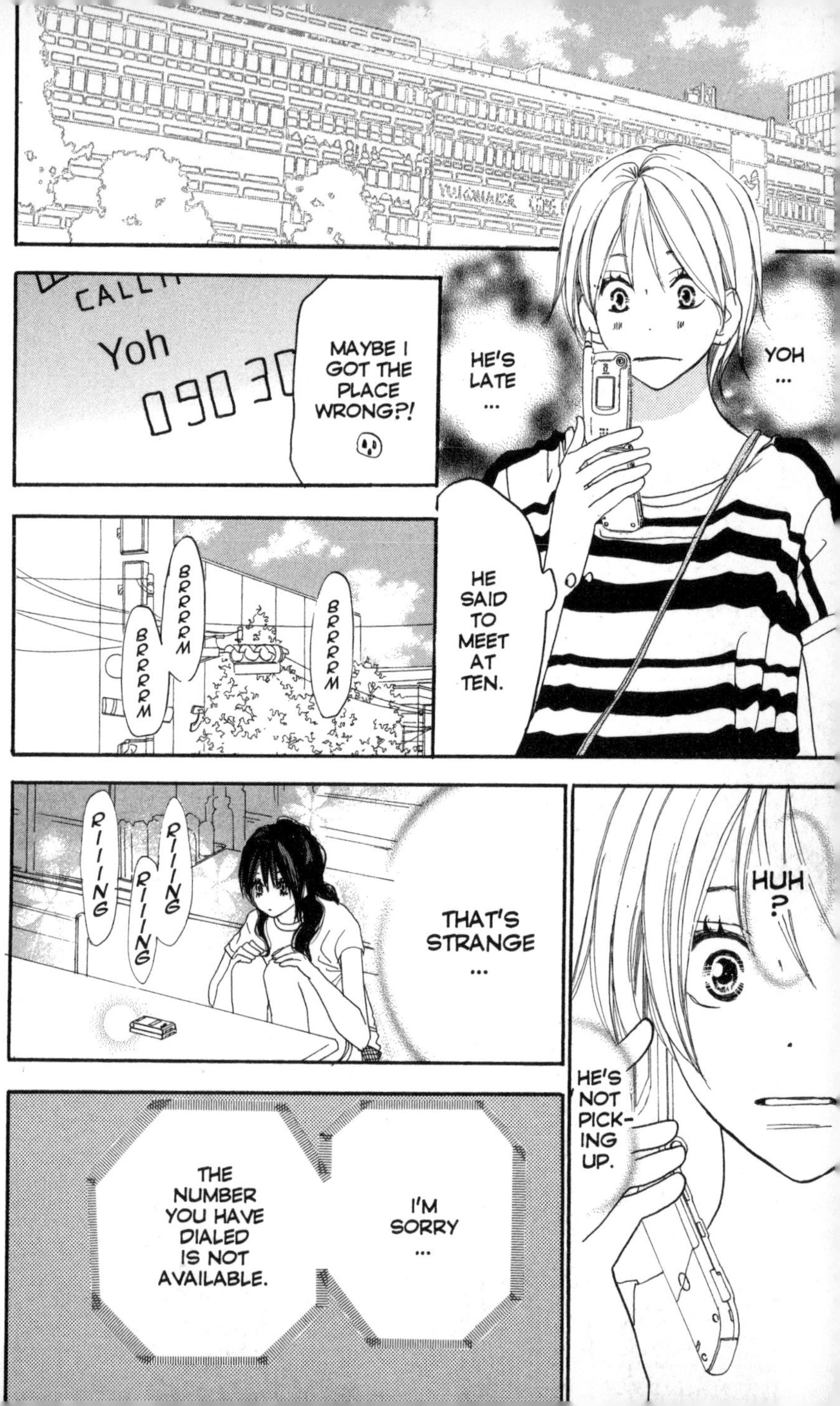
YOH ...
HE'S LATE ...
HE SAID TO MEET AT TEN.
CALL
Yoh
090 30
MAYBE I GOT THE PLACE WRONG?!
BRRRRM
BRRRRM
BRRRRM
HUH?
HE'S NOT PICKING UP.
THAT'S STRANGE ...
RIIING
RIIING
RIIING
I'M SORRY ...
THE NUMBER YOU HAVE DIALED IS NOT AVAILABLE.

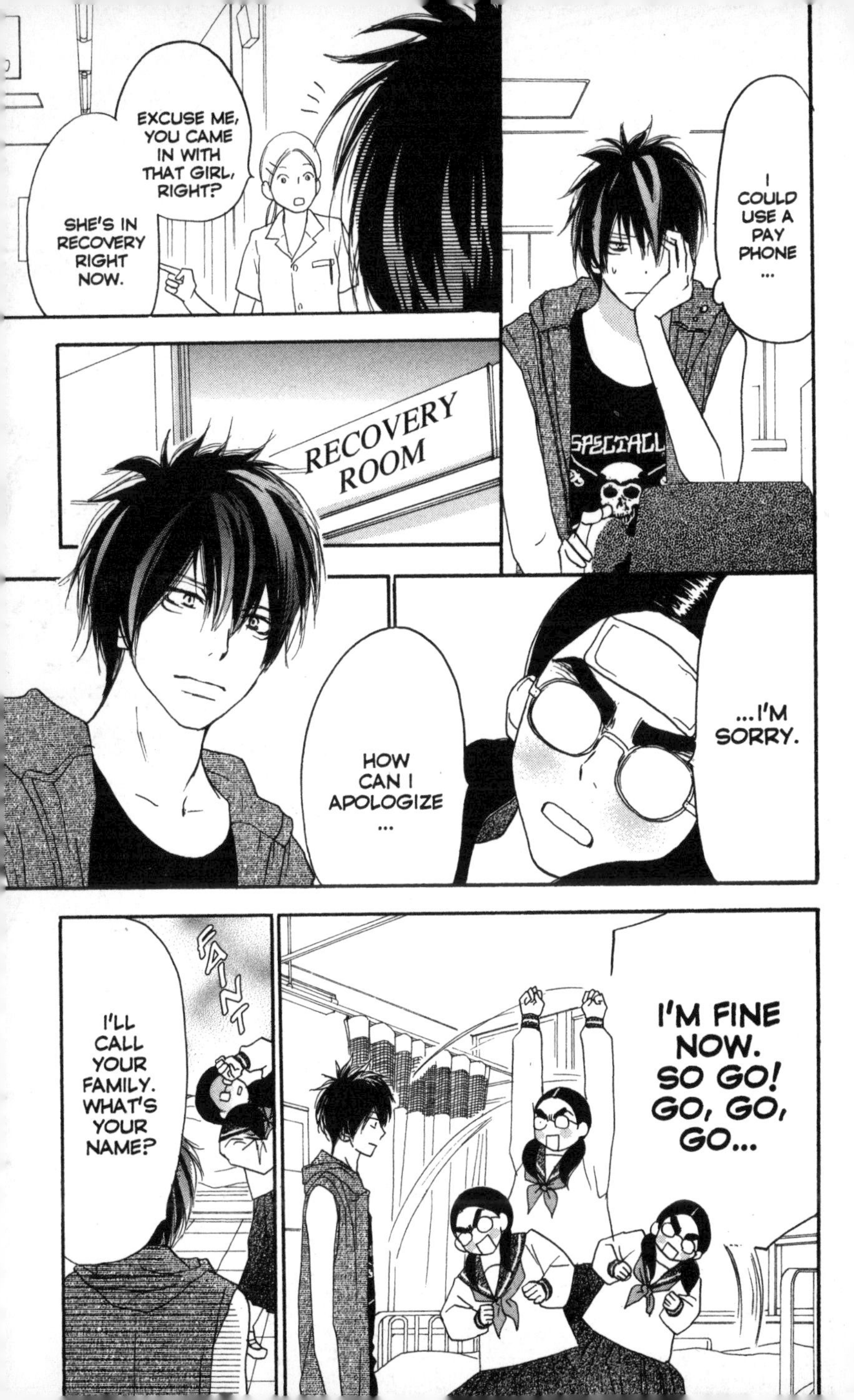
I COULD USE A PAY PHONE ...
EXCUSE ME, YOU CAME IN WITH THAT GIRL, RIGHT?
SHE'S IN RECOVERY RIGHT NOW.
RECOVERY ROOM
...I'M SORRY.
HOW CAN I APOLOGIZE ...
I'M FINE NOW. SO GO! GO, GO, GO...
I'LL CALL YOUR FAMILY. WHAT'S YOUR NAME?

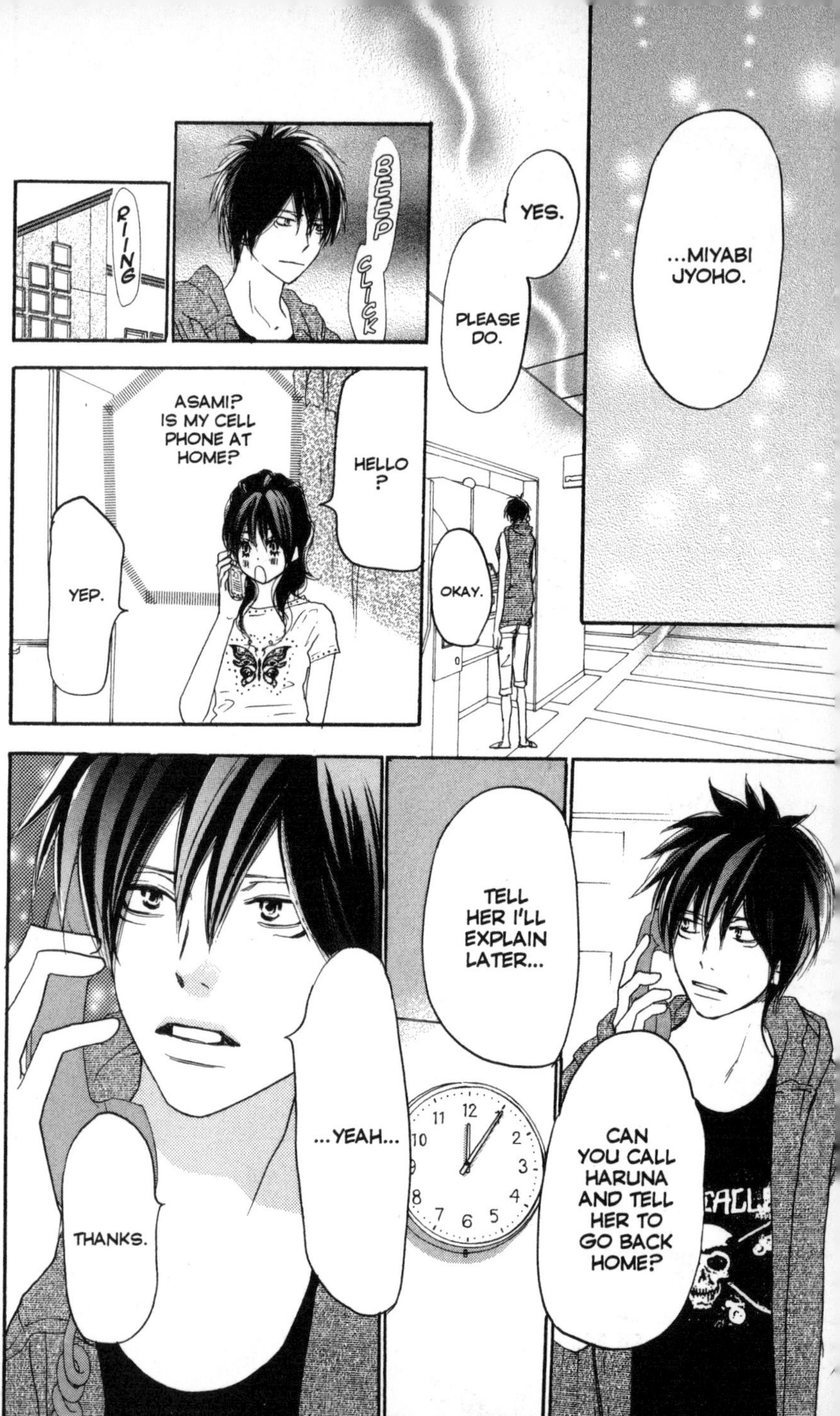
...MIYABI JYOHO.
YES.
PLEASE DO.
BEEP CLICK
RIIING
HELLO?
ASAMI? IS MY CELL PHONE AT HOME?
YEP.
OKAY.
CAN YOU CALL HARUNA AND TELL HER TO GO BACK HOME?
TELL HER I'LL EXPLAIN LATER...
...YEAH...
THANKS.

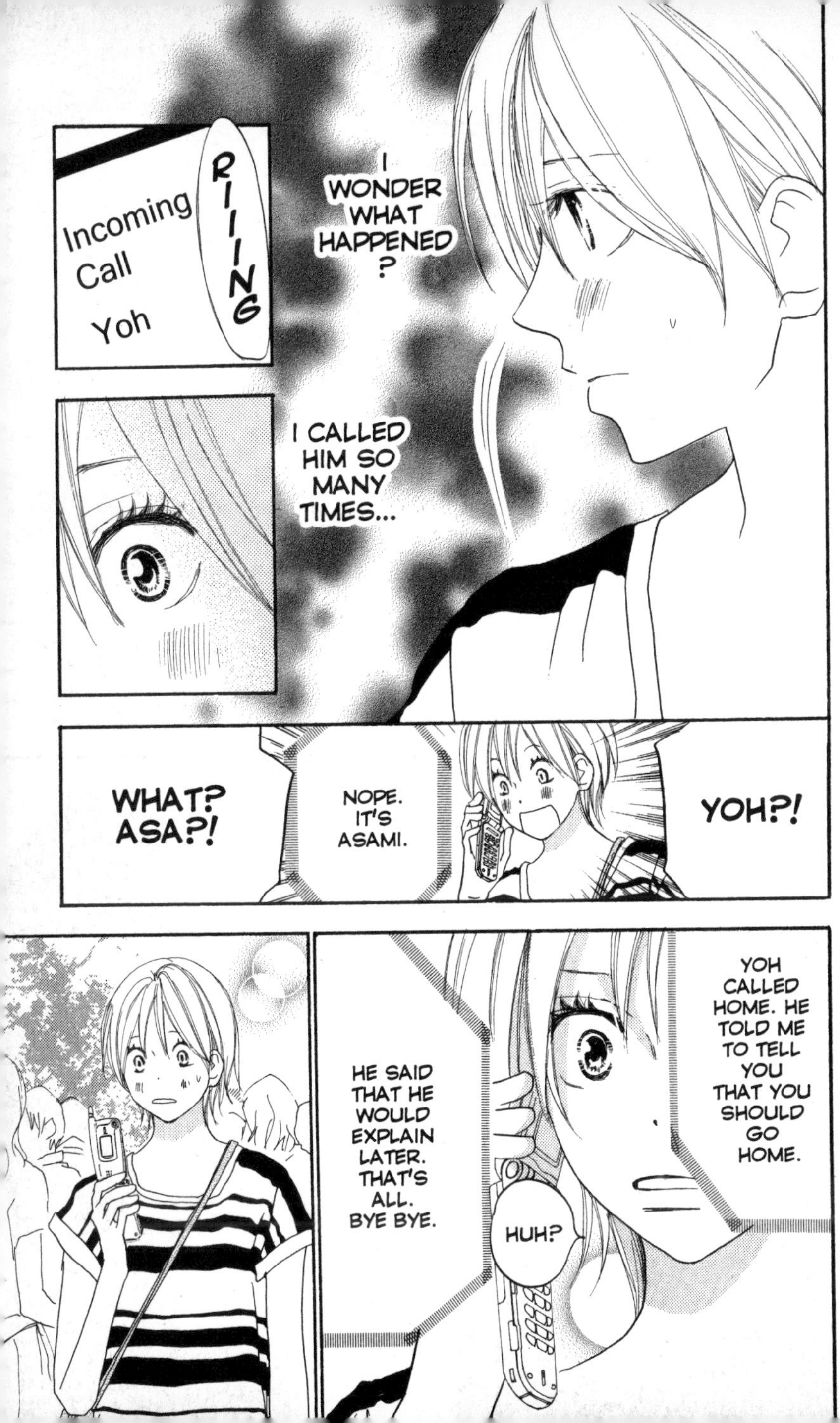
I WONDER WHAT HAPPENED?
I CALLED HIM SO MANY TIMES...
Incoming Call Yoh
RIIING
YOH?!
NOPE. IT'S ASAMI.
WHAT? ASA?!
YOH CALLED HOME. HE TOLD ME TO TELL YOU THAT YOU SHOULD GO HOME.
HUH?
HE SAID THAT HE WOULD EXPLAIN LATER. THAT'S ALL. BYE BYE.

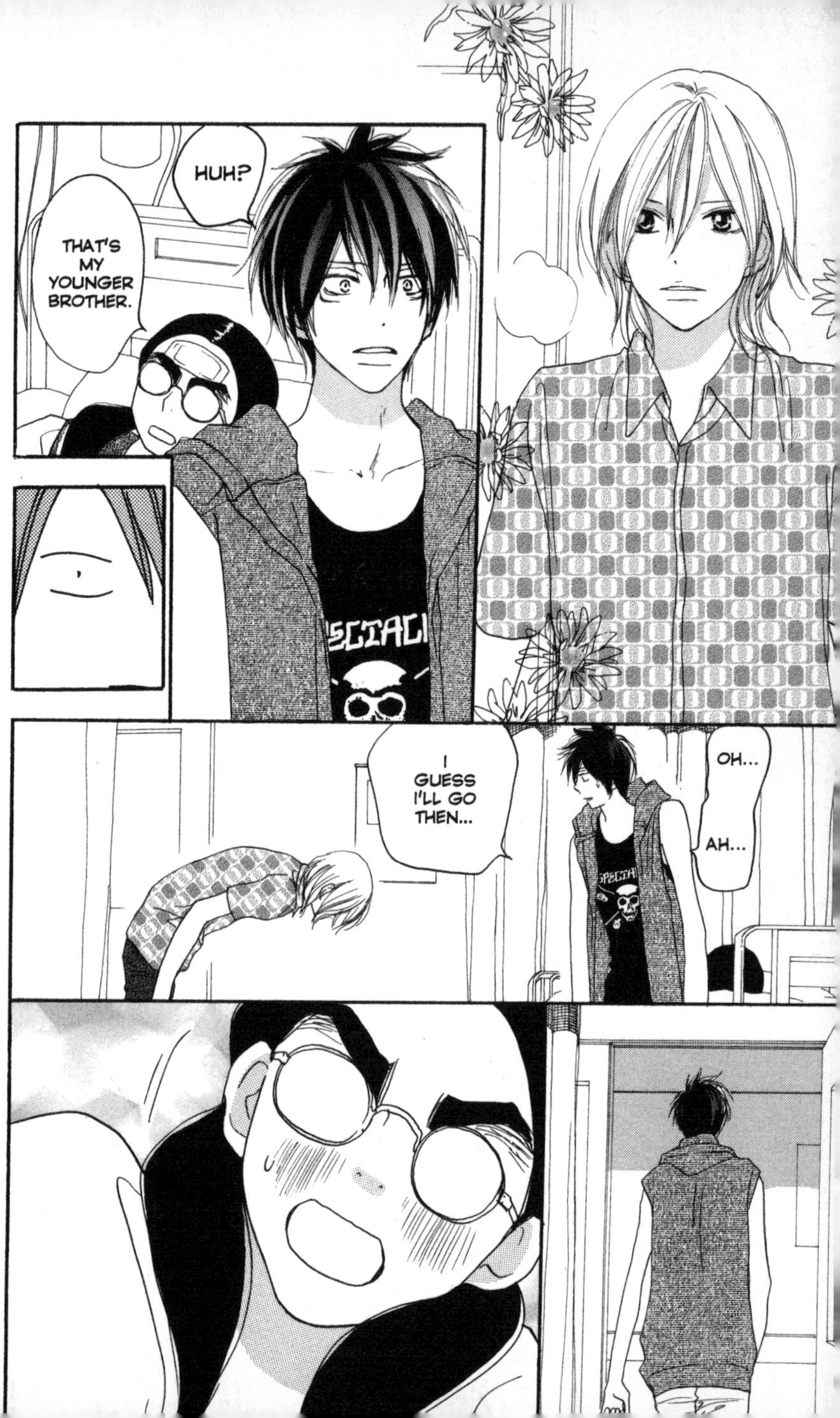
HUH?
THAT'S MY YOUNGER BROTHER.
OH...
AH...
I GUESS I'LL GO THEN...

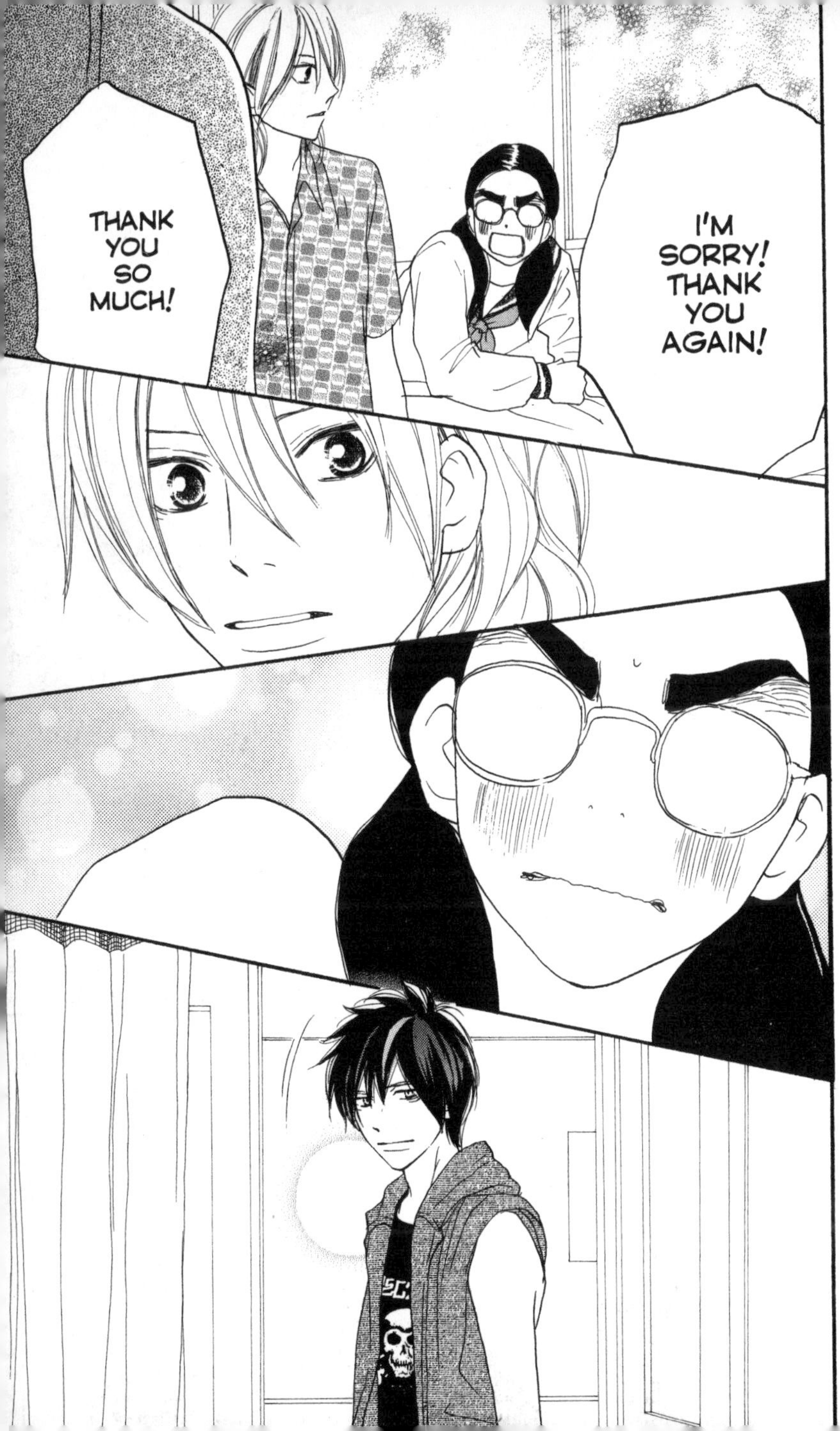
I'M SORRY! THANK YOU AGAIN!
THANK YOU SO MUCH!

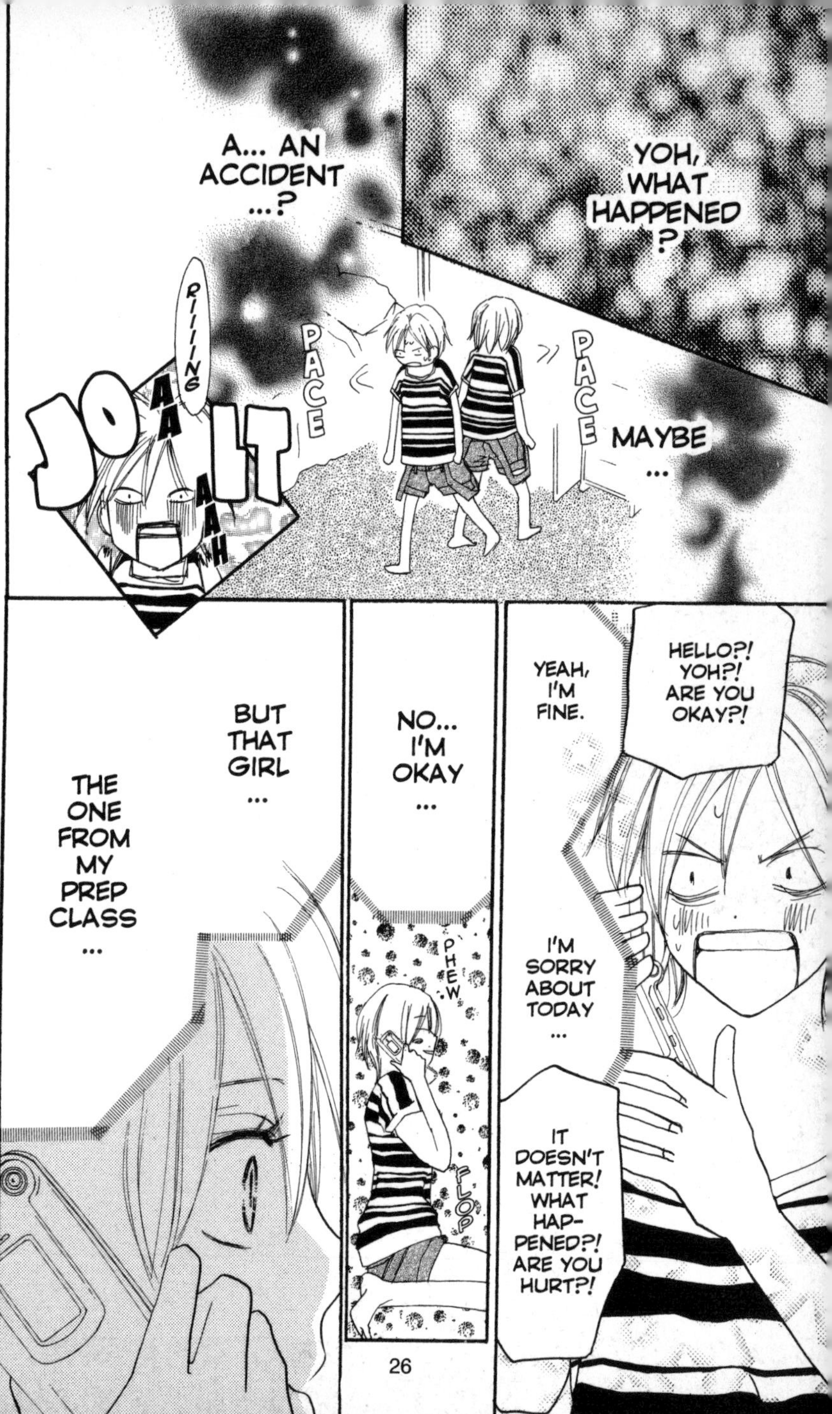
YOH, WHAT HAPPENED?
A... AN ACCIDENT...?
MAYBE...
PACE
PACE
RIIIING
JOLT
AAAAAH
HELLO?! YOH?! ARE YOU OKAY?!
YEAH, I'M FINE.
I'M SORRY ABOUT TODAY...
IT DOESN'T MATTER! WHAT HAP-PENED?! ARE YOU HURT?!
NO... I'M OKAY...
PHEW
FLOP
BUT THAT GIRL...
THE ONE FROM MY PREP CLASS...

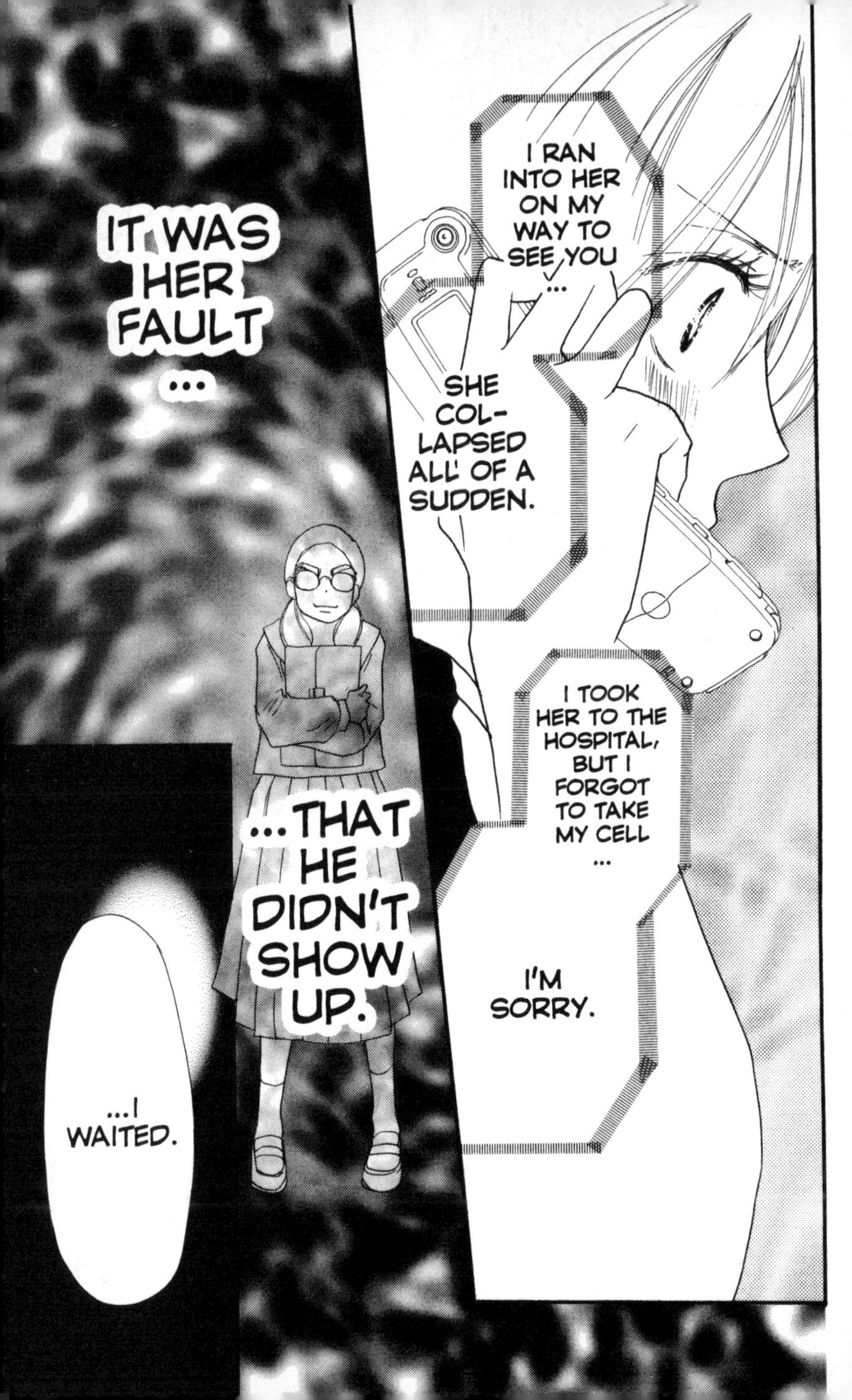
I RAN INTO HER ON MY WAY TO SEE YOU...
SHE COL-LAPSED ALL OF A SUDDEN.
I TOOK HER TO THE HOSPITAL, BUT I FORGOT TO TAKE MY CELL...
I'M SORRY.
IT WAS HER FAULT...
...THAT HE DIDN'T SHOW UP.
...I WAITED.

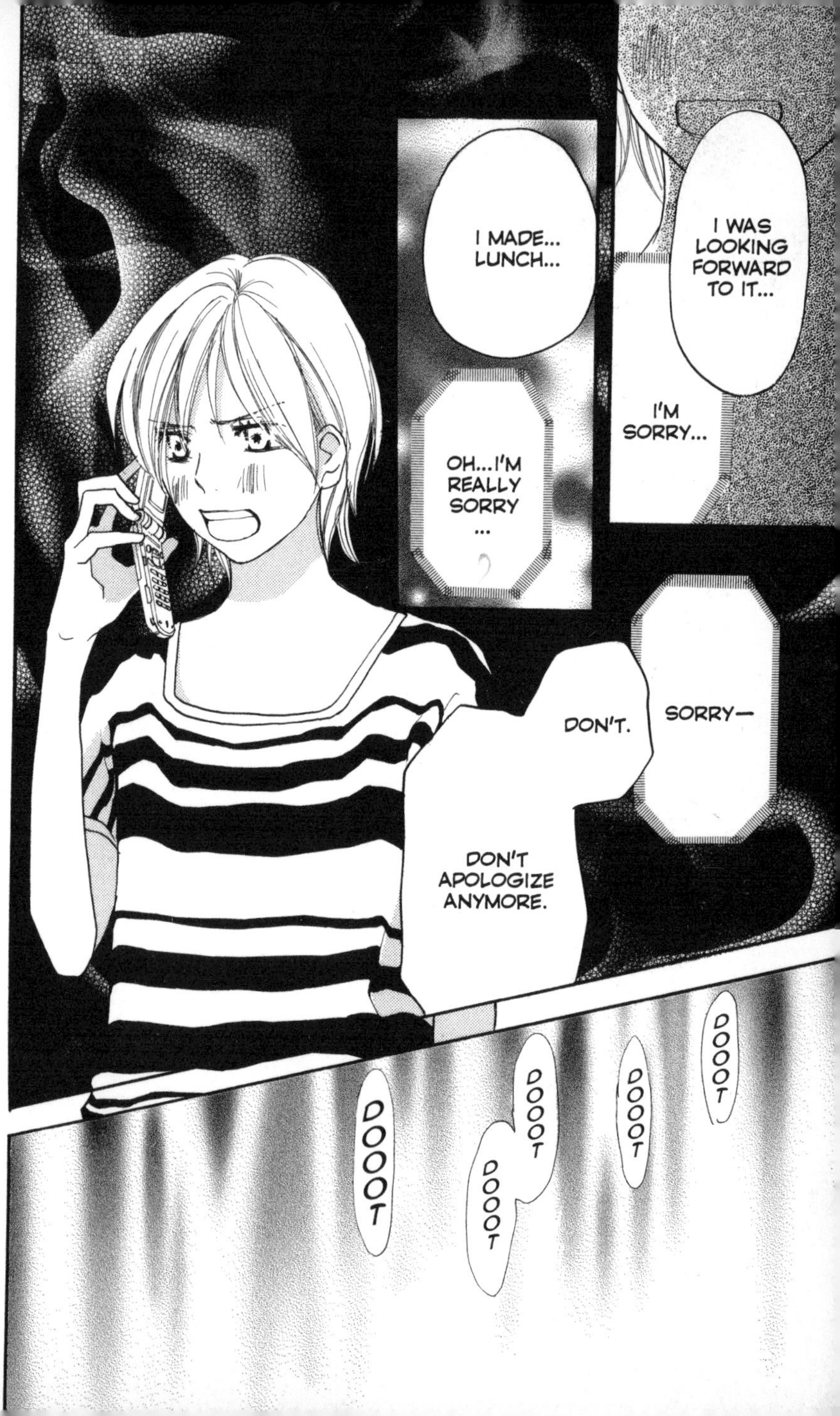
I WAS LOOKING FORWARD TO IT...
I'M SORRY...
I MADE... LUNCH...
OH...I'M REALLY SORRY ...
SORRY—
DON'T.
DON'T APOLOGIZE ANYMORE.
DOOOT
DOOOT
DOOOT
DOOOT
DOOOT

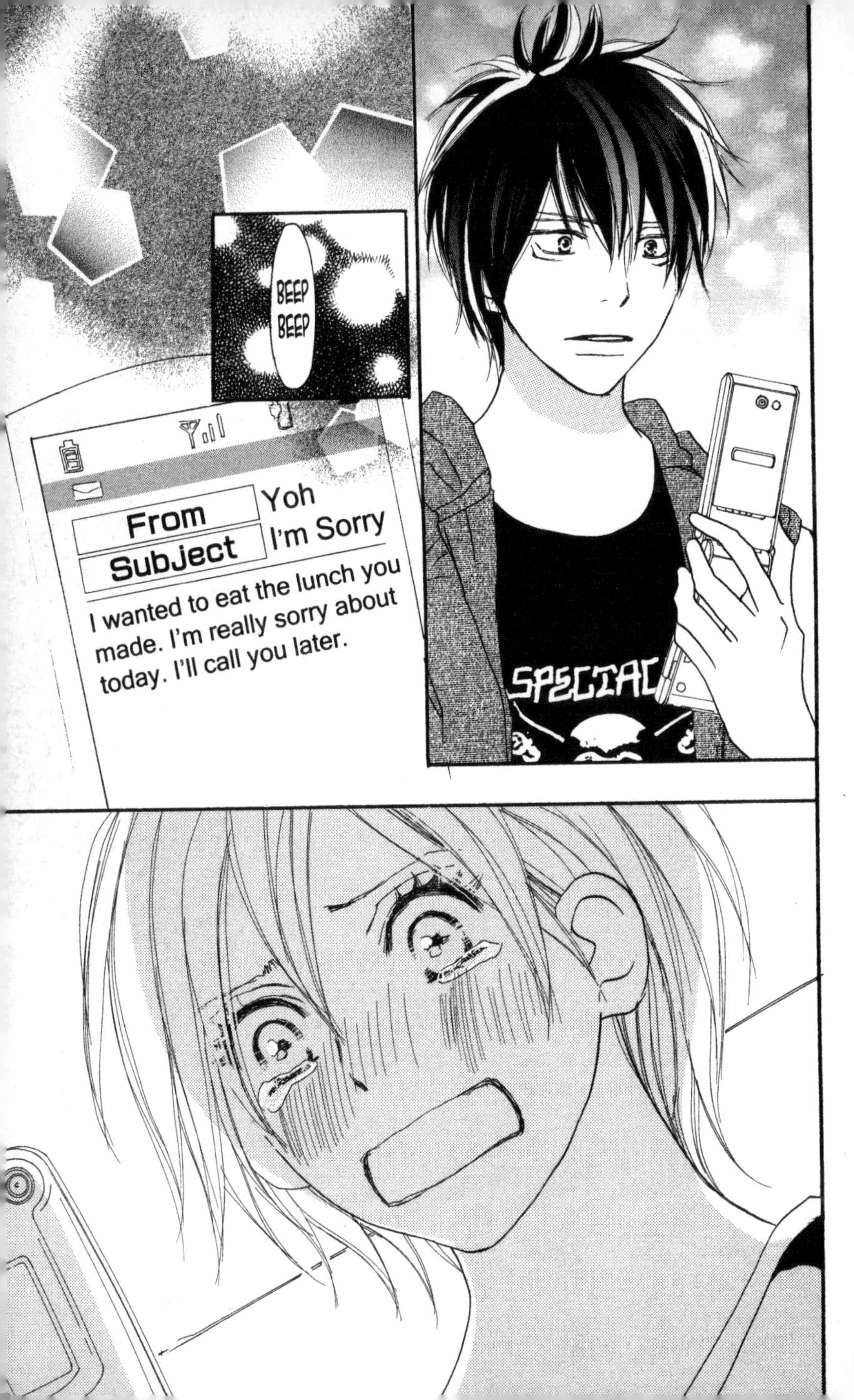
BEEP BEEP
From
Yoh
Subject
I'm Sorry
I wanted to eat the lunch you made. I'm really sorry about today. I'll call you later.
SPECIAL

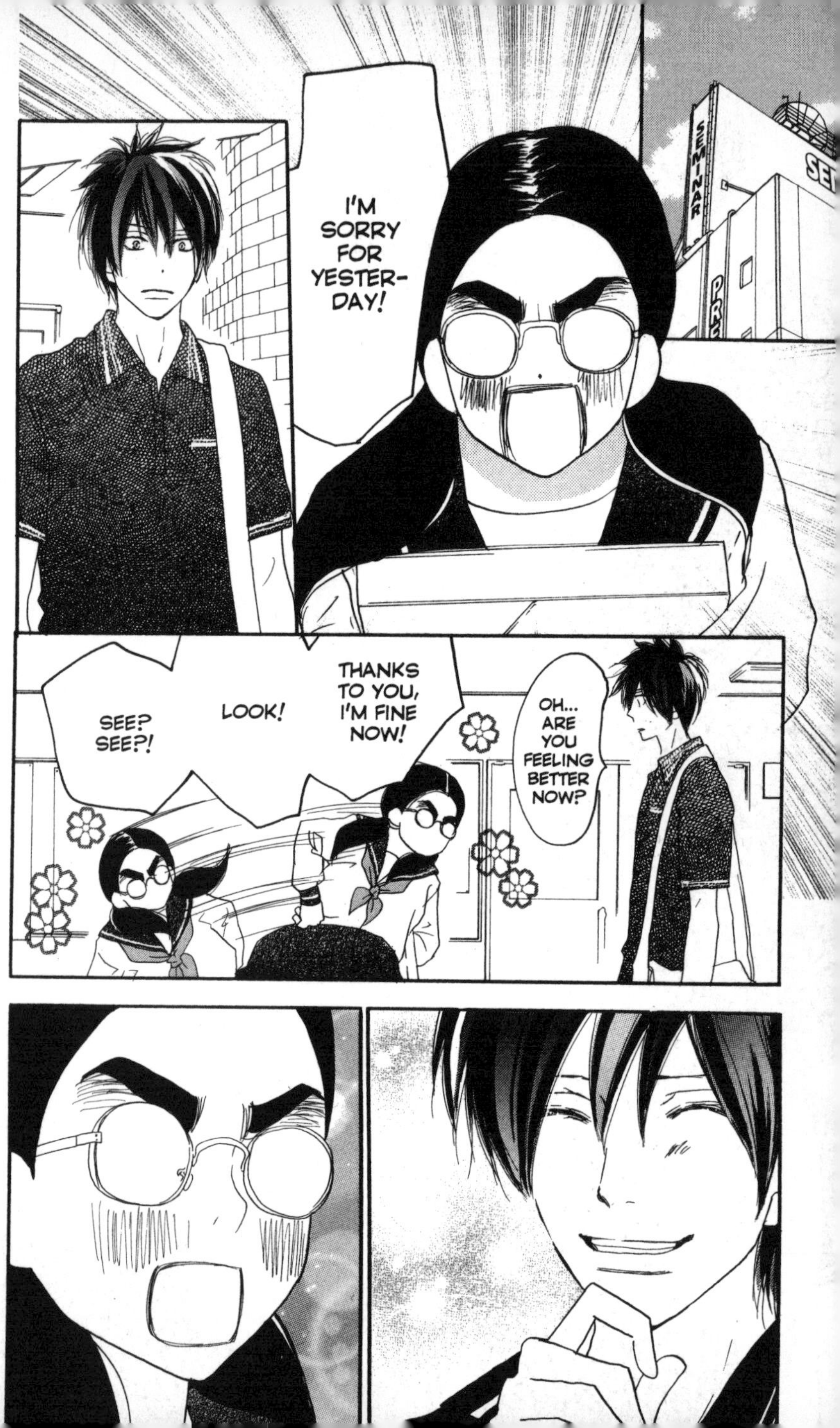
I'M SORRY FOR YESTER-DAY!
SEMINAR
OH... ARE YOU FEELING BETTER NOW?
THANKS TO YOU, I'M FINE NOW!
LOOK!
SEE? SEE?!

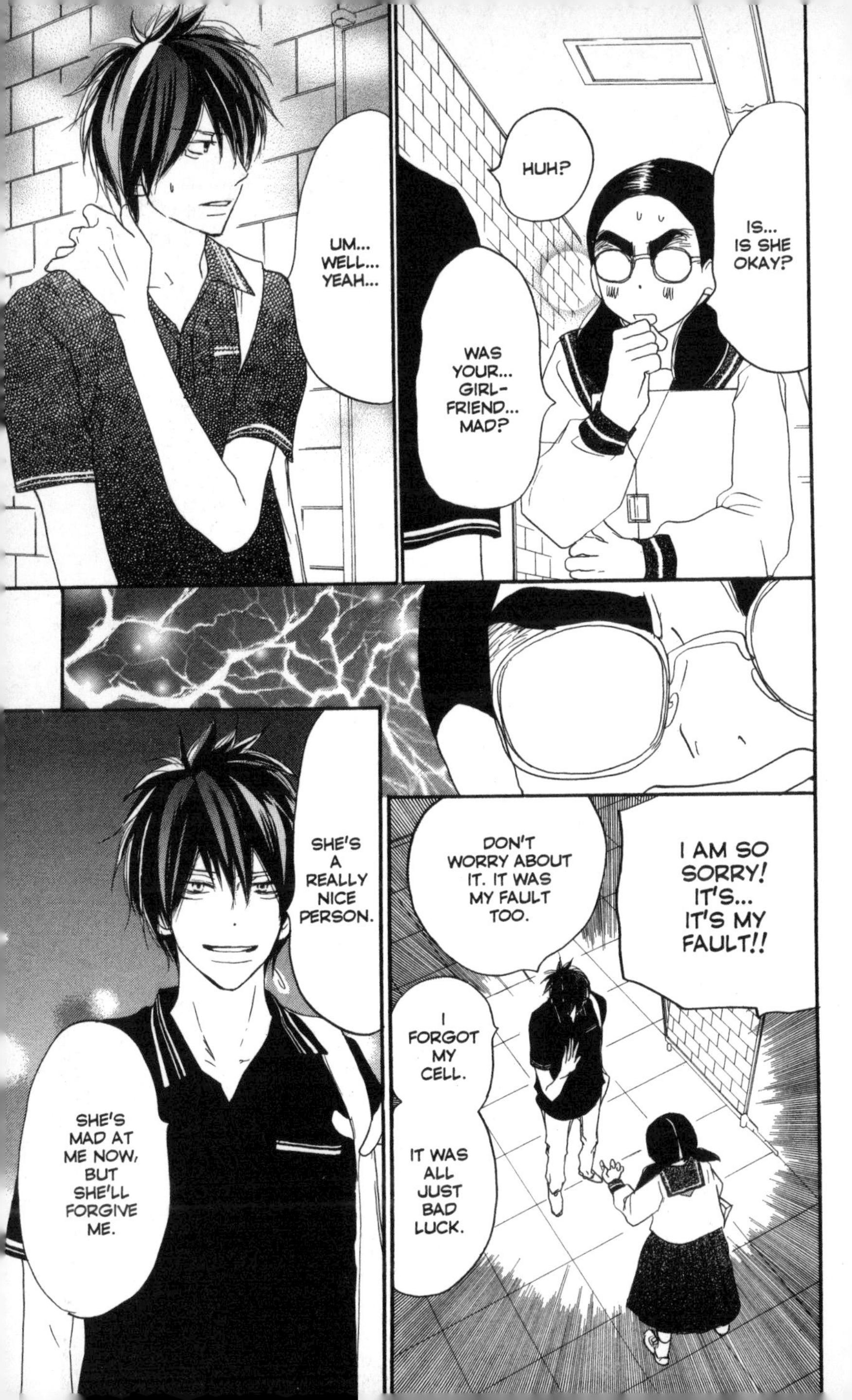
IS... IS SHE OKAY?
HUH?
WAS YOUR... GIRL-FRIEND... MAD?
UM... WELL... YEAH...
I AM SO SORRY! IT'S... IT'S MY FAULT!!
DON'T WORRY ABOUT IT. IT WAS MY FAULT TOO.
I FORGOT MY CELL.
IT WAS ALL JUST BAD LUCK.
SHE'S A REALLY NICE PERSON.
SHE'S MAD AT ME NOW, BUT SHE'LL FORGIVE ME.

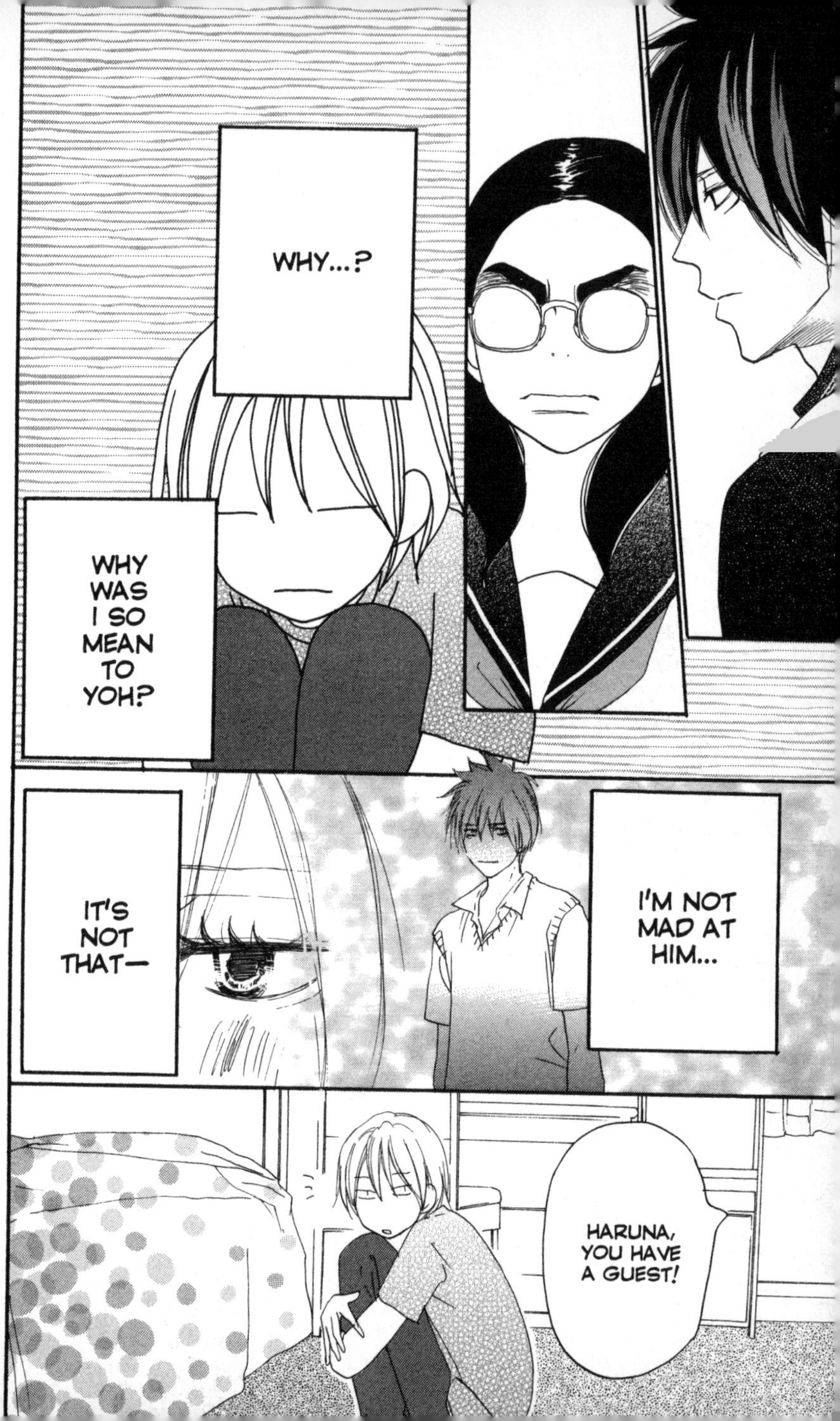
WHY...?
WHY WAS I SO MEAN TO YOH?
I'M NOT MAD AT HIM...
IT'S NOT THAT—
HARUNA, YOU HAVE A GUEST!

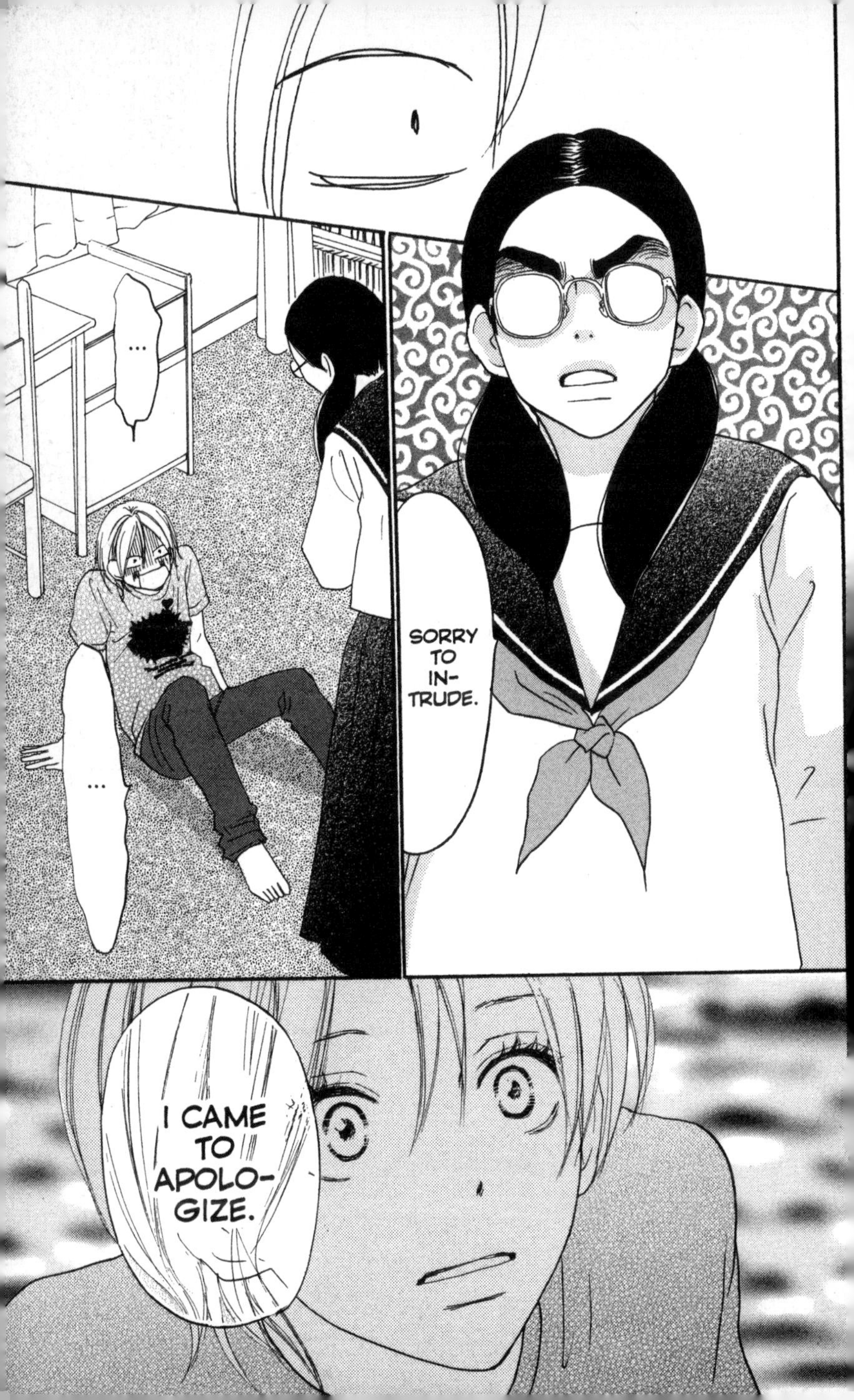
SORRY TO IN-TRUDE.
...
...
I CAME TO APOLO-GIZE.

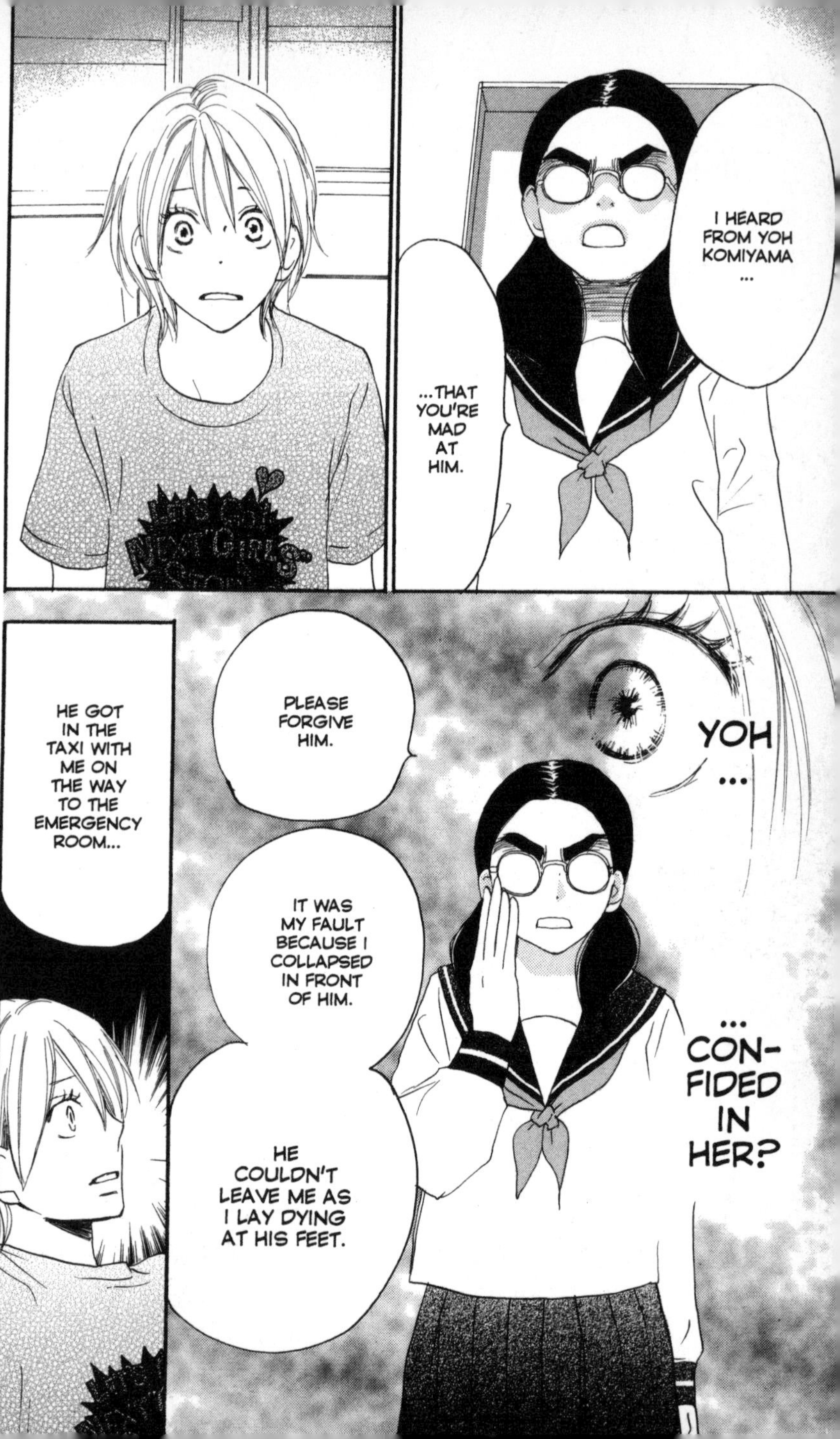
I HEARD FROM YOH KOMIYAMA ...
...THAT YOU'RE MAD AT HIM.
YOH ...
... CON-FIDED IN HER?
PLEASE FORGIVE HIM.
IT WAS MY FAULT BECAUSE I COLLAPSED IN FRONT OF HIM.
HE COULDN'T LEAVE ME AS I LAY DYING AT HIS FEET.
HE GOT IN THE TAXI WITH ME ON THE WAY TO THE EMERGENCY ROOM...

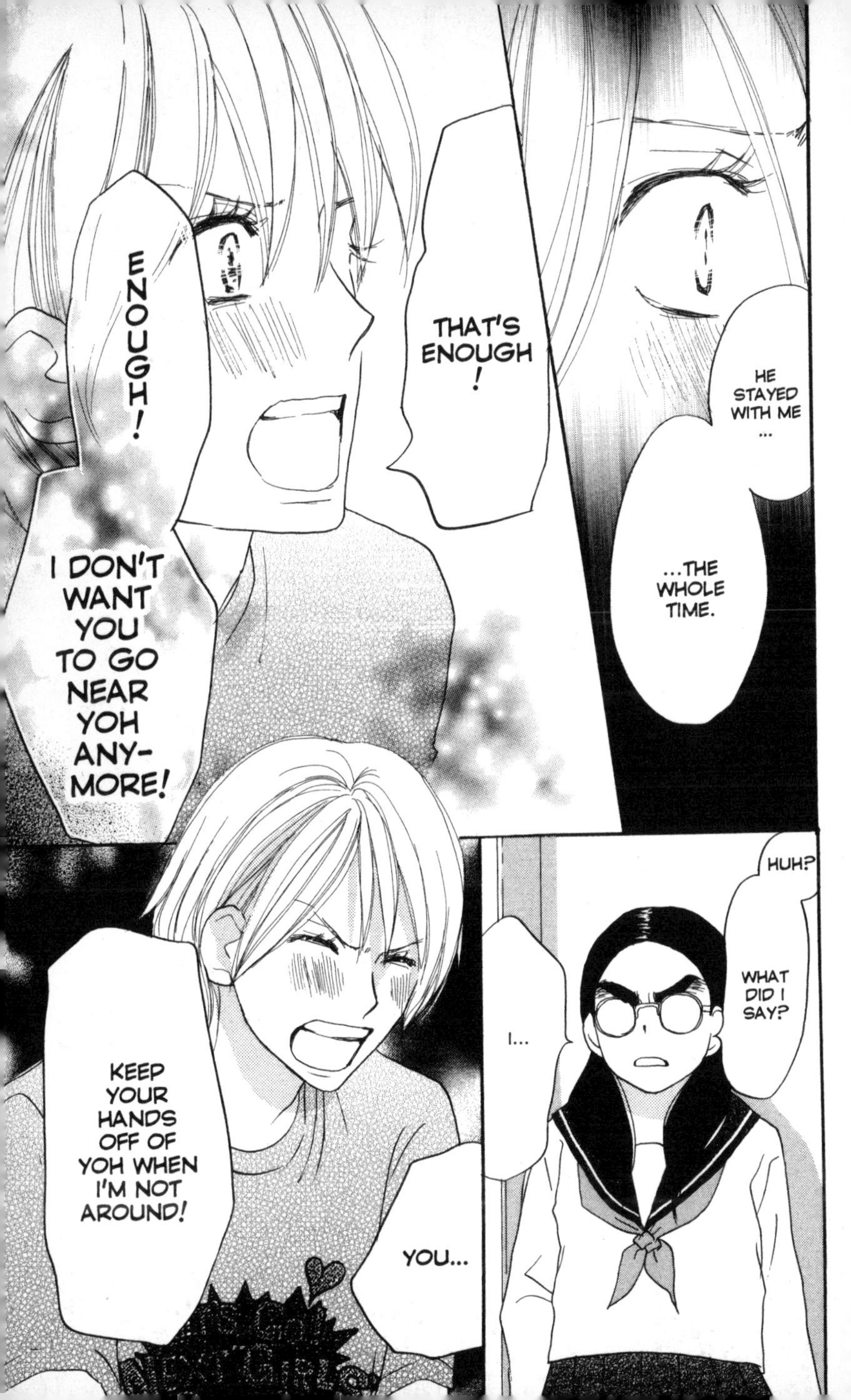
HE STAYED WITH ME ...
...THE WHOLE TIME.
THAT'S ENOUGH!
ENOUGH!
I DON'T WANT YOU TO GO NEAR YOH ANY-MORE!
HUH?
WHAT DID I SAY?
I...
KEEP YOUR HANDS OFF OF YOH WHEN I'M NOT AROUND!
YOU...

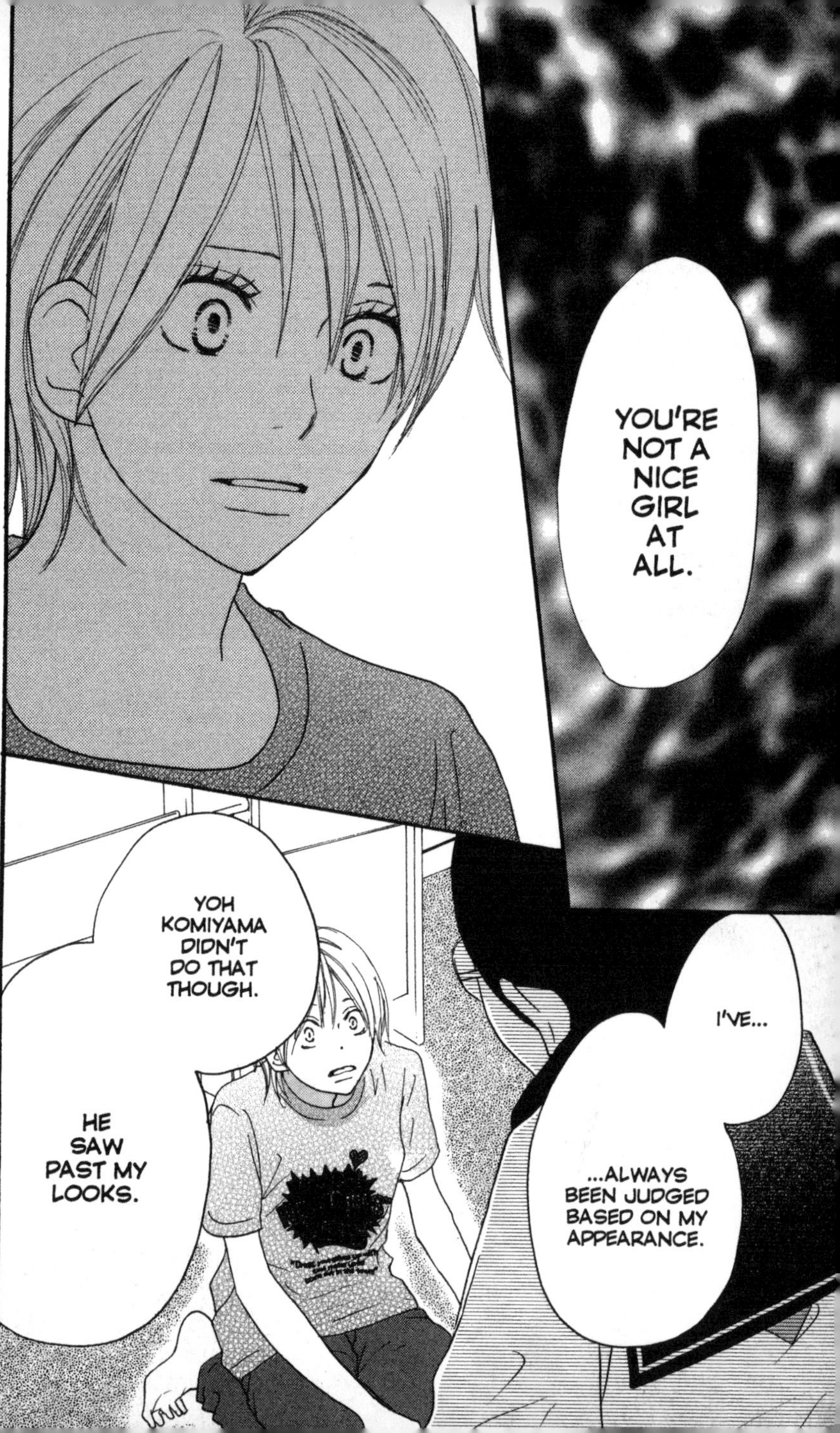
YOU'RE NOT A NICE GIRL AT ALL.
I'VE...
...ALWAYS BEEN JUDGED BASED ON MY APPEARANCE.
YOH KOMIYAMA DIDN'T DO THAT THOUGH.
HE SAW PAST MY LOOKS.

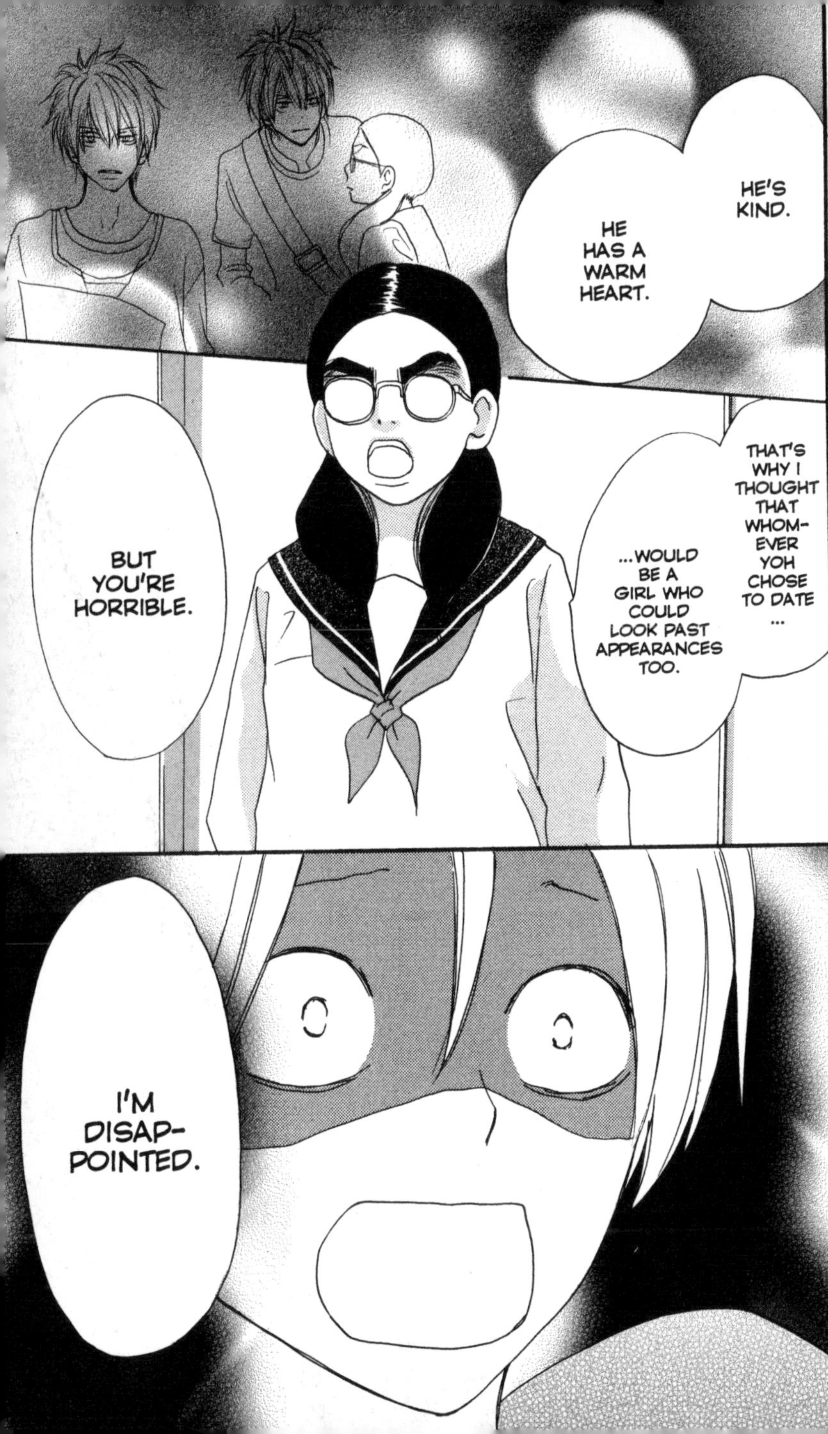
HE'S KIND.
HE HAS A WARM HEART.
THAT'S WHY I THOUGHT THAT WHOM-EVER YOH CHOSE TO DATE ...
...WOULD BE A GIRL WHO COULD LOOK PAST APPEARANCES TOO.
BUT YOU'RE HORRIBLE.
I'M DISAP-POINTED.

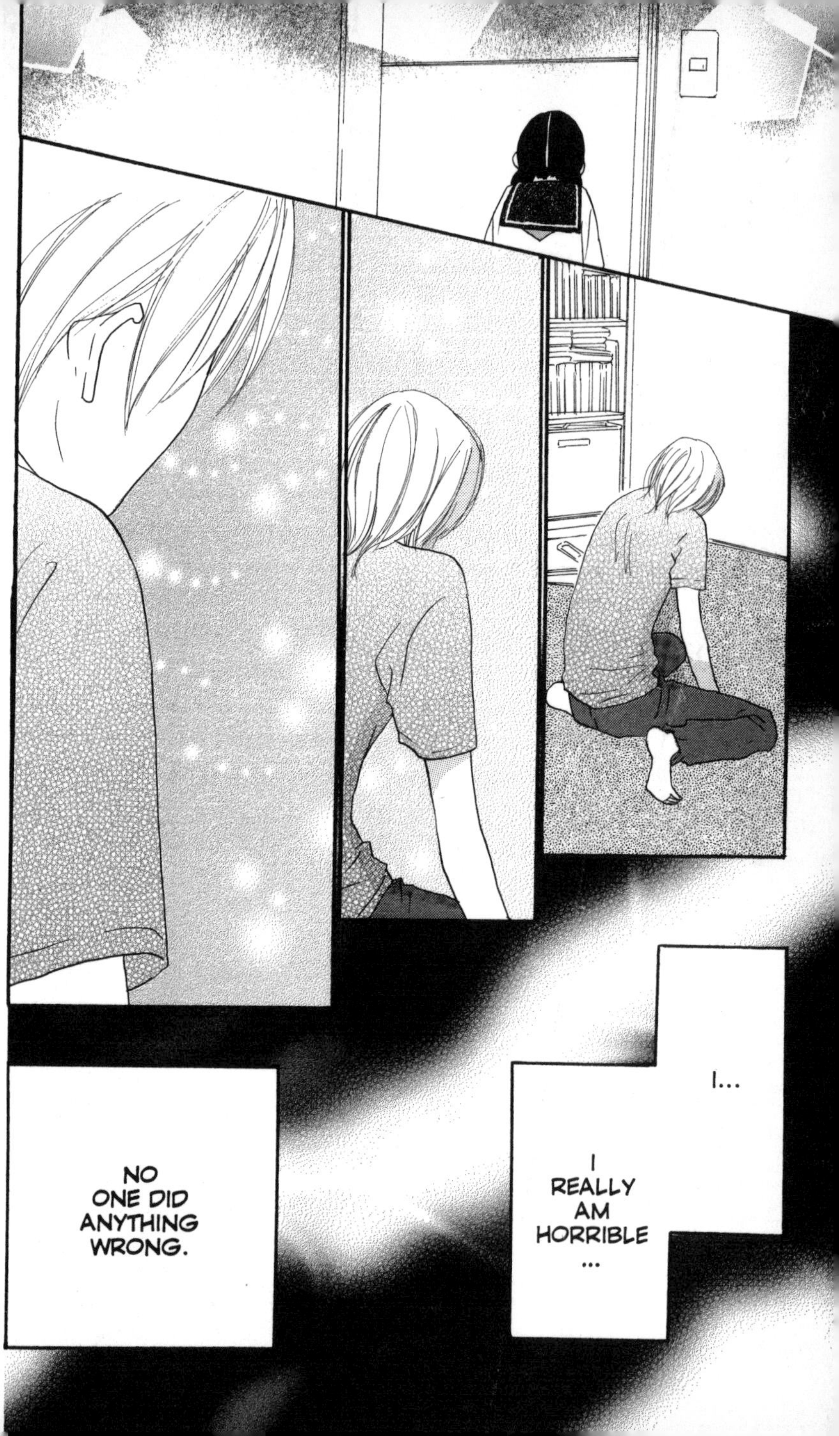
I...
I REALLY AM HORRIBLE ...
NO ONE DID ANYTHING WRONG.

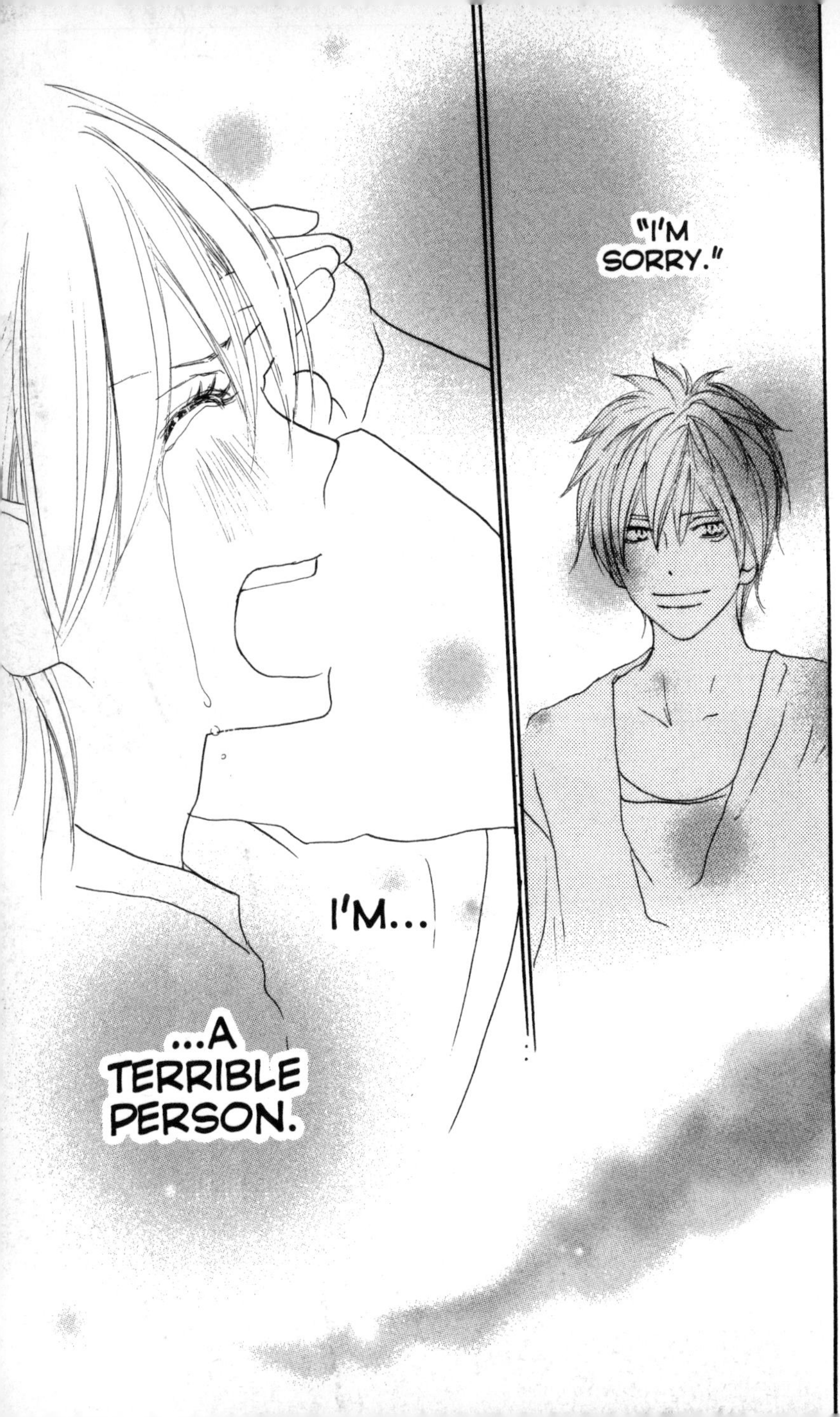
"I'M SORRY."
I'M...
...A TERRIBLE PERSON.

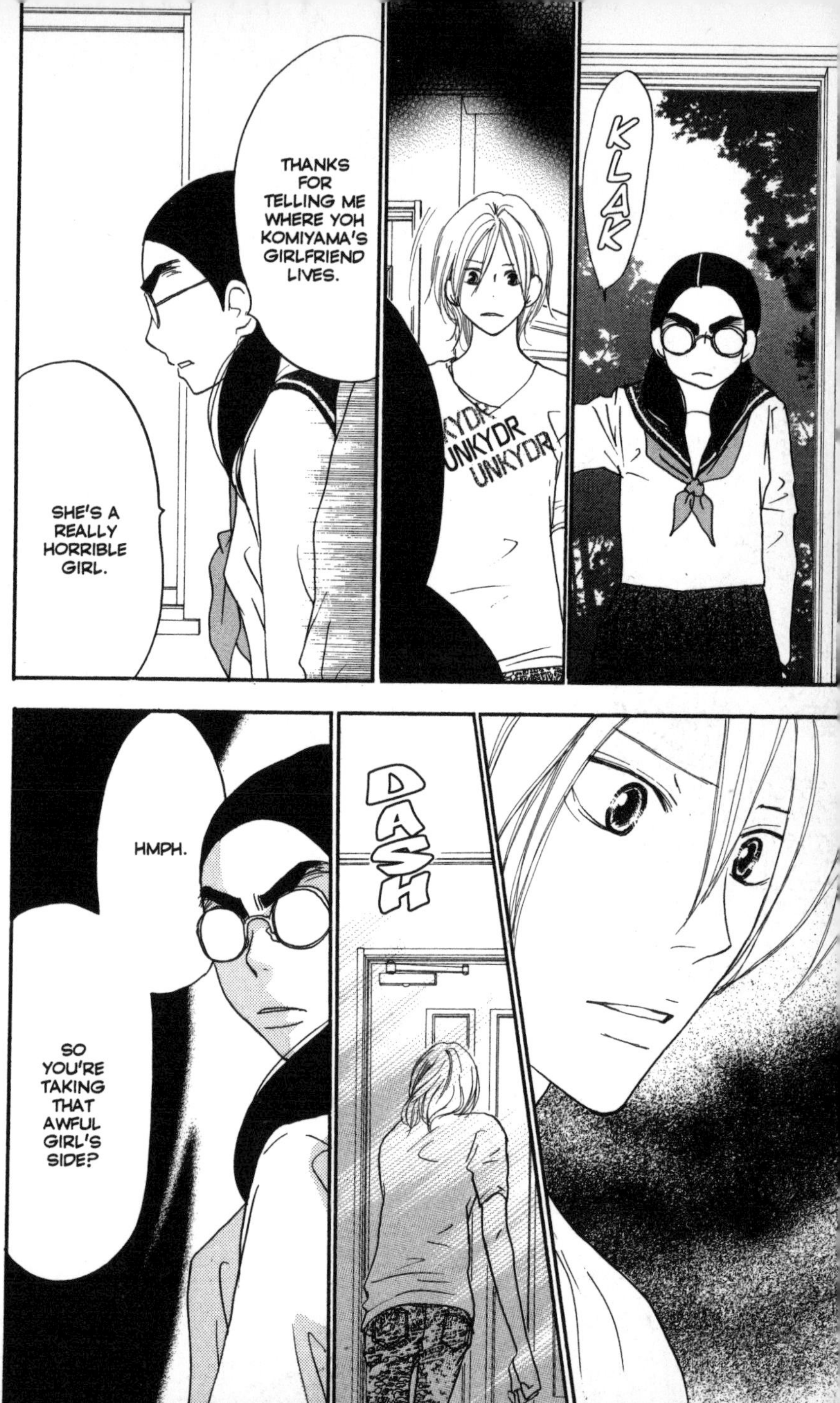
KLAK
THANKS FOR TELLING ME WHERE YOH KOMIYAMA'S GIRLFRIEND LIVES.
SHE'S A REALLY HORRIBLE GIRL.
DASH
HMPH.
SO YOU'RE TAKING THAT AWFUL GIRL'S SIDE?

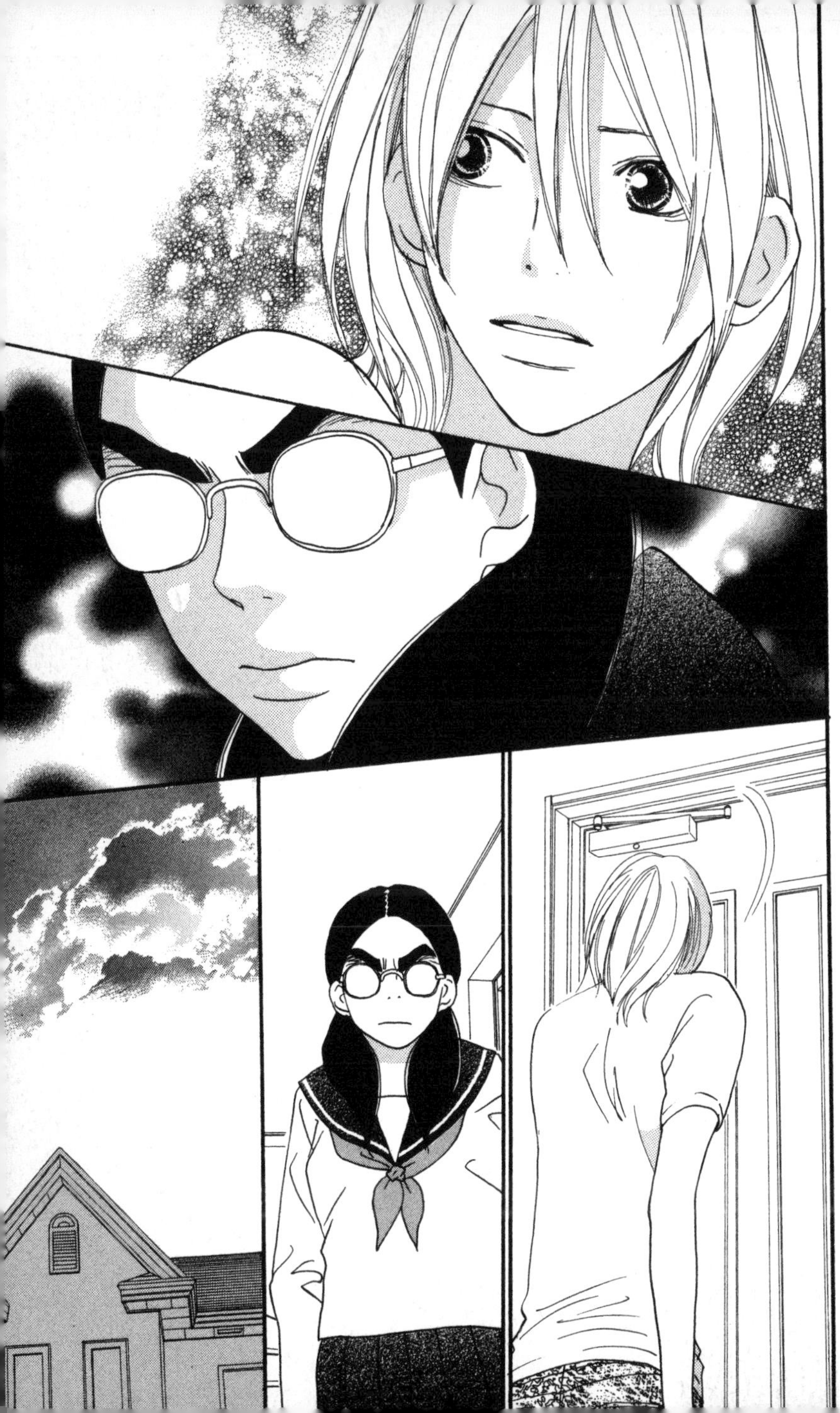

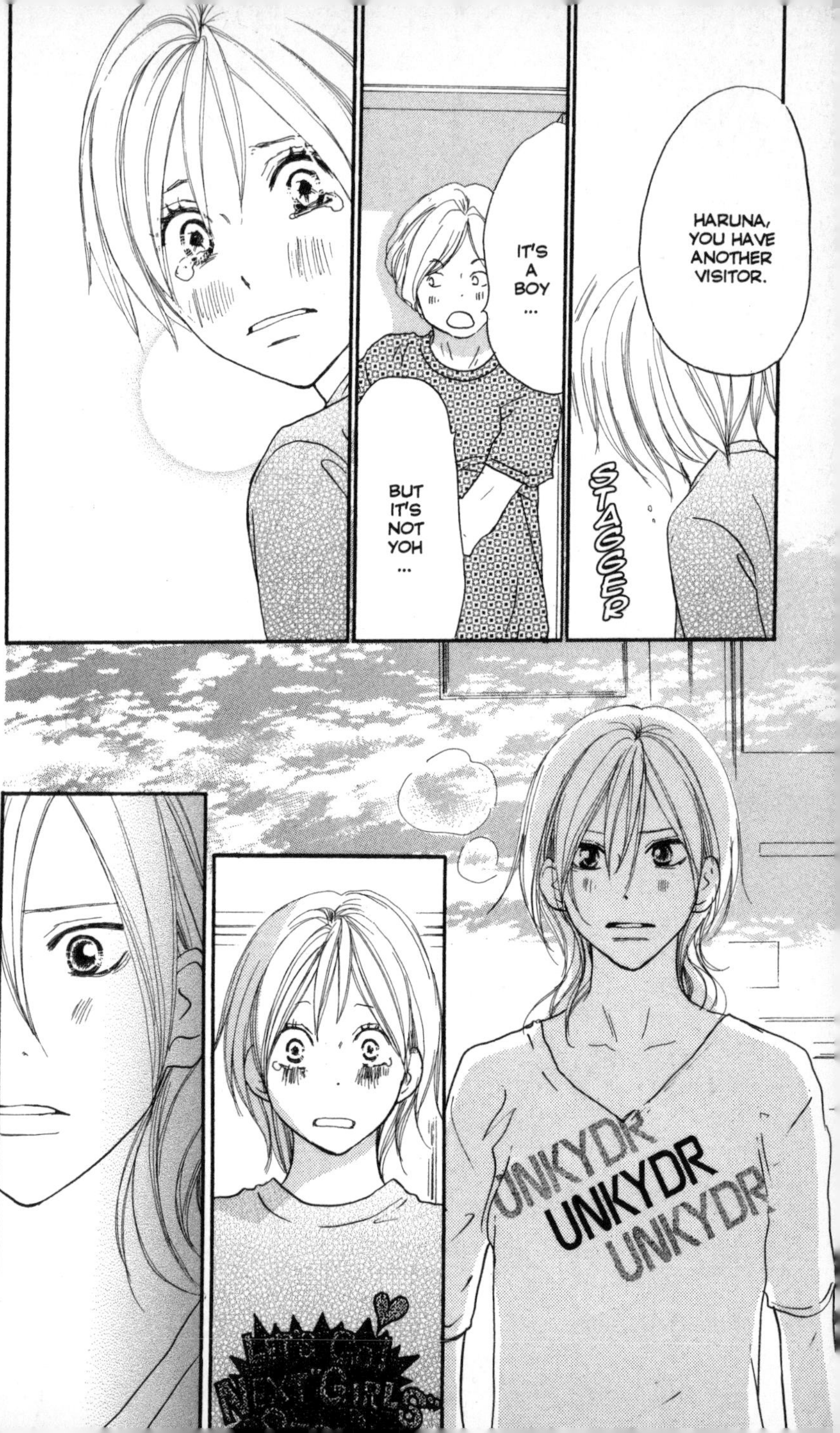
HARUNA, YOU HAVE ANOTHER VISITOR.
STAGGER
IT'S A BOY ...
BUT IT'S NOT YOH ...

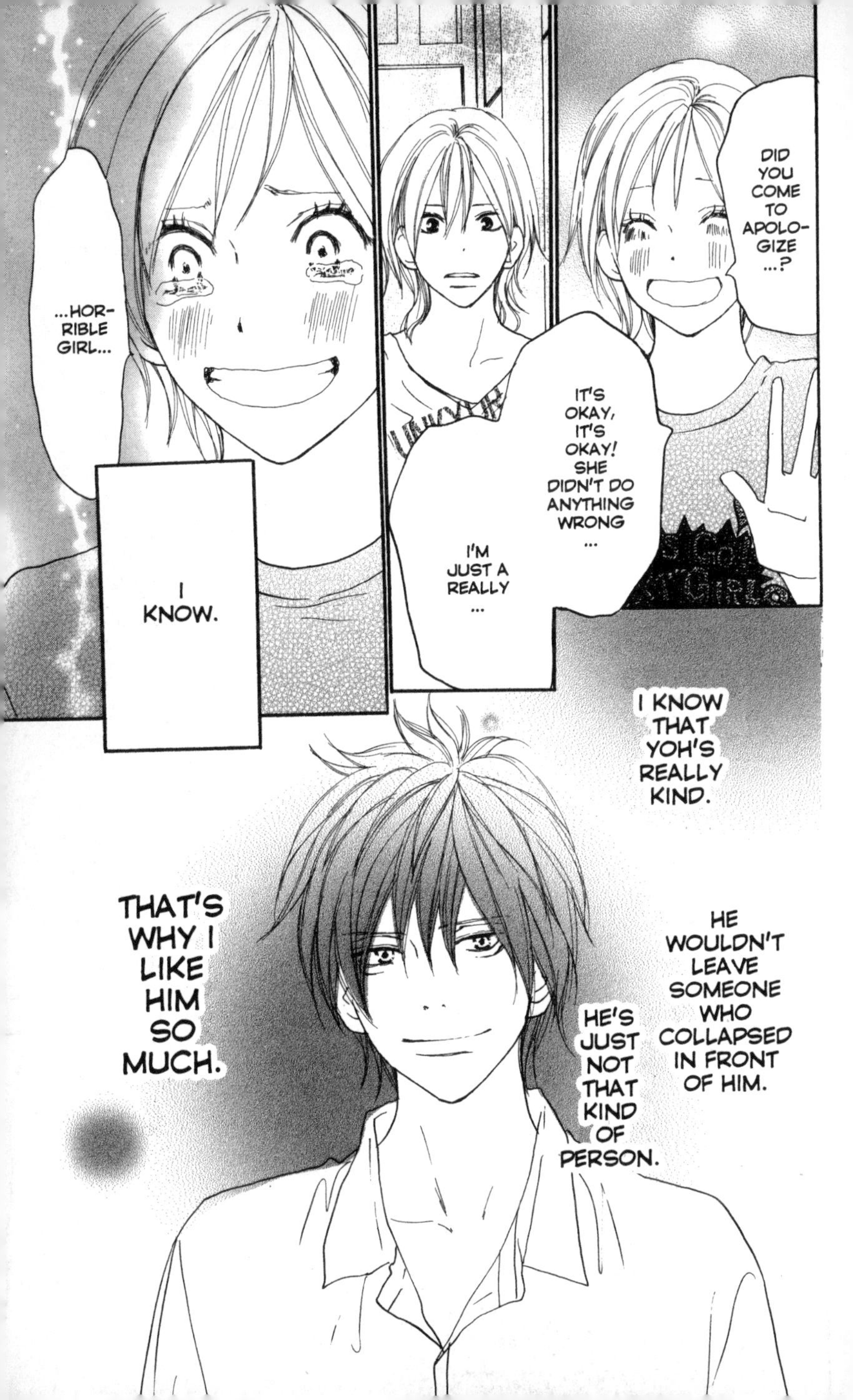
DID YOU COME TO APOLO-GIZE ...?
IT'S OKAY, IT'S OKAY! SHE DIDN'T DO ANYTHING WRONG ...
I'M JUST A REALLY ...
...HOR-RIBLE GIRL...
I KNOW.
I KNOW THAT YOH'S REALLY KIND.
HE WOULDN'T LEAVE SOMEONE WHO COLLAPSED IN FRONT OF HIM.
HE'S JUST NOT THAT KIND OF PERSON.
THAT'S WHY I LIKE HIM SO MUCH.

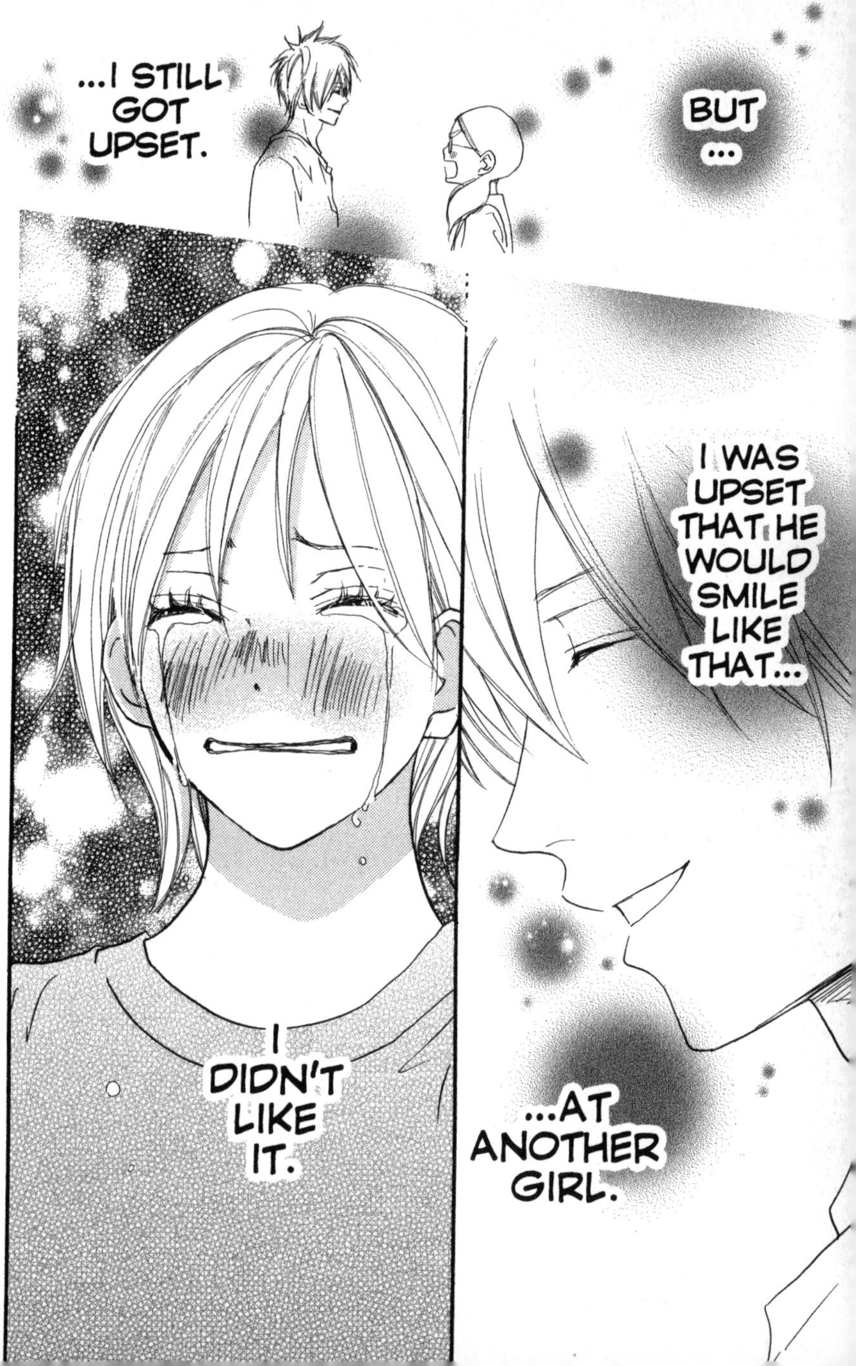
BUT ...
...I STILL GOT UPSET.
I WAS UPSET THAT HE WOULD SMILE LIKE THAT...
...AT ANOTHER GIRL.
I DIDN'T LIKE IT.

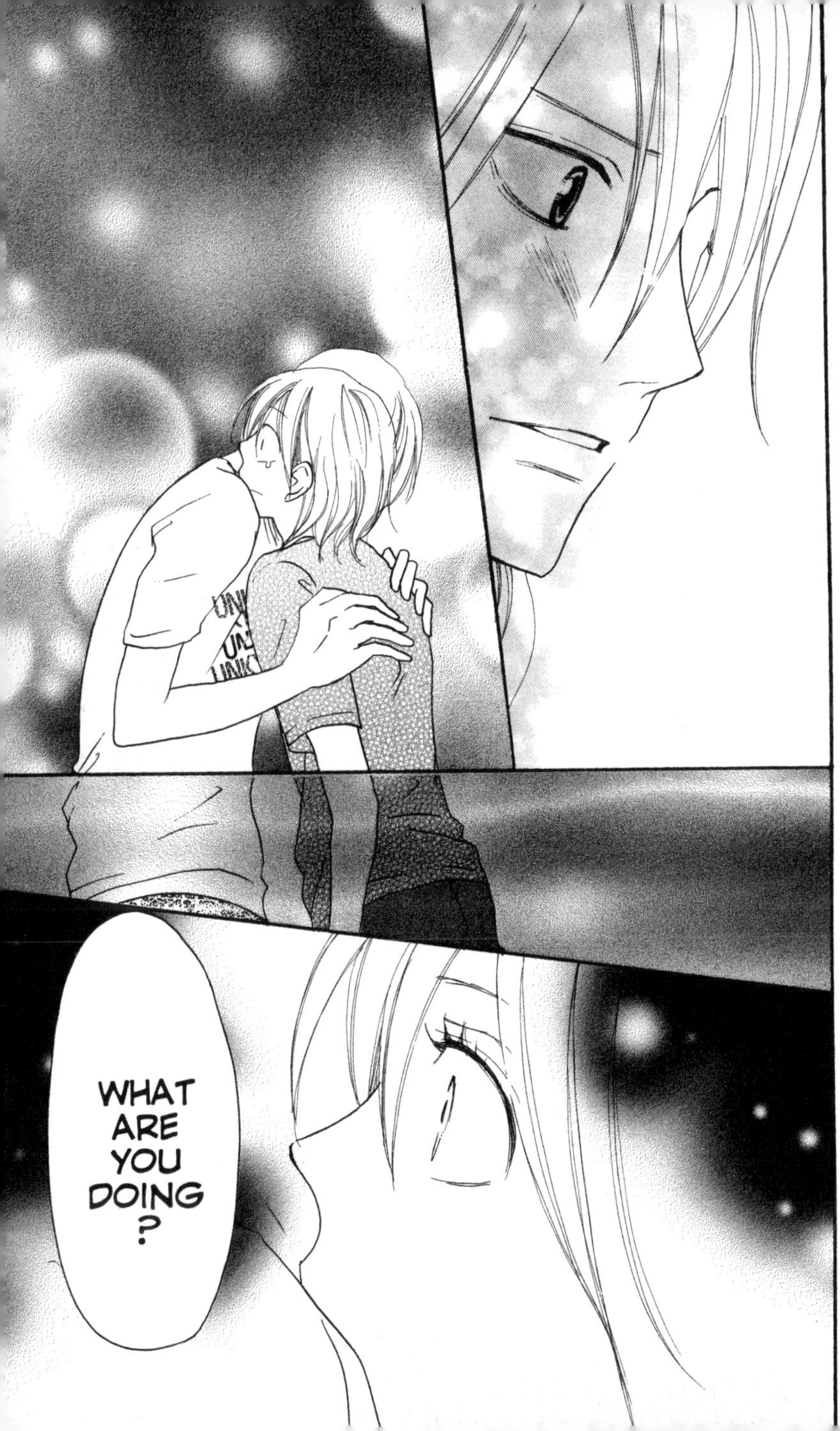
WHAT ARE YOU DOING?

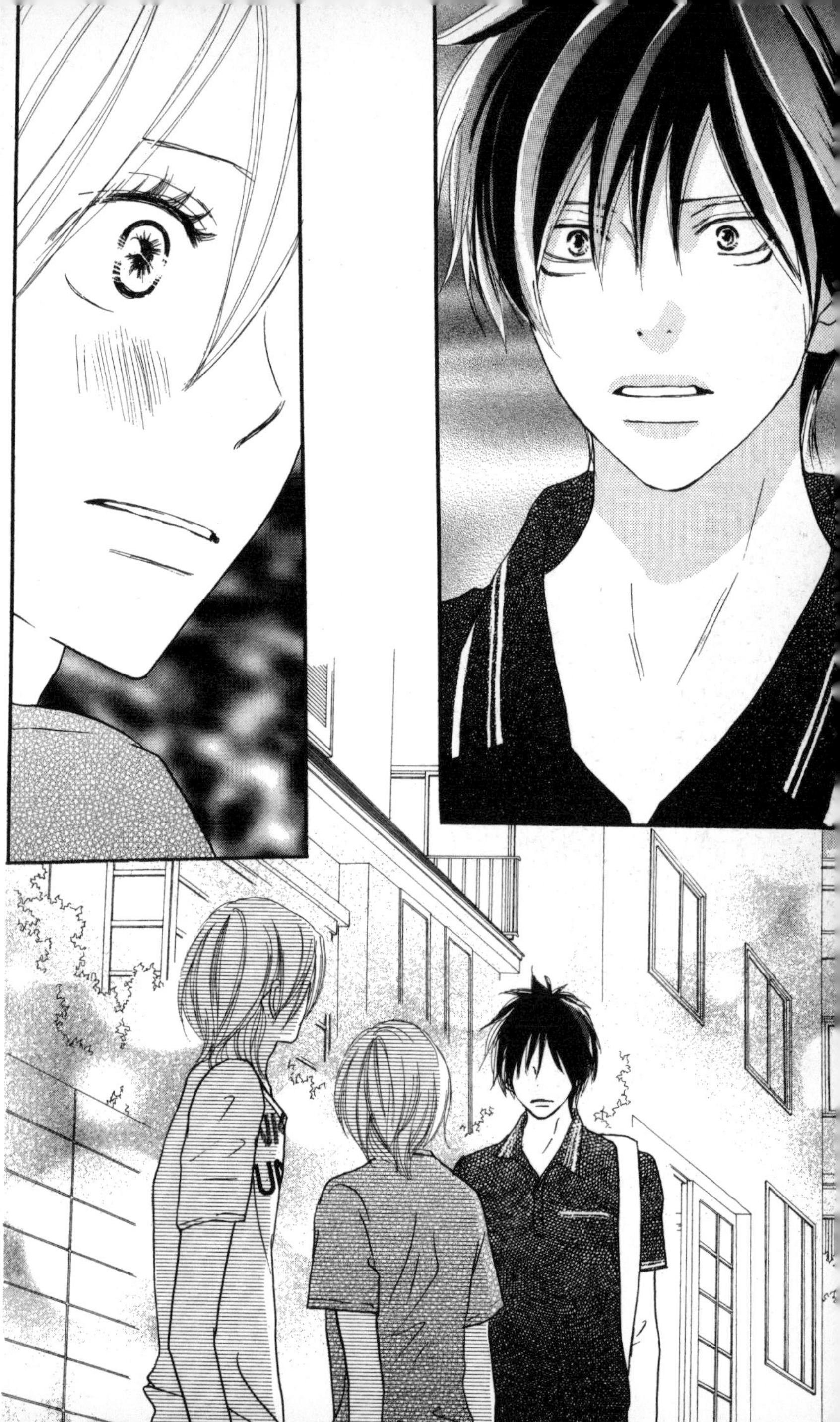

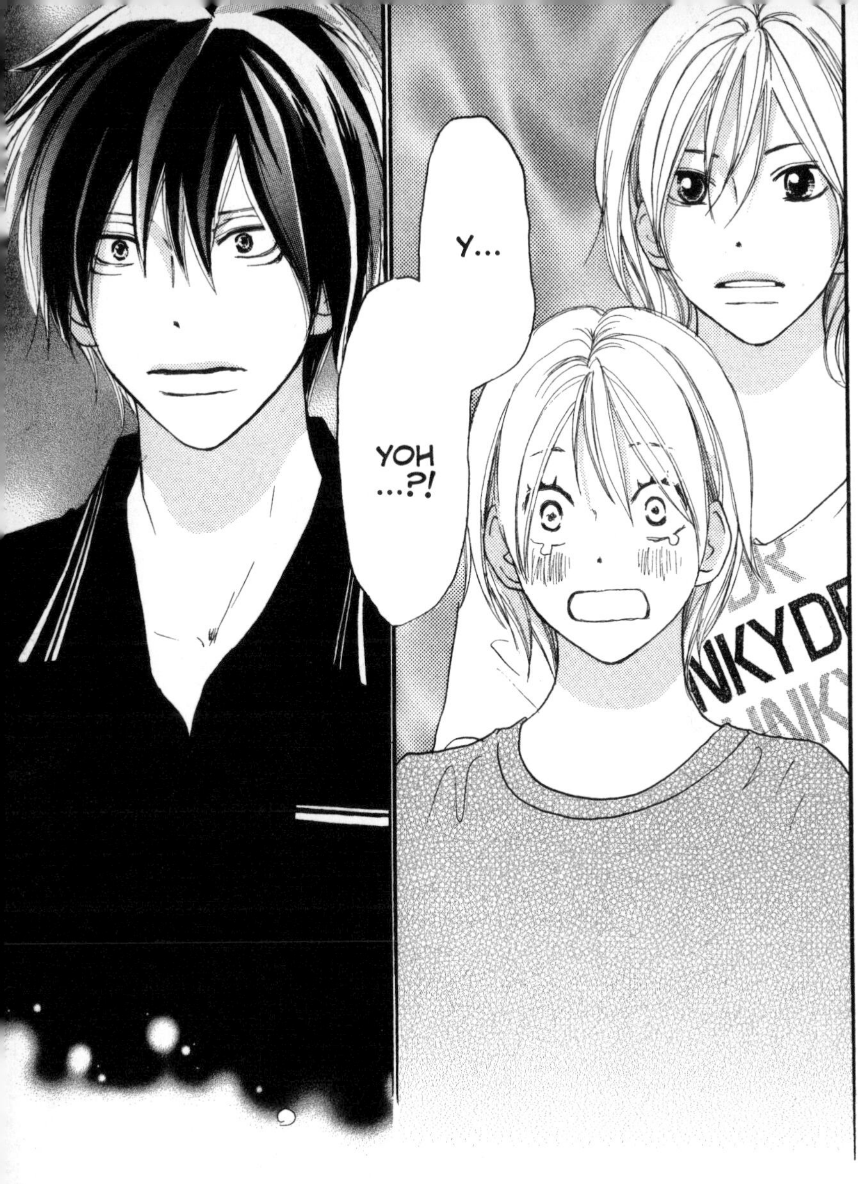
Y... YOH ...?!

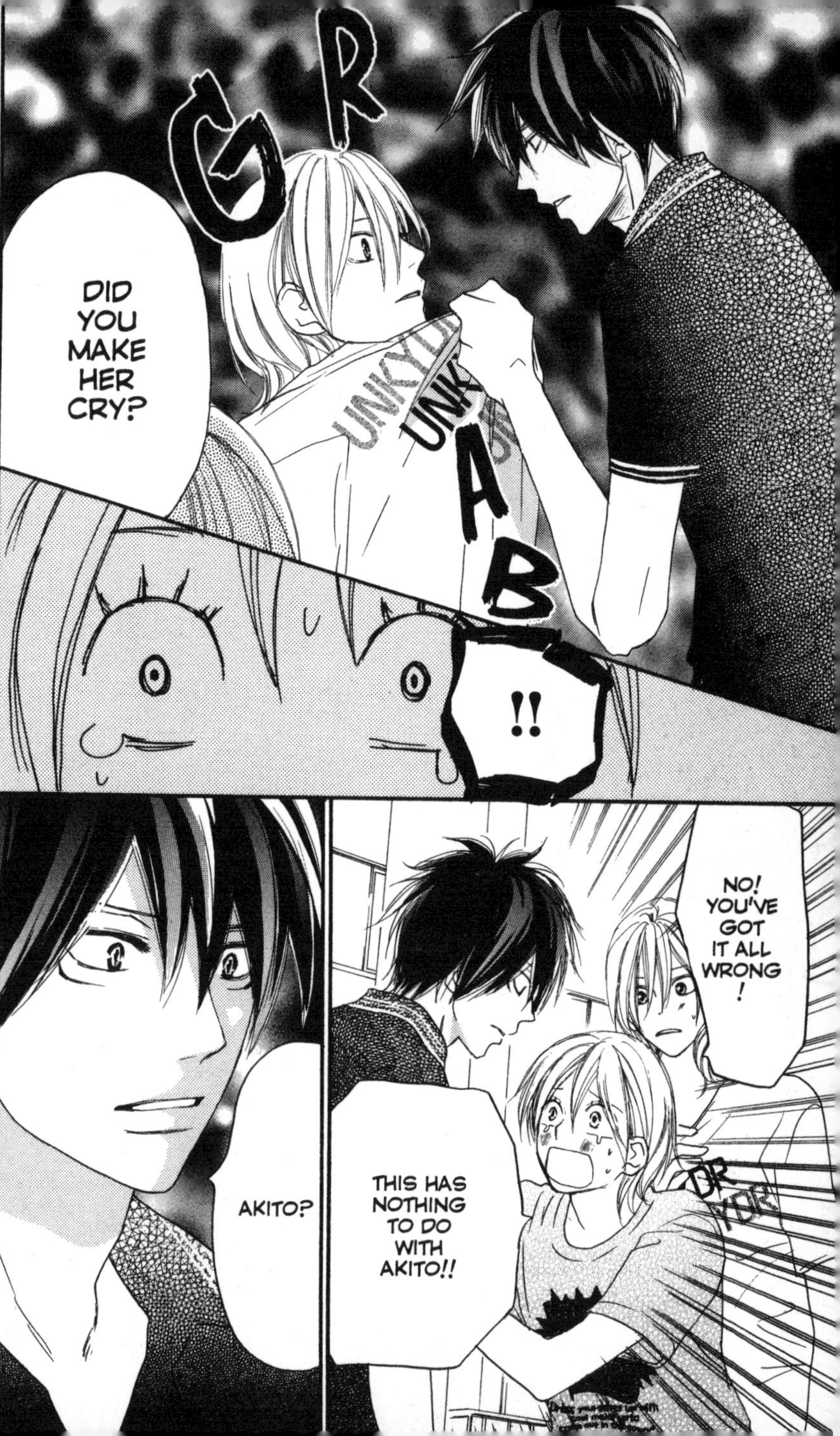
GRAB
DID YOU MAKE HER CRY?
!!
NO! YOU'VE GOT IT ALL WRONG!
THIS HAS NOTHING TO DO WITH AKITO!!
AKITO?

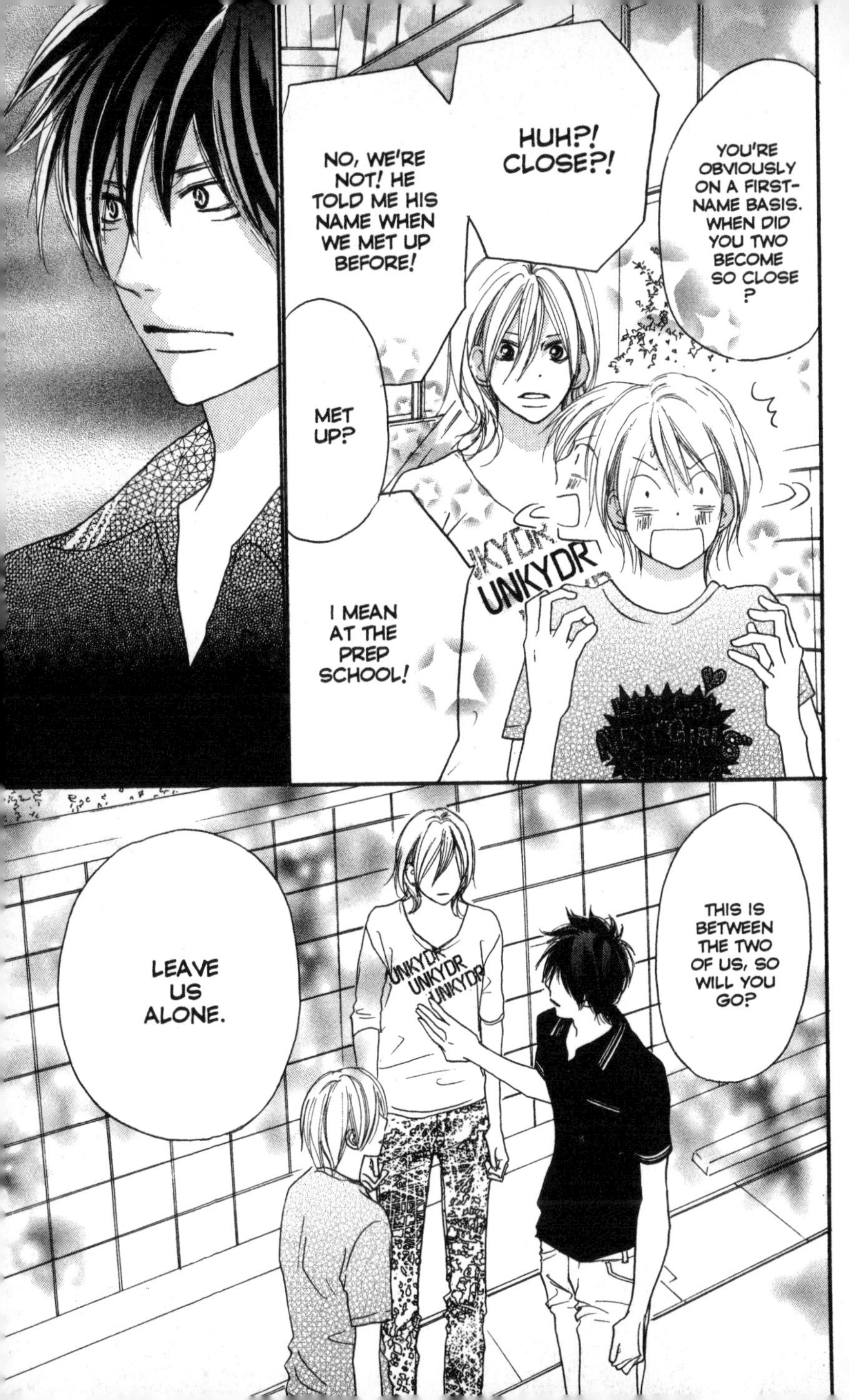
YOU'RE OBVIOUSLY ON A FIRST-NAME BASIS. WHEN DID YOU TWO BECOME SO CLOSE?
HUH?! CLOSE?!
NO, WE'RE NOT! HE TOLD ME HIS NAME WHEN WE MET UP BEFORE!
MET UP?
I MEAN AT THE PREP SCHOOL!
UNKYDR
THIS IS BETWEEN THE TWO OF US, SO WILL YOU GO?
LEAVE US ALONE.

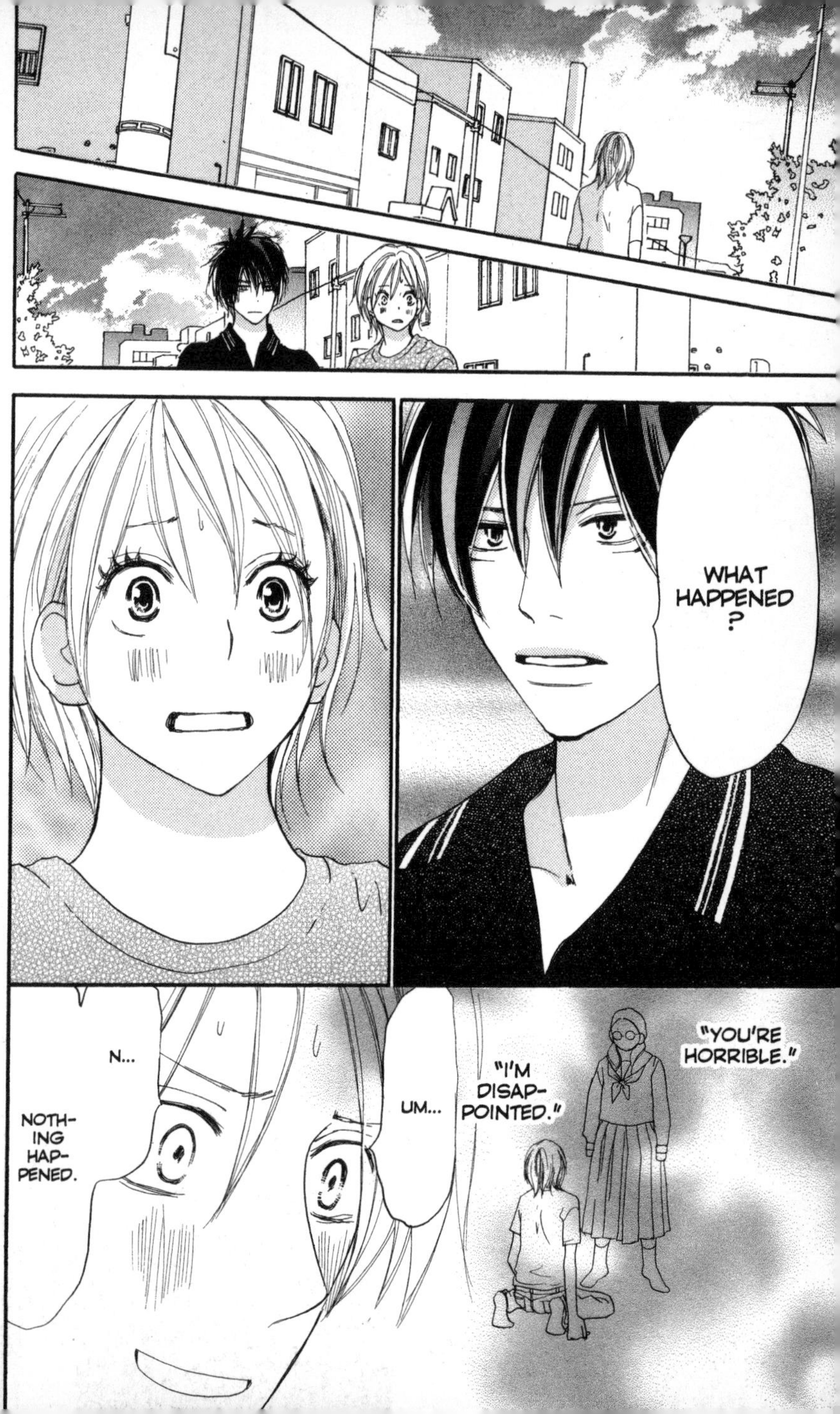
WHAT HAPPENED?
"YOU'RE HORRIBLE."
"I'M DISAPPOINTED."
UM...
N...
NOTHING HAPPENED.

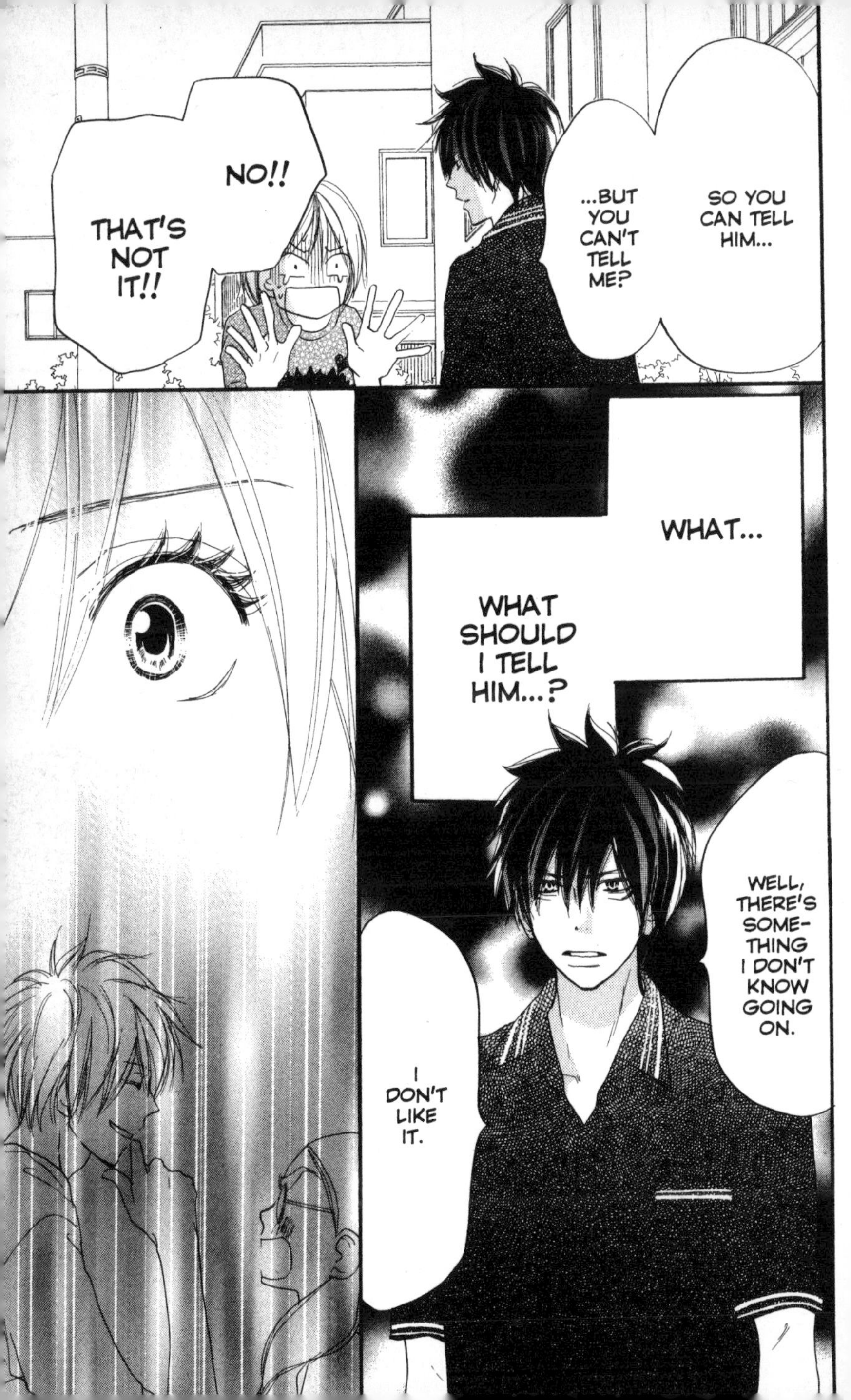
SO YOU CAN TELL HIM...
...BUT YOU CAN'T TELL ME?
NO!!
THAT'S NOT IT!!
WHAT...
WHAT SHOULD I TELL HIM...?
WELL, THERE'S SOME-THING I DON'T KNOW GOING ON.
I DON'T LIKE IT.

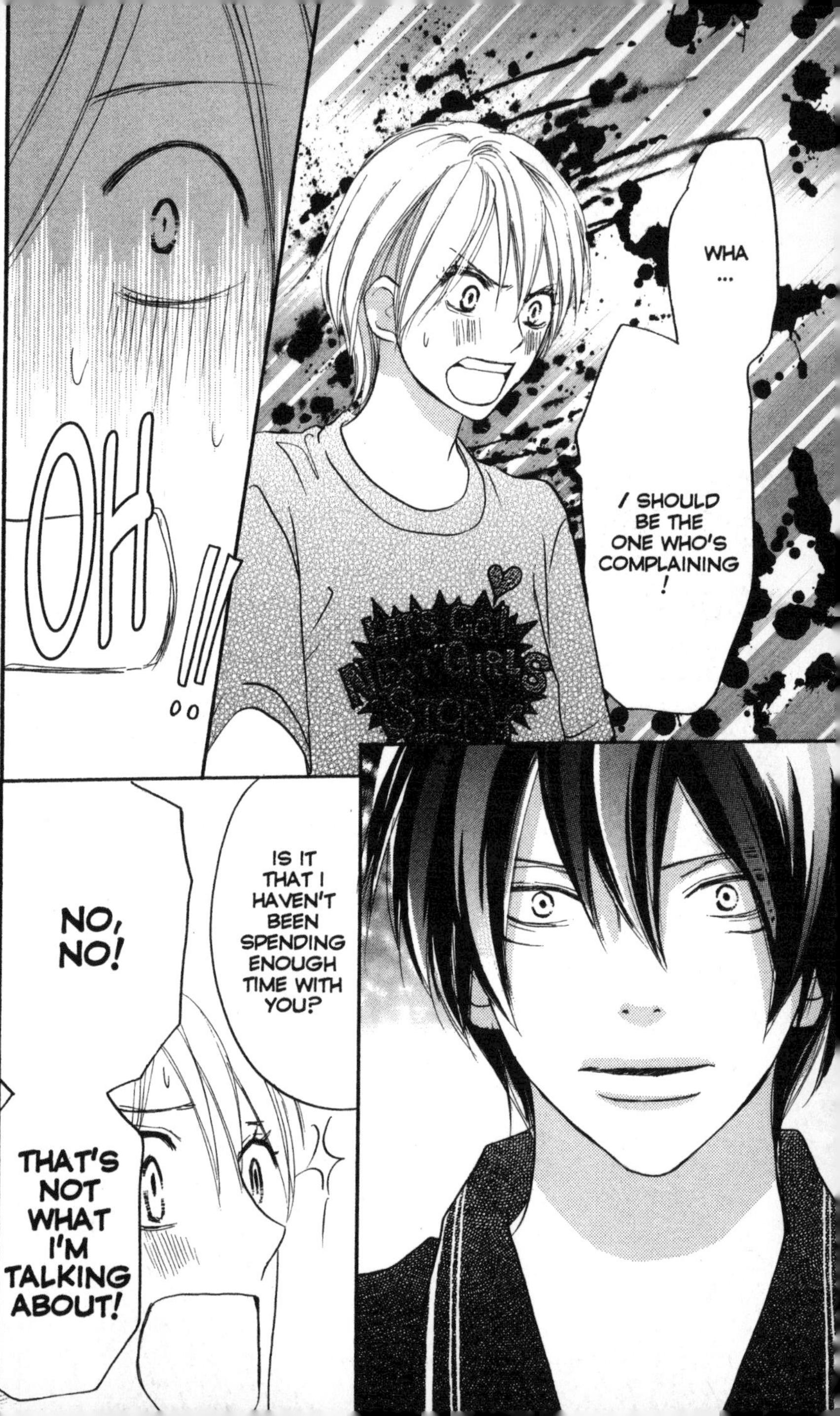
WHA ...
I SHOULD BE THE ONE WHO'S COMPLAINING!
OH!!
IS IT THAT I HAVEN'T BEEN SPENDING ENOUGH TIME WITH YOU?
NO, NO!
THAT'S NOT WHAT I'M TALKING ABOUT!

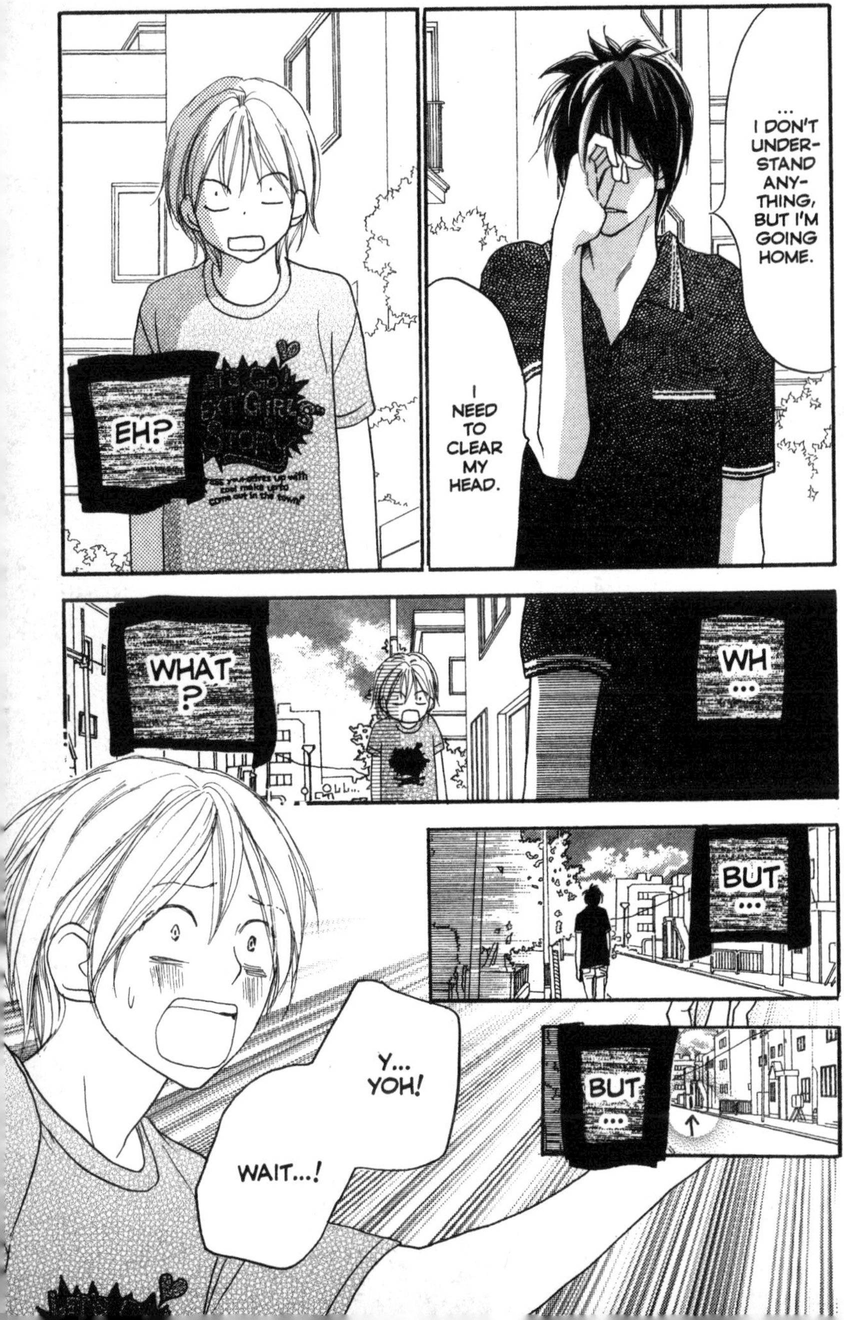
... I DON'T UNDER-STAND ANY-THING, BUT I'M GOING HOME.
I NEED TO CLEAR MY HEAD.
EH?
WH...
WHAT?
BUT...
BUT...
Y... YOH!
WAIT...!

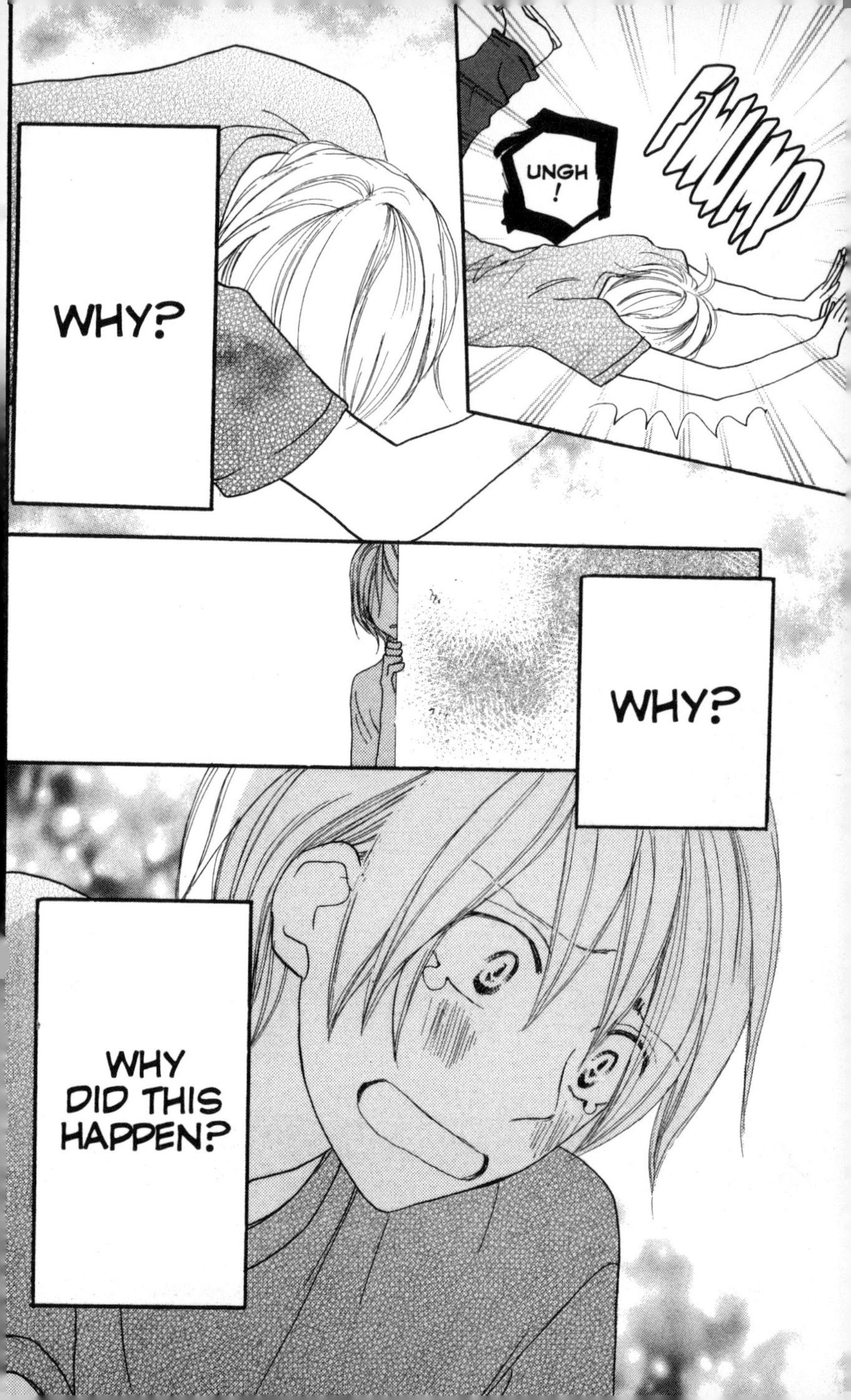
FWUMP
UNGH!
WHY?
WHY?
WHY DID THIS HAPPEN?

2

The food was really good in New Zealand. ✧✧

The best was the fresh blueberries. Every day, I went to the supermarket near my friend's home to buy them. They were so sweet and juicy! My descriptions can't do them justice...

Even now that I'm back in Japan, I still think of them sometimes.

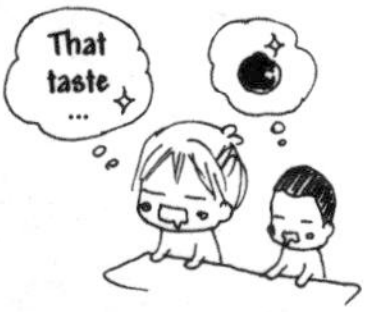
That taste ...

All the other food in New Zealand was great too! ✧✧

The sandwiches in the cafés were a really strange color, but they tasted so good! ✧✧

The soup was delicious. The bread too... ✧✧

I want to go back and experience those flavors again!

Oh yes, and on the beach...

There were little transparent things like these floating. When I dipped my foot in the water, my foot went numb... They were jellyfish.

This isn't important, but the food on the plane was great too...

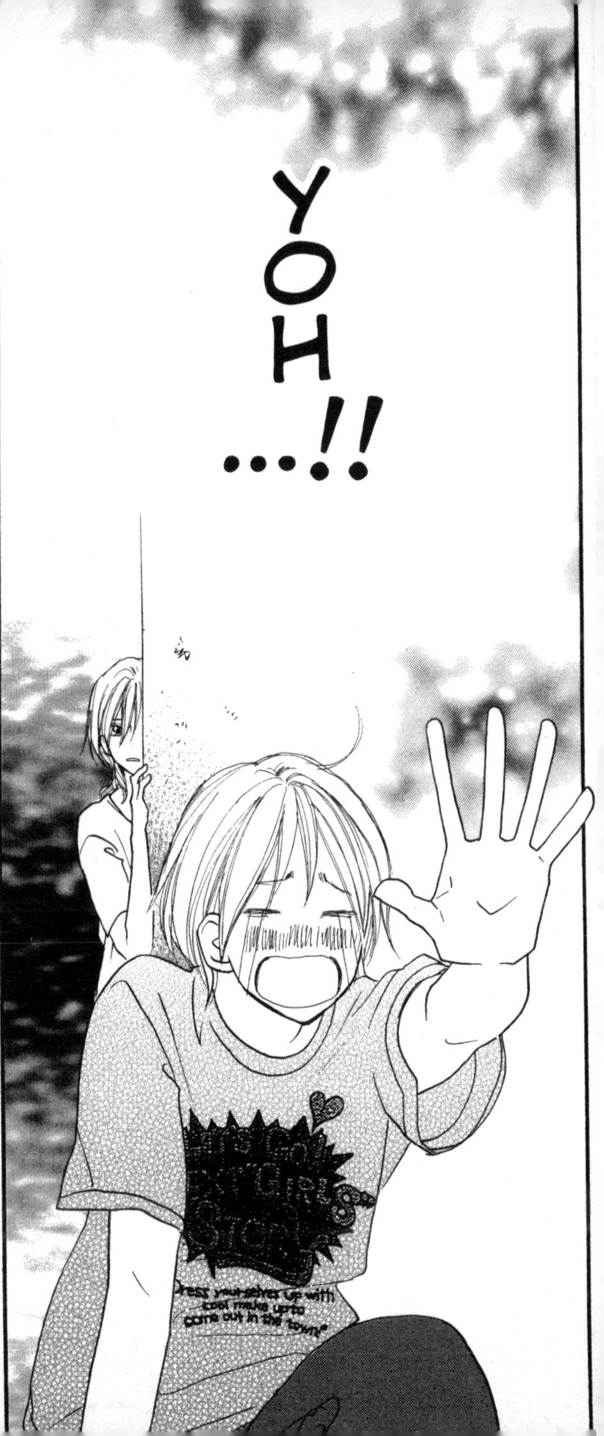
YOH...!!
Dress yourselves up with cool make up to come out in the town!

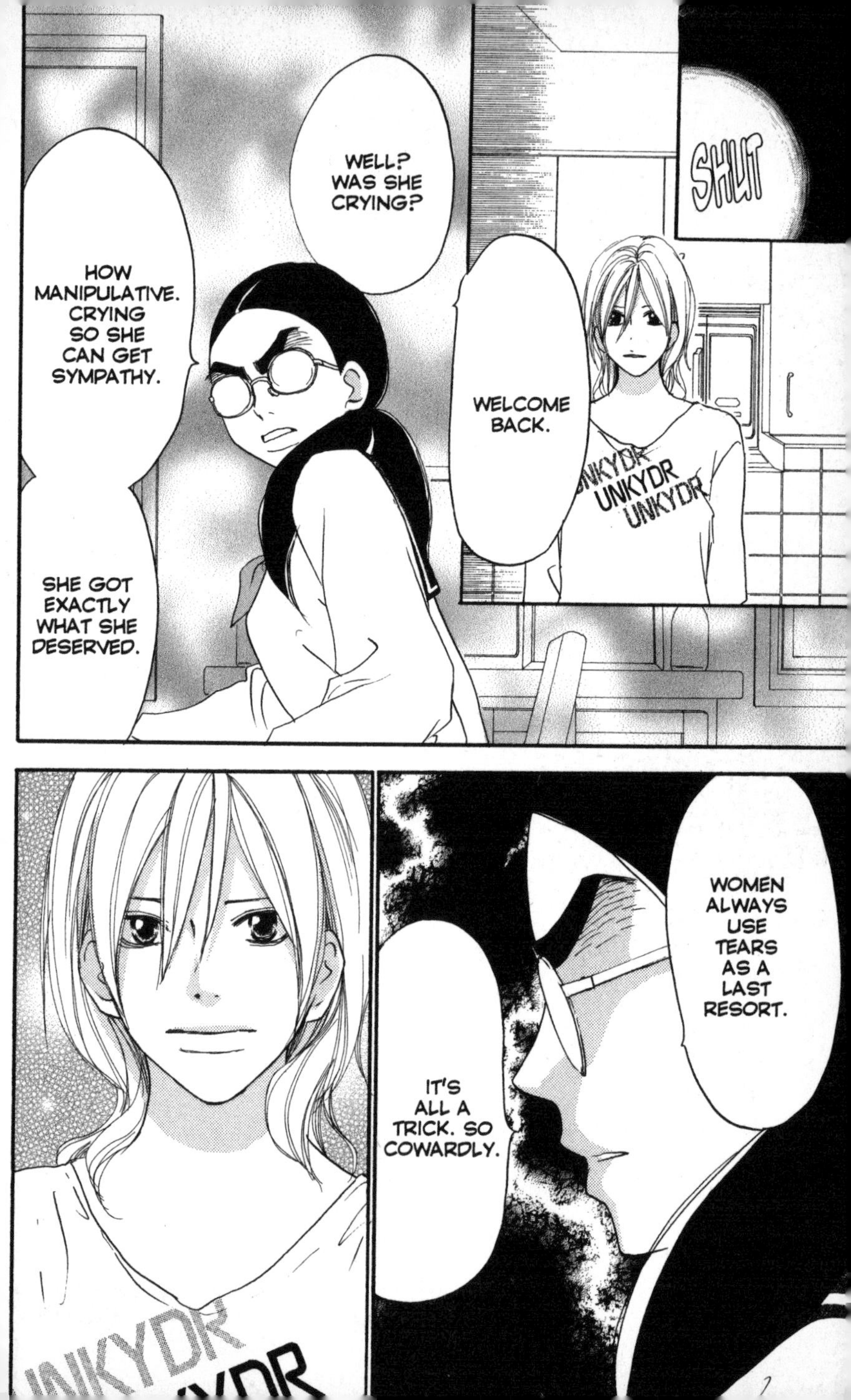
SHUT
WELCOME BACK.
UNKYDR UNKYDR UNKYDR
WELL? WAS SHE CRYING?
HOW MANIPULATIVE. CRYING SO SHE CAN GET SYMPATHY.
SHE GOT EXACTLY WHAT SHE DESERVED.
WOMEN ALWAYS USE TEARS AS A LAST RESORT.
IT'S ALL A TRICK. SO COWARDLY.

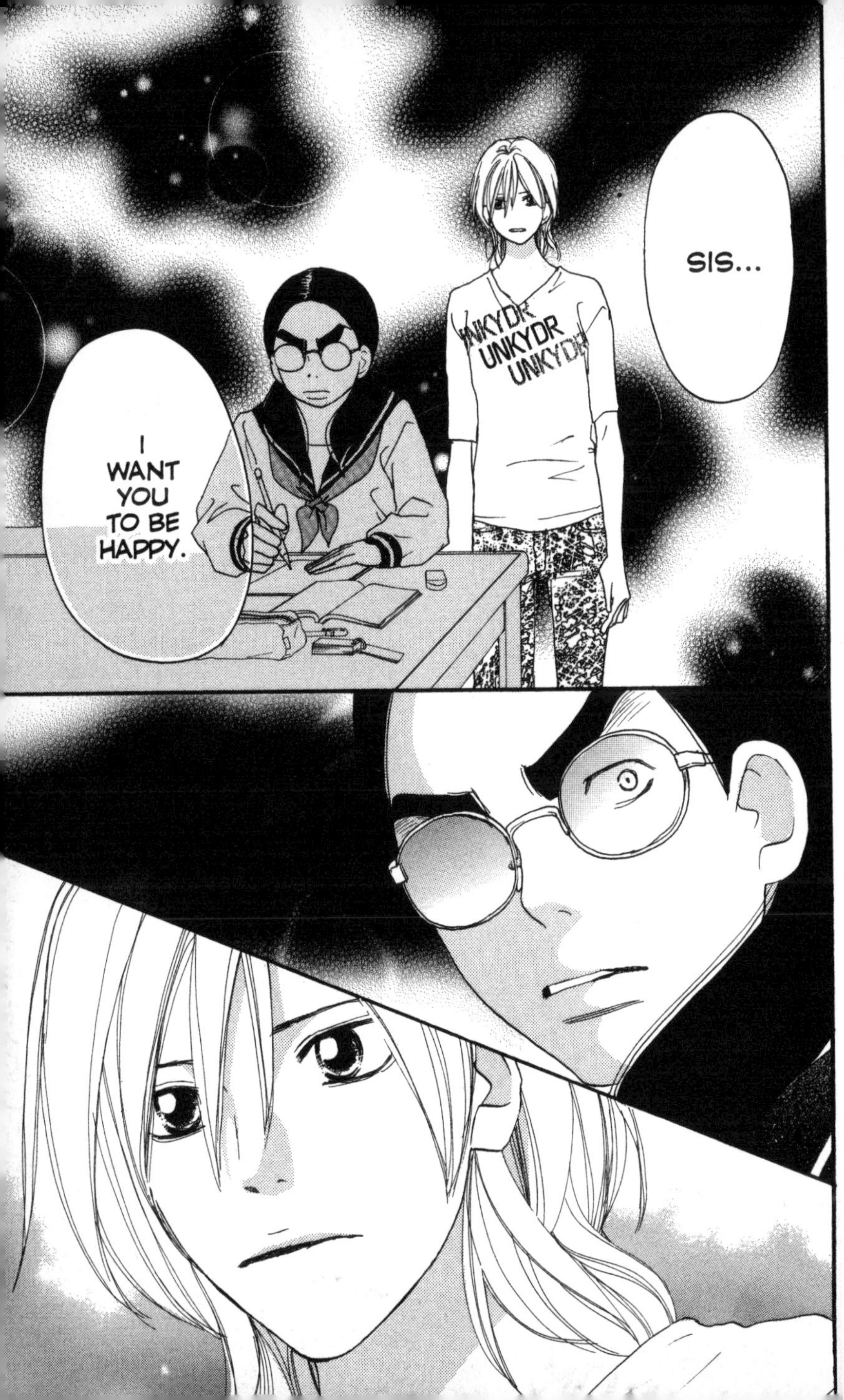
SIS...
I WANT YOU TO BE HAPPY.

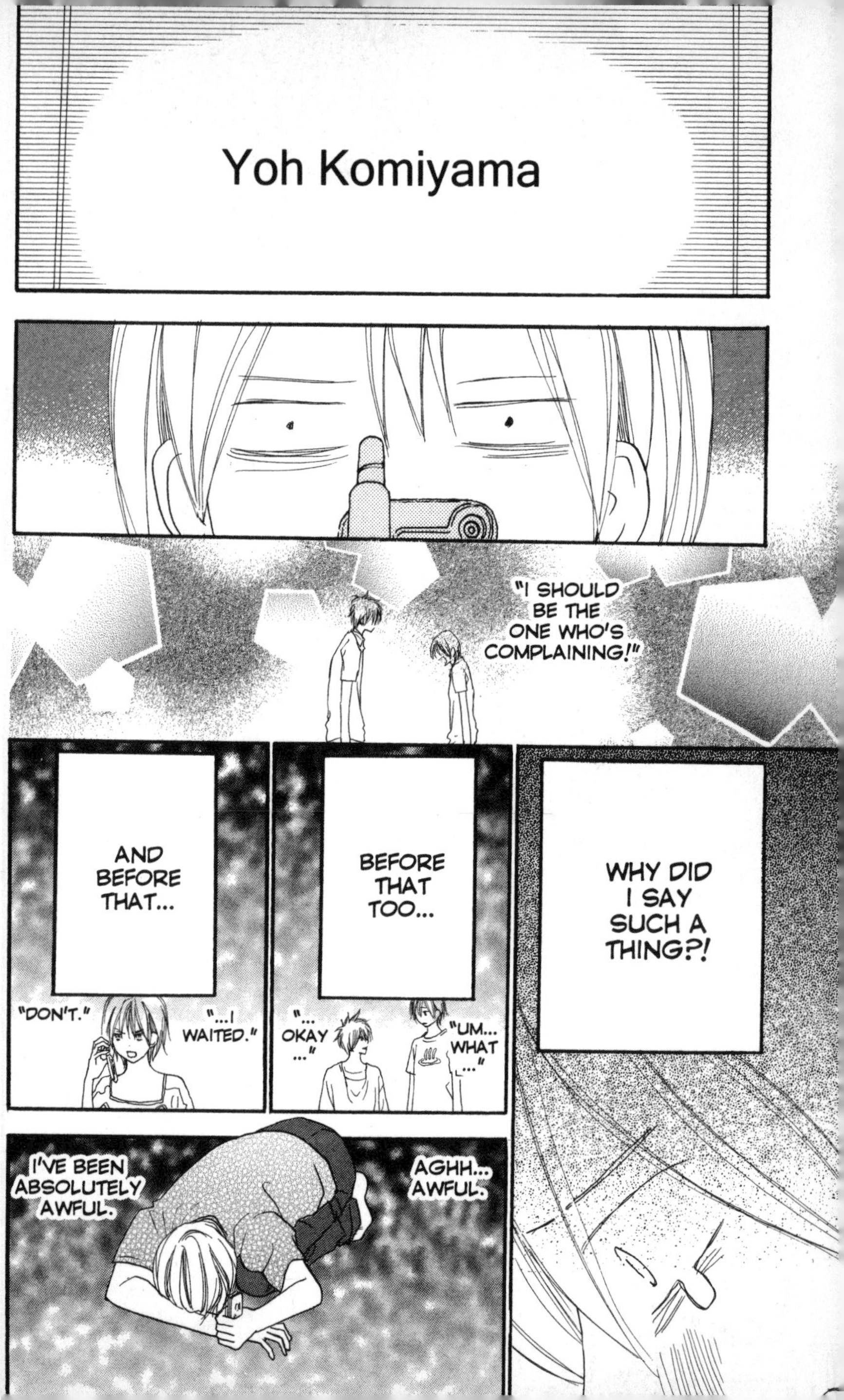
Yoh Komiyama
"I SHOULD BE THE ONE WHO'S COMPLAINING!"
WHY DID I SAY SUCH A THING?!
BEFORE THAT TOO...
"UM... WHAT..."
"...OKAY..."
AND BEFORE THAT...
"...I WAITED."
"DON'T."
AGHH... AWFUL.
I'VE BEEN ABSOLUTELY AWFUL.

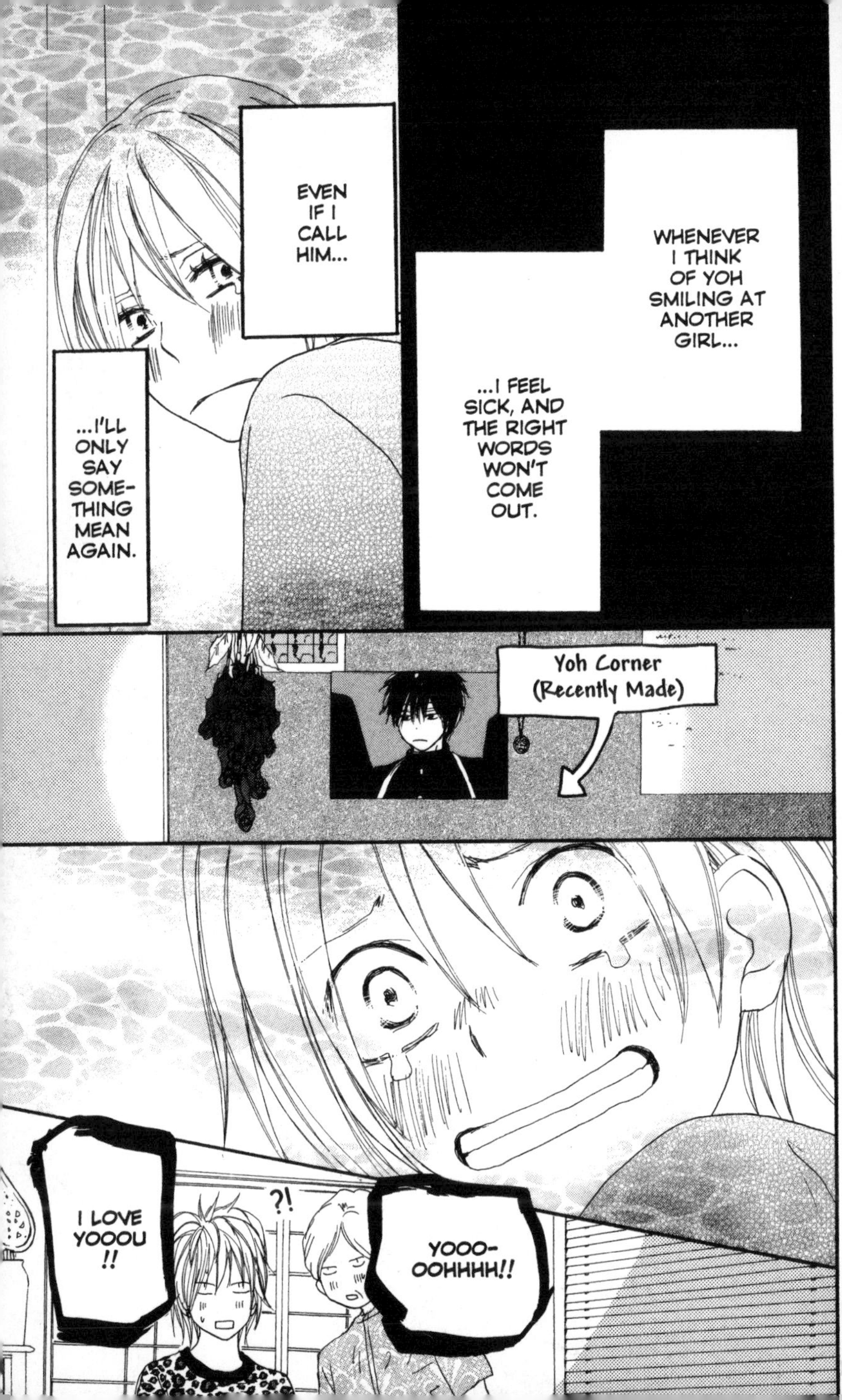
WHENEVER I THINK OF YOH SMILING AT ANOTHER GIRL...
...I FEEL SICK, AND THE RIGHT WORDS WON'T COME OUT.
EVEN IF I CALL HIM...
...I'LL ONLY SAY SOME-THING MEAN AGAIN.
Yoh Corner (Recently Made)
YOOO-OOHHHH!!
?!
I LOVE YOOOU!!

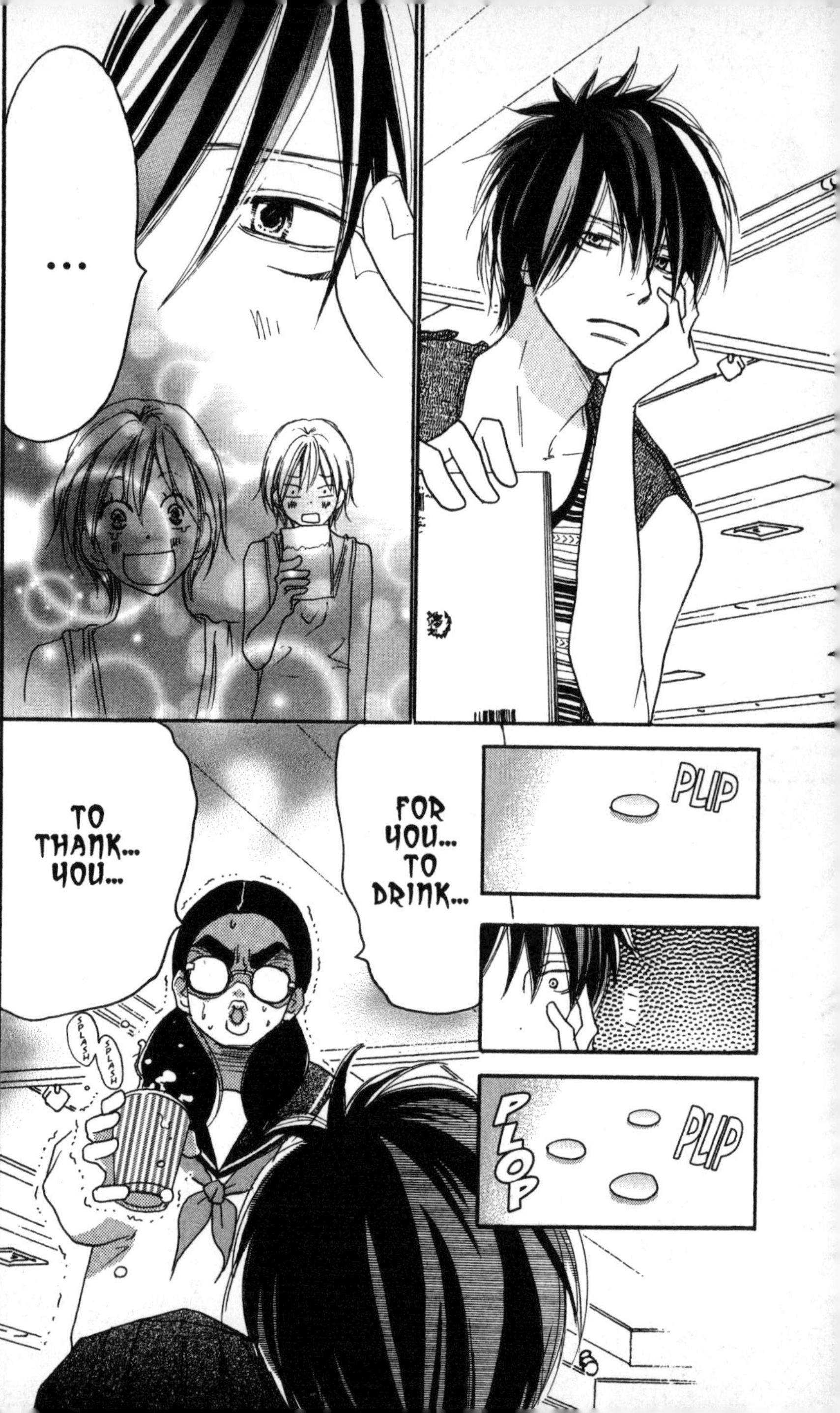
...
PLIP
PLOP
PLIP
FOR YOU... TO DRINK...
TO THANK... YOU...
SPLASH
SPLASH

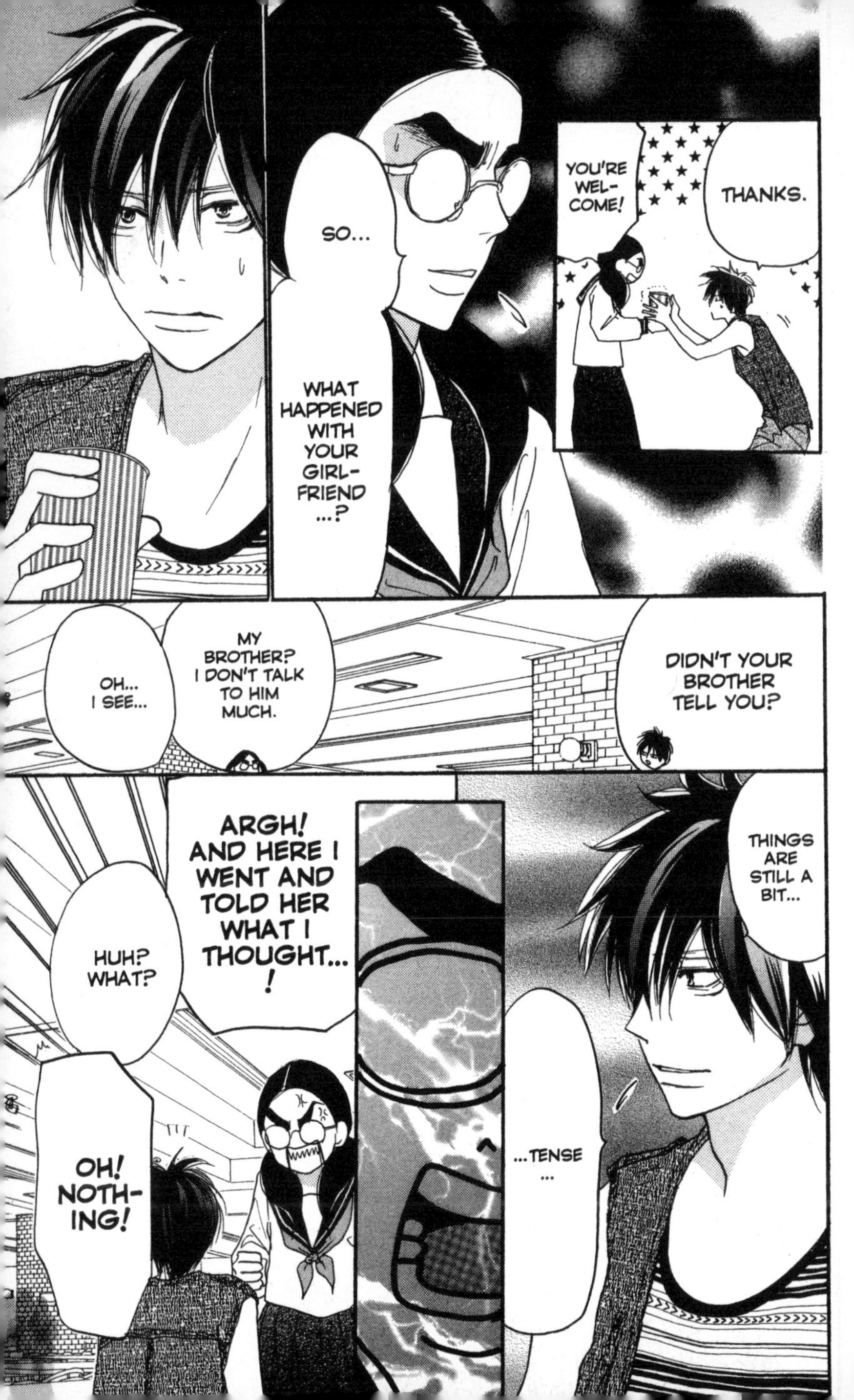
THANKS.
YOU'RE WELCOME!
SO...
WHAT HAPPENED WITH YOUR GIRLFRIEND...?
DIDN'T YOUR BROTHER TELL YOU?
MY BROTHER? I DON'T TALK TO HIM MUCH.
OH... I SEE...
THINGS ARE STILL A BIT...
...TENSE...
ARGH! AND HERE I WENT AND TOLD HER WHAT I THOUGHT...!
HUH? WHAT?
OH! NOTHING!

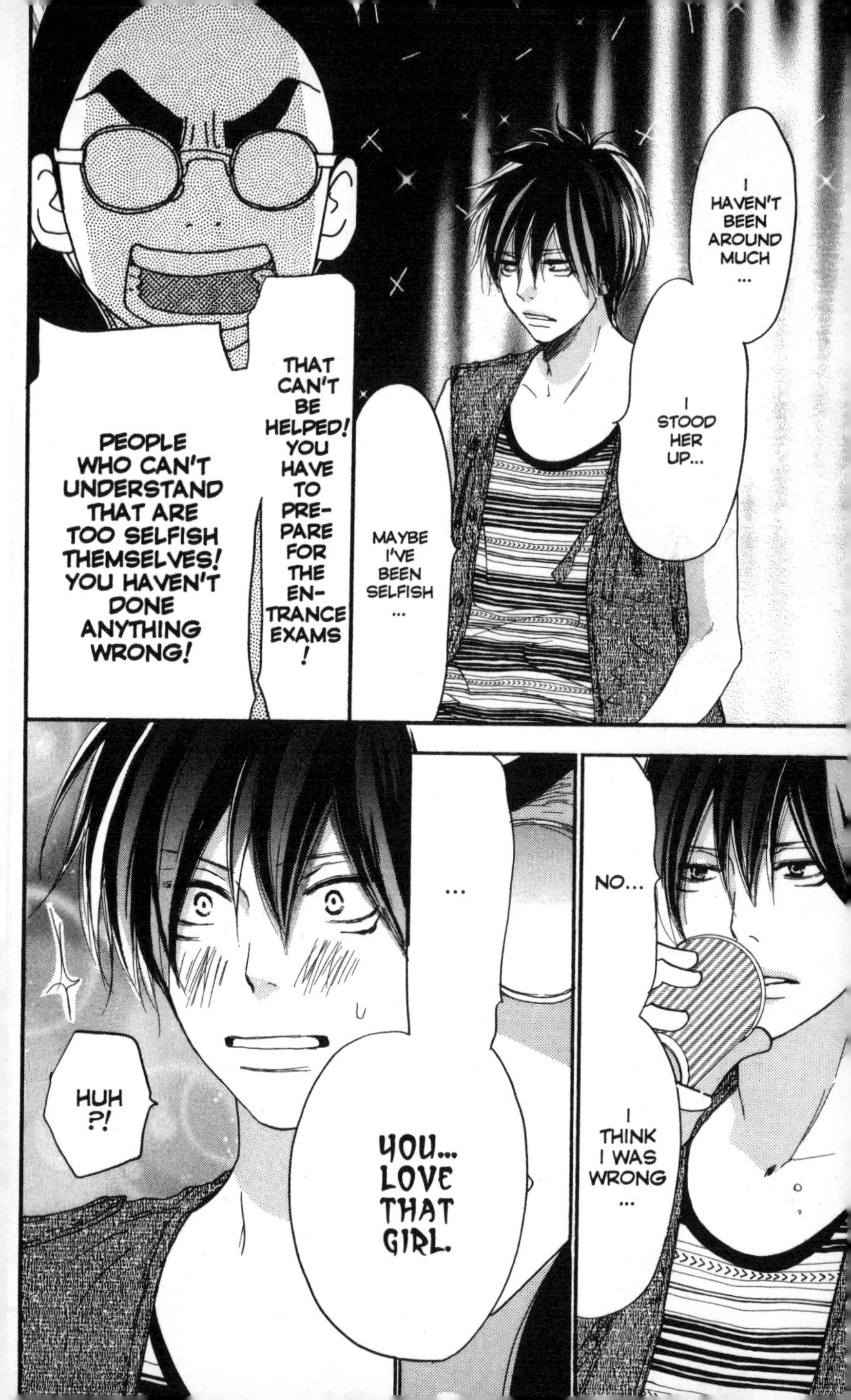
I HAVEN'T BEEN AROUND MUCH...
I STOOD HER UP...
MAYBE I'VE BEEN SELFISH...
THAT CAN'T BE HELPED! YOU HAVE TO PRE-PARE FOR THE EN-TRANCE EXAMS!
PEOPLE WHO CAN'T UNDERSTAND THAT ARE TOO SELFISH THEMSELVES! YOU HAVEN'T DONE ANYTHING WRONG!
NO...
I THINK I WAS WRONG...
...
YOU... LOVE THAT GIRL.
HUH?!

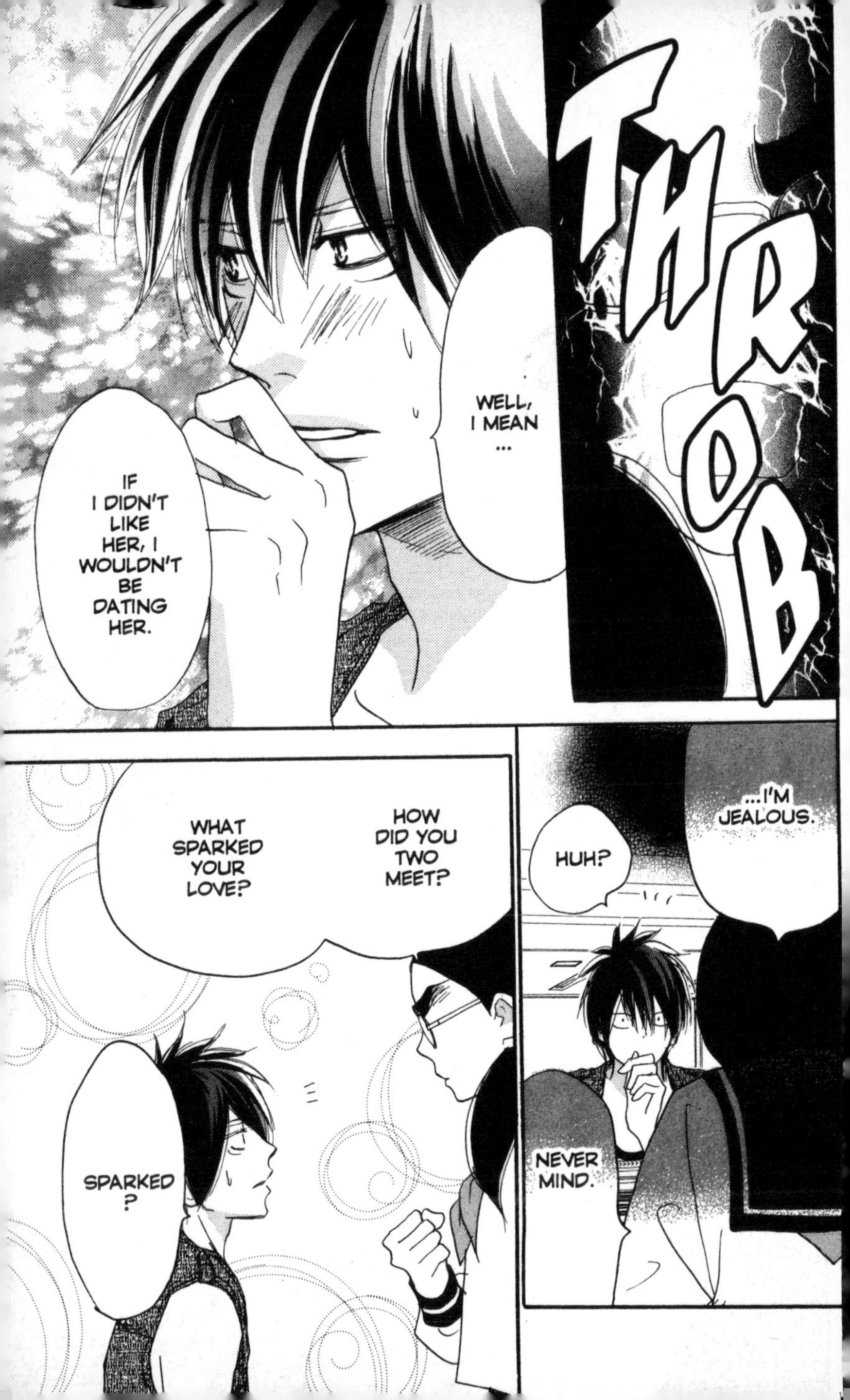
THROB
WELL, I MEAN ...
IF I DIDN'T LIKE HER, I WOULDN'T BE DATING HER.
...I'M JEALOUS.
HUH?
NEVER MIND.
HOW DID YOU TWO MEET?
WHAT SPARKED YOUR LOVE?
SPARKED?

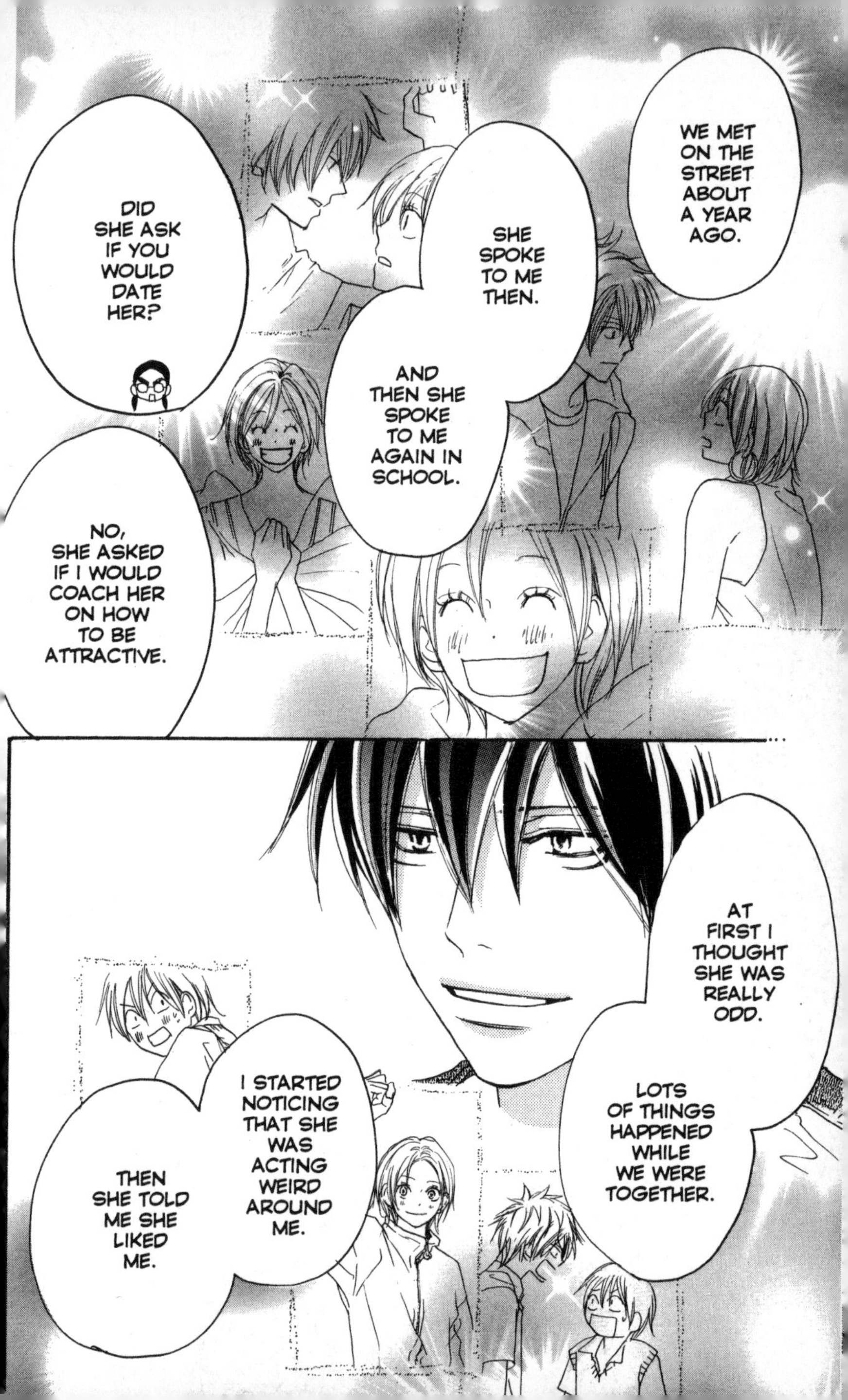
WE MET ON THE STREET ABOUT A YEAR AGO.
SHE SPOKE TO ME THEN.
AND THEN SHE SPOKE TO ME AGAIN IN SCHOOL.
DID SHE ASK IF YOU WOULD DATE HER?
NO, SHE ASKED IF I WOULD COACH HER ON HOW TO BE ATTRACTIVE.
AT FIRST I THOUGHT SHE WAS REALLY ODD.
LOTS OF THINGS HAPPENED WHILE WE WERE TOGETHER.
I STARTED NOTICING THAT SHE WAS ACTING WEIRD AROUND ME.
THEN SHE TOLD ME SHE LIKED ME.

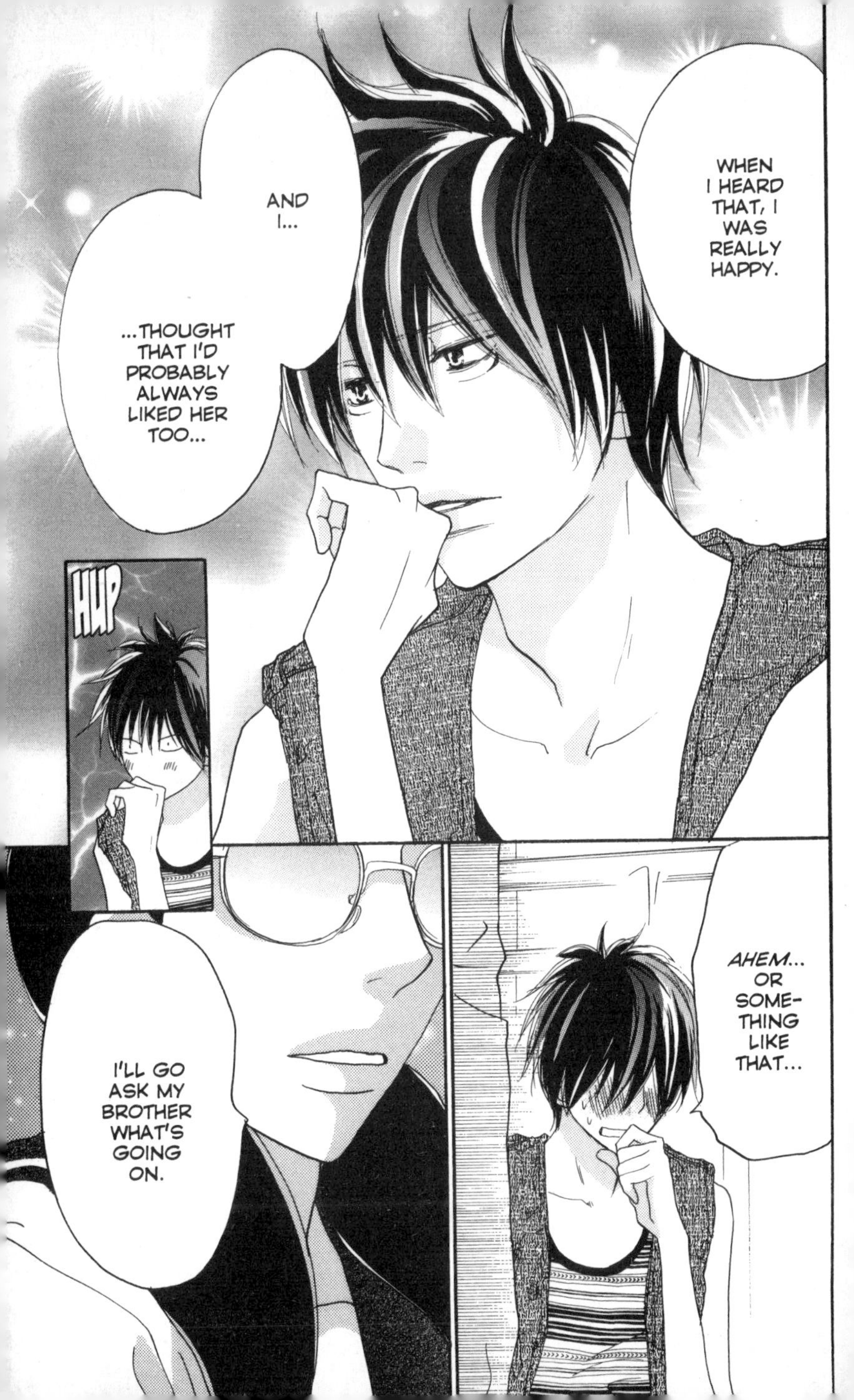
WHEN I HEARD THAT, I WAS REALLY HAPPY.
AND I...
...THOUGHT THAT I'D PROBABLY ALWAYS LIKED HER TOO...
HUP
AHEM... OR SOME-THING LIKE THAT...
I'LL GO ASK MY BROTHER WHAT'S GOING ON.

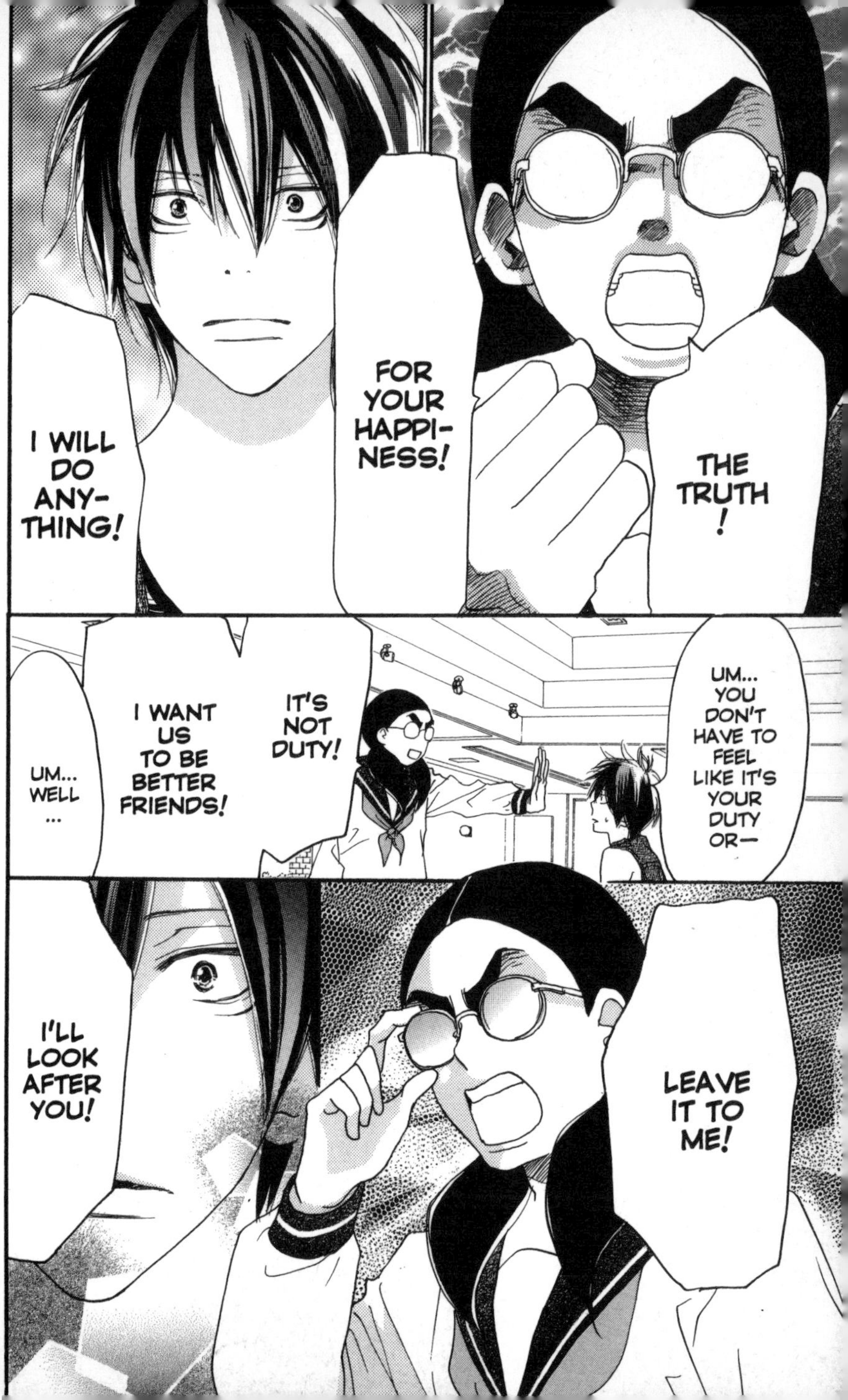
THE TRUTH!
FOR YOUR HAPPINESS!
I WILL DO ANYTHING!
UM... YOU DON'T HAVE TO FEEL LIKE IT'S YOUR DUTY OR—
IT'S NOT DUTY!
I WANT US TO BE BETTER FRIENDS!
UM... WELL ...
LEAVE IT TO ME!
I'LL LOOK AFTER YOU!

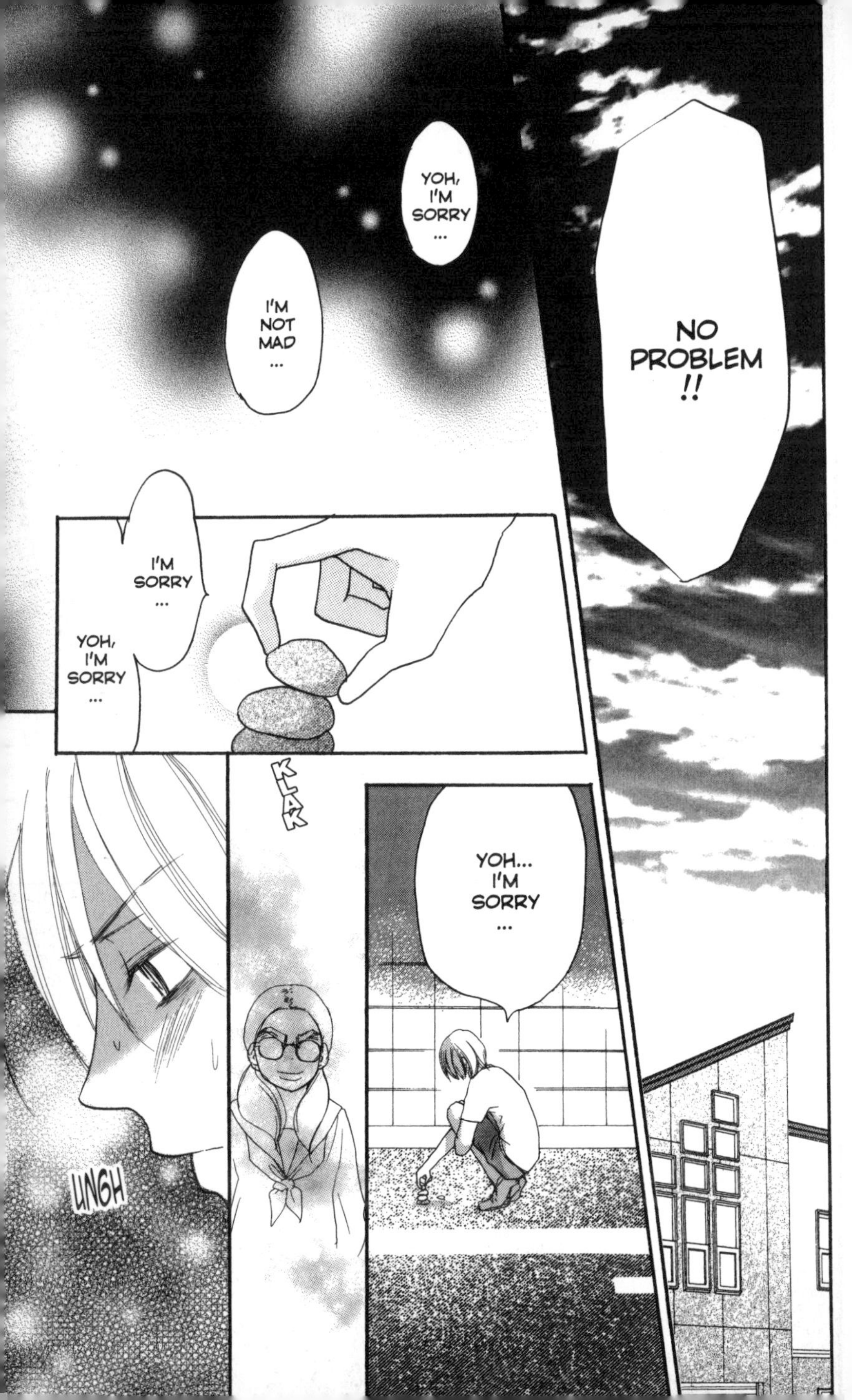
NO PROBLEM!!
YOH, I'M SORRY...
I'M NOT MAD...
I'M SORRY...
YOH, I'M SORRY...
YOH... I'M SORRY...
KLAK
UNGH

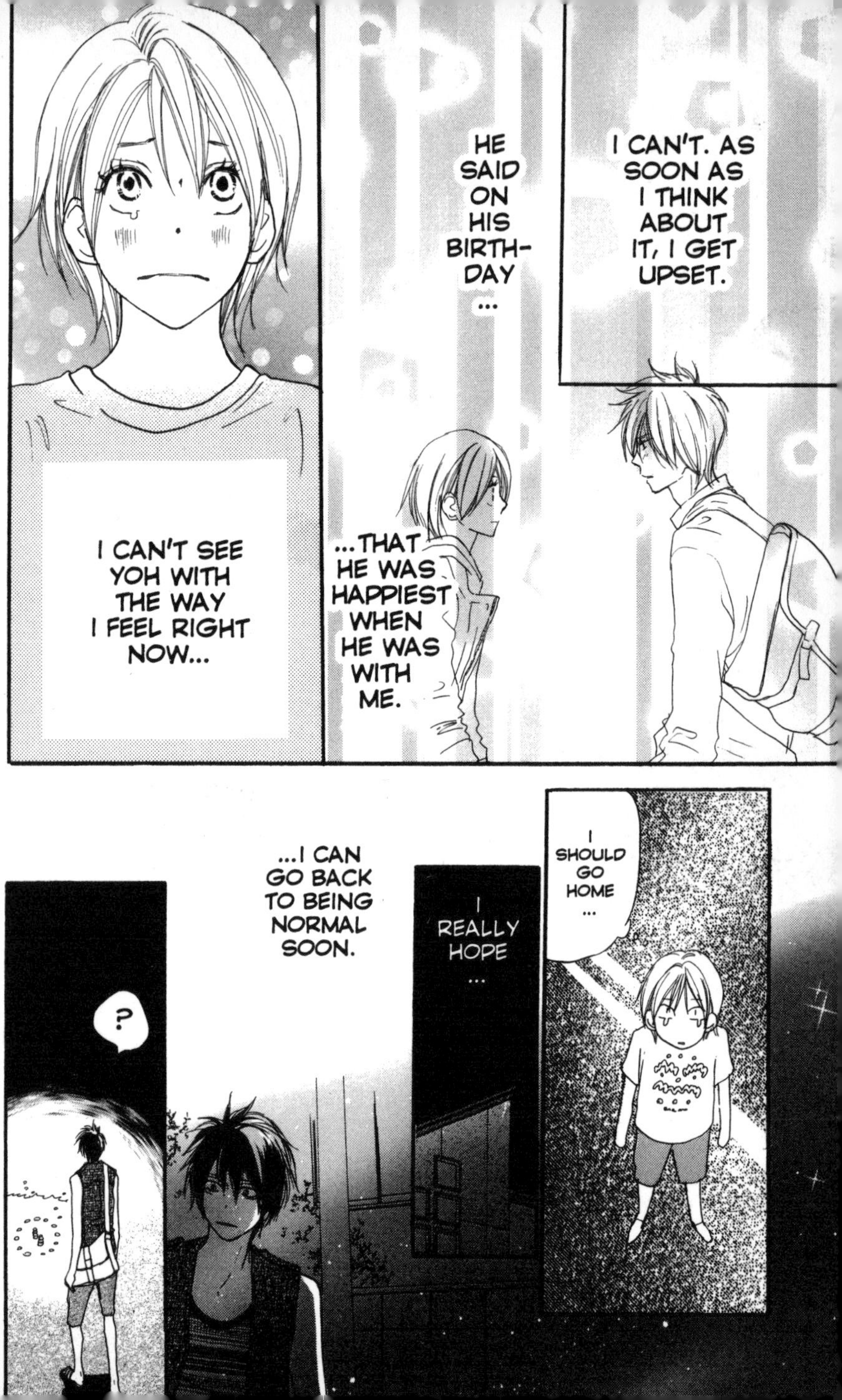
I CAN'T. AS SOON AS I THINK ABOUT IT, I GET UPSET.
HE SAID ON HIS BIRTH-DAY...
...THAT HE WAS HAPPIEST WHEN HE WAS WITH ME.
I CAN'T SEE YOH WITH THE WAY I FEEL RIGHT NOW...
I SHOULD GO HOME...
I REALLY HOPE...
...I CAN GO BACK TO BEING NORMAL SOON.
?

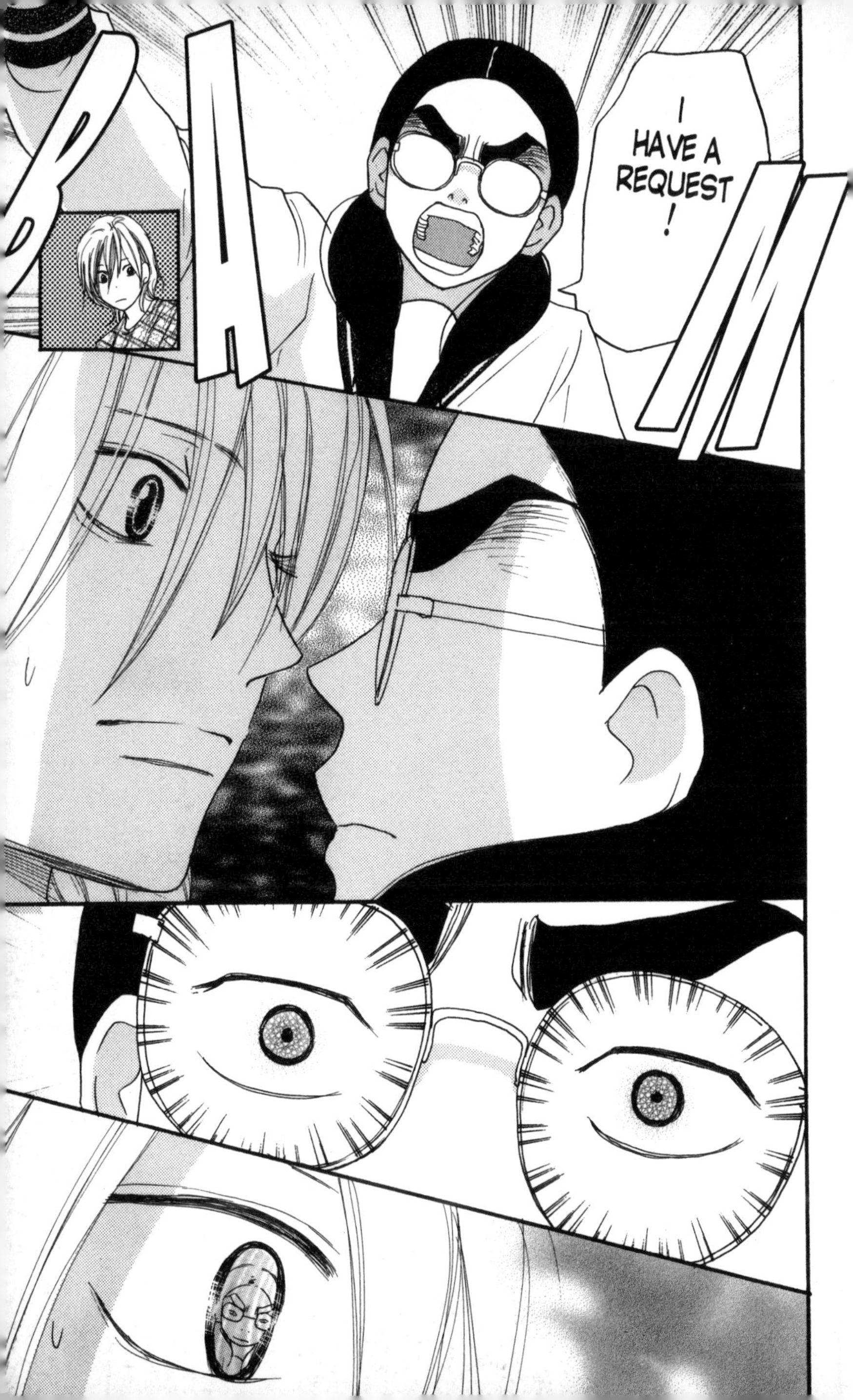
I HAVE A REQUEST!
BAM

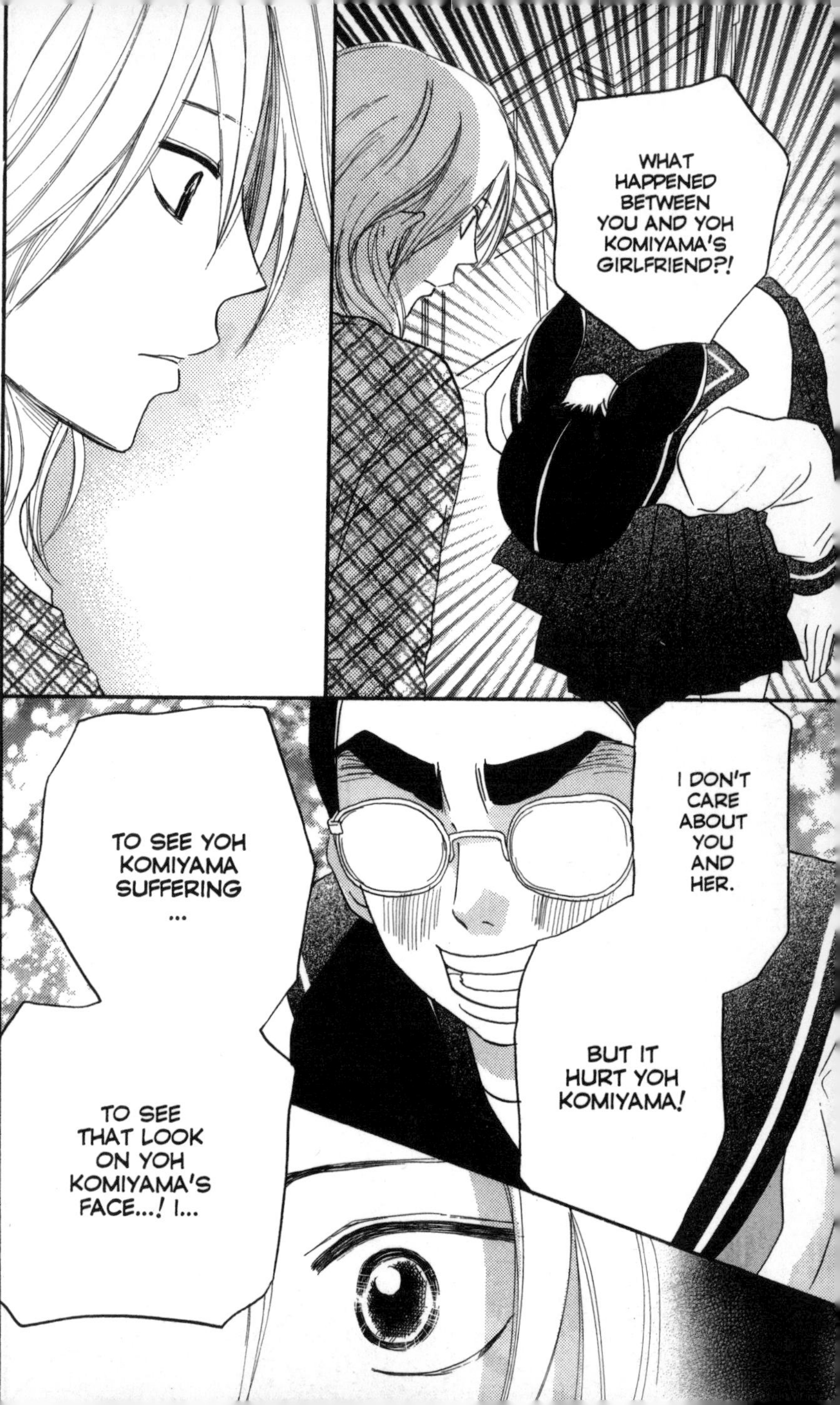
WHAT HAPPENED BETWEEN YOU AND YOH KOMIYAMA'S GIRLFRIEND?!
I DON'T CARE ABOUT YOU AND HER.
BUT IT HURT YOH KOMIYAMA!
TO SEE YOH KOMIYAMA SUFFERING ...
TO SEE THAT LOOK ON YOH KOMIYAMA'S FACE...! I...

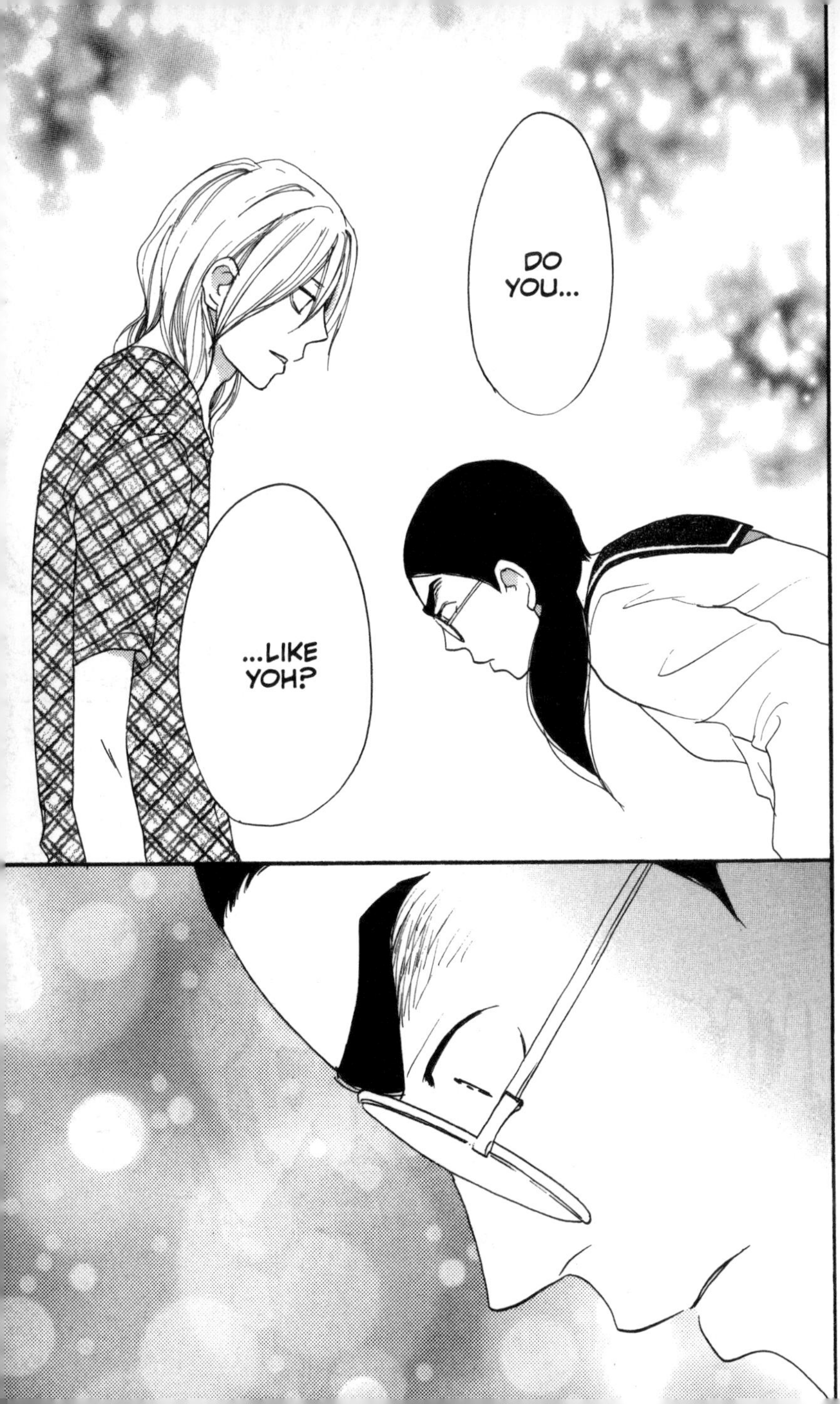
DO YOU...
...LIKE YOH?

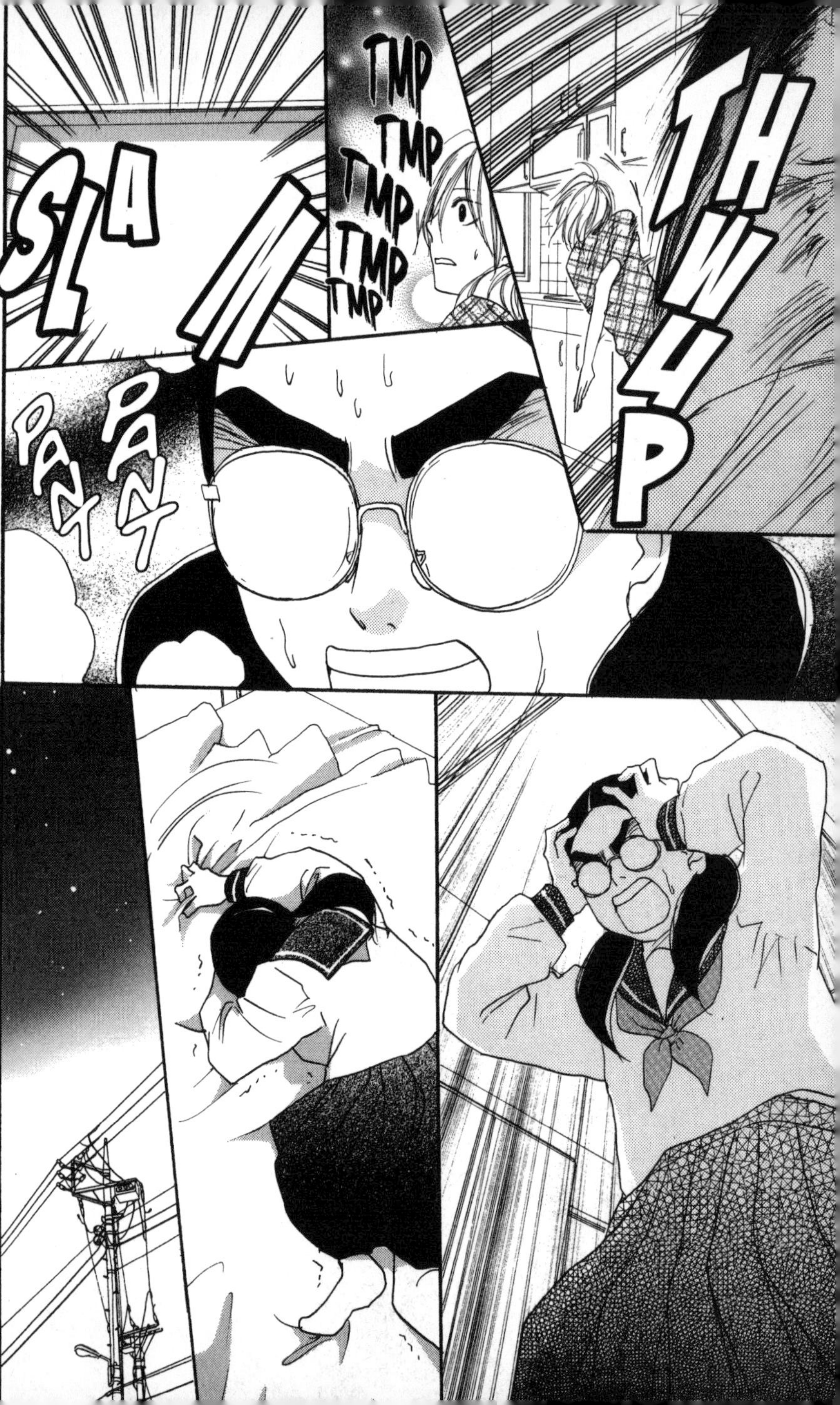
THWUMP
TMP TMP TMP TMP TMP TMP
SLAM
PANT PANT

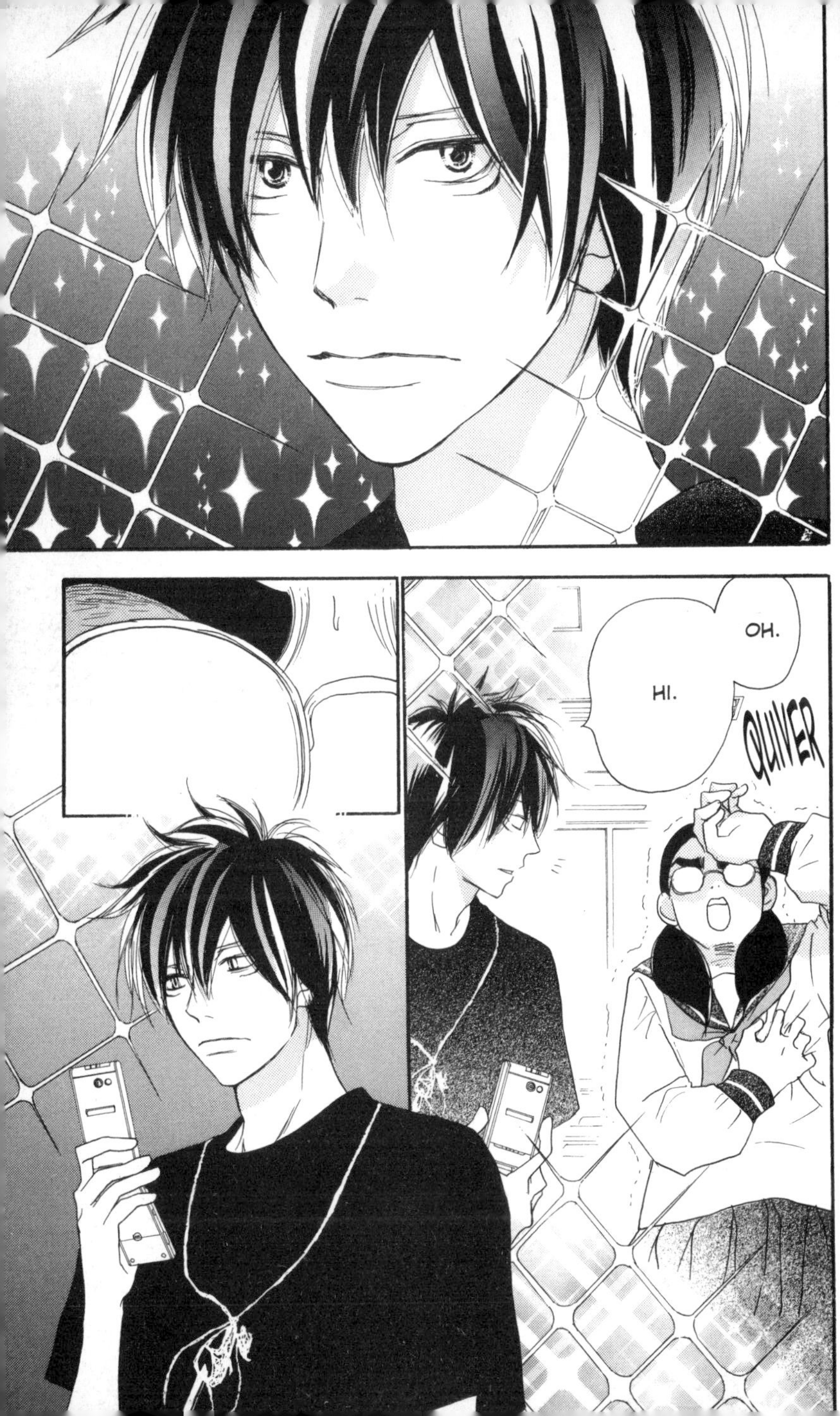
OH.
HI.
QUIVER

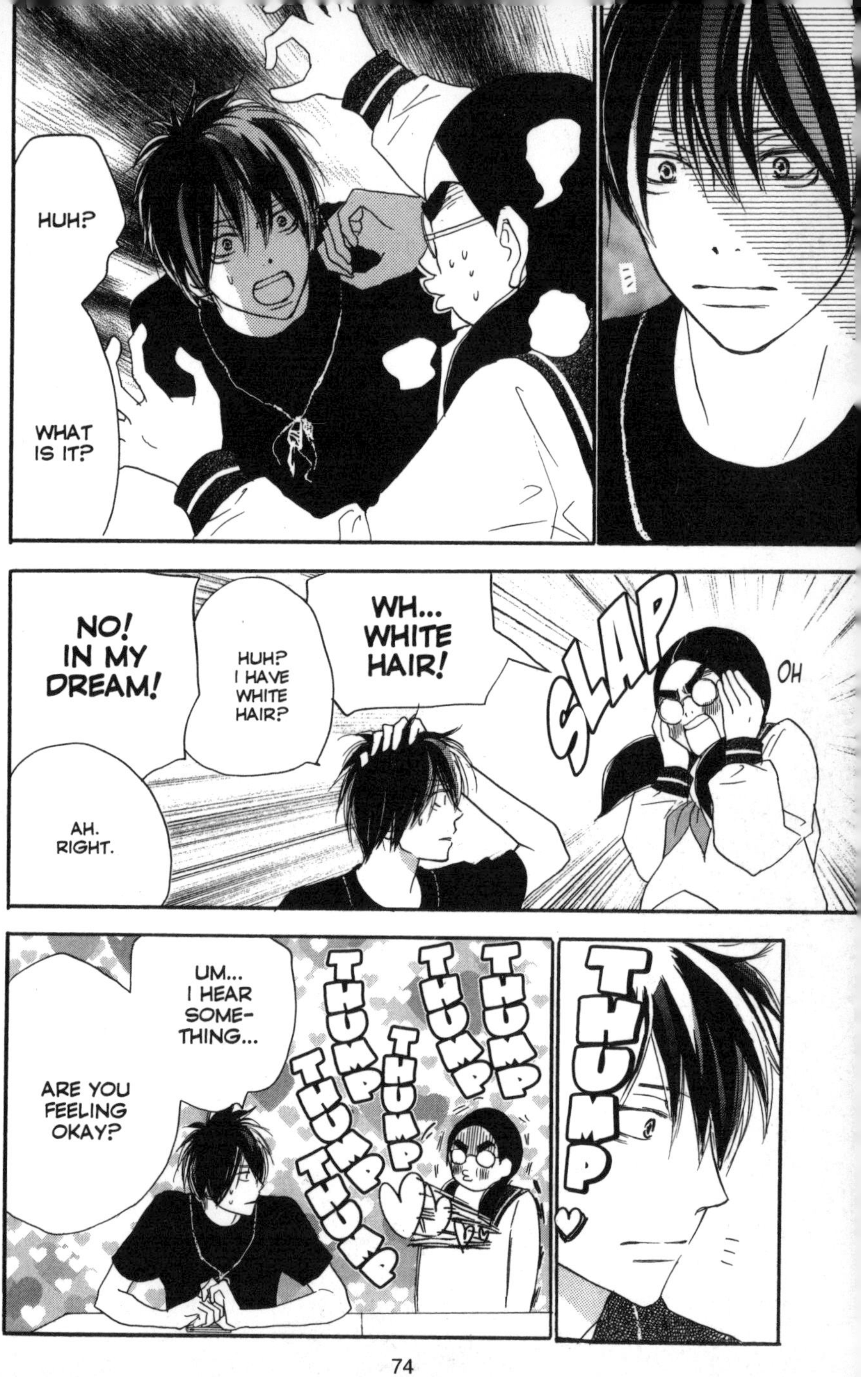
HUH?
WHAT IS IT?
OH
SLAP
WH... WHITE HAIR!
HUH? I HAVE WHITE HAIR?
NO! IN MY DREAM!
AH. RIGHT.
THUMP
THUMP
THUMP
THUMP
THUMP
THUMP
THUMP
UM... I HEAR SOME-THING...
ARE YOU FEELING OKAY?

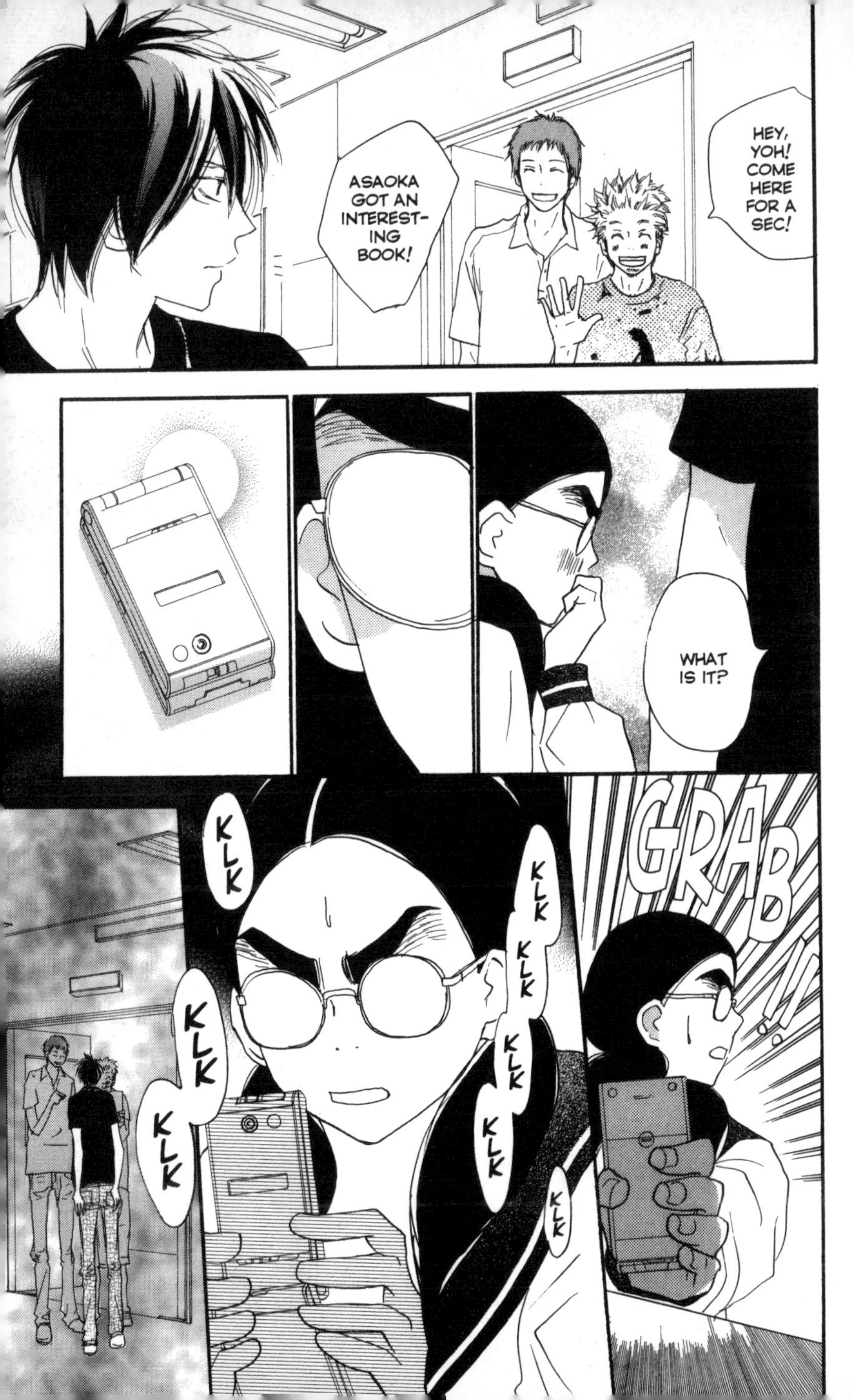
HEY, YOH! COME HERE FOR A SEC!
ASAOKA GOT AN INTERESTING BOOK!
WHAT IS IT?
GRAB
KLK KLK KLK KLK KLK KLK KLK KLK KLK KLK

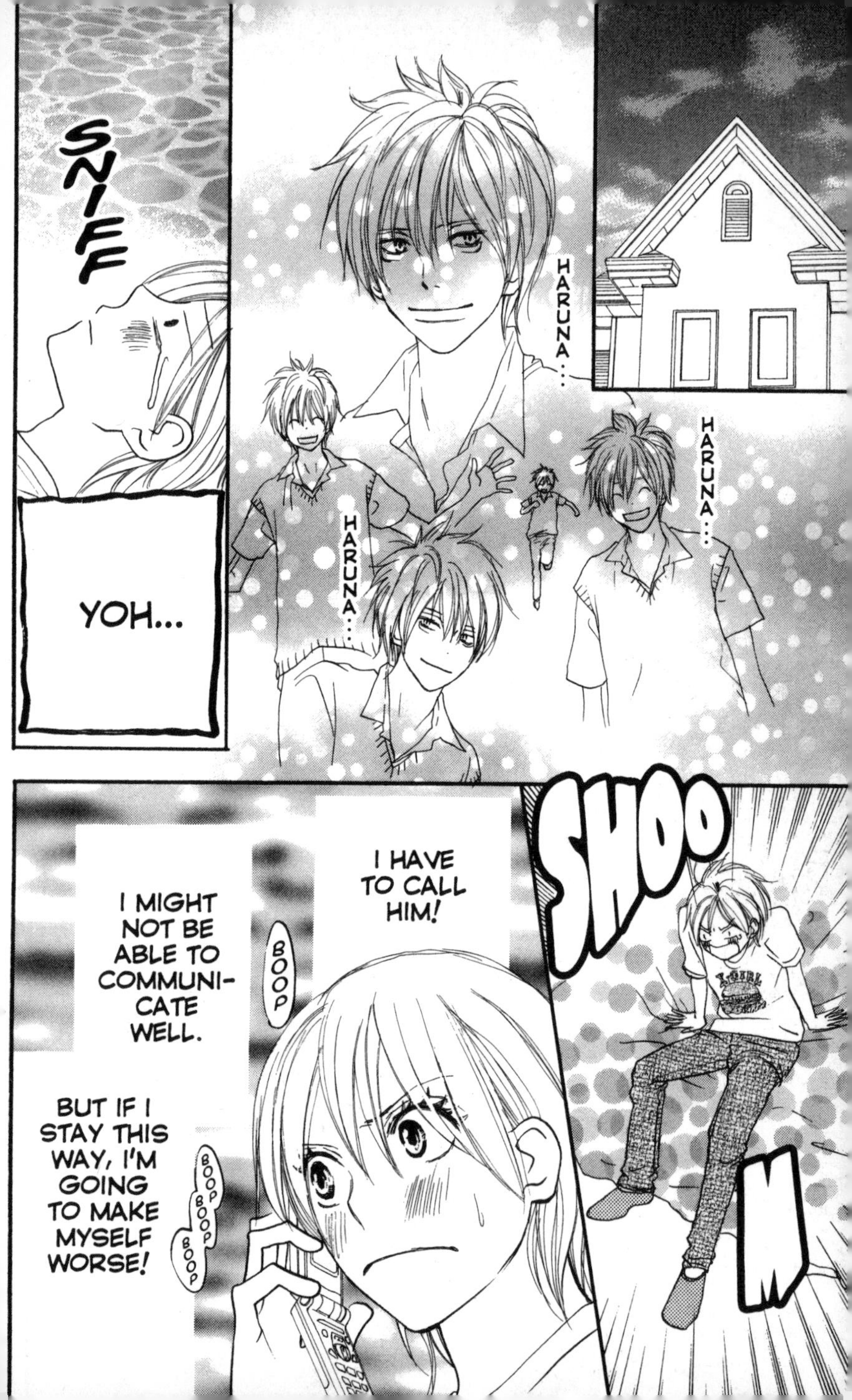
HARUNA...
HARUNA...
HARUNA...
SNIFF
YOH...
SHOOM
I HAVE TO CALL HIM!
BOOP
I MIGHT NOT BE ABLE TO COMMUNICATE WELL.
BOOP BOOP BOOP
BUT IF I STAY THIS WAY, I'M GOING TO MAKE MYSELF WORSE!

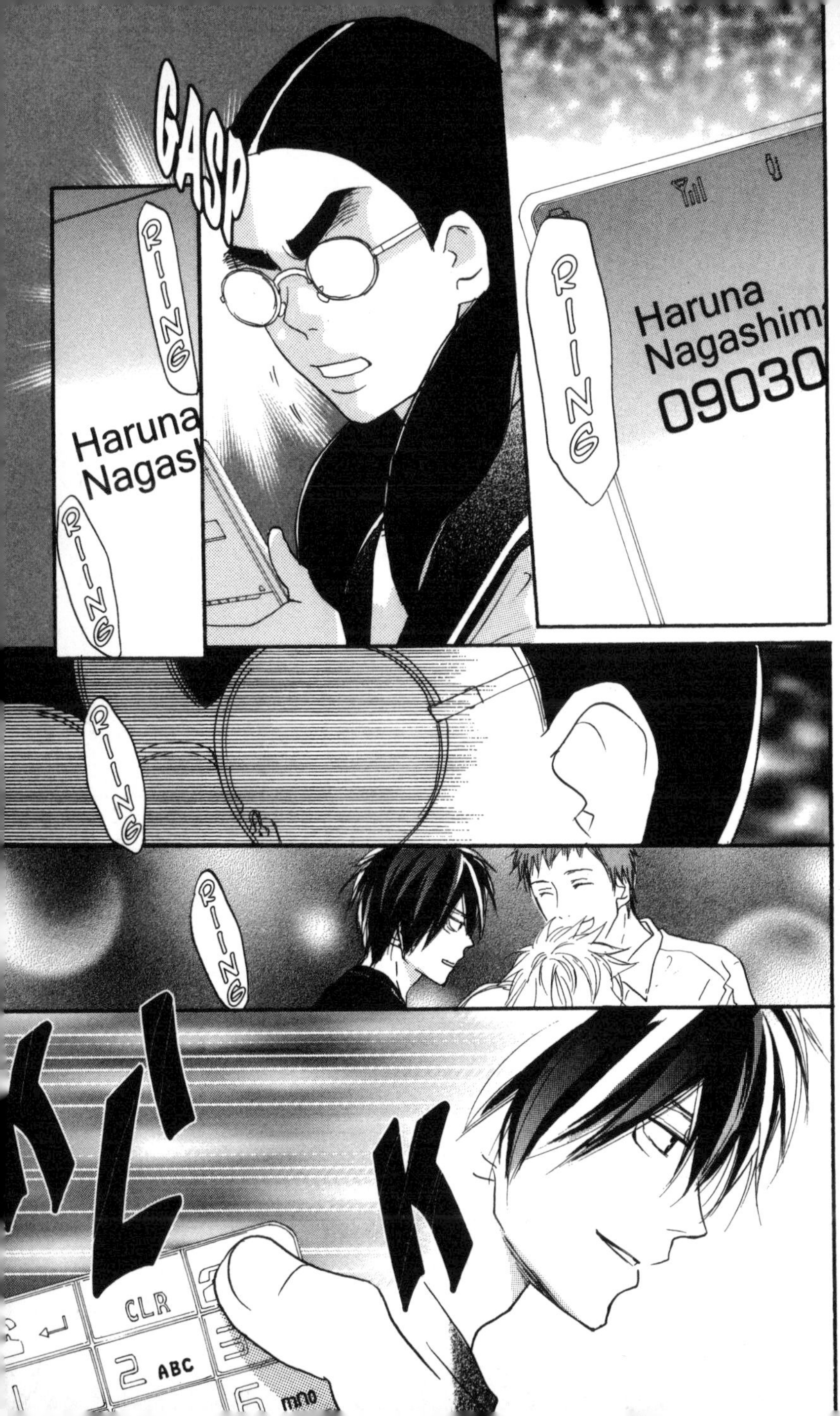
RIIING
Haruna
Nagashim
09030
GASP
RIIING
Haruna
Nagas
RIIING
RIIING
RIIING
CLR
2 ABC
mno

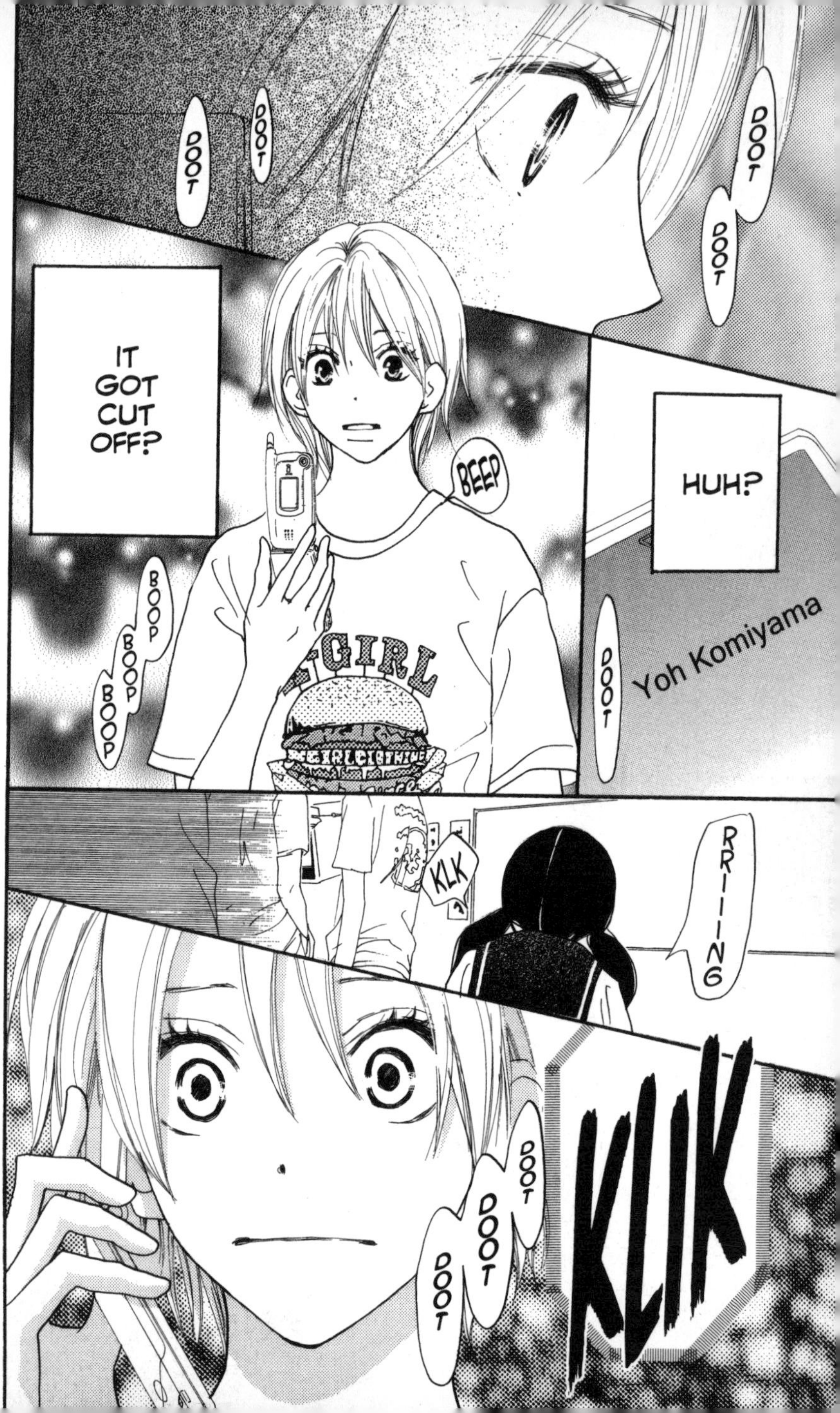
DOOT
DOOT
DOOT
DOOT
HUH?
DOOT
IT GOT CUT OFF?
BEEP
BOOP BOOP BOOP
RRIIING
KLK
KLIK
DOOT DOOT DOOT

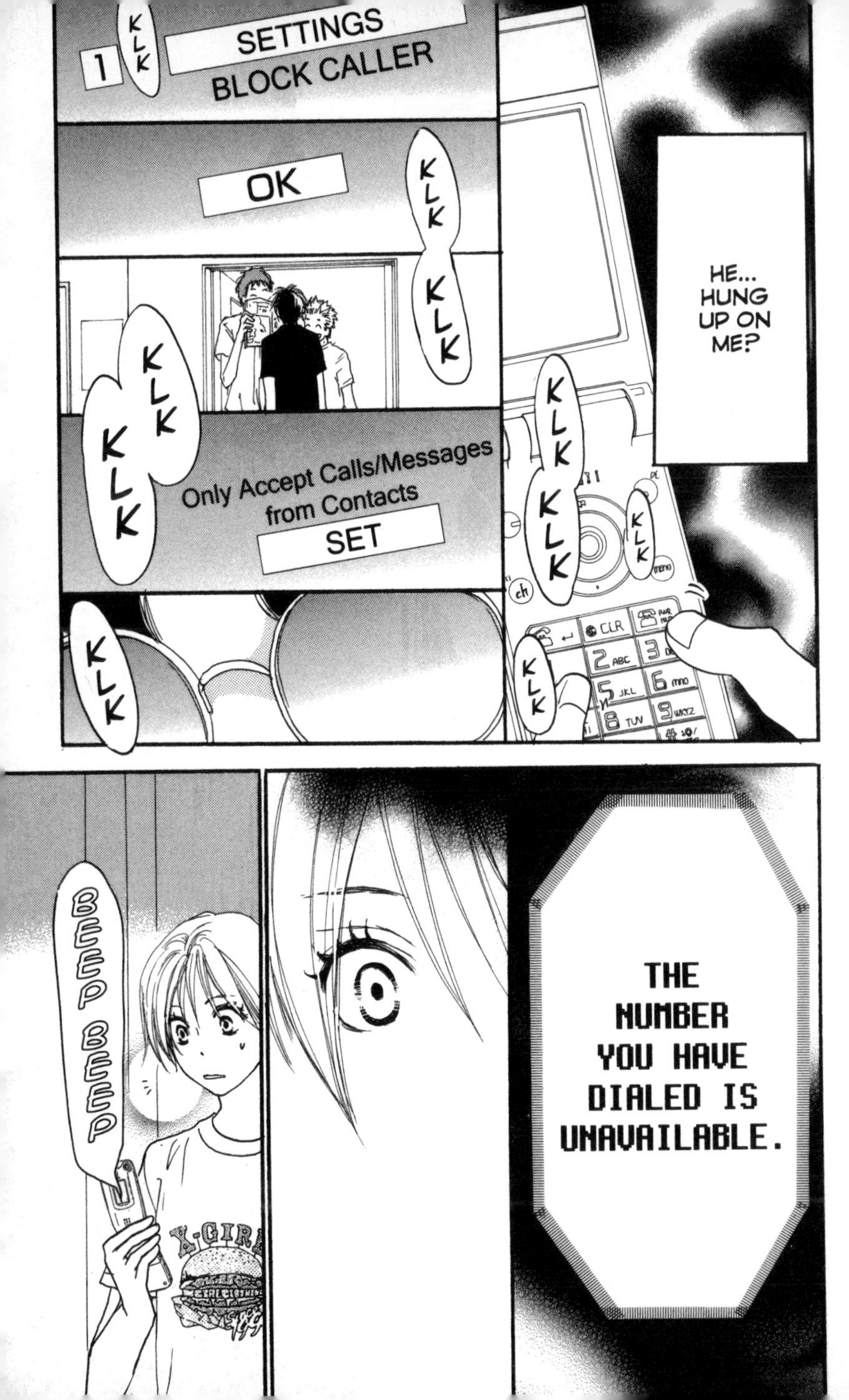
HE... HUNG UP ON ME?
KLK
KLK
KLK
KLK
1
KLK
SETTINGS
BLOCK CALLER
OK
KLK
KLK
KLK
KLK
Only Accept Calls/Messages from Contacts
SET
KLK
THE NUMBER YOU HAVE DIALED IS UNAVAILABLE.
BEEP BEEP

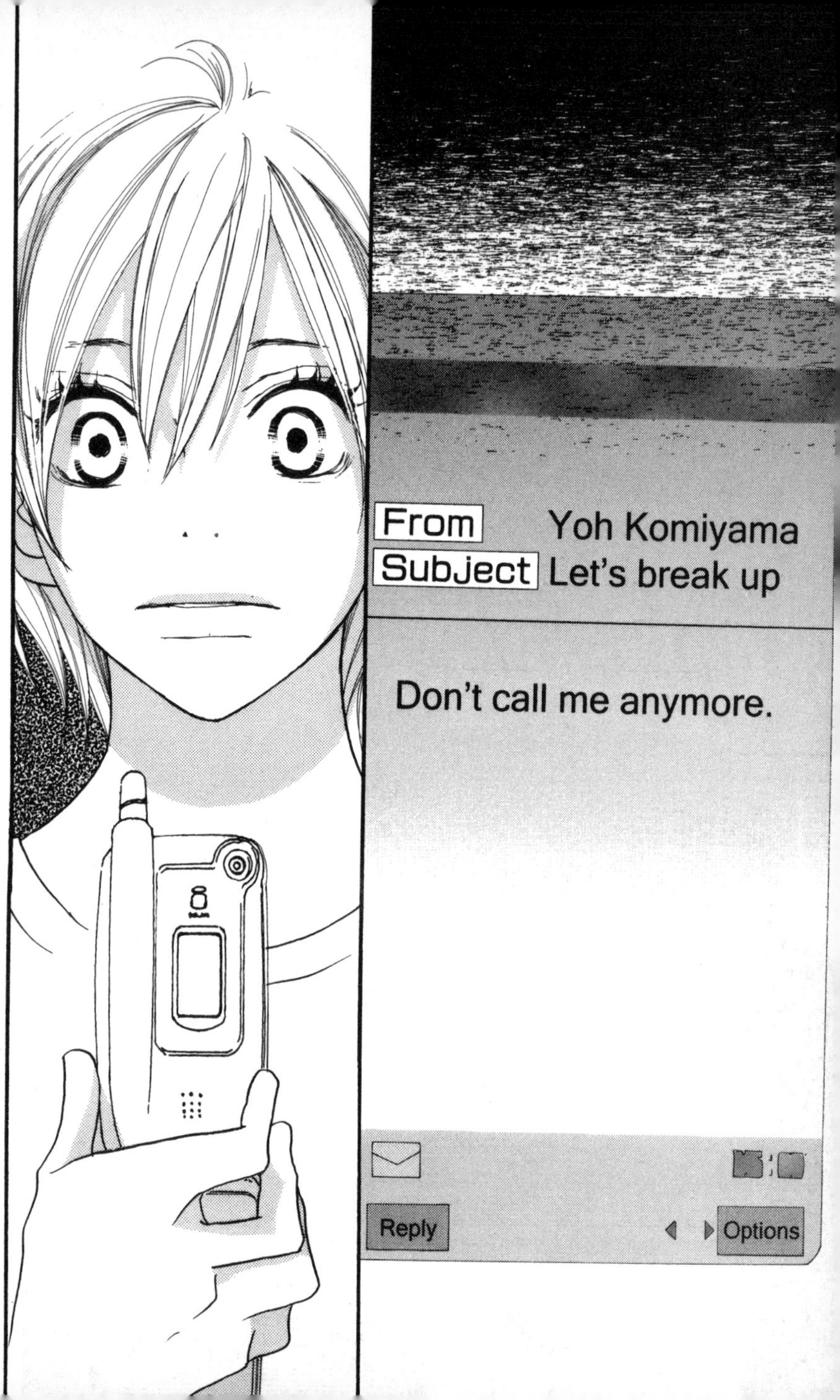
From Yoh Komiyama
Subject Let's break up
Don't call me anymore.
Reply
Options

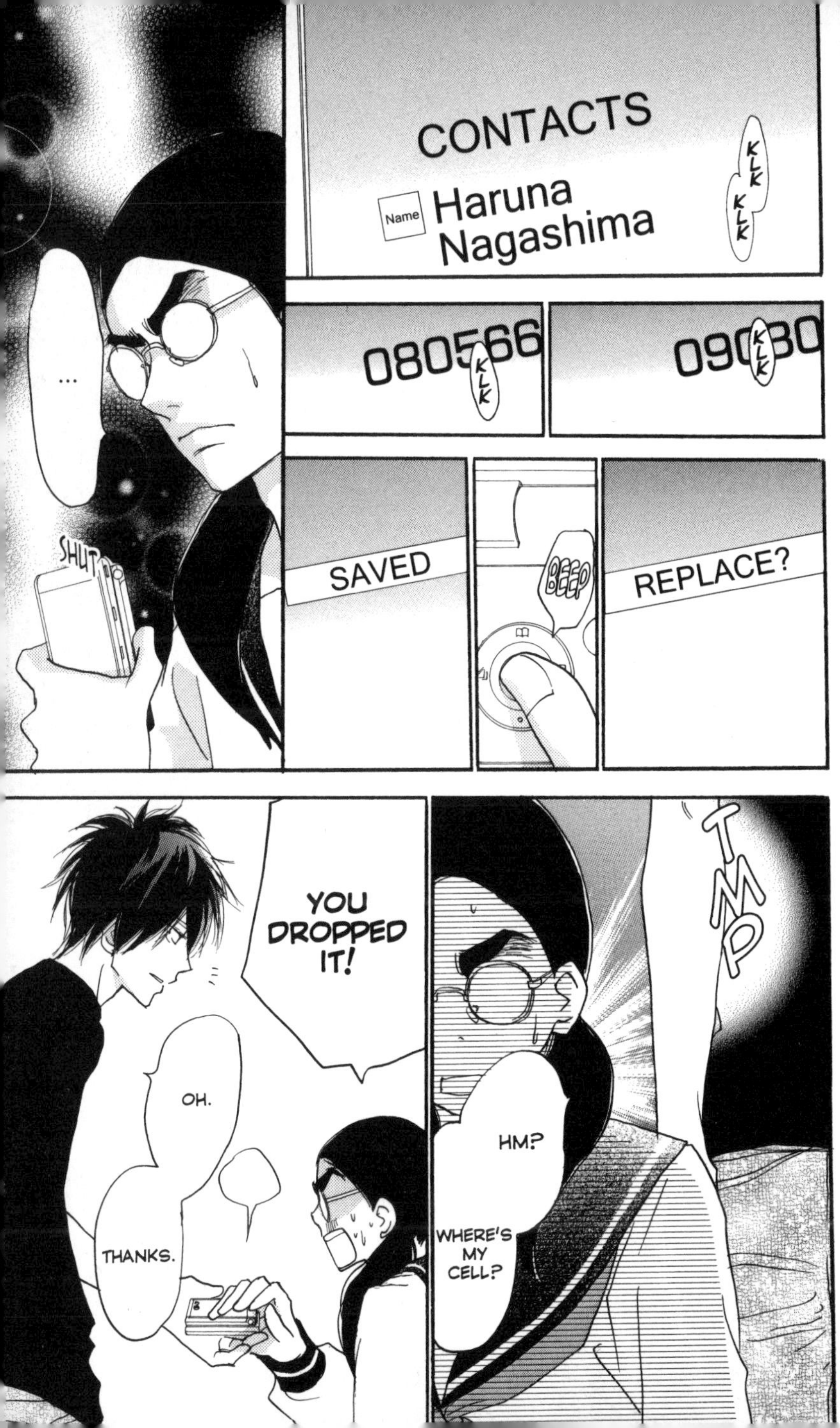
CONTACTS
Name Haruna Nagashima
KLK
KLK
090
KLK
080566
KLK
REPLACE?
BEEP
SAVED
...
SHUT
TMP
HM?
WHERE'S MY CELL?
YOU DROPPED IT!
OH.
THANKS.

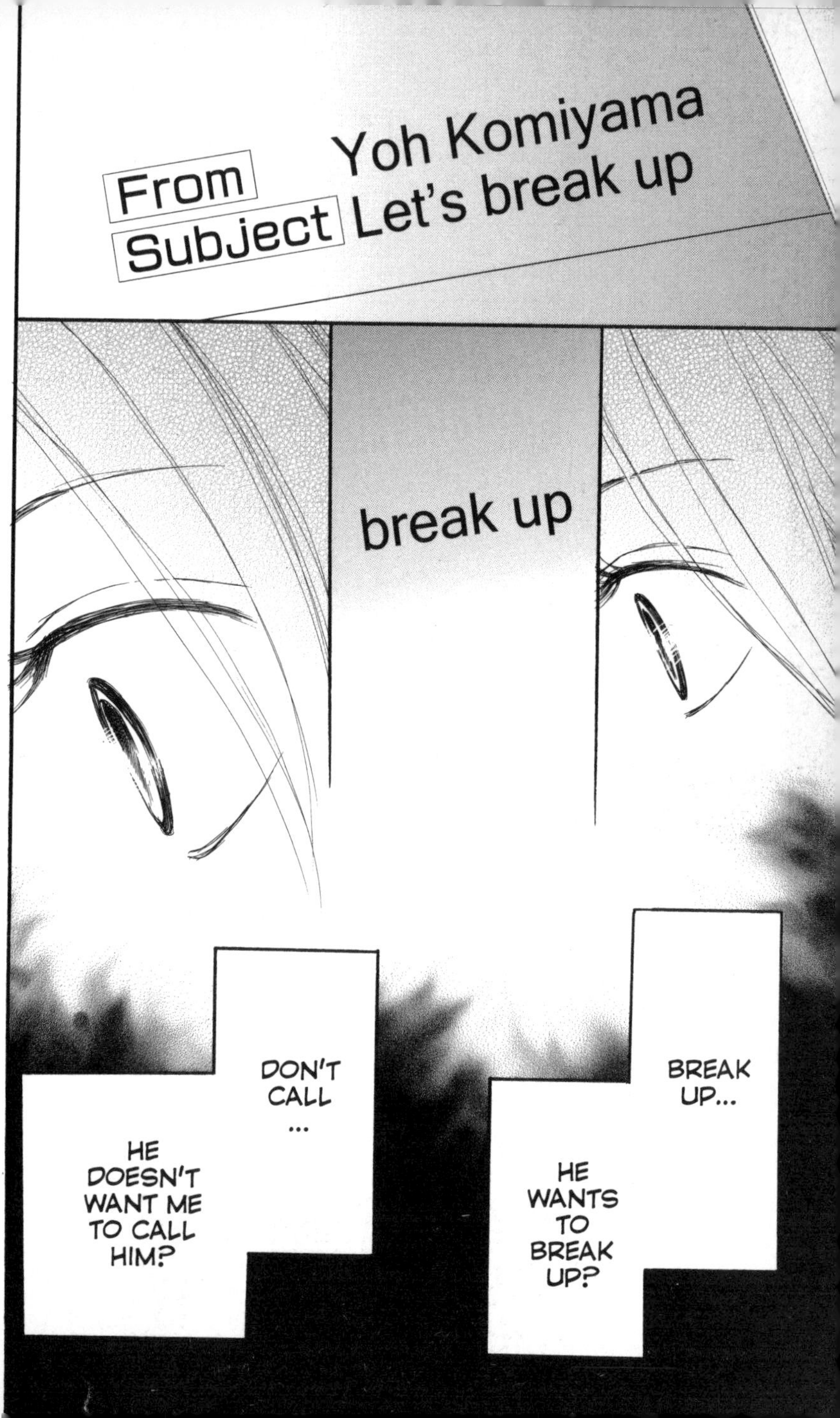
From Yoh Komiyama
Subject Let's break up
break up
BREAK UP...
HE WANTS TO BREAK UP?
DON'T CALL ...
HE DOESN'T WANT ME TO CALL HIM?

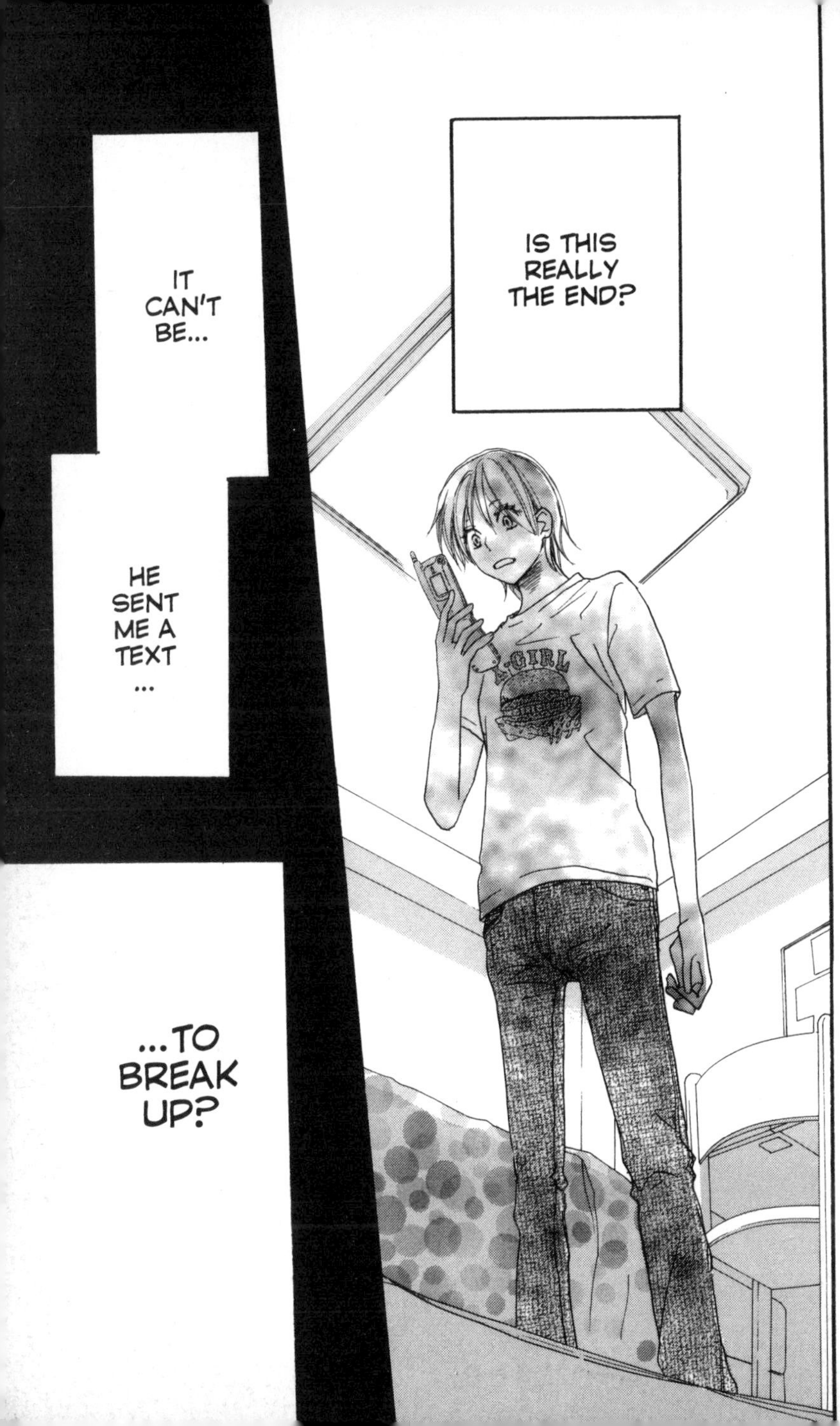
IS THIS REALLY THE END?
IT CAN'T BE...
HE SENT ME A TEXT ...
...TO BREAK UP?

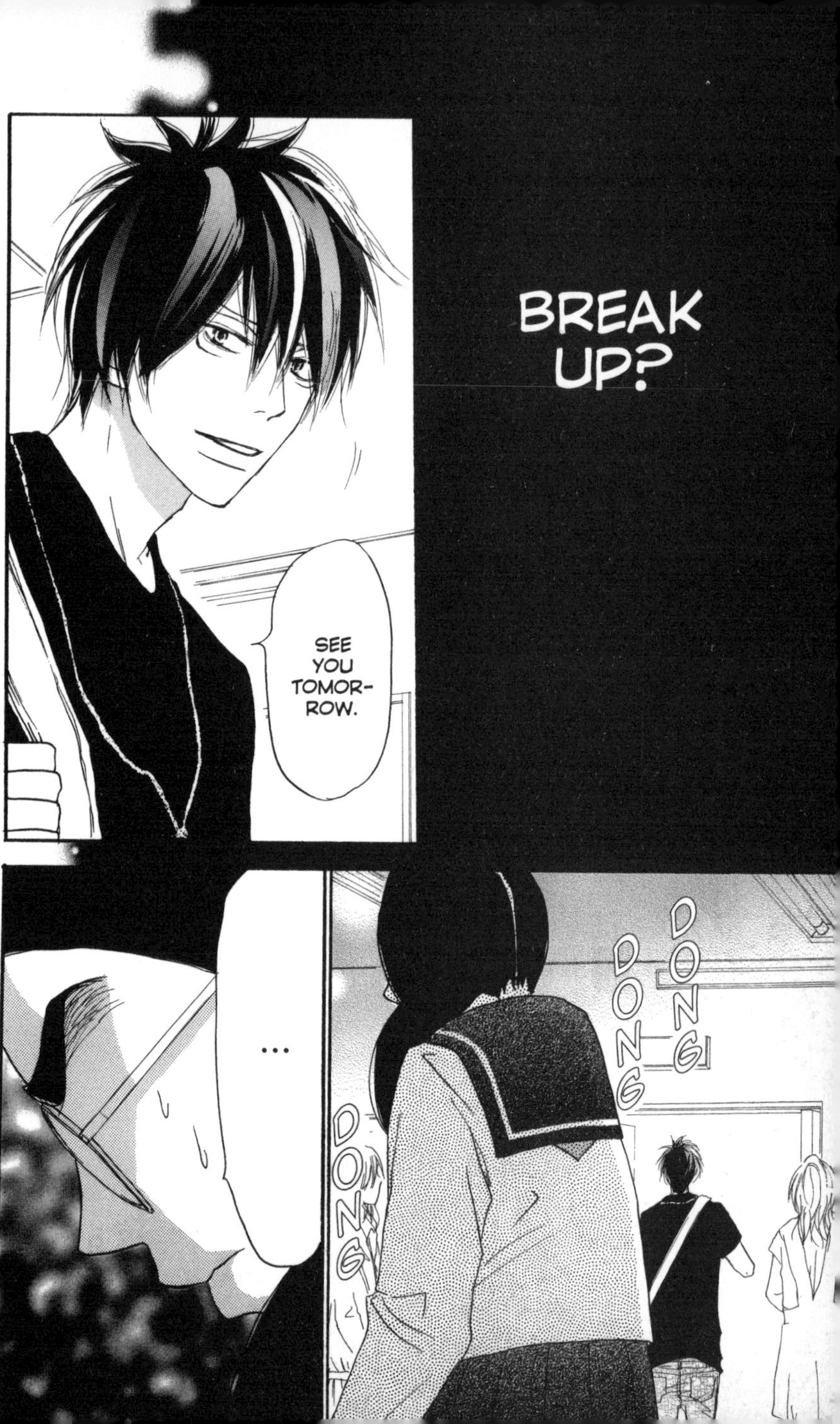
BREAK UP?
SEE YOU TOMORROW.
DONG
DONG
DONG
...

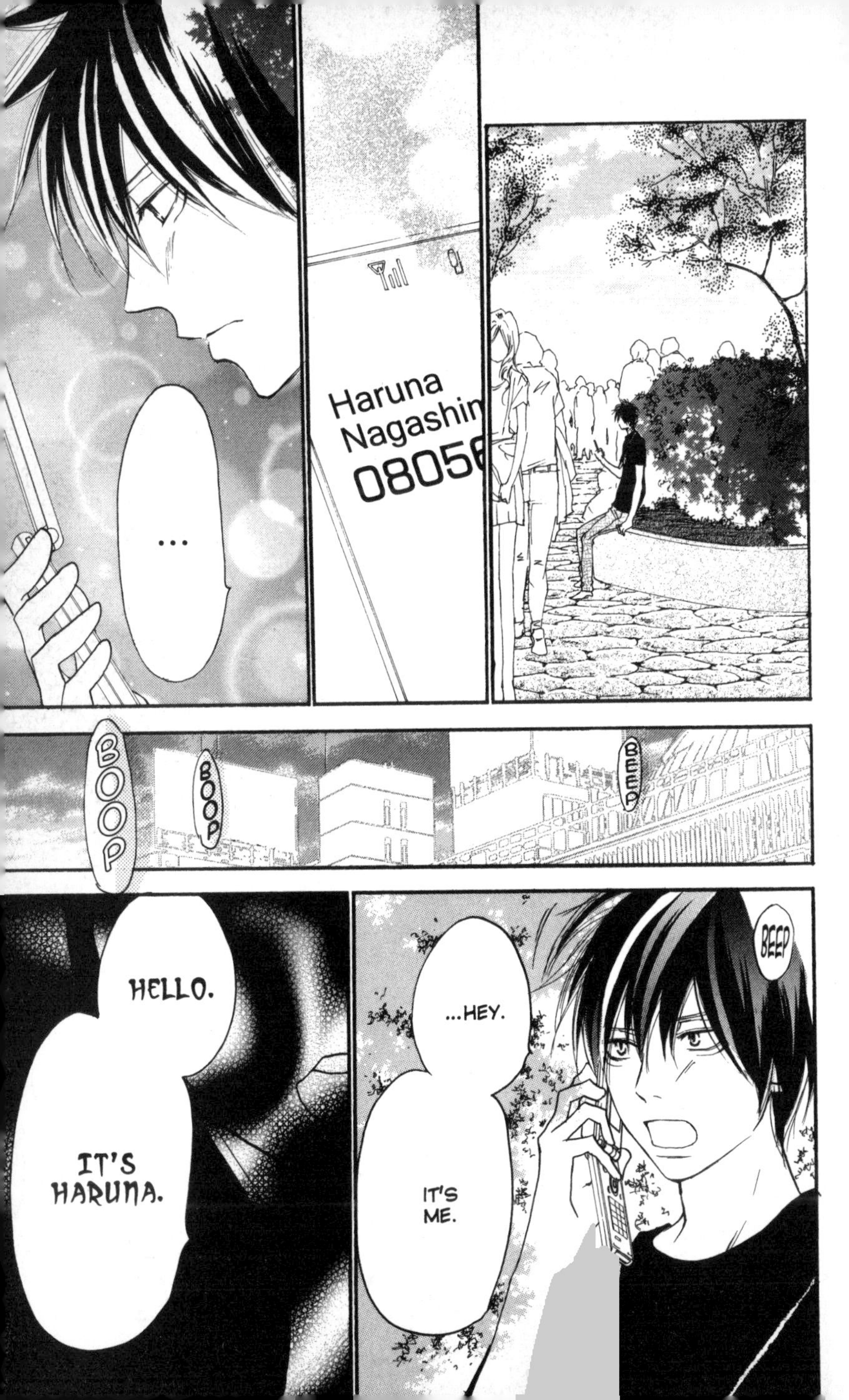
Haruna Nagashim
08056
...
BEEP
BOOP
BOOP
BEEP
...HEY.
IT'S ME.
HELLO.
IT'S HARUNA.

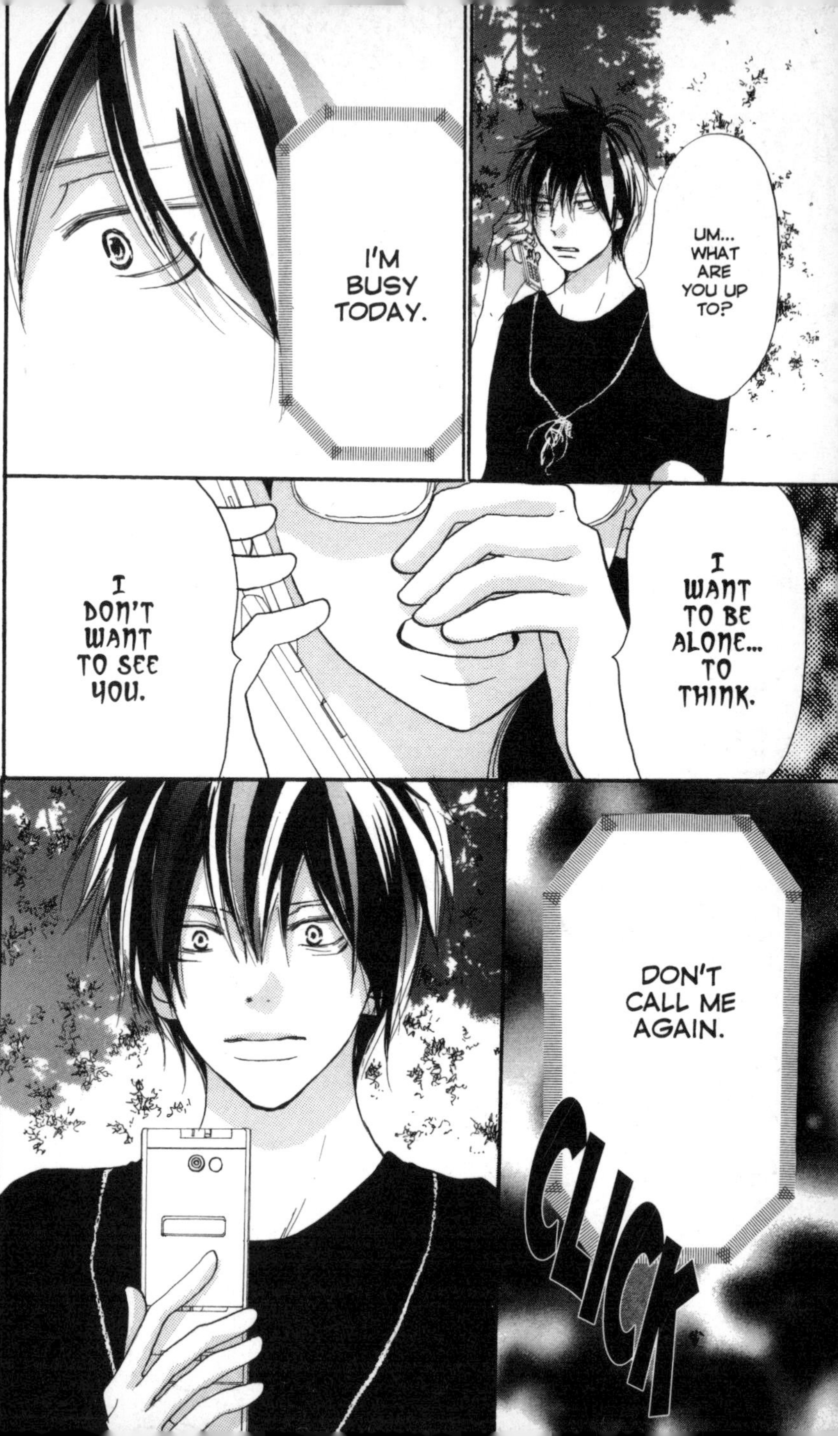
UM... WHAT ARE YOU UP TO?
I'M BUSY TODAY.
I WANT TO BE ALONE... TO THINK.
I DON'T WANT TO SEE YOU.
DON'T CALL ME AGAIN.
CLICK

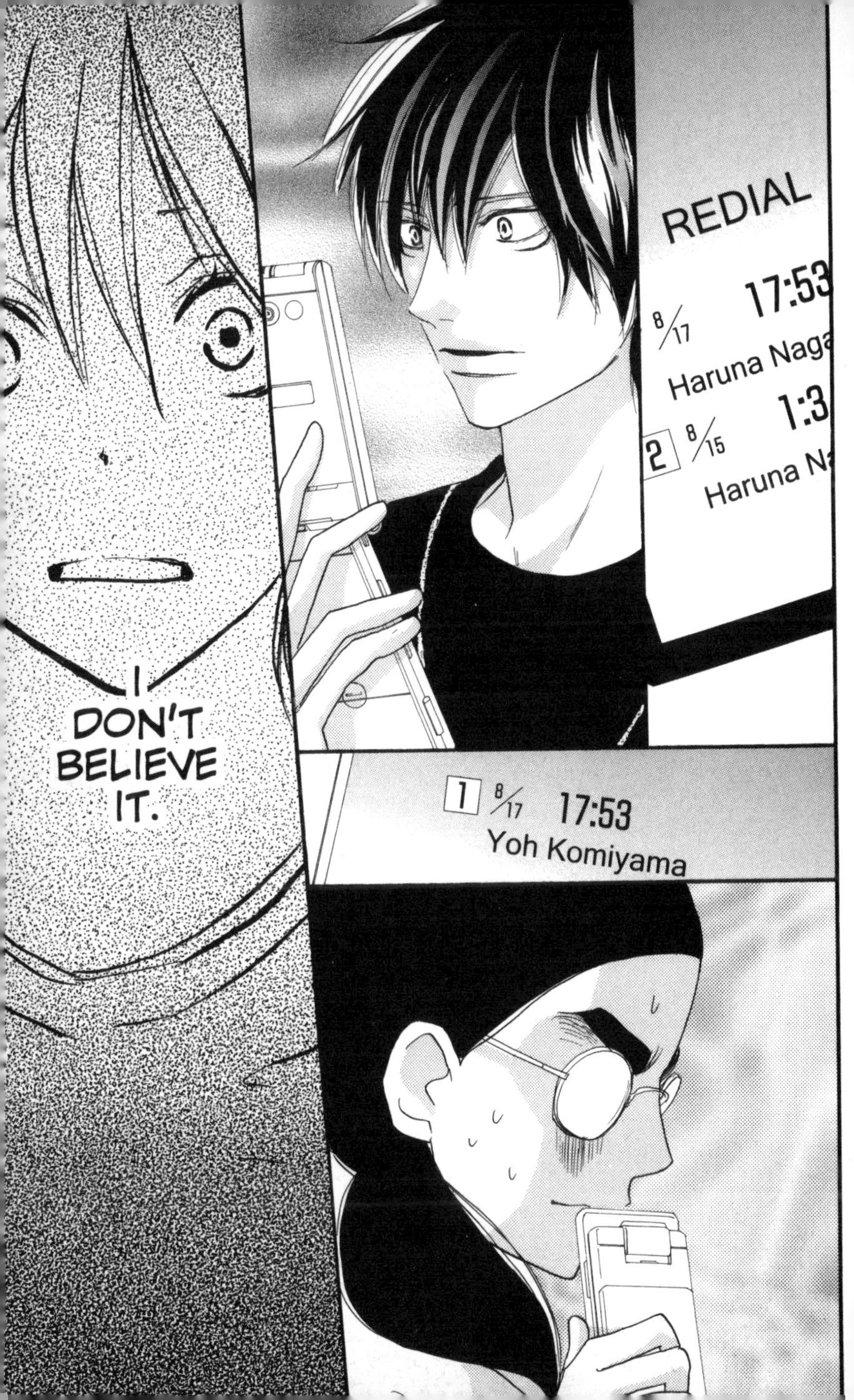
REDIAL
8/17 17:53
Haruna Naga
2 8/15 1:3
Haruna Na
1 8/17 17:53
Yoh Komiyama
I DON'T BELIEVE IT.

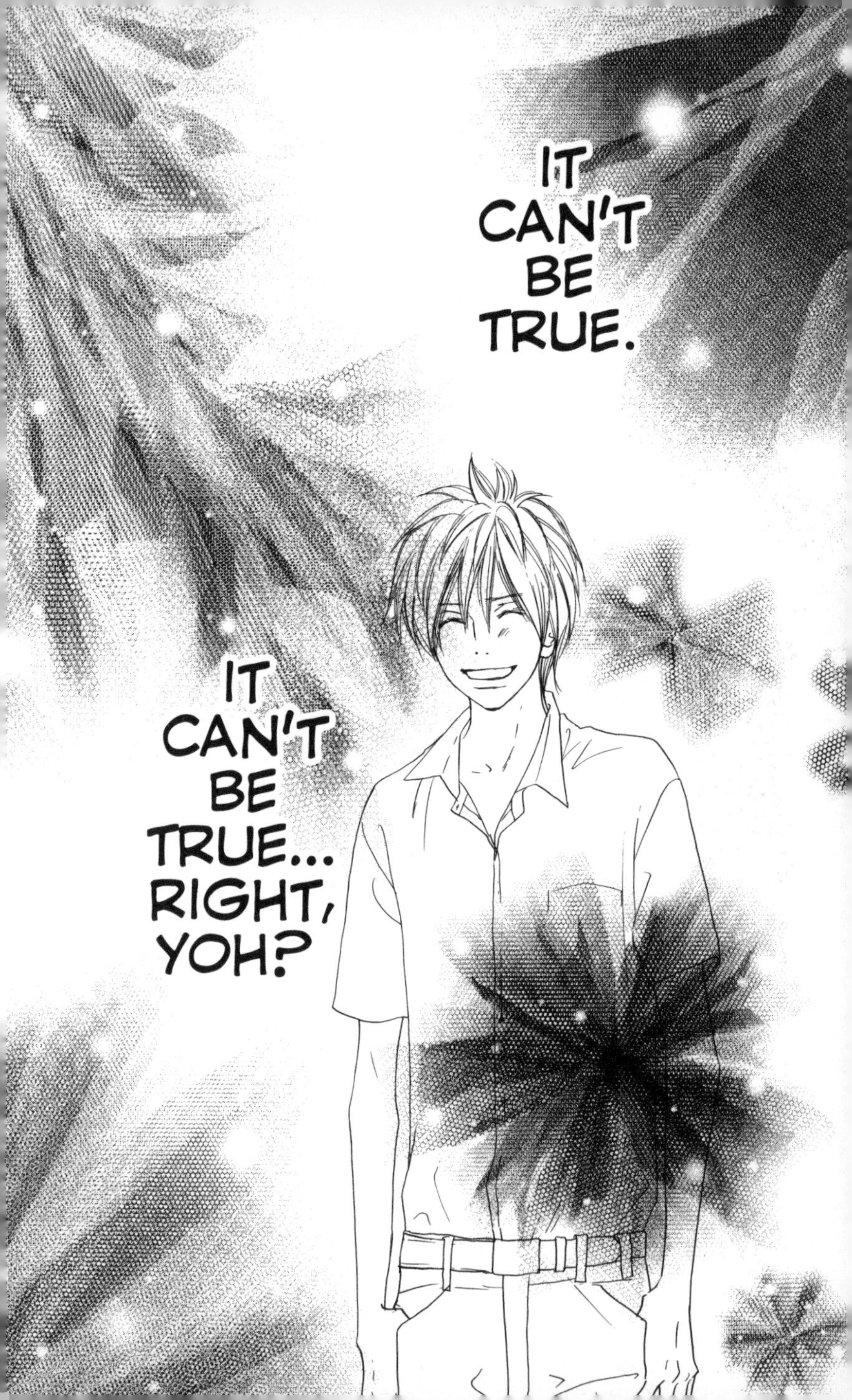
IT CAN'T BE TRUE.
IT CAN'T BE TRUE... RIGHT, YOH?

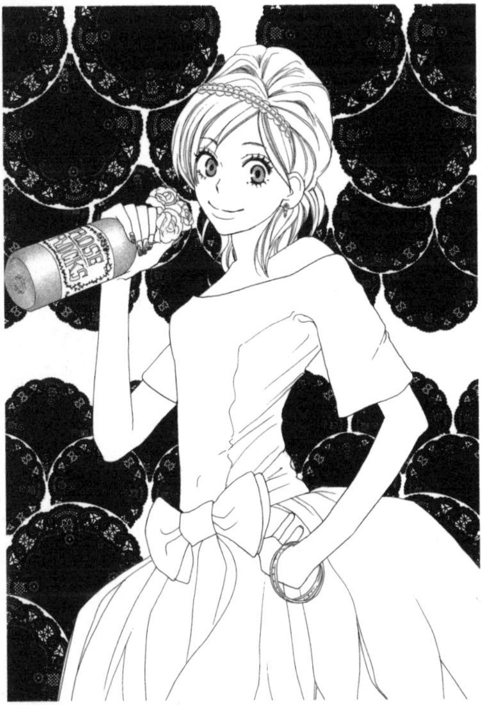
ROSE ROCKS

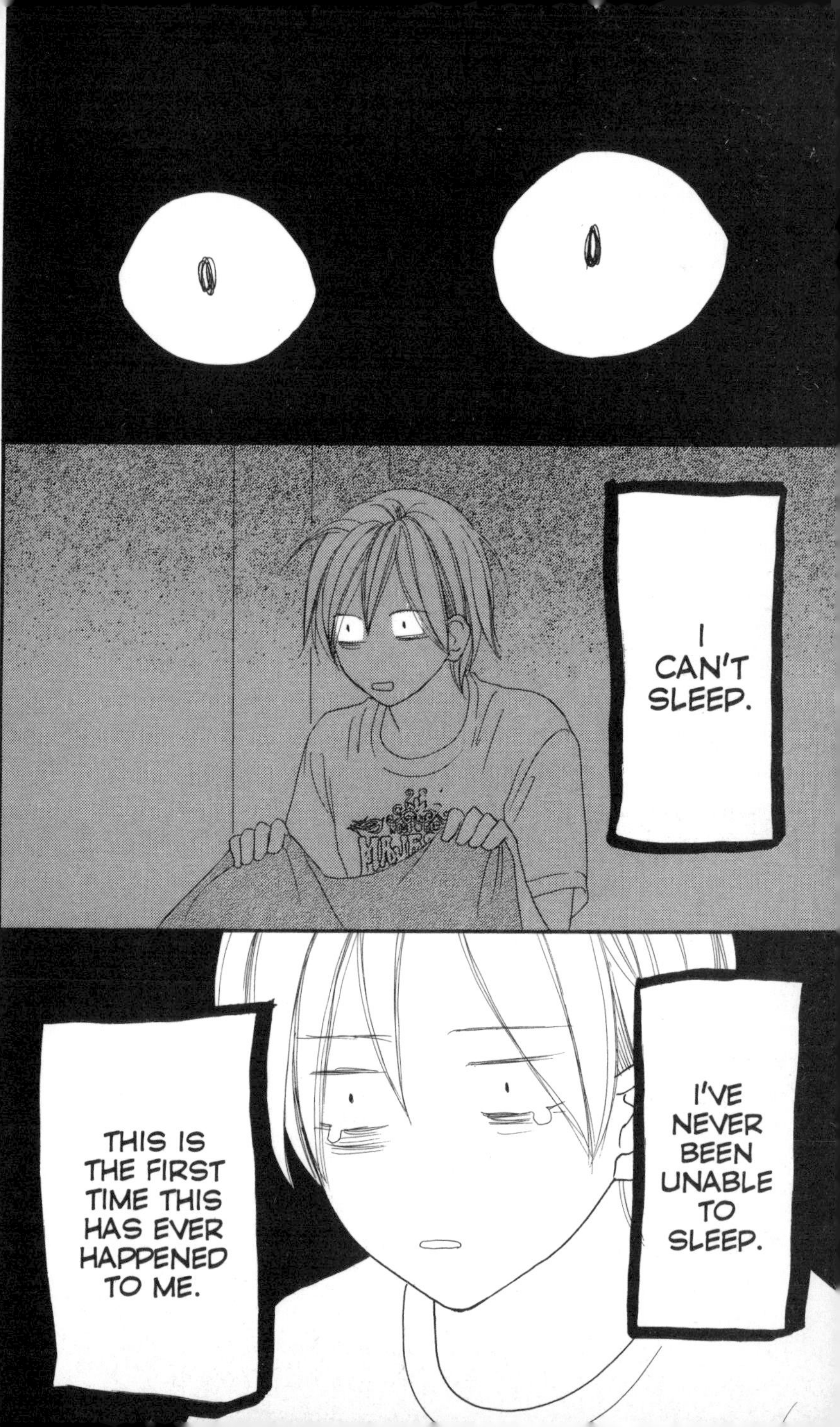
I CAN'T SLEEP.
I'VE NEVER BEEN UNABLE TO SLEEP.
THIS IS THE FIRST TIME THIS HAS EVER HAPPENED TO ME.

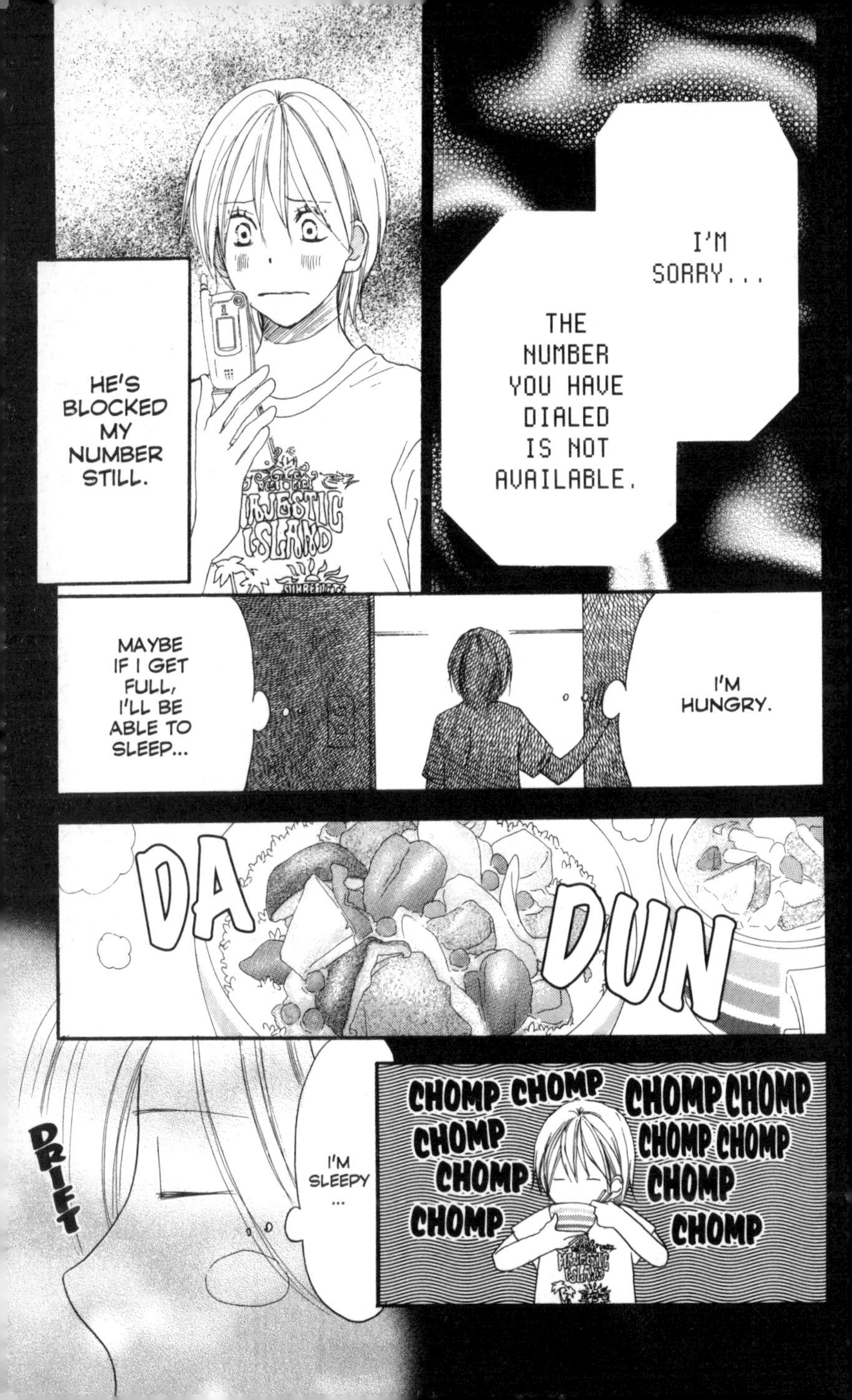
I'M SORRY...
THE NUMBER YOU HAVE DIALED IS NOT AVAILABLE.
HE'S BLOCKED MY NUMBER STILL.
I'M HUNGRY.
MAYBE IF I GET FULL, I'LL BE ABLE TO SLEEP...
DA
DUN
CHOMP CHOMP CHOMP CHOMP
CHOMP CHOMP CHOMP
CHOMP CHOMP
CHOMP CHOMP
I'M SLEEPY ...
DRIFT

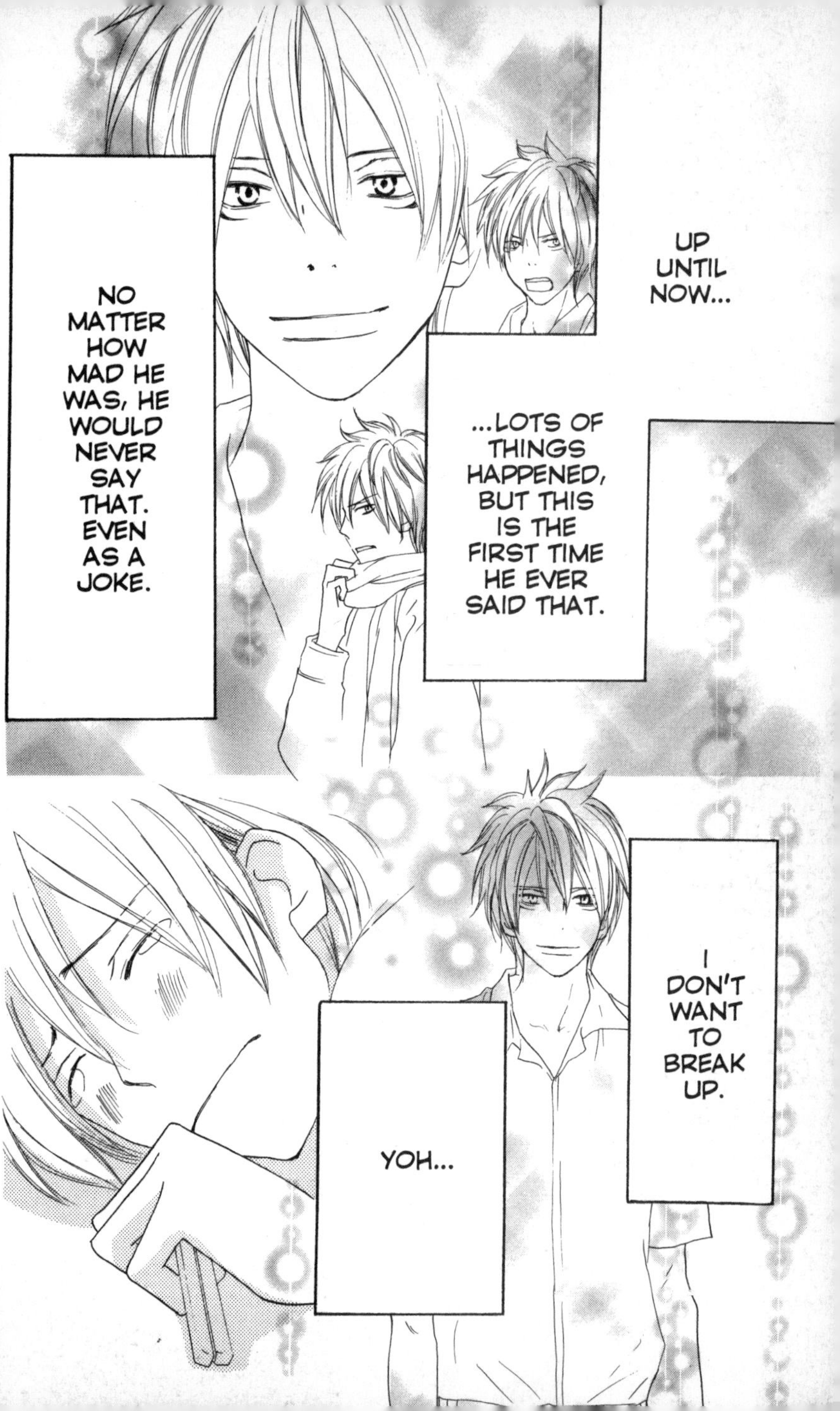
UP UNTIL NOW...
...LOTS OF THINGS HAPPENED, BUT THIS IS THE FIRST TIME HE EVER SAID THAT.
NO MATTER HOW MAD HE WAS, HE WOULD NEVER SAY THAT. EVEN AS A JOKE.
I DON'T WANT TO BREAK UP.
YOH...

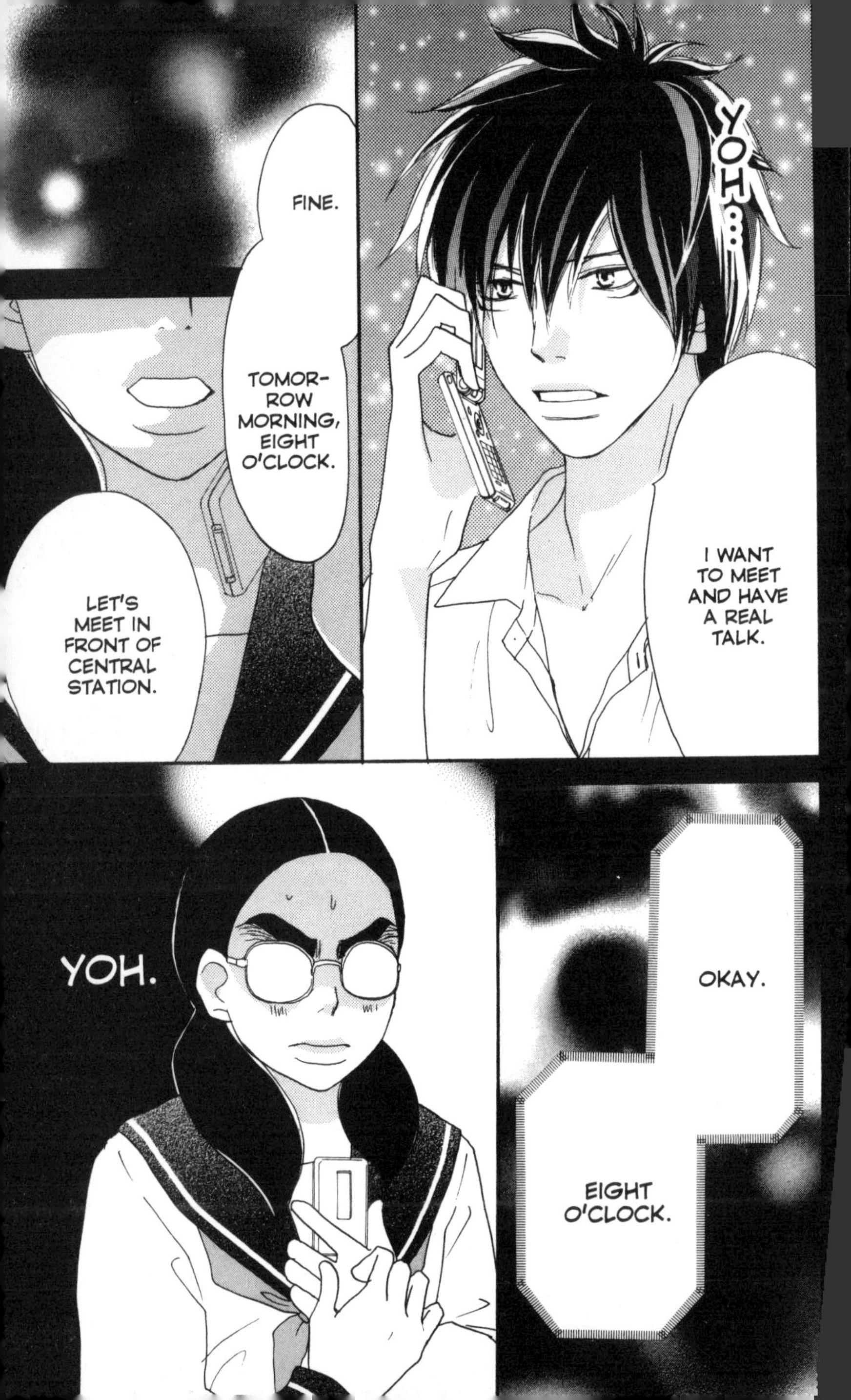
YOH...
I WANT TO MEET AND HAVE A REAL TALK.
FINE.
TOMOR-ROW MORNING, EIGHT O'CLOCK.
LET'S MEET IN FRONT OF CENTRAL STATION.
OKAY.
EIGHT O'CLOCK.
YOH.

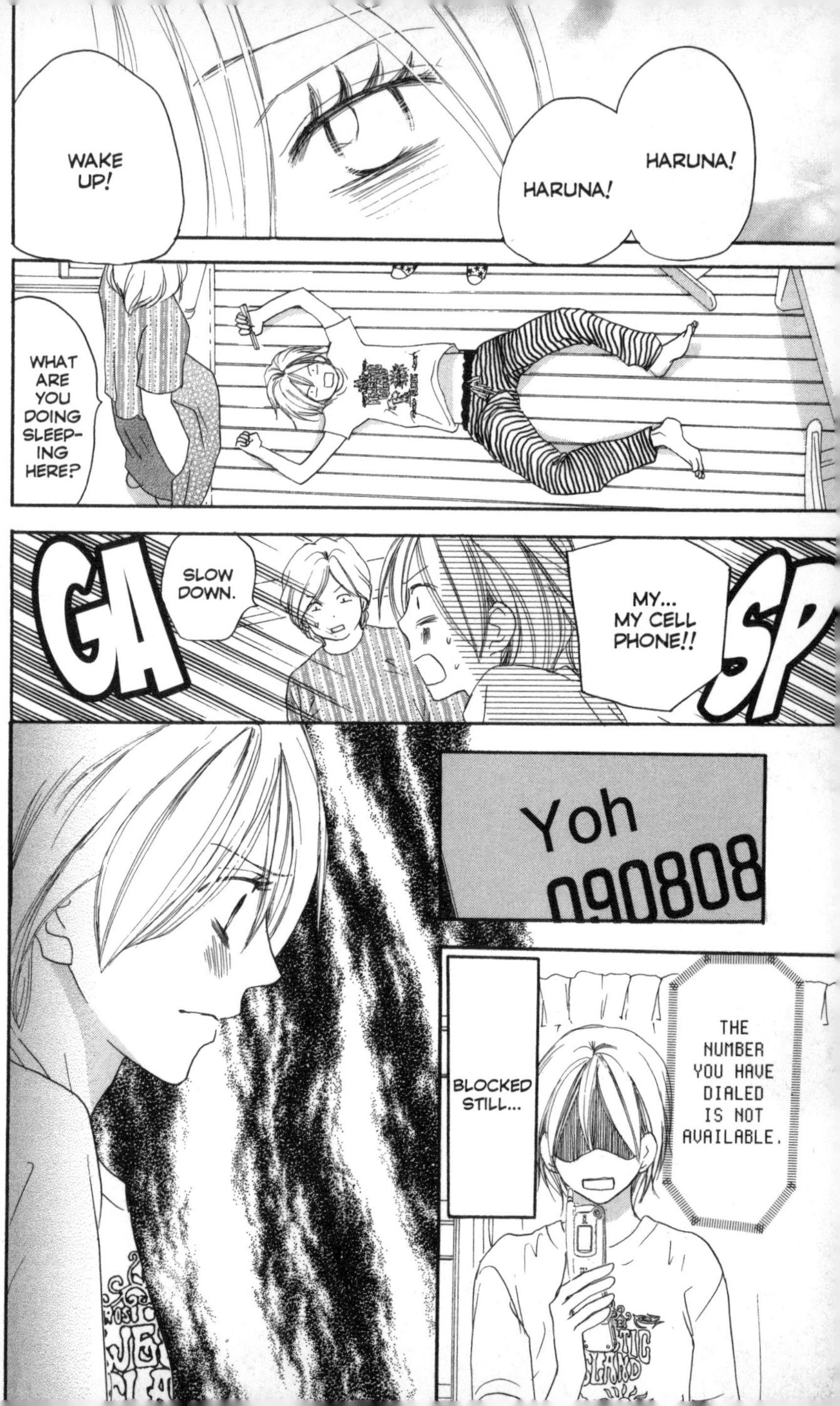
HARUNA! HARUNA!
WAKE UP!
WHAT ARE YOU DOING SLEEPING HERE?
GA
SP
MY... MY CELL PHONE!!
SLOW DOWN.
Yoh
090808
THE NUMBER YOU HAVE DIALED IS NOT AVAILABLE.
BLOCKED STILL...

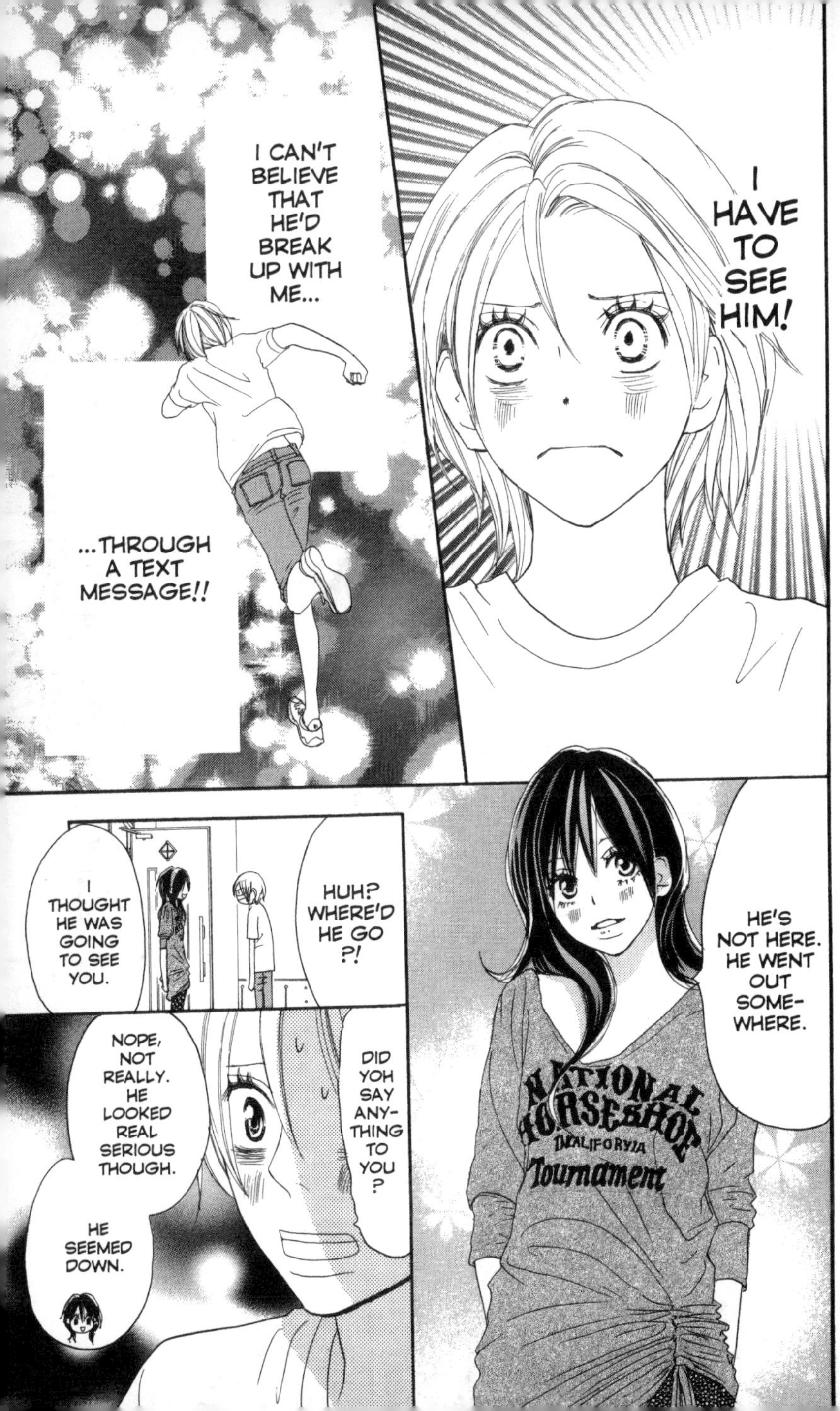
I HAVE TO SEE HIM!
I CAN'T BELIEVE THAT HE'D BREAK UP WITH ME...
...THROUGH A TEXT MESSAGE!!
HE'S NOT HERE. HE WENT OUT SOME-WHERE.
HUH? WHERE'D HE GO ?!
I THOUGHT HE WAS GOING TO SEE YOU.
DID YOH SAY ANY-THING TO YOU ?
NOPE, NOT REALLY. HE LOOKED REAL SERIOUS THOUGH.
HE SEEMED DOWN.

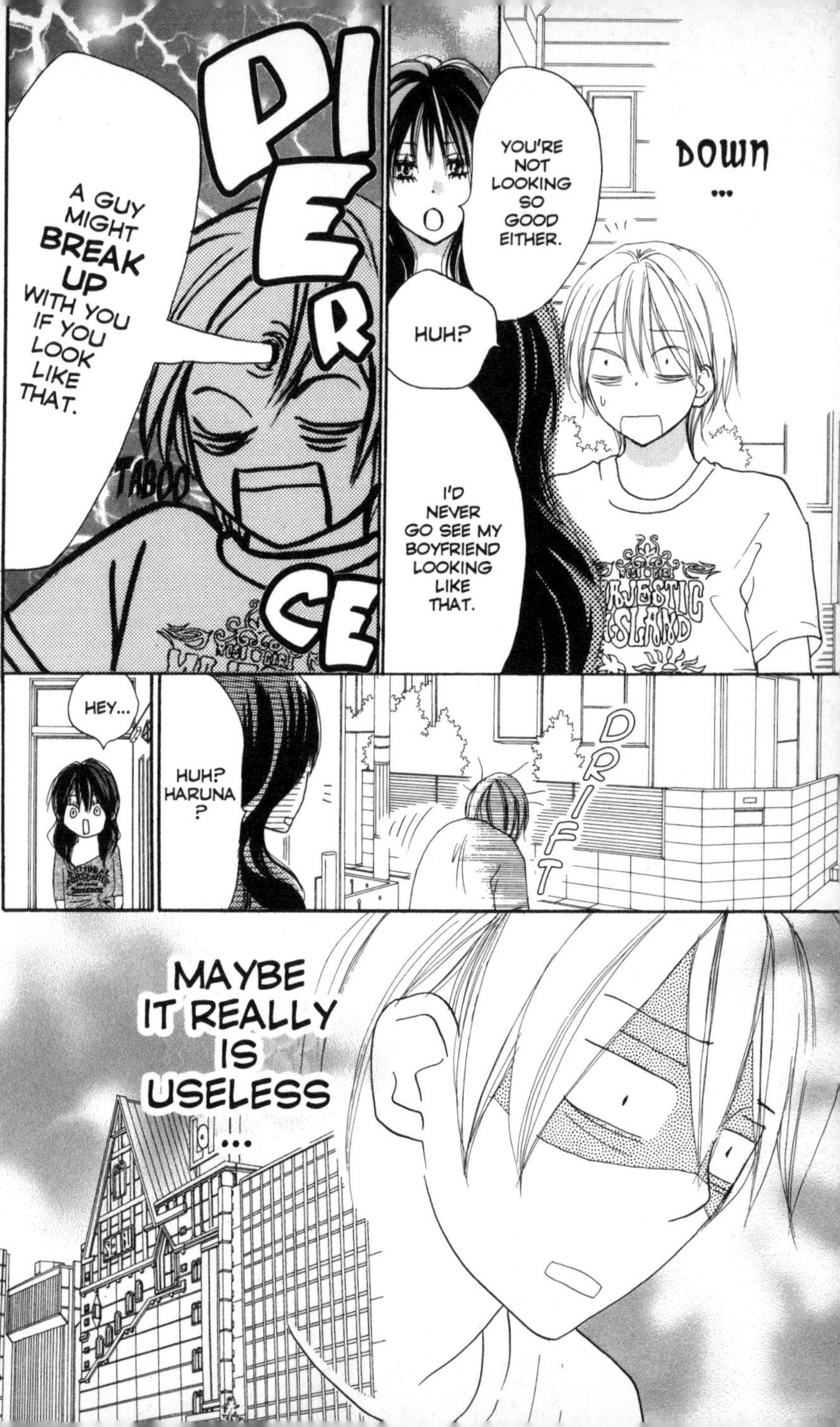
DOWN...
YOU'RE NOT LOOKING SO GOOD EITHER.
HUH?
I'D NEVER GO SEE MY BOYFRIEND LOOKING LIKE THAT.
PIERCE
A GUY MIGHT BREAK UP WITH YOU IF YOU LOOK LIKE THAT.
TABOO
DRIFT
HUH? HARUNA?
HEY...
MAYBE IT REALLY IS USELESS...

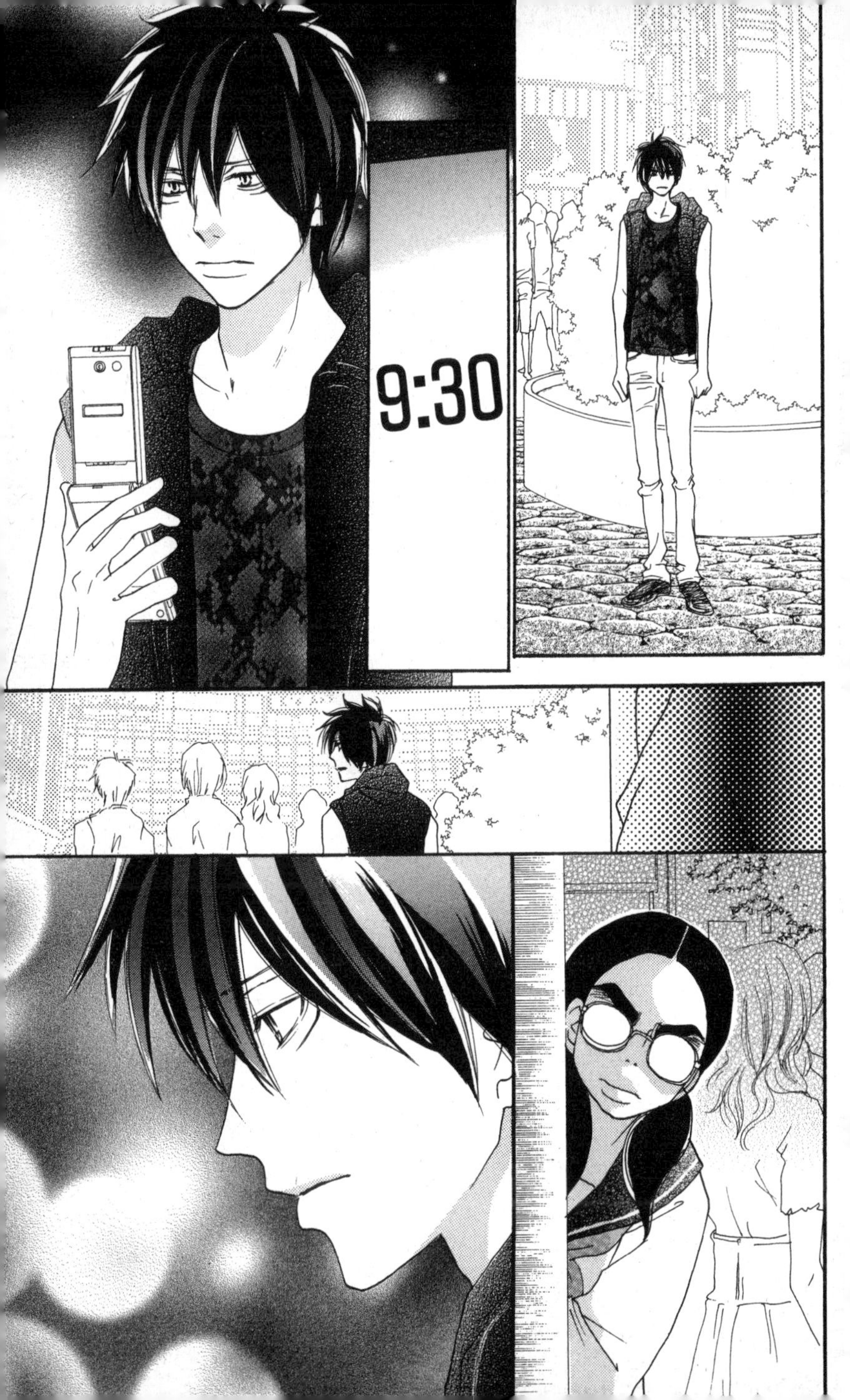
9:30

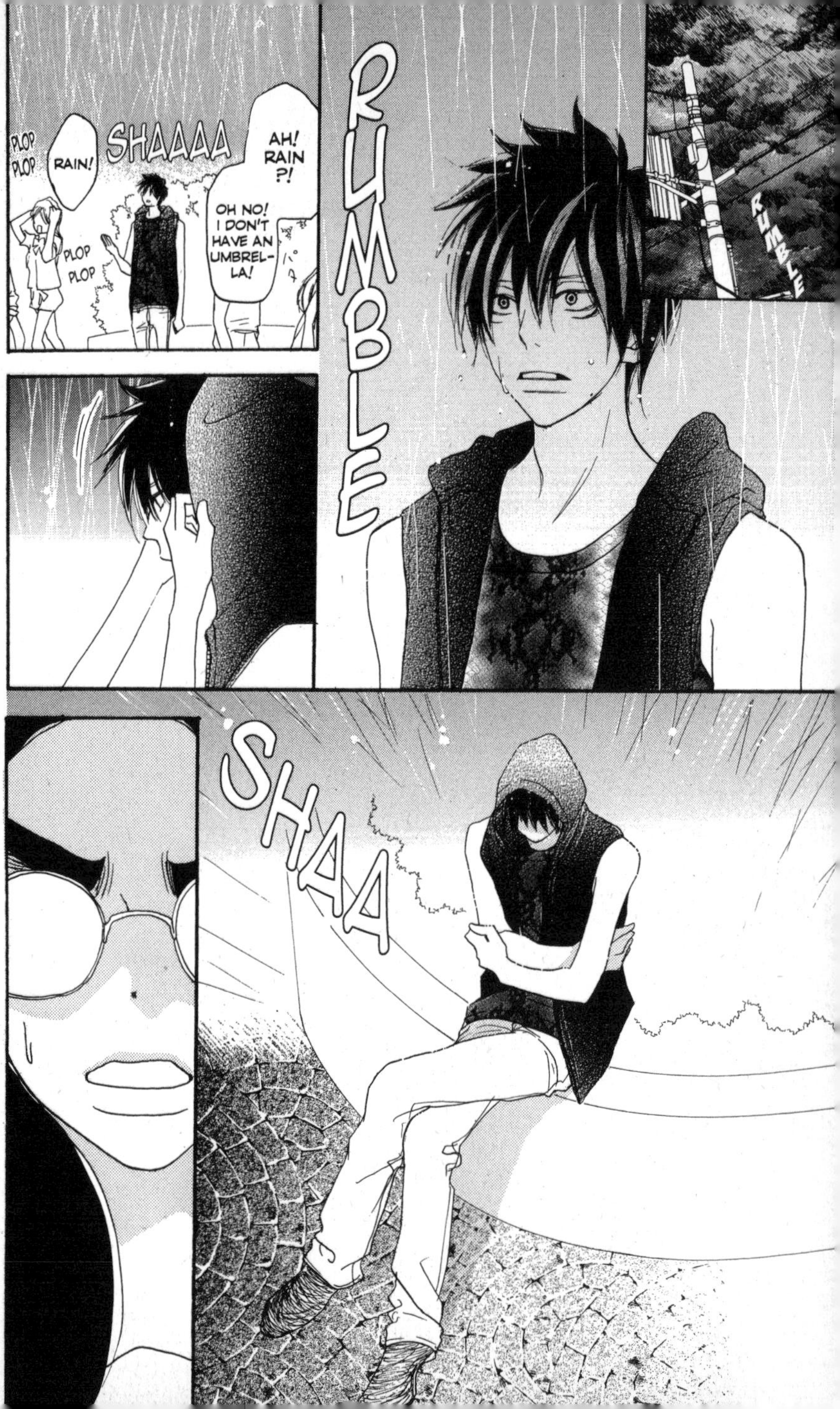
RUMBLE
RUMBLE
AH! RAIN?!
OH NO! I DON'T HAVE AN UMBREL-LA!
SHAAAA
RAIN!
PLOP PLOP
PLOP PLOP
SHAA

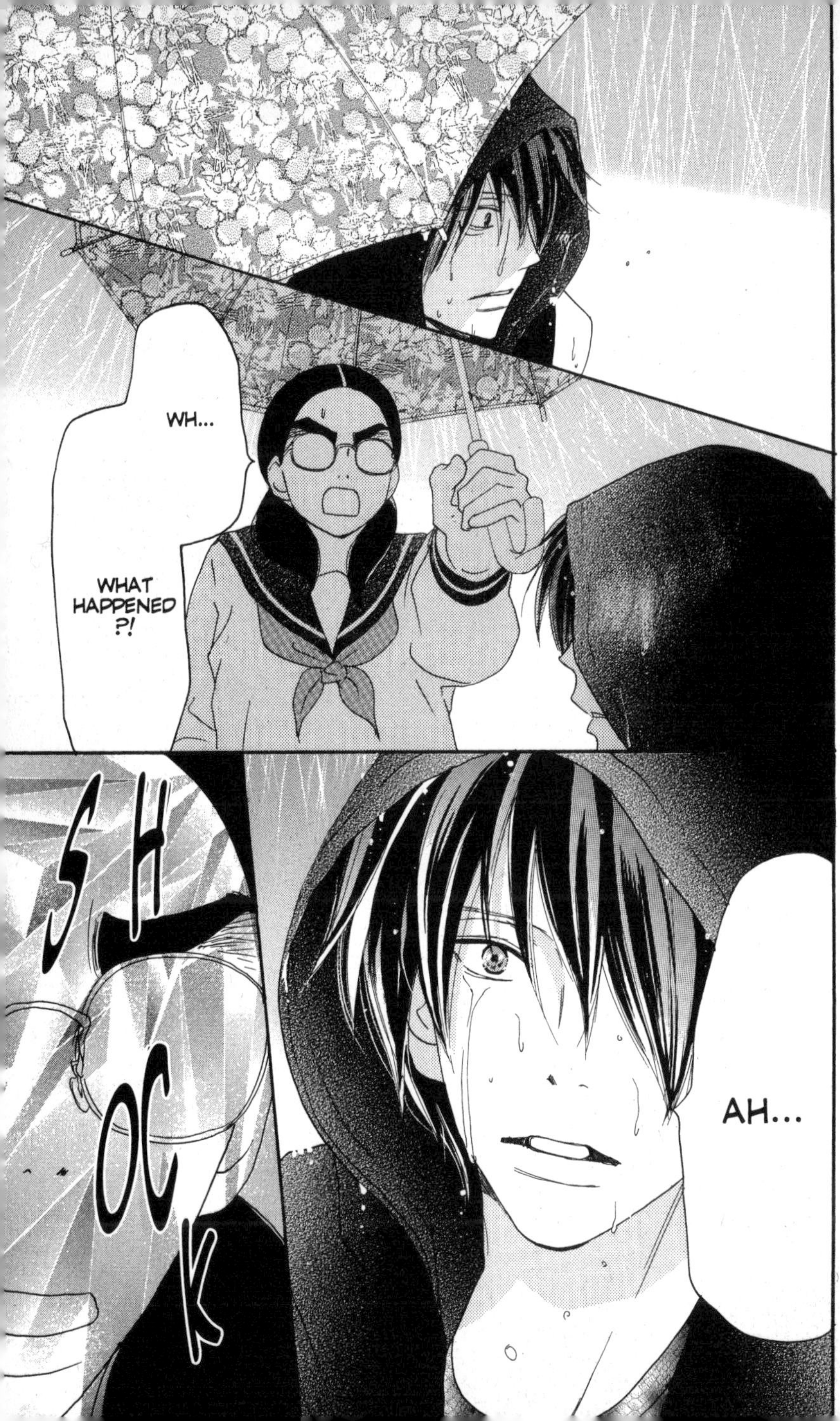
WH...
WHAT HAPPENED ?!
AH...
SHOCK

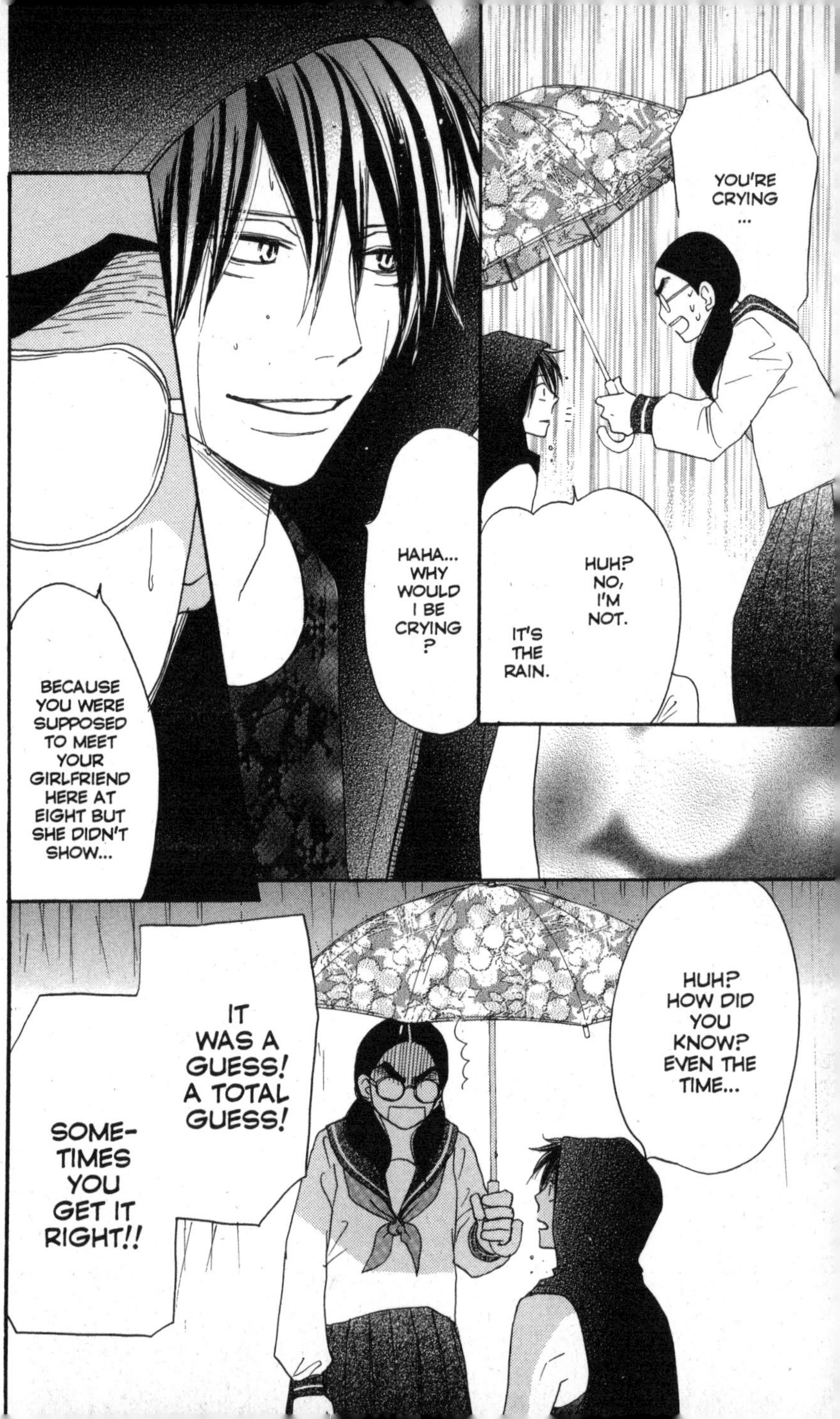
YOU'RE CRYING ...
HUH? NO, I'M NOT.
IT'S THE RAIN.
HAHA... WHY WOULD I BE CRYING?
BECAUSE YOU WERE SUPPOSED TO MEET YOUR GIRLFRIEND HERE AT EIGHT BUT SHE DIDN'T SHOW...
HUH? HOW DID YOU KNOW? EVEN THE TIME...
IT WAS A GUESS! A TOTAL GUESS!
SOME-TIMES YOU GET IT RIGHT!!

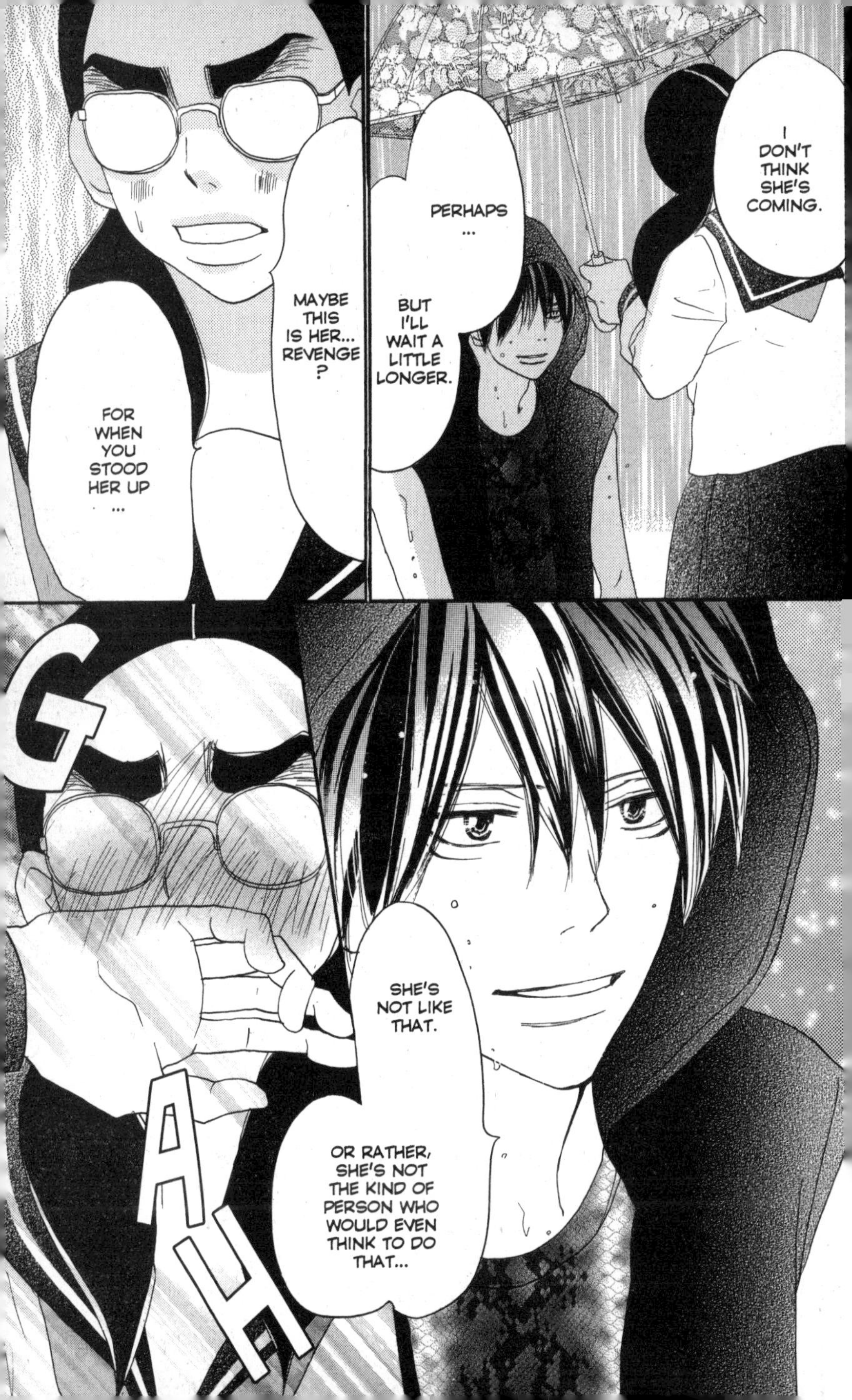
I DON'T THINK SHE'S COMING.
PERHAPS...
BUT I'LL WAIT A LITTLE LONGER.
MAYBE THIS IS HER... REVENGE?
FOR WHEN YOU STOOD HER UP...
GAH
SHE'S NOT LIKE THAT.
OR RATHER, SHE'S NOT THE KIND OF PERSON WHO WOULD EVEN THINK TO DO THAT...

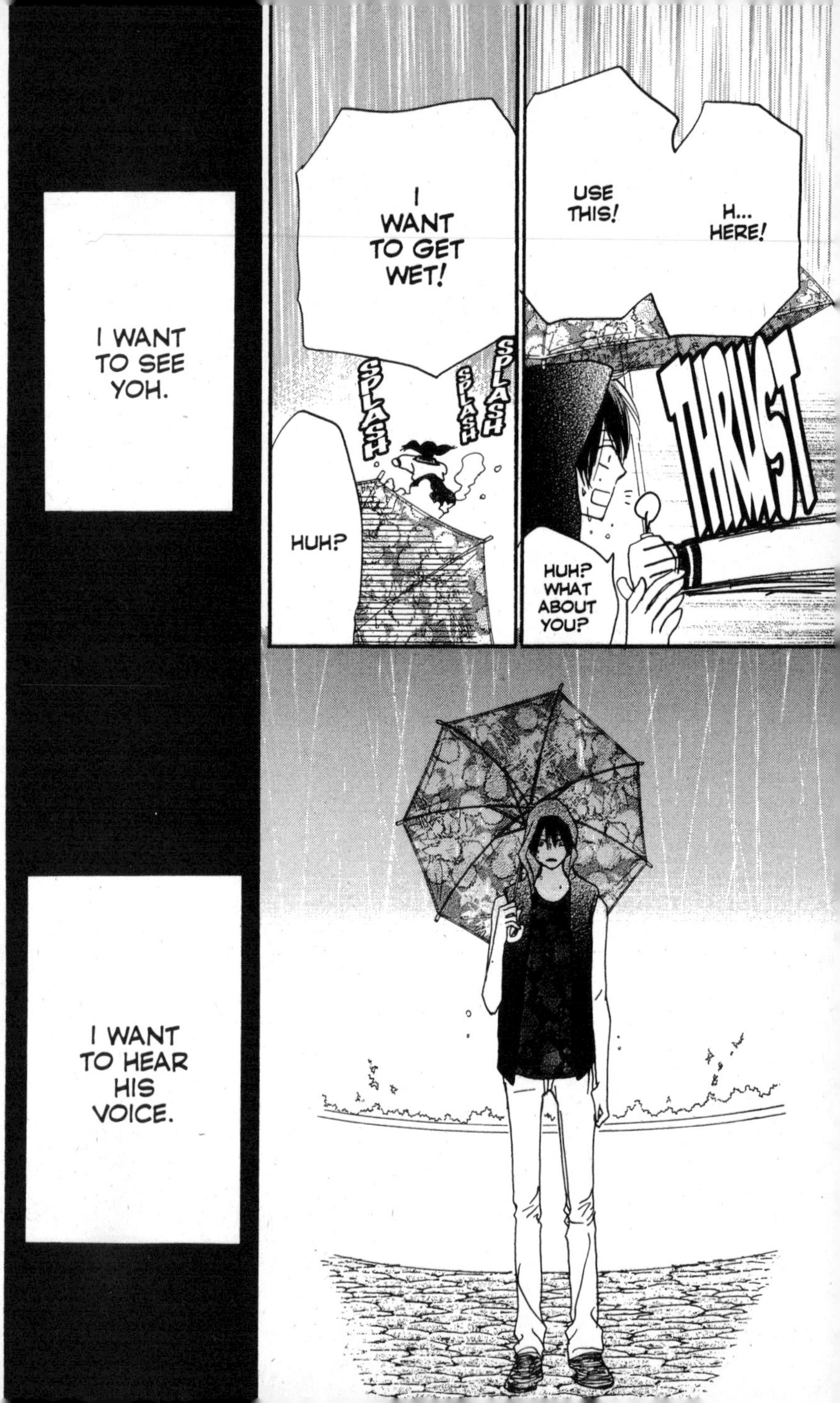
H... HERE!
USE THIS!
THRUST
HUH? WHAT ABOUT YOU?
I WANT TO GET WET!
SPLASH
SPLASH
SPLASH
HUH?
I WANT TO SEE YOH.
I WANT TO HEAR HIS VOICE.

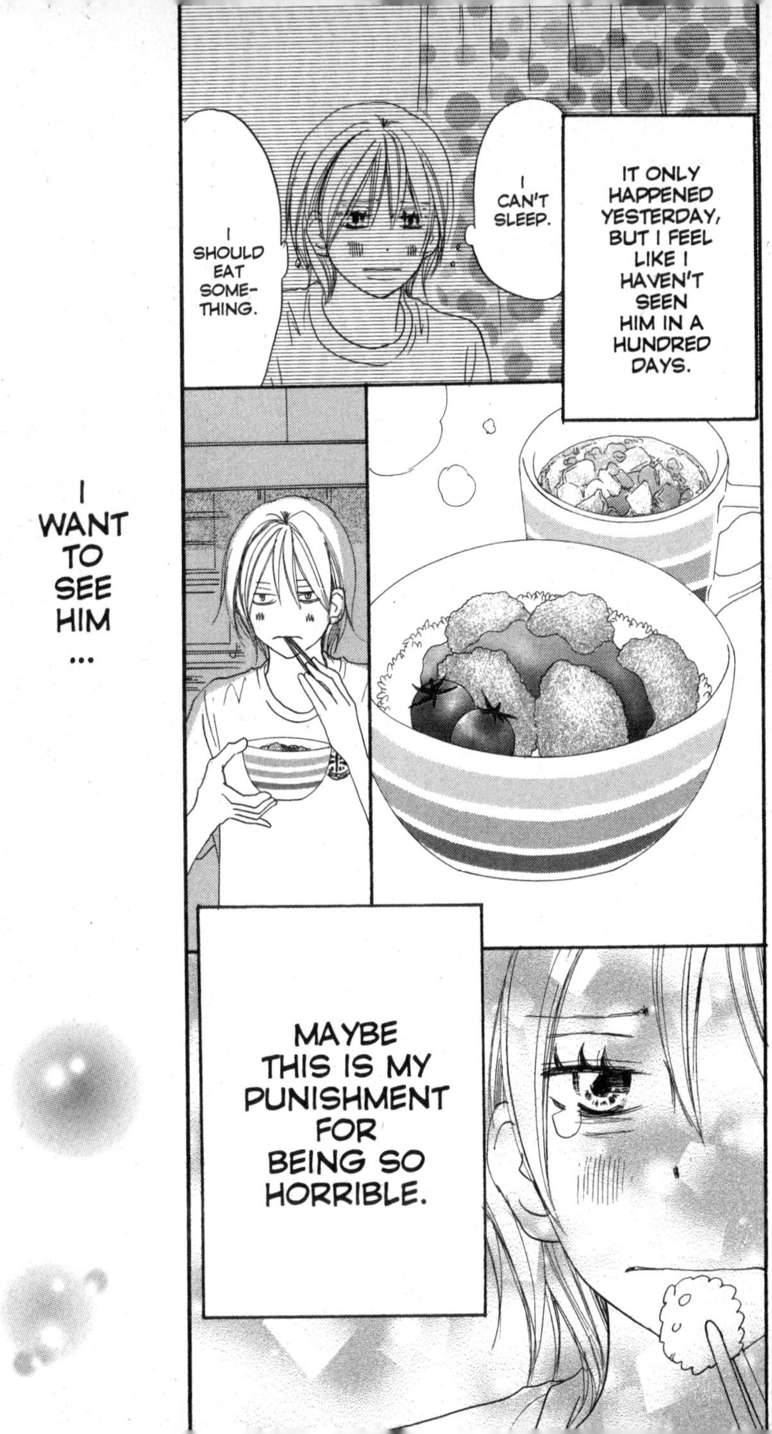
IT ONLY HAPPENED YESTERDAY, BUT I FEEL LIKE I HAVEN'T SEEN HIM IN A HUNDRED DAYS.
I CAN'T SLEEP.
I SHOULD EAT SOME-THING.
I WANT TO SEE HIM...
MAYBE THIS IS MY PUNISHMENT FOR BEING SO HORRIBLE.

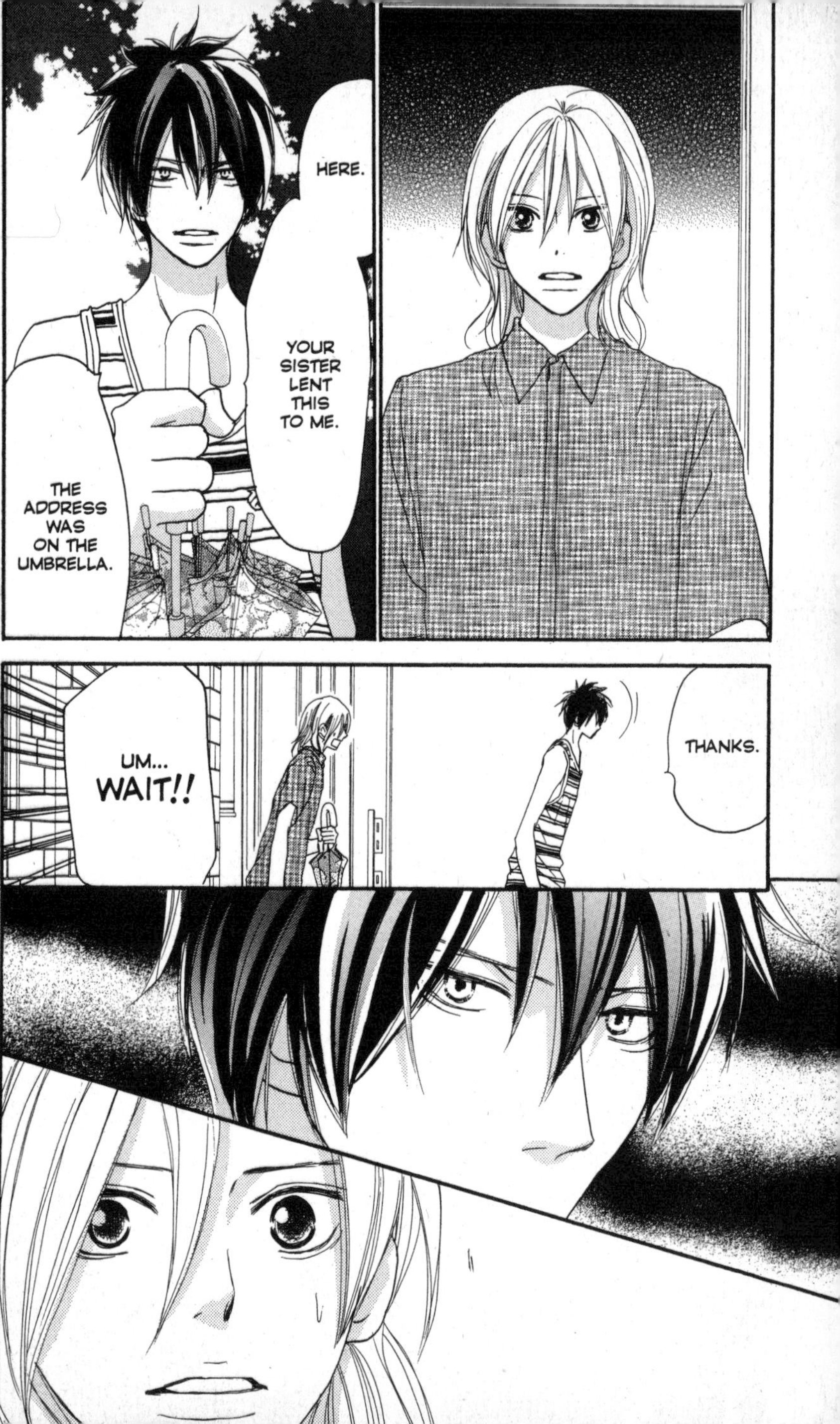
HERE.
YOUR SISTER LENT THIS TO ME.
THE ADDRESS WAS ON THE UMBRELLA.
THANKS.
UM... WAIT!!

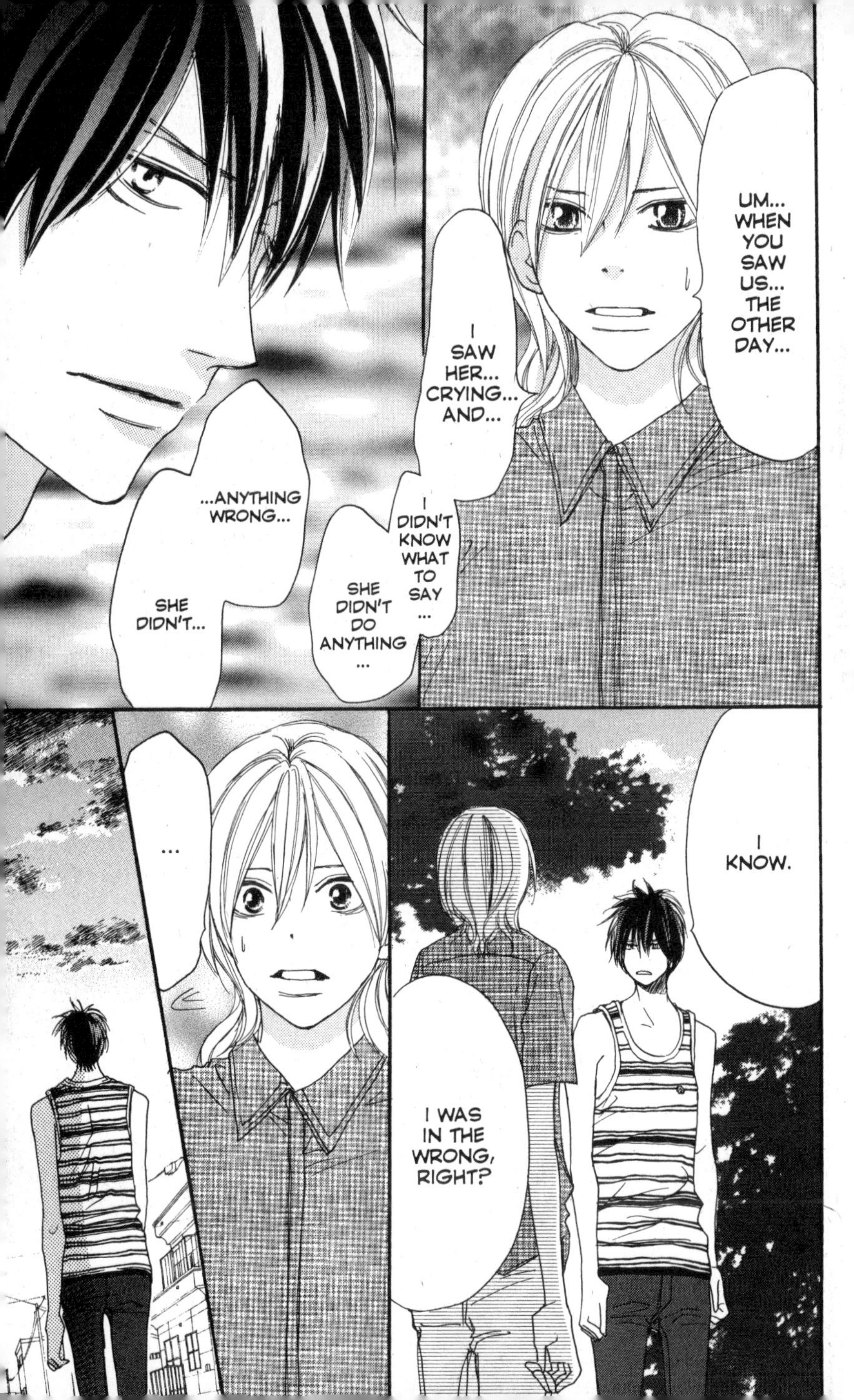
UM... WHEN YOU SAW US... THE OTHER DAY...
I SAW HER... CRYING... AND...
I DIDN'T KNOW WHAT TO SAY...
SHE DIDN'T DO ANYTHING...
SHE DIDN'T...
...ANYTHING WRONG...
I KNOW.
I WAS IN THE WRONG, RIGHT?
...

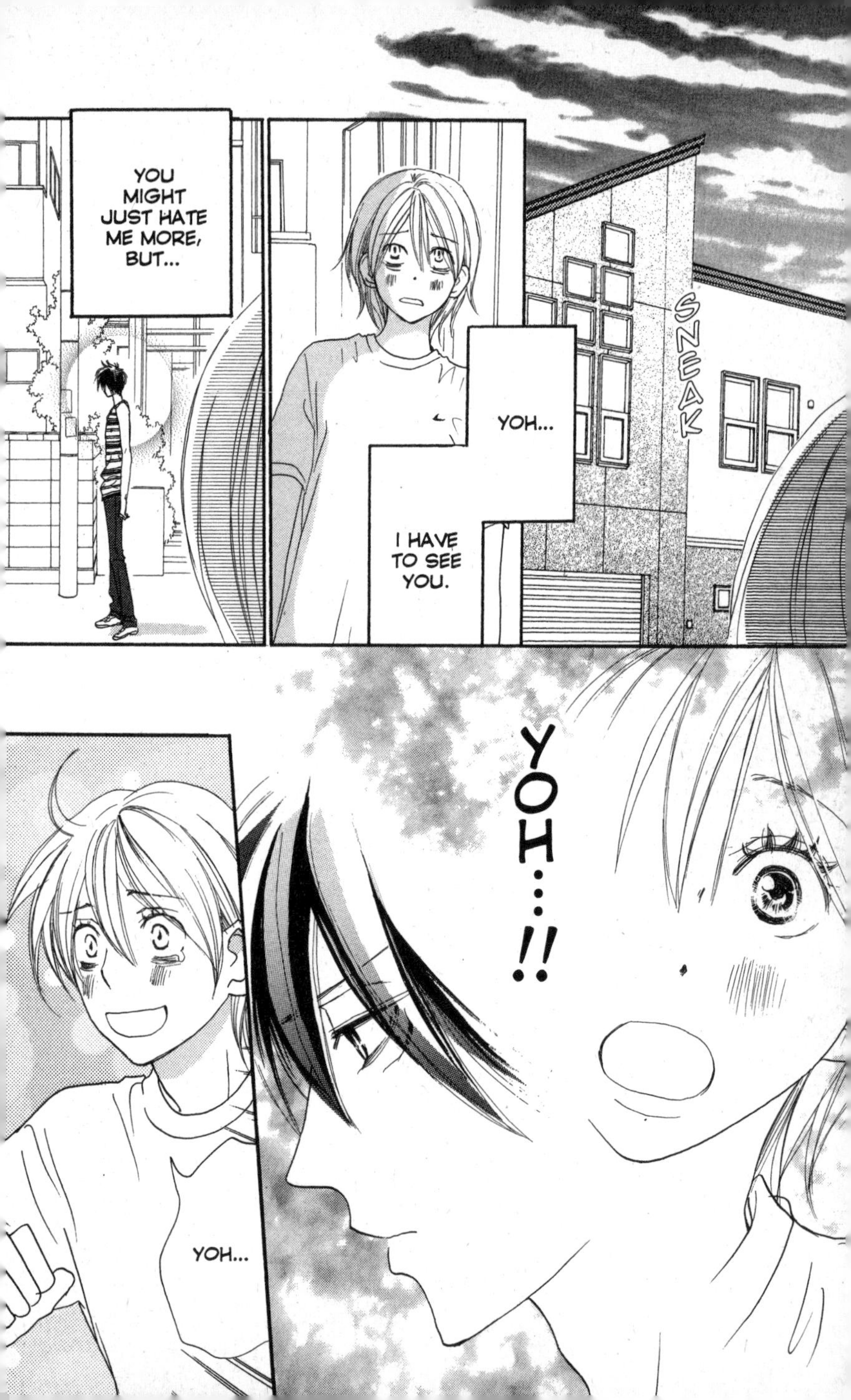
SNEAK
YOH...
I HAVE TO SEE YOU.
YOU MIGHT JUST HATE ME MORE, BUT...
YOH...!!
YOH...

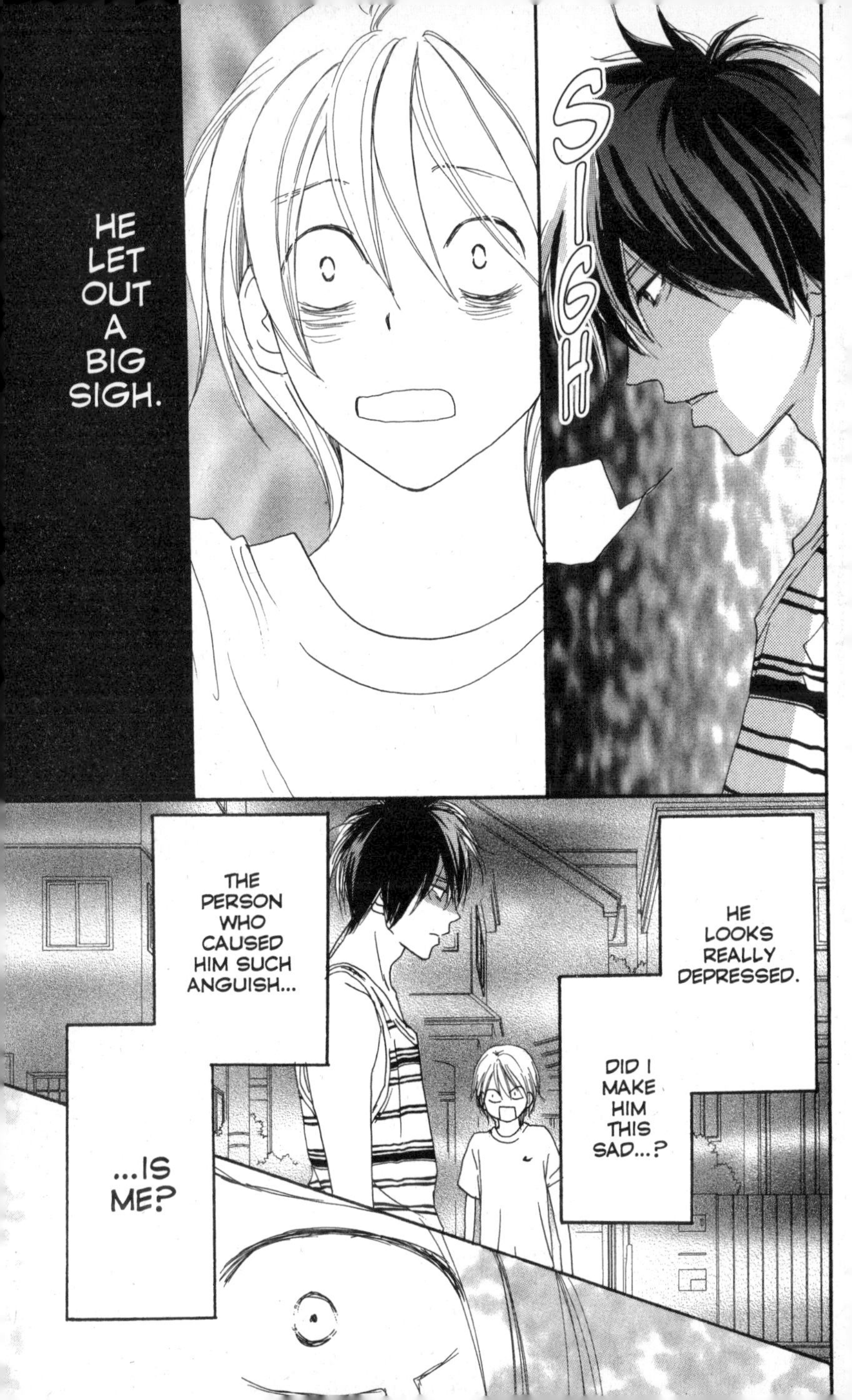
SIGH
HE LET OUT A BIG SIGH.
HE LOOKS REALLY DEPRESSED.
DID I MAKE HIM THIS SAD...?
THE PERSON WHO CAUSED HIM SUCH ANGUISH...
...IS ME?

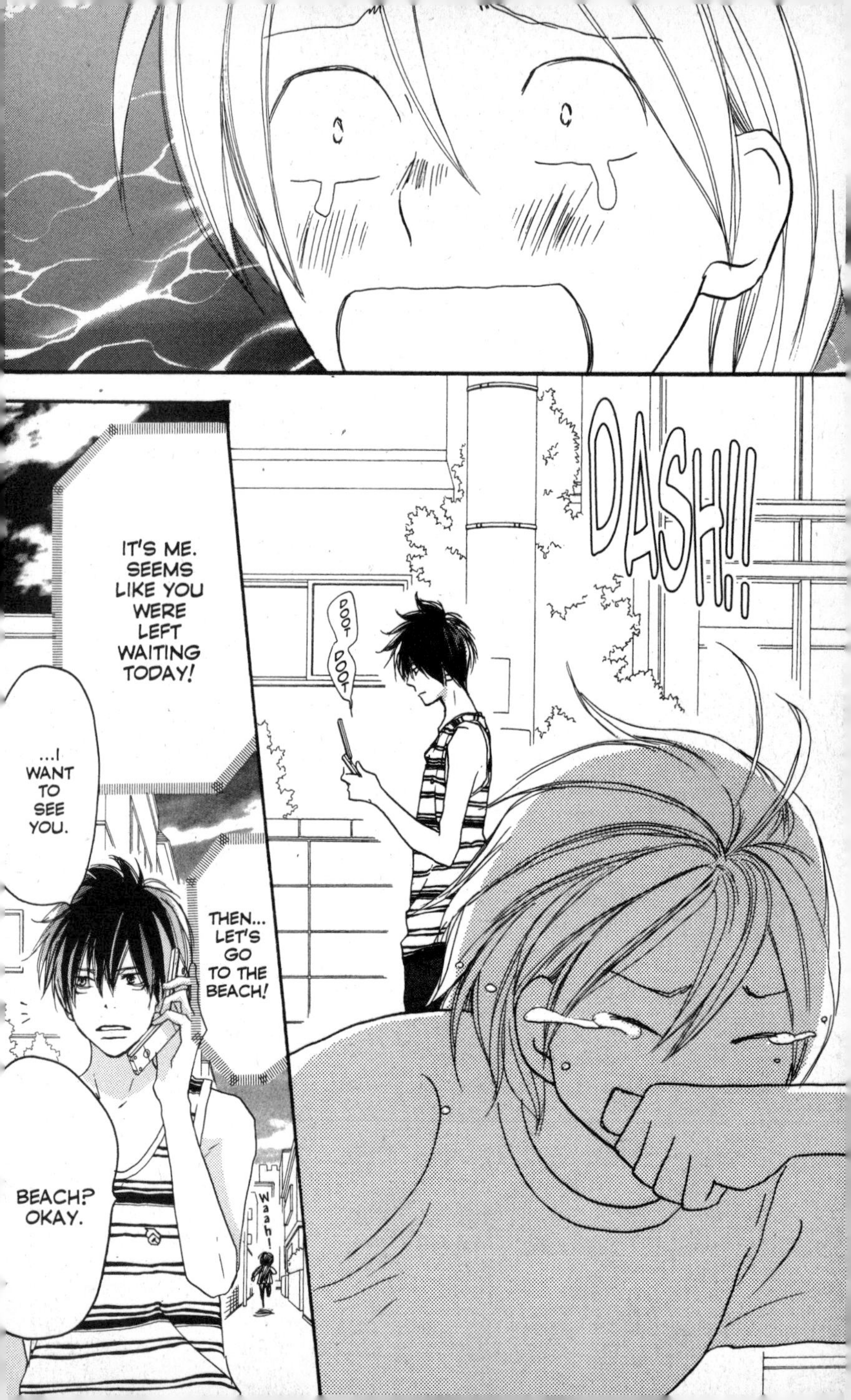
DASH!!
DOOT DOOT
IT'S ME. SEEMS LIKE YOU WERE LEFT WAITING TODAY!
...I WANT TO SEE YOU.
THEN... LET'S GO TO THE BEACH!
Waah!
BEACH? OKAY.

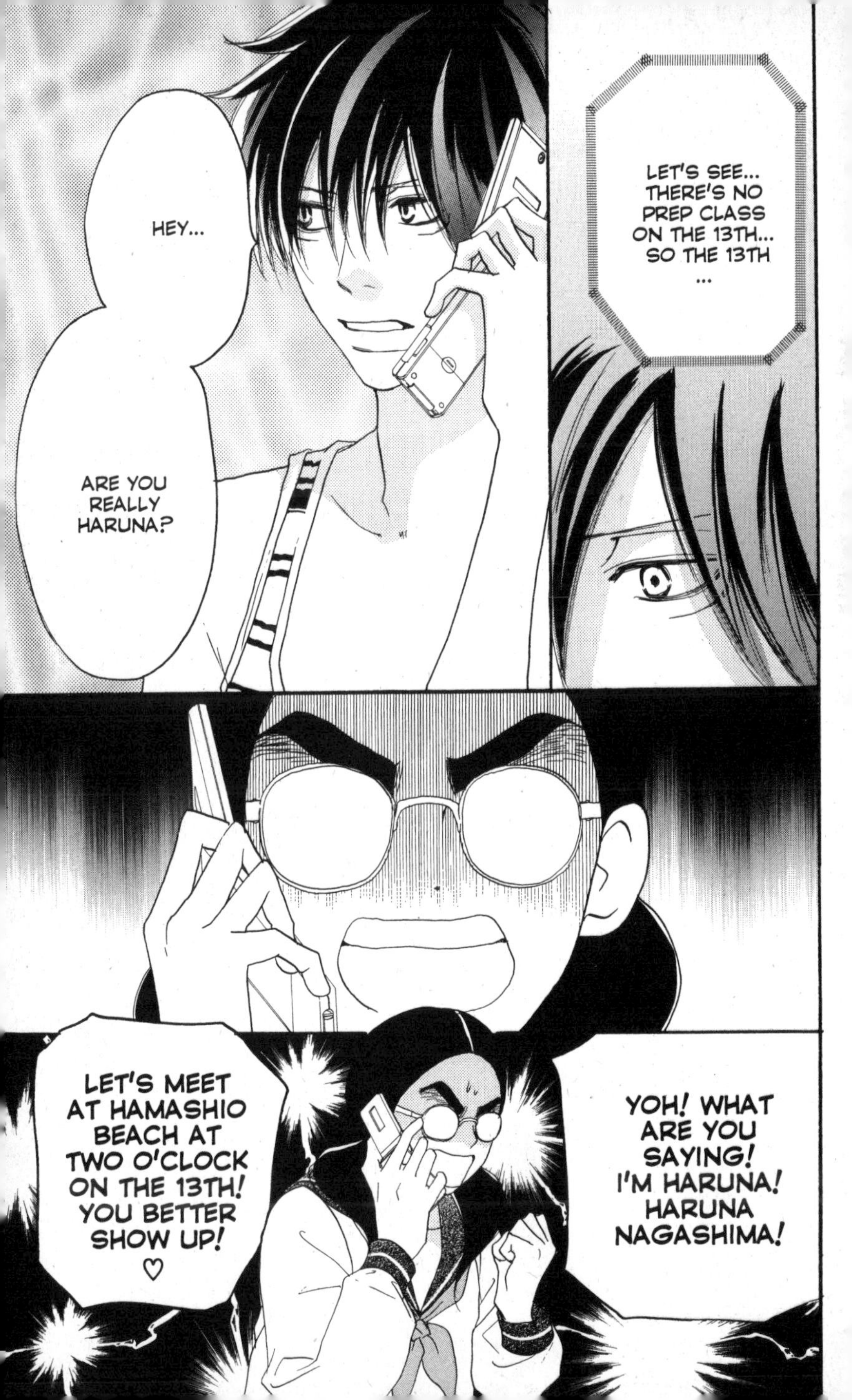
LET'S SEE... THERE'S NO PREP CLASS ON THE 13TH... SO THE 13TH ...
HEY...
ARE YOU REALLY HARUNA?
YOH! WHAT ARE YOU SAYING! I'M HARUNA! HARUNA NAGASHIMA!
LET'S MEET AT HAMASHIO BEACH AT TWO O'CLOCK ON THE 13TH! YOU BETTER SHOW UP! ♡

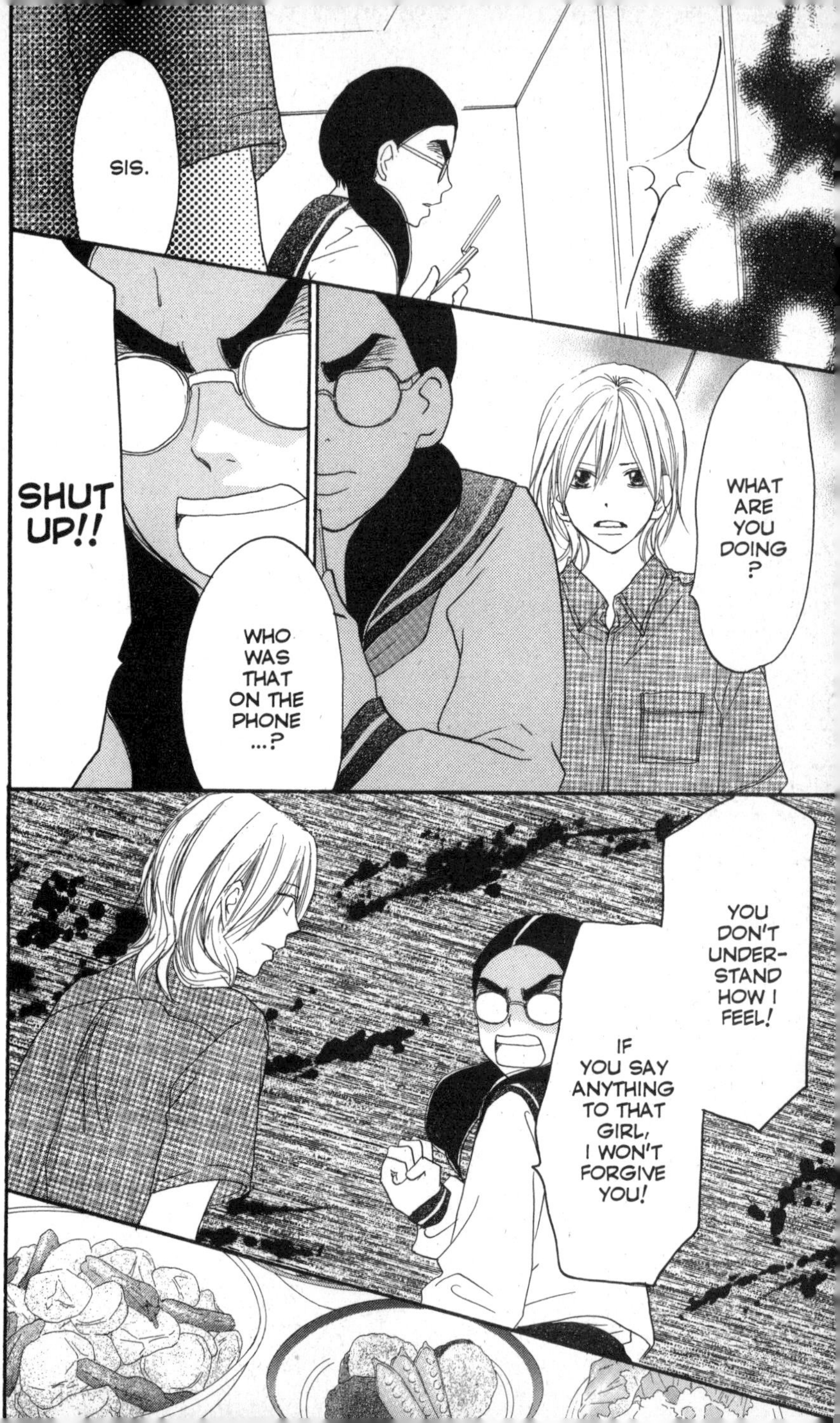
SIS.
WHAT ARE YOU DOING?
WHO WAS THAT ON THE PHONE...?
SHUT UP!!
YOU DON'T UNDER-STAND HOW I FEEL!
IF YOU SAY ANYTHING TO THAT GIRL, I WON'T FORGIVE YOU!

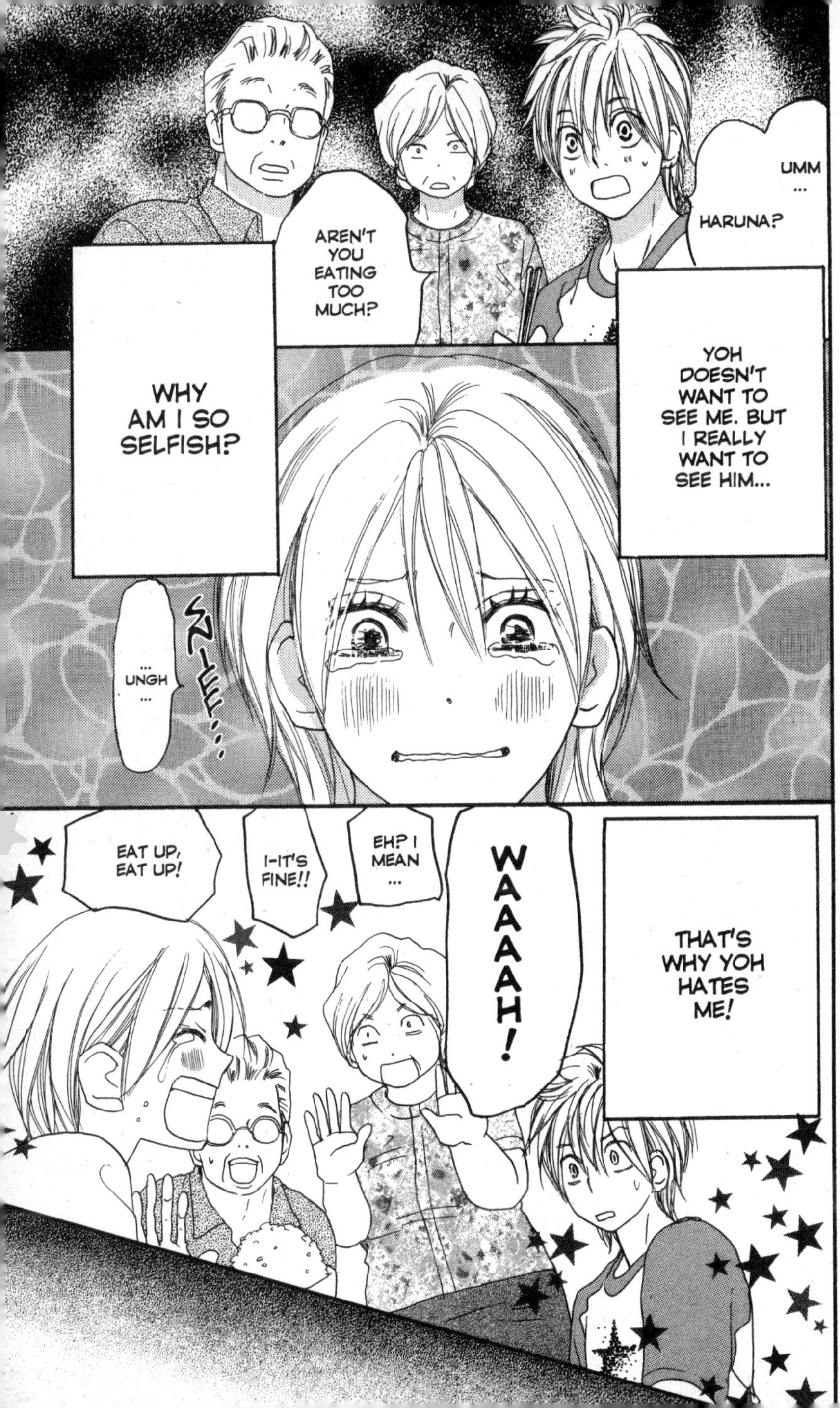
UMM ...
HARUNA?
AREN'T YOU EATING TOO MUCH?
YOH DOESN'T WANT TO SEE ME. BUT I REALLY WANT TO SEE HIM...
WHY AM I SO SELFISH?
... UNGH ...
THAT'S WHY YOH HATES ME!
WAAAAAH!
EH? I MEAN ...
I-IT'S FINE!!
EAT UP, EAT UP!

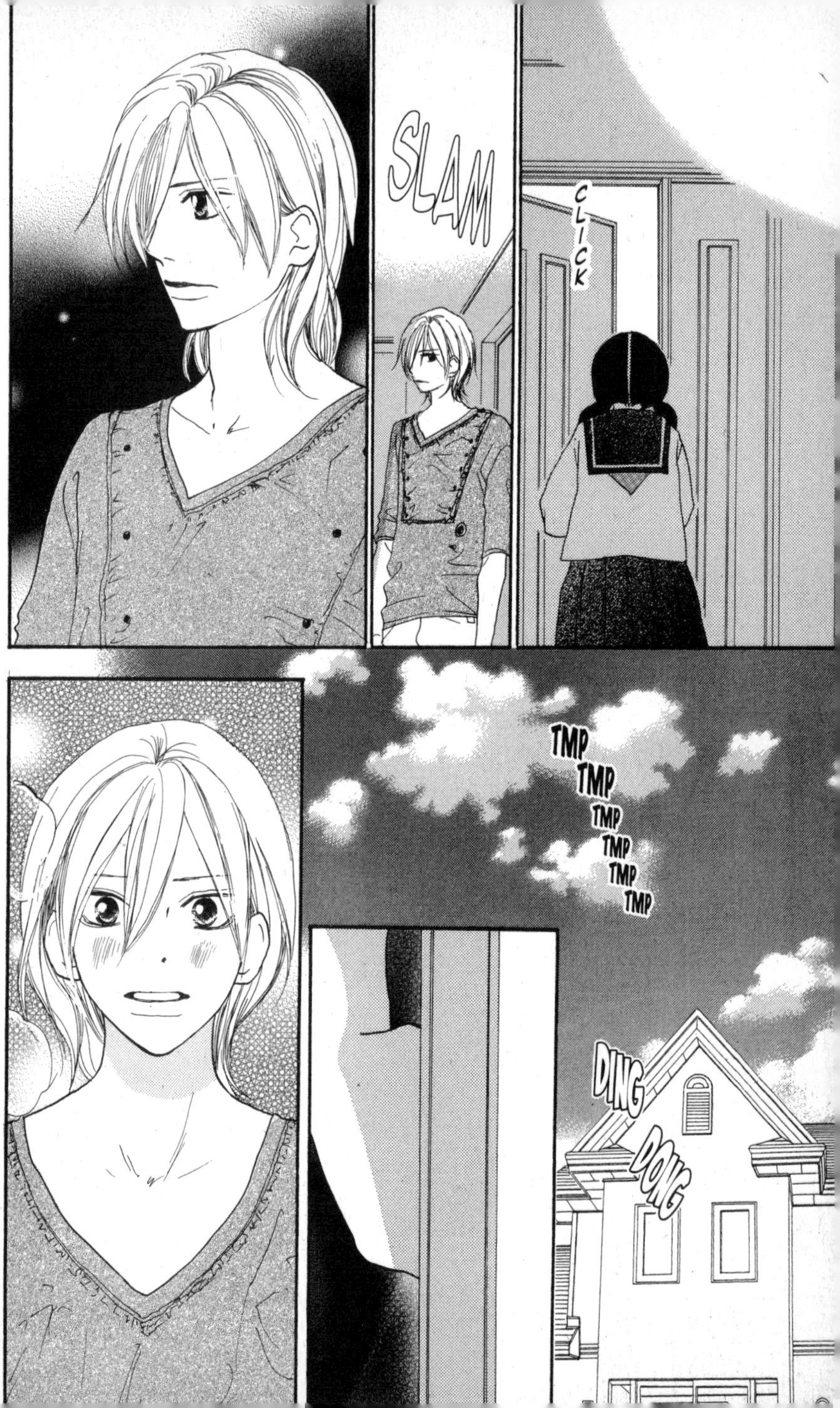
CLICK
SLAM
TMP TMP TMP TMP TMP TMP
DING DONG

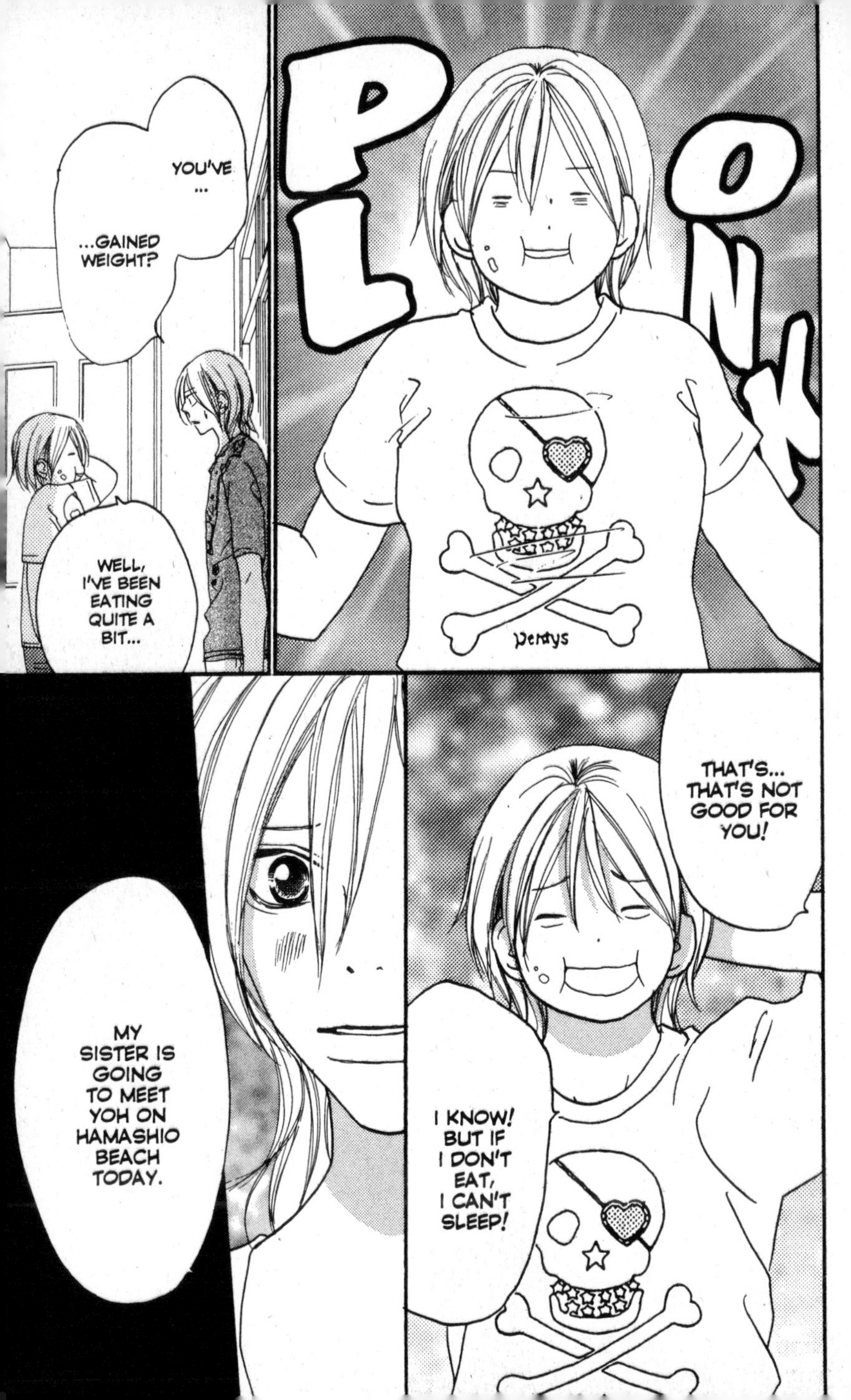
PLONK
YOU'VE ...
...GAINED WEIGHT?
WELL, I'VE BEEN EATING QUITE A BIT...
THAT'S... THAT'S NOT GOOD FOR YOU!
I KNOW! BUT IF I DON'T EAT, I CAN'T SLEEP!
MY SISTER IS GOING TO MEET YOH ON HAMASHIO BEACH TODAY.

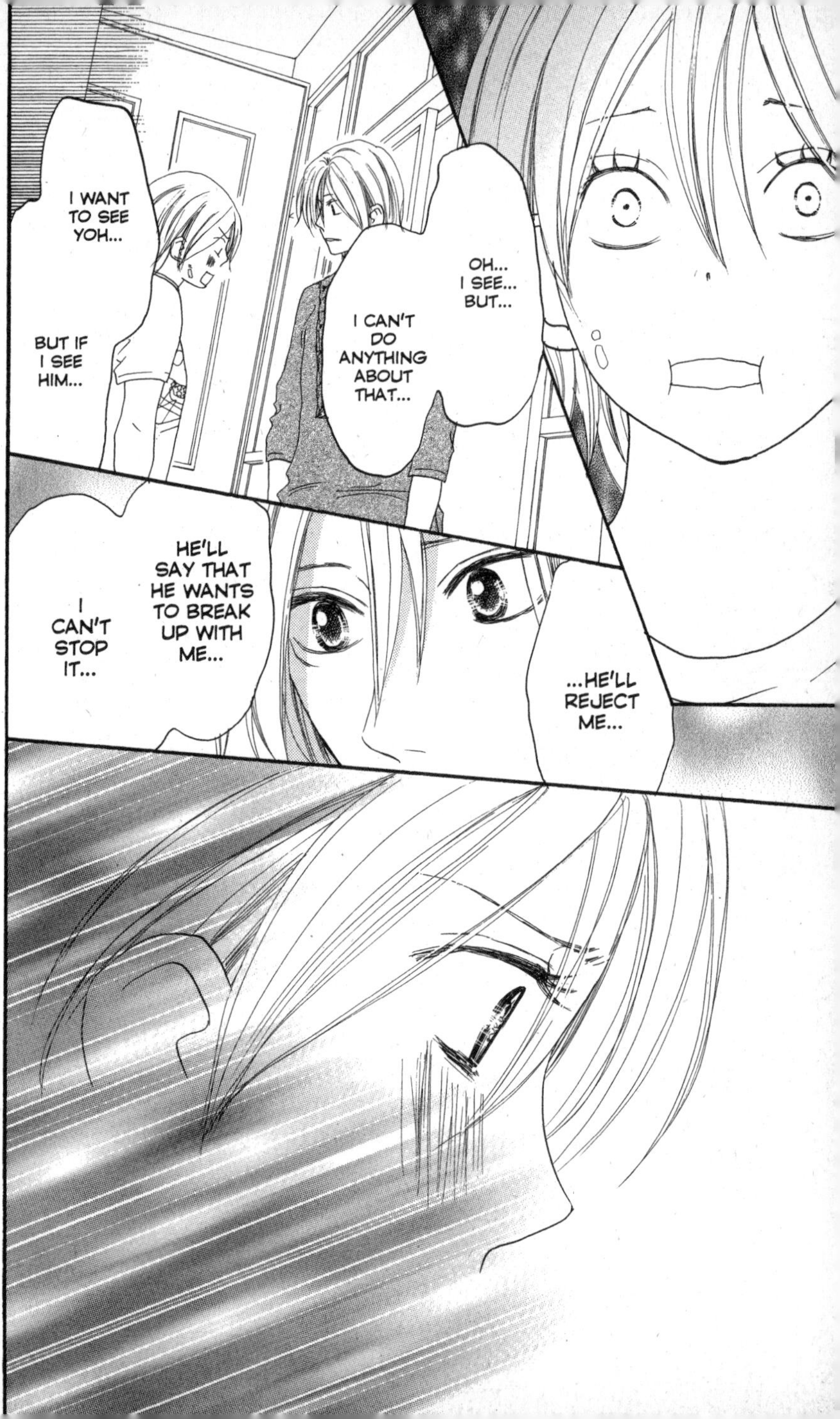
I WANT TO SEE YOH...
OH... I SEE... BUT...
I CAN'T DO ANYTHING ABOUT THAT...
BUT IF I SEE HIM...
...HE'LL REJECT ME...
HE'LL SAY THAT HE WANTS TO BREAK UP WITH ME...
I CAN'T STOP IT...

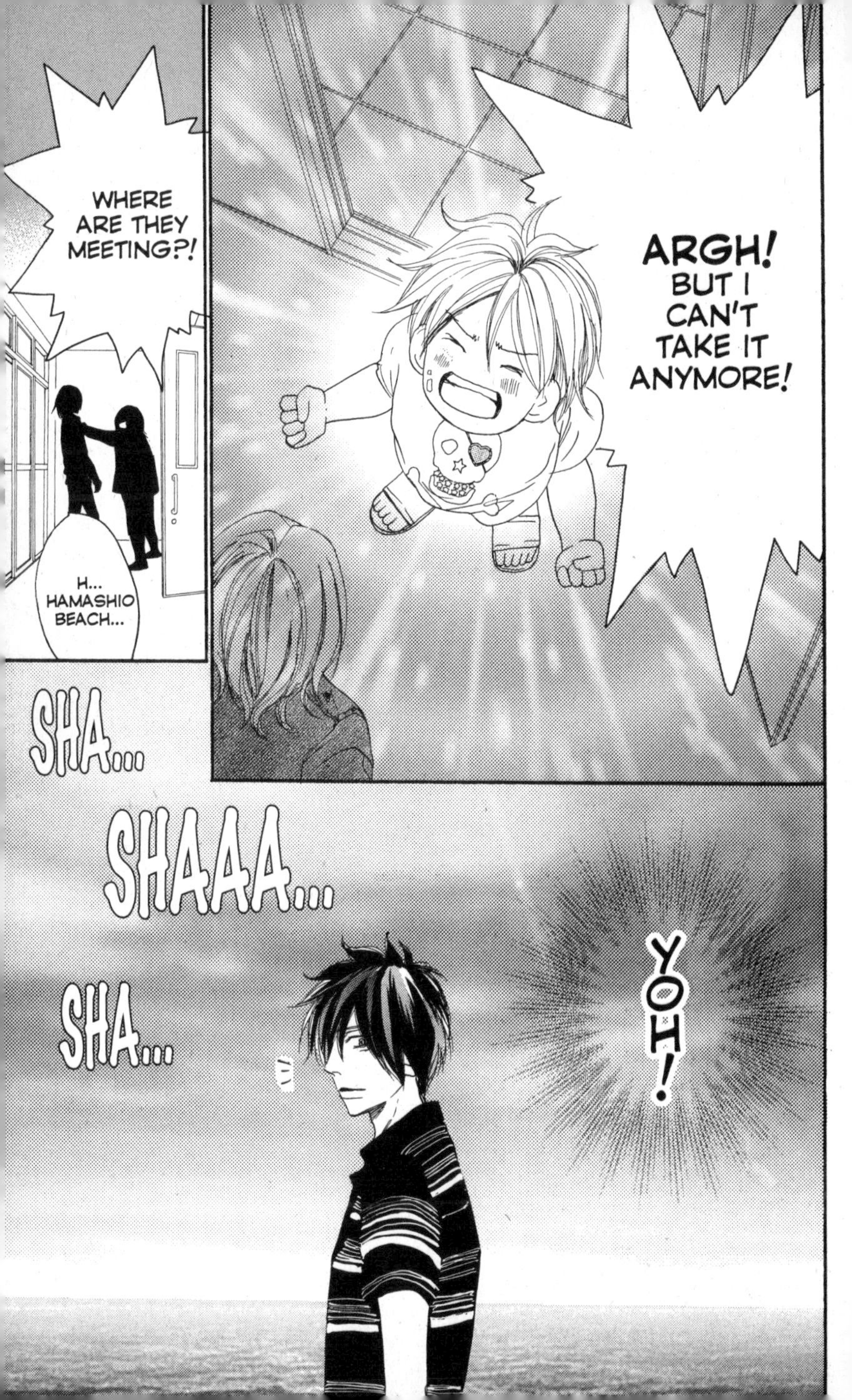
ARGH! BUT I CAN'T TAKE IT ANYMORE!
WHERE ARE THEY MEETING?!
H... HAMASHIO BEACH...
SHA...
SHAAA...
SHA...
YOH!

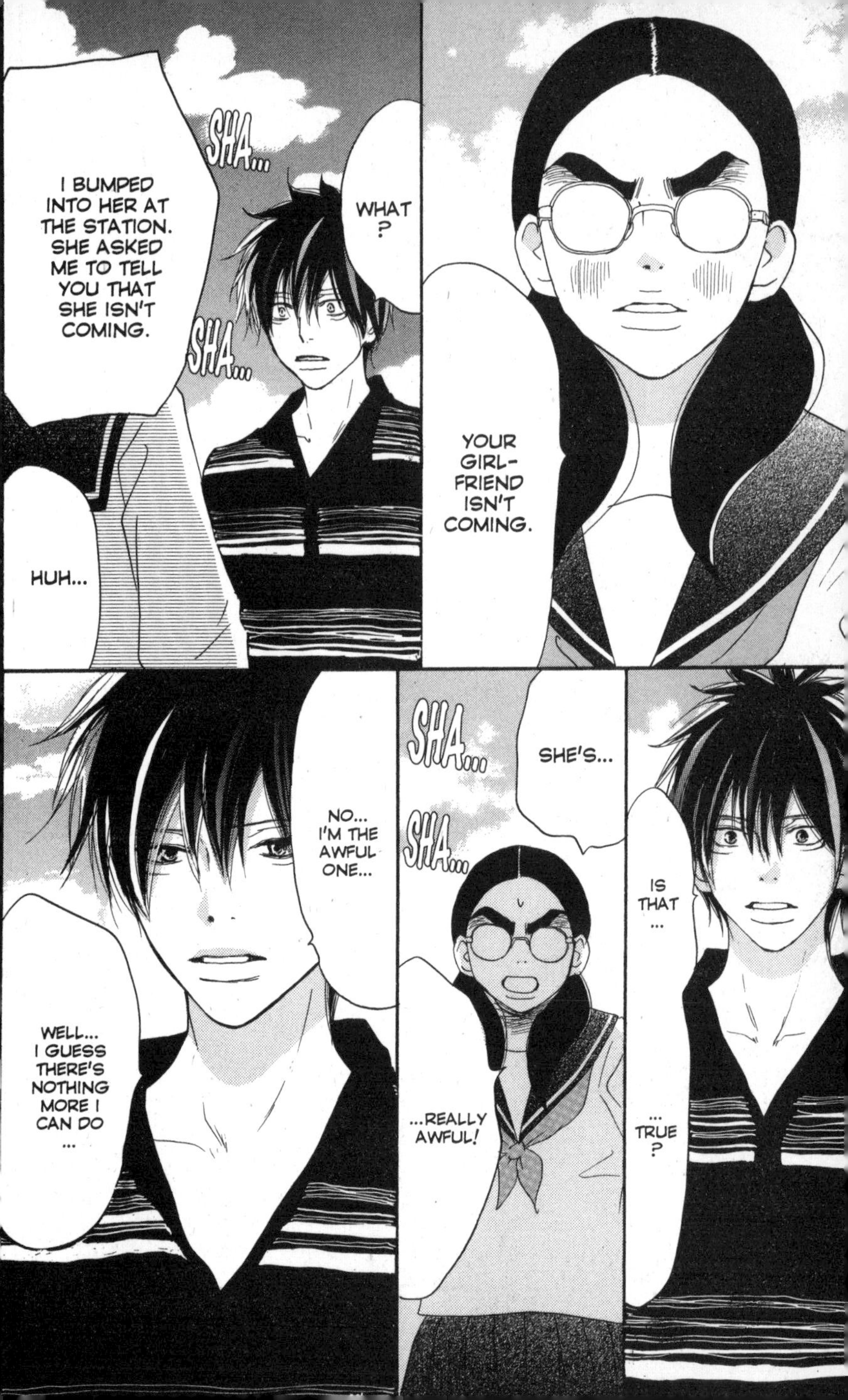
YOUR GIRL-FRIEND ISN'T COMING.
WHAT ?
SHA...
I BUMPED INTO HER AT THE STATION. SHE ASKED ME TO TELL YOU THAT SHE ISN'T COMING.
SHA...
HUH...
IS THAT ... ... TRUE ?
SHE'S...
SHA...
SHA...
...REALLY AWFUL!
NO... I'M THE AWFUL ONE...
WELL... I GUESS THERE'S NOTHING MORE I CAN DO ...

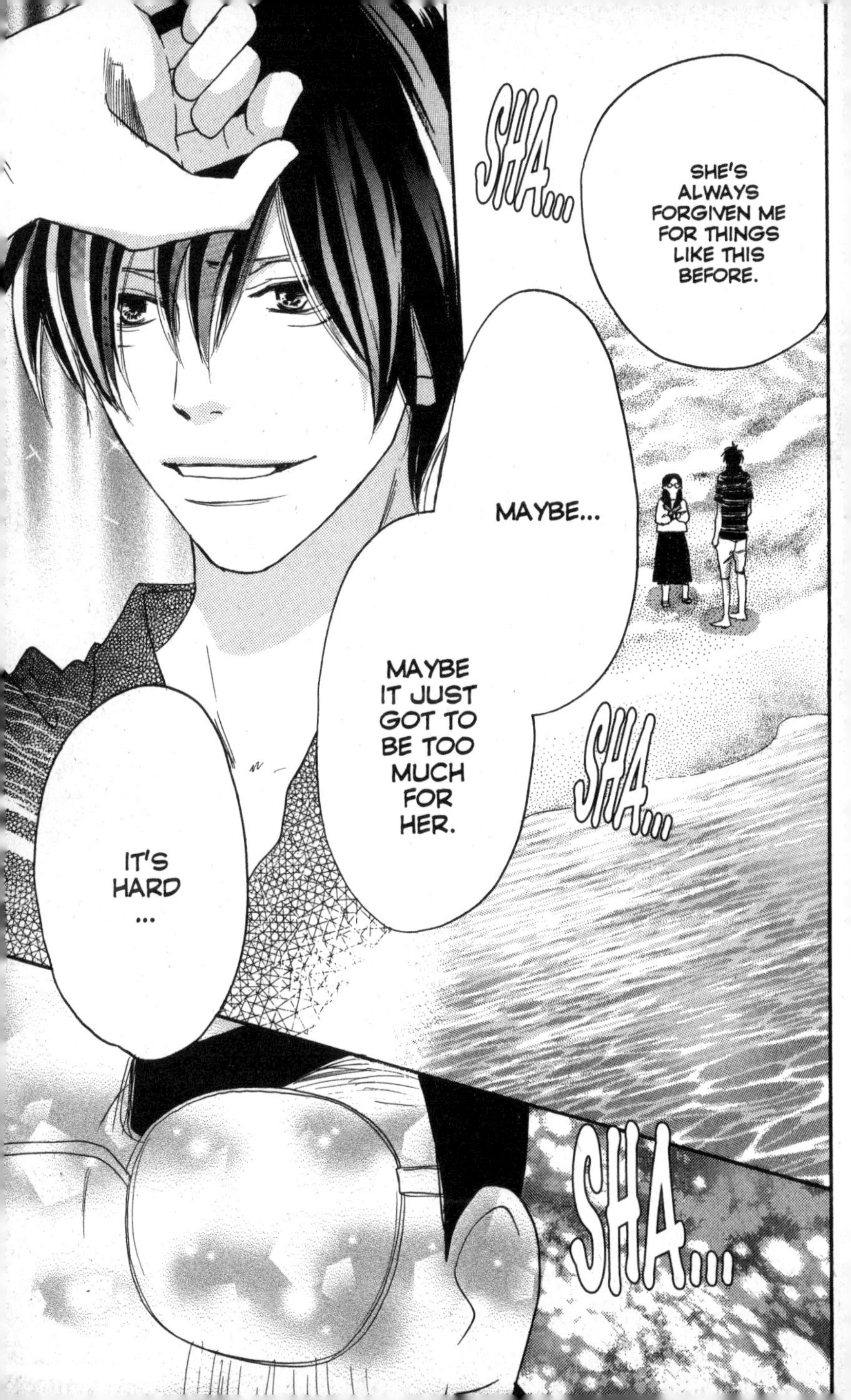
SHE'S ALWAYS FORGIVEN ME FOR THINGS LIKE THIS BEFORE.
SHA...
MAYBE...
MAYBE IT JUST GOT TO BE TOO MUCH FOR HER.
SHA...
IT'S HARD ...
SHA...

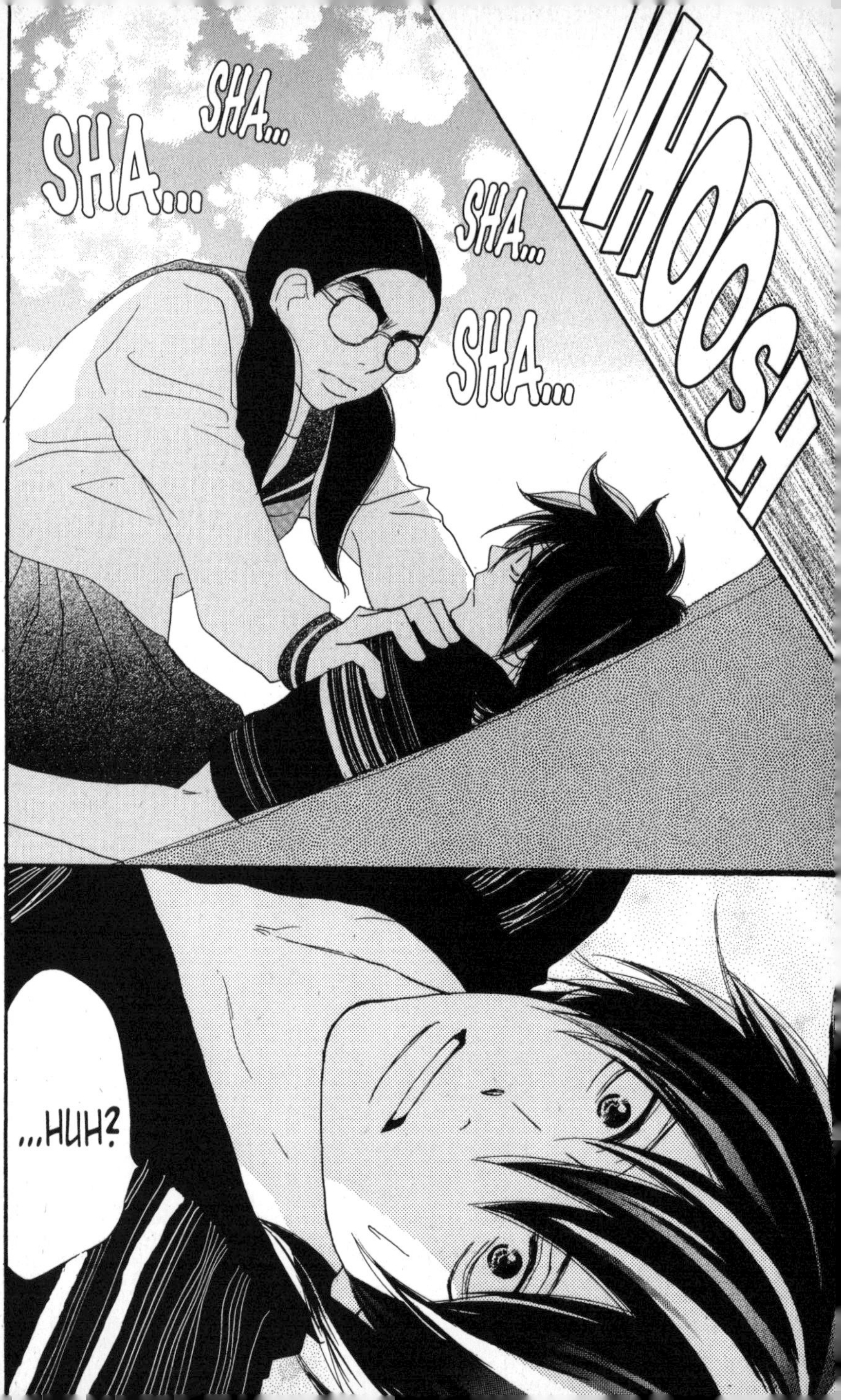
WHOOSH
SHA...
SHA...
SHA...
SHA...
...HUH?

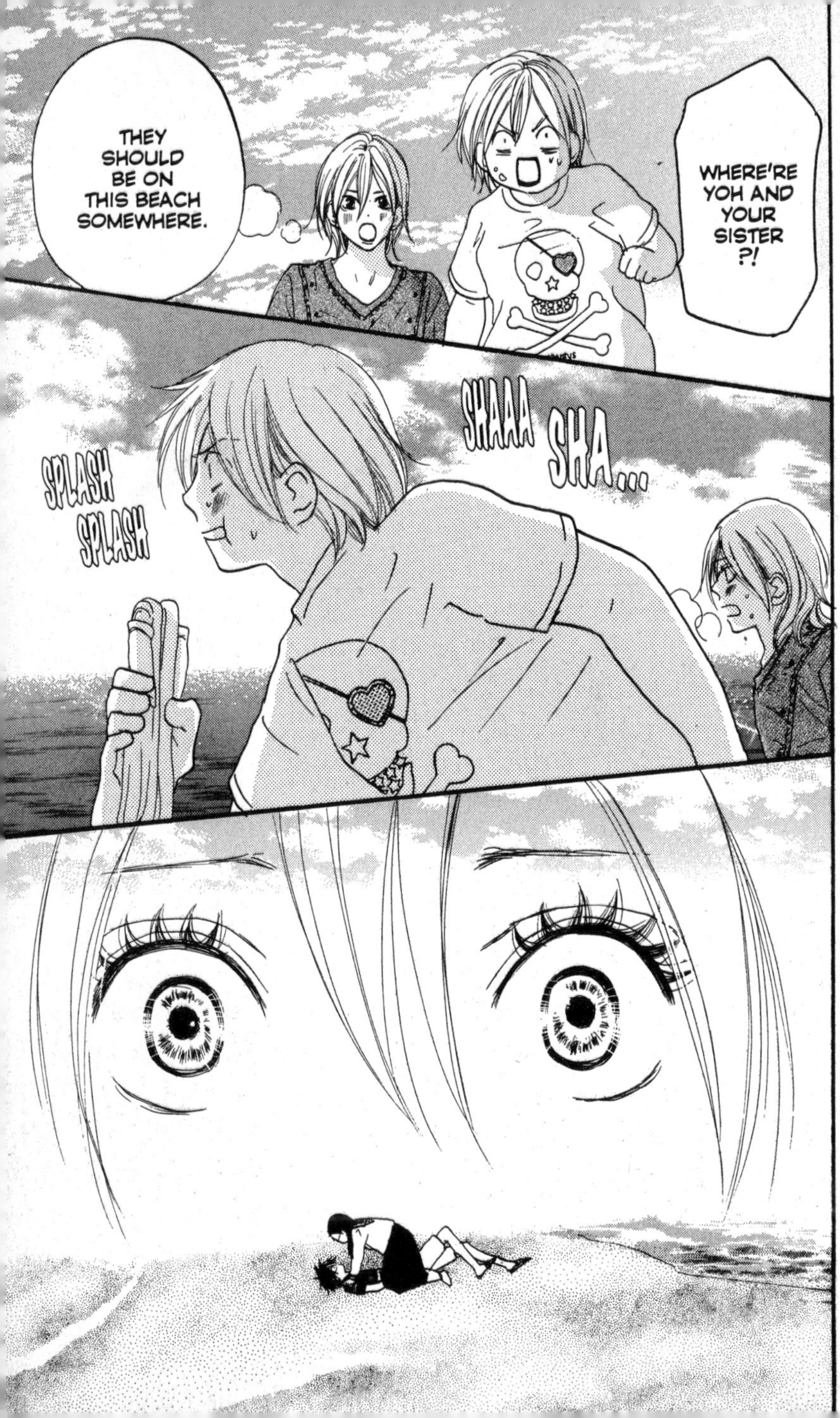
WHERE'RE YOH AND YOUR SISTER ?!
THEY SHOULD BE ON THIS BEACH SOMEWHERE.
SHAAA SHA...
SPLASH SPLASH

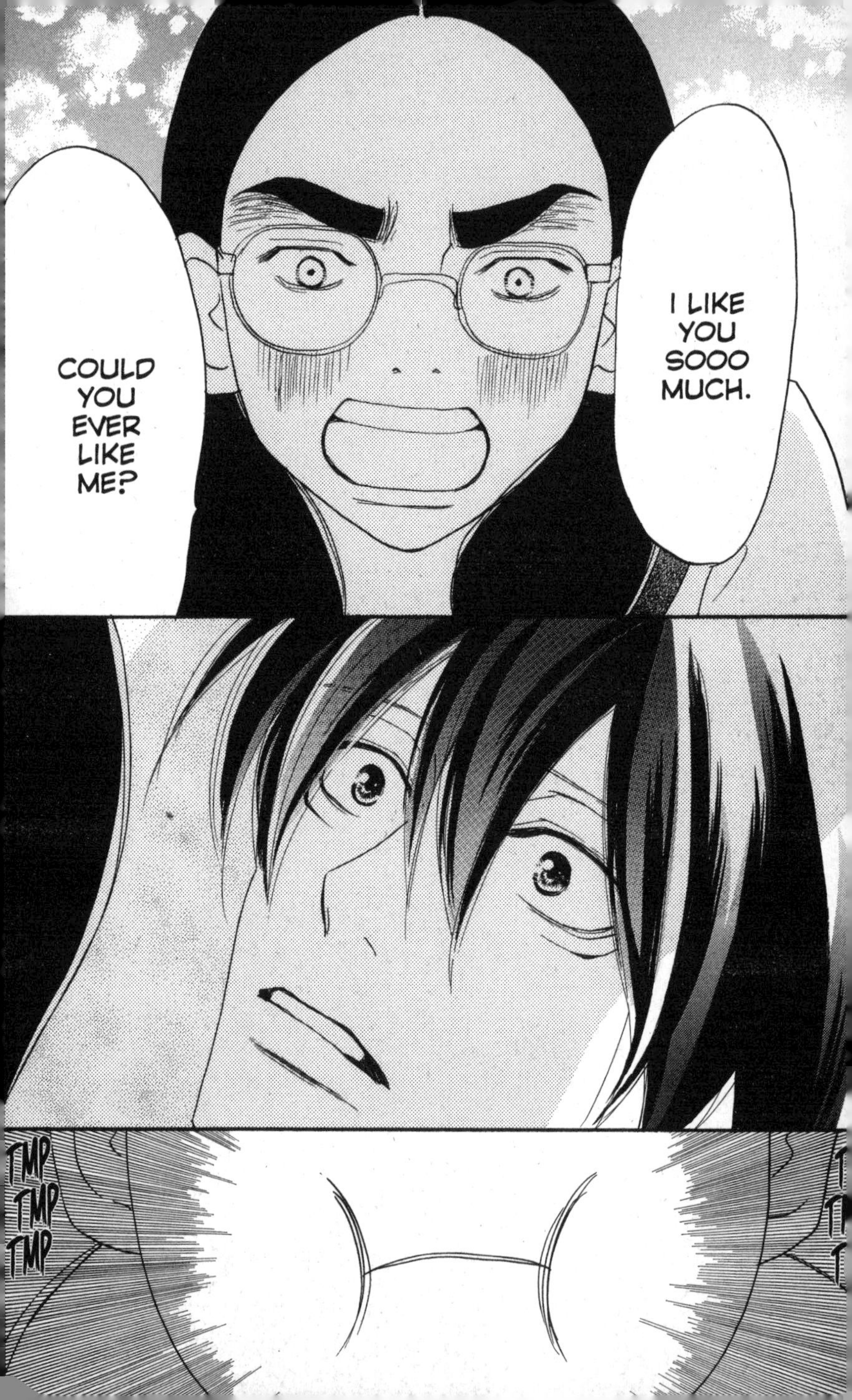
I LIKE YOU SOOO MUCH.
COULD YOU EVER LIKE ME?
TMP TMP TMP TMP

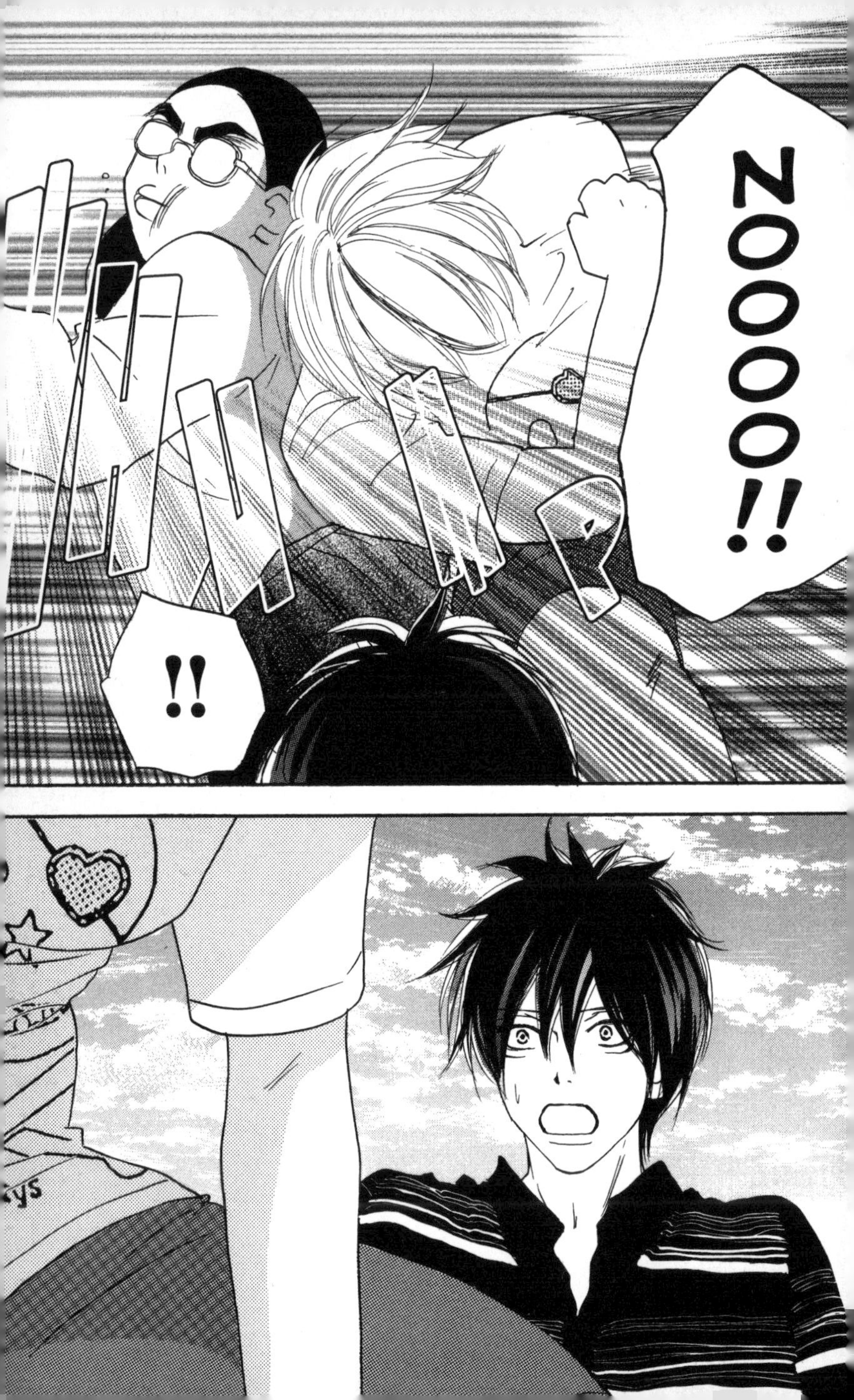
NOOOO!!
!!

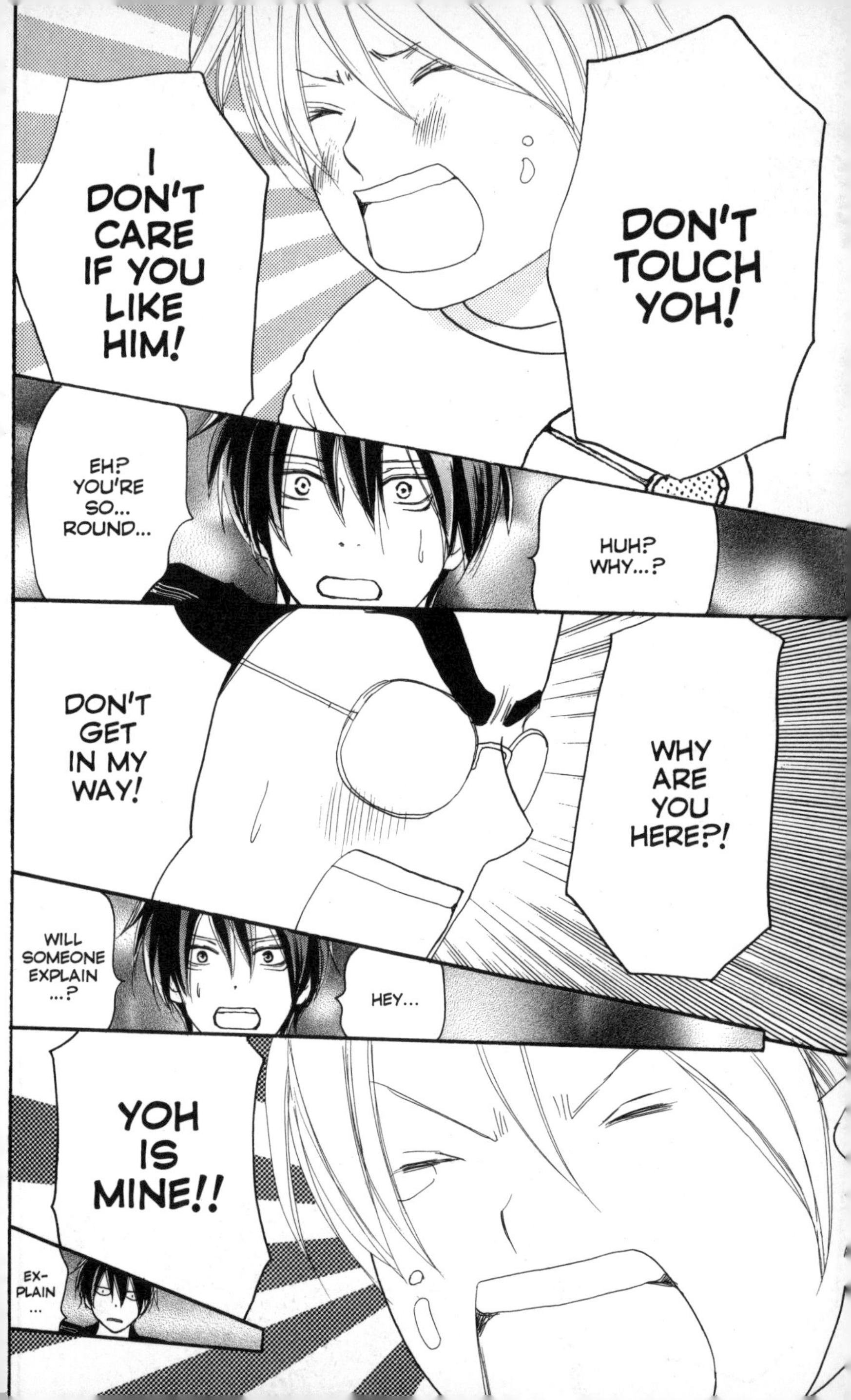
DON'T TOUCH YOH!
I DON'T CARE IF YOU LIKE HIM!
HUH? WHY...?
EH? YOU'RE SO... ROUND...
WHY ARE YOU HERE?!
DON'T GET IN MY WAY!
HEY...
WILL SOMEONE EXPLAIN ...?
YOH IS MINE!!
EX-PLAIN ...

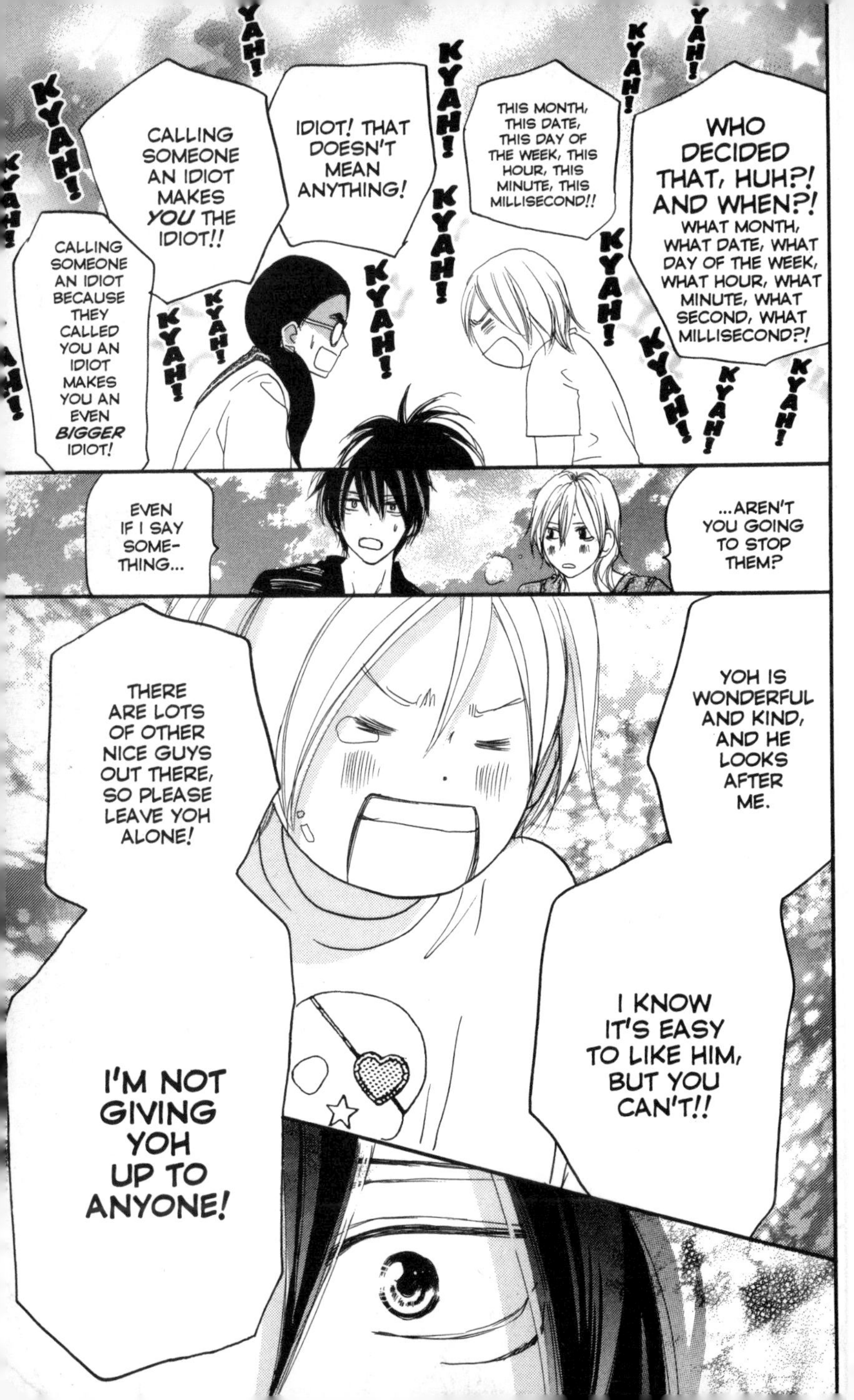
YAH!
KYAH!
WHO DECIDED THAT, HUH?! AND WHEN?! WHAT MONTH, WHAT DATE, WHAT DAY OF THE WEEK, WHAT HOUR, WHAT MINUTE, WHAT SECOND, WHAT MILLISECOND?!
THIS MONTH, THIS DATE, THIS DAY OF THE WEEK, THIS HOUR, THIS MINUTE, THIS MILLISECOND!!
IDIOT! THAT DOESN'T MEAN ANYTHING!
CALLING SOMEONE AN IDIOT MAKES *YOU* THE IDIOT!!
CALLING SOMEONE AN IDIOT BECAUSE THEY CALLED YOU AN IDIOT MAKES YOU AN EVEN ***BIGGER*** IDIOT!
KYAH! KYAH! KYAH! KYAH! KYAH! KYAH! KYAH! KYAH! KYAH! KYAH! KYAH!
...AREN'T YOU GOING TO STOP THEM?
EVEN IF I SAY SOME-THING...
YOH IS WONDERFUL AND KIND, AND HE LOOKS AFTER ME.
THERE ARE LOTS OF OTHER NICE GUYS OUT THERE, SO PLEASE LEAVE YOH ALONE!
I KNOW IT'S EASY TO LIKE HIM, BUT YOU CAN'T!!
I'M NOT GIVING YOH UP TO ANYONE!

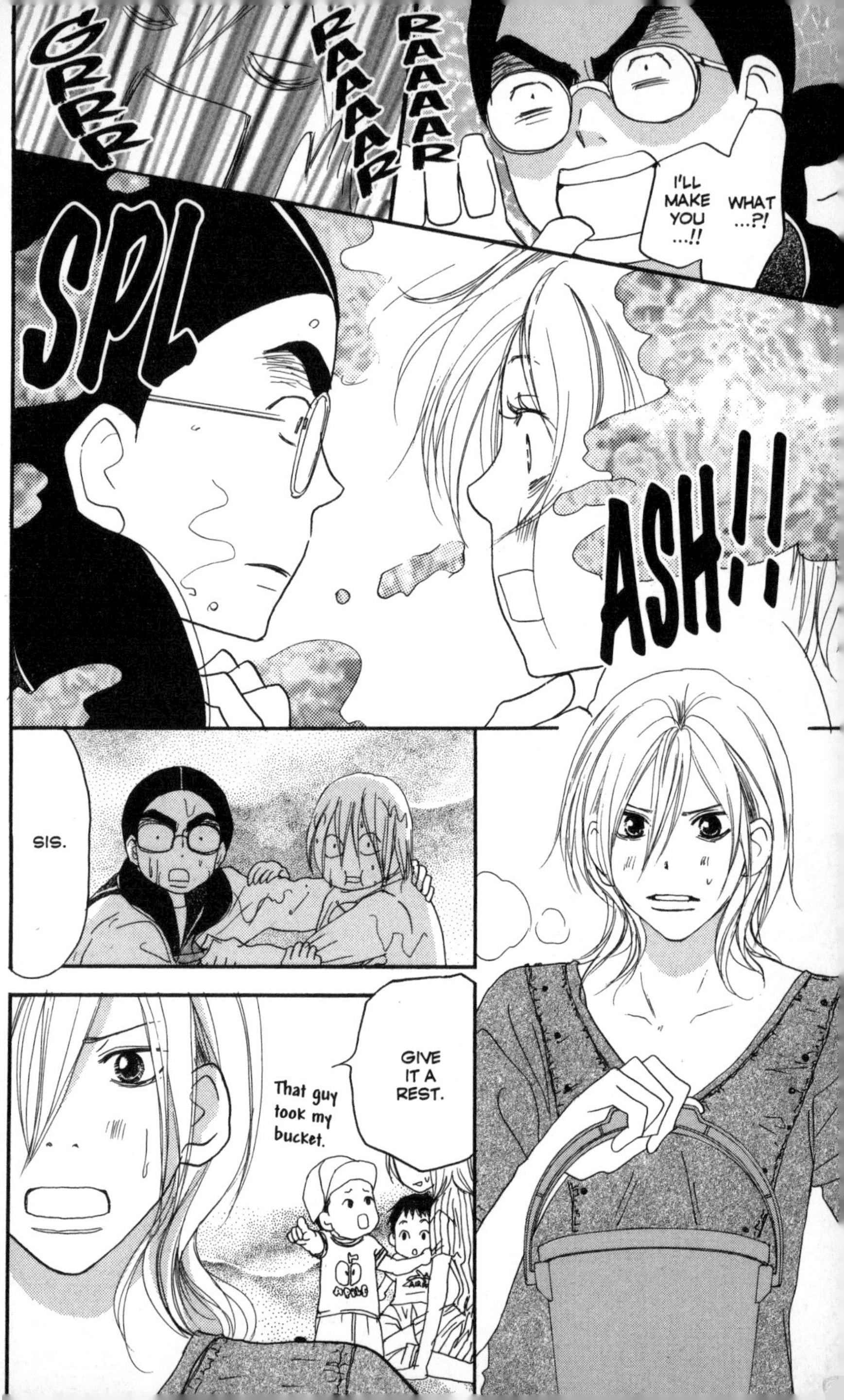
RAAAAR
RAAAAR
GRRRR
WHAT ...?!
I'LL MAKE YOU ...!!
SPL
ASH!!!
SIS.
GIVE IT A REST.
That guy took my bucket.

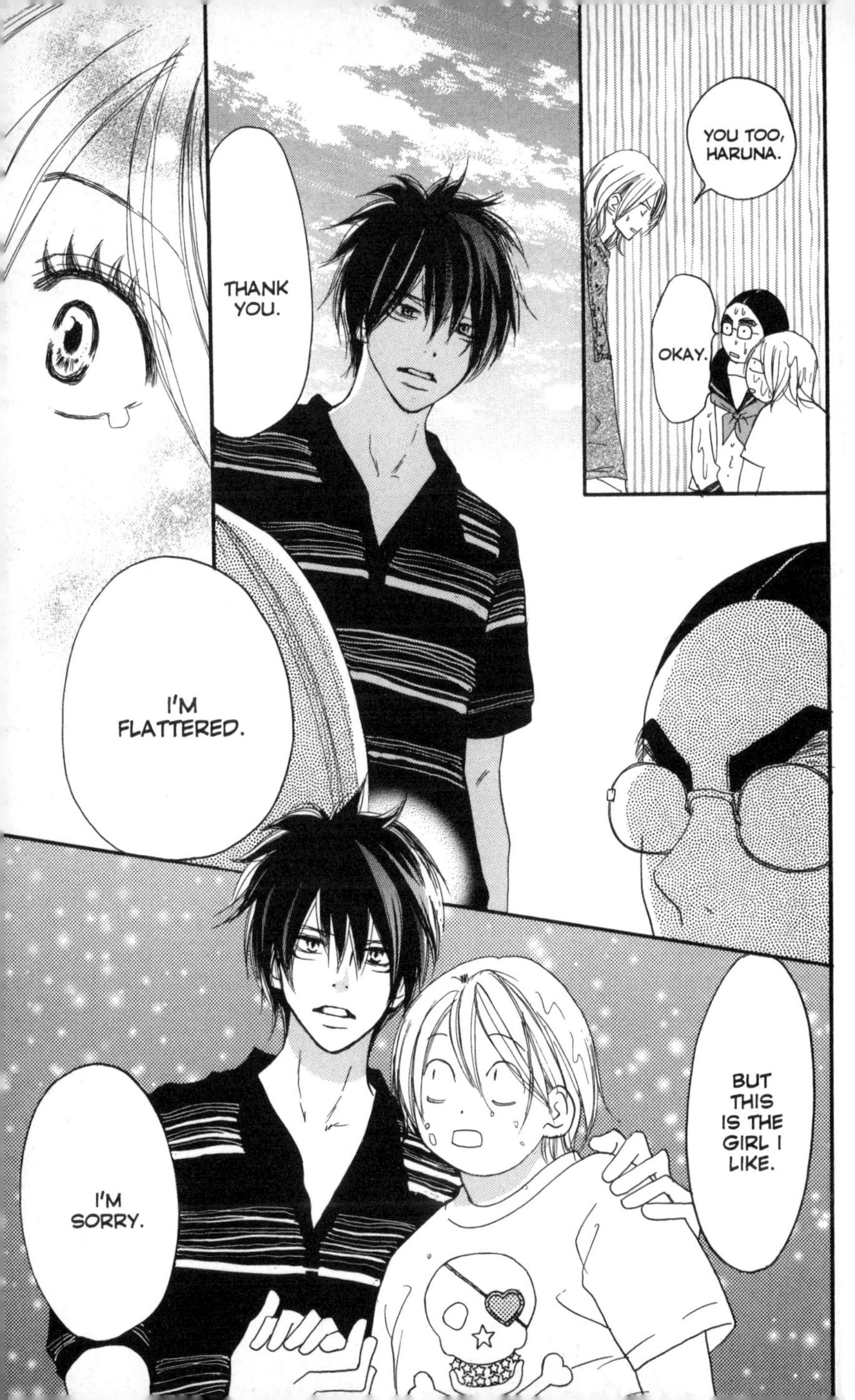
YOU TOO, HARUNA.
OKAY.
THANK YOU.
I'M FLATTERED.
BUT THIS IS THE GIRL I LIKE.
I'M SORRY.

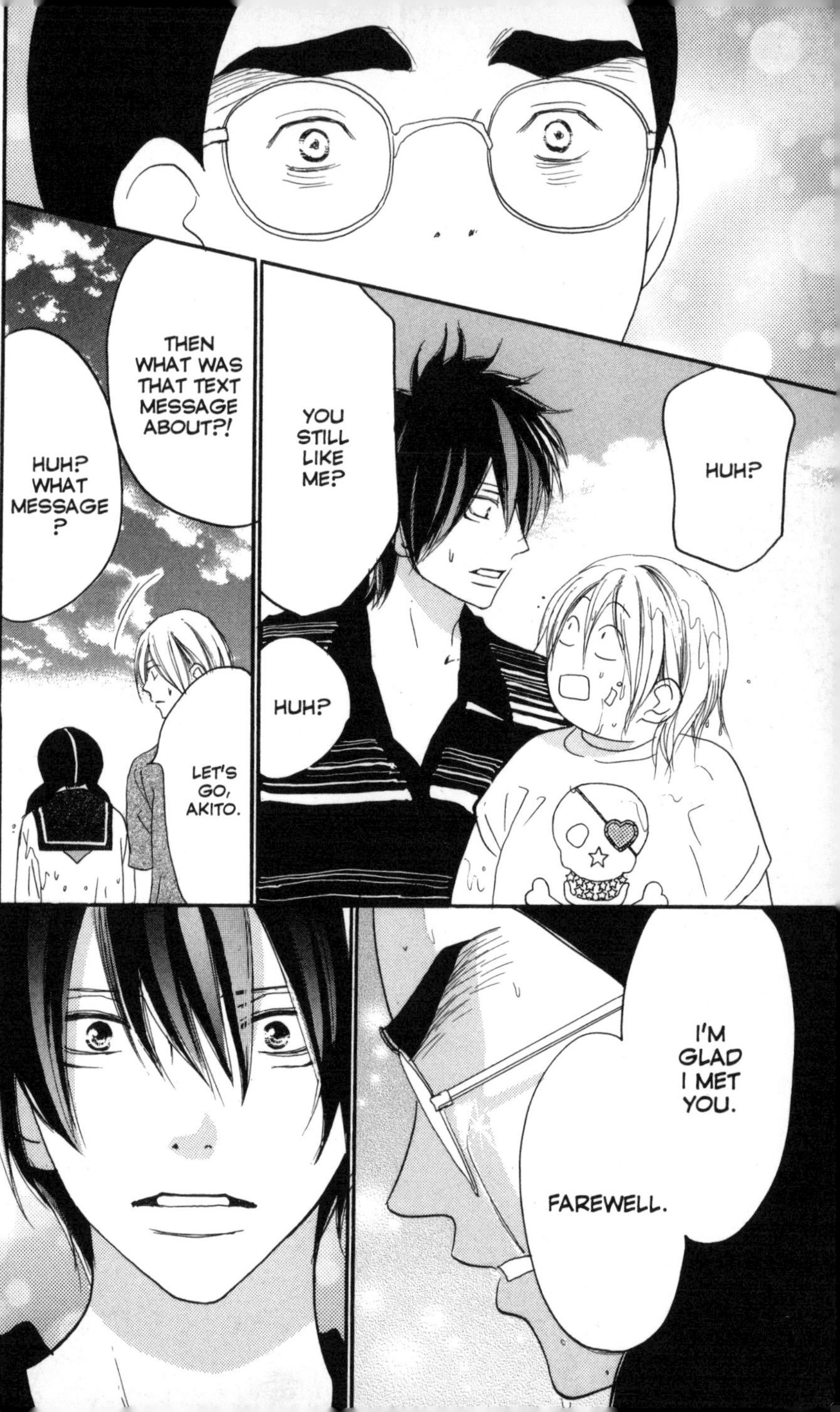
HUH?
YOU STILL LIKE ME?
HUH?
THEN WHAT WAS THAT TEXT MESSAGE ABOUT?!
HUH? WHAT MESSAGE ?
LET'S GO, AKITO.
I'M GLAD I MET YOU.
FAREWELL.

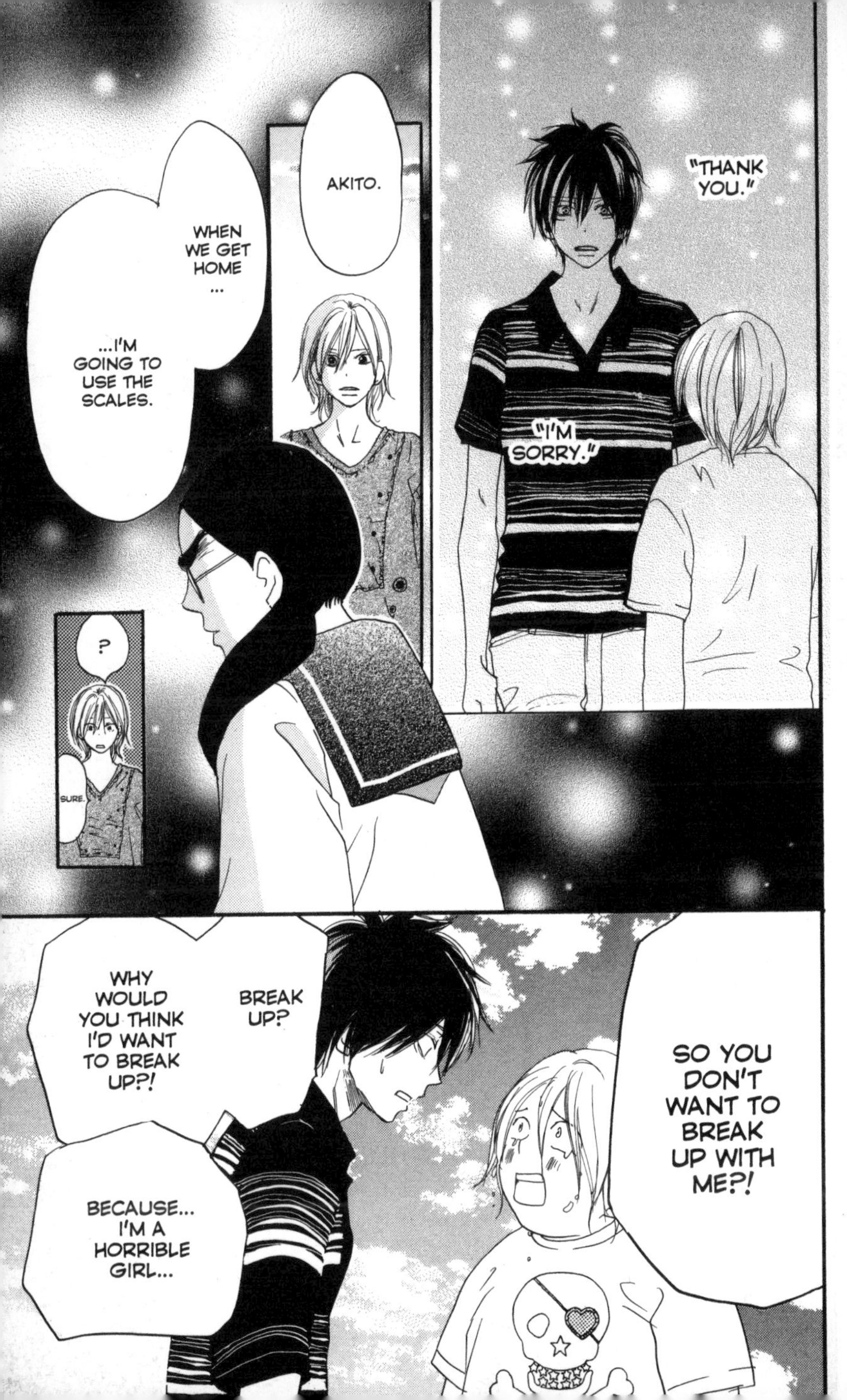
"THANK YOU."
"I'M SORRY."
AKITO.
WHEN WE GET HOME ...
...I'M GOING TO USE THE SCALES.
?
SURE.
SO YOU DON'T WANT TO BREAK UP WITH ME?!
BREAK UP?
WHY WOULD YOU THINK I'D WANT TO BREAK UP?!
BECAUSE... I'M A HORRIBLE GIRL...

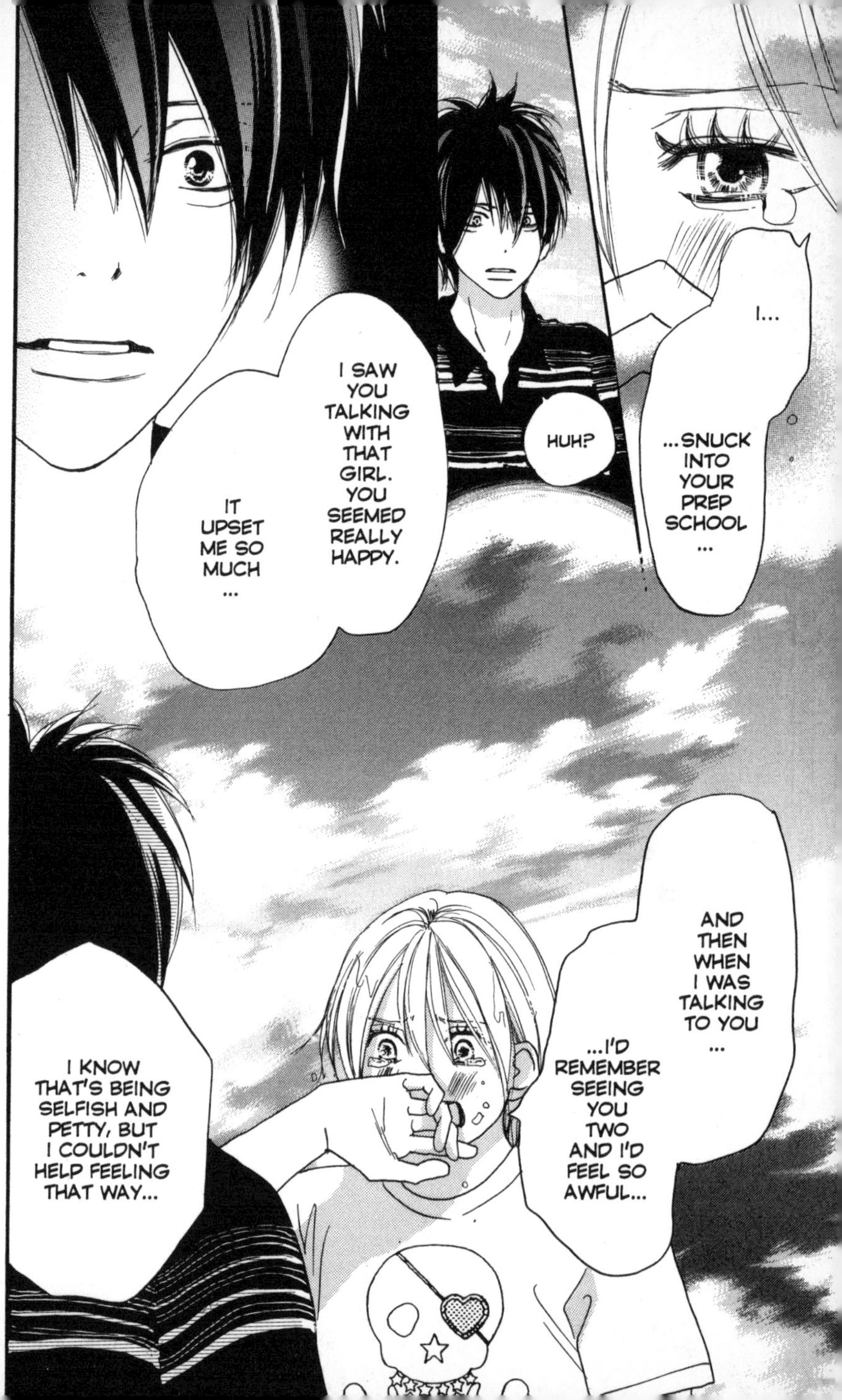
I...
...SNUCK INTO YOUR PREP SCHOOL...
HUH?
I SAW YOU TALKING WITH THAT GIRL. YOU SEEMED REALLY HAPPY.
IT UPSET ME SO MUCH...
AND THEN WHEN I WAS TALKING TO YOU...
...I'D REMEMBER SEEING YOU TWO AND I'D FEEL SO AWFUL...
I KNOW THAT'S BEING SELFISH AND PETTY, BUT I COULDN'T HELP FEELING THAT WAY...

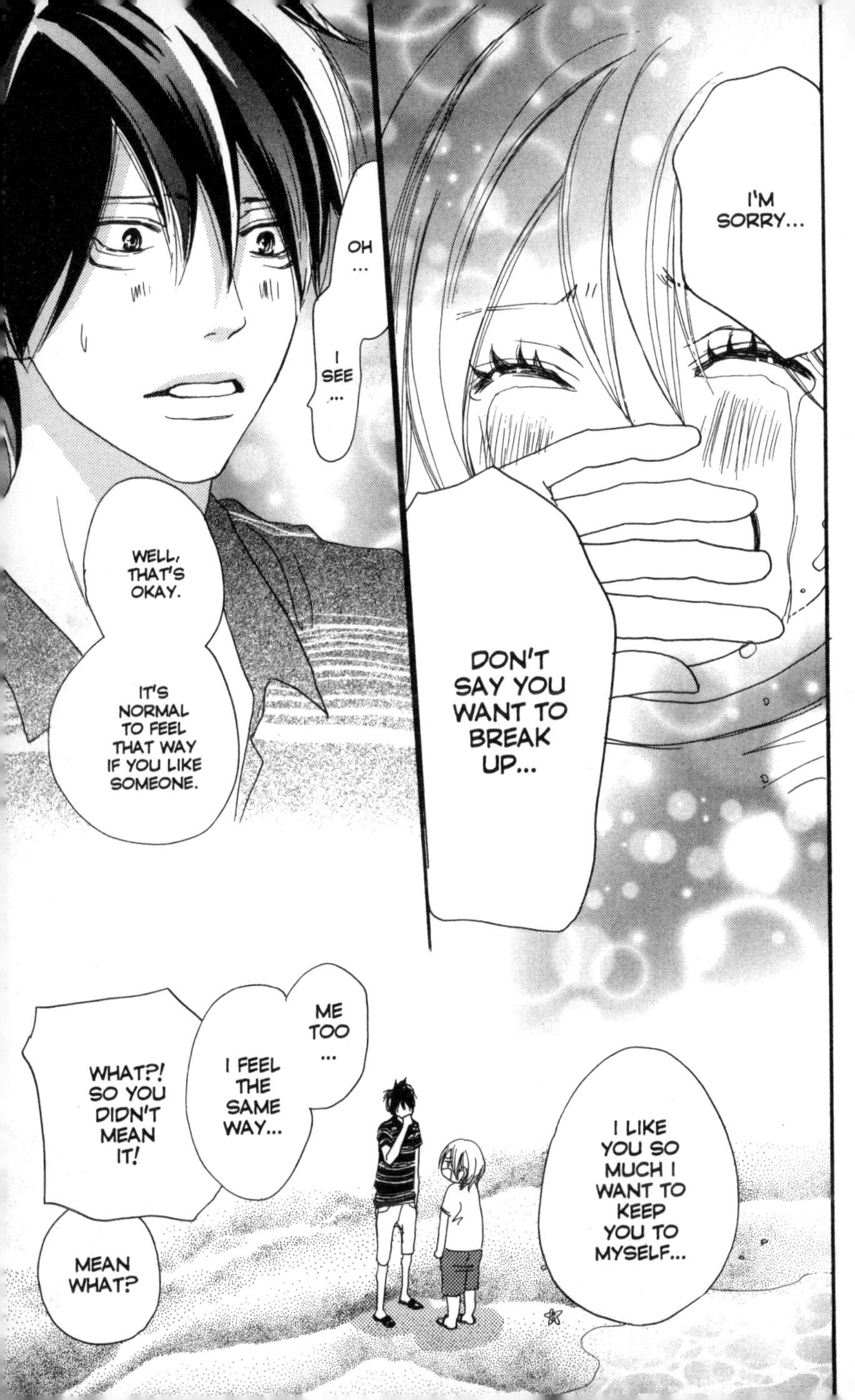
I'M SORRY...
DON'T SAY YOU WANT TO BREAK UP...
OH ... I SEE ...
WELL, THAT'S OKAY.
IT'S NORMAL TO FEEL THAT WAY IF YOU LIKE SOMEONE.
I LIKE YOU SO MUCH I WANT TO KEEP YOU TO MYSELF...
ME TOO ...
I FEEL THE SAME WAY...
WHAT?! SO YOU DIDN'T MEAN IT!
MEAN WHAT?

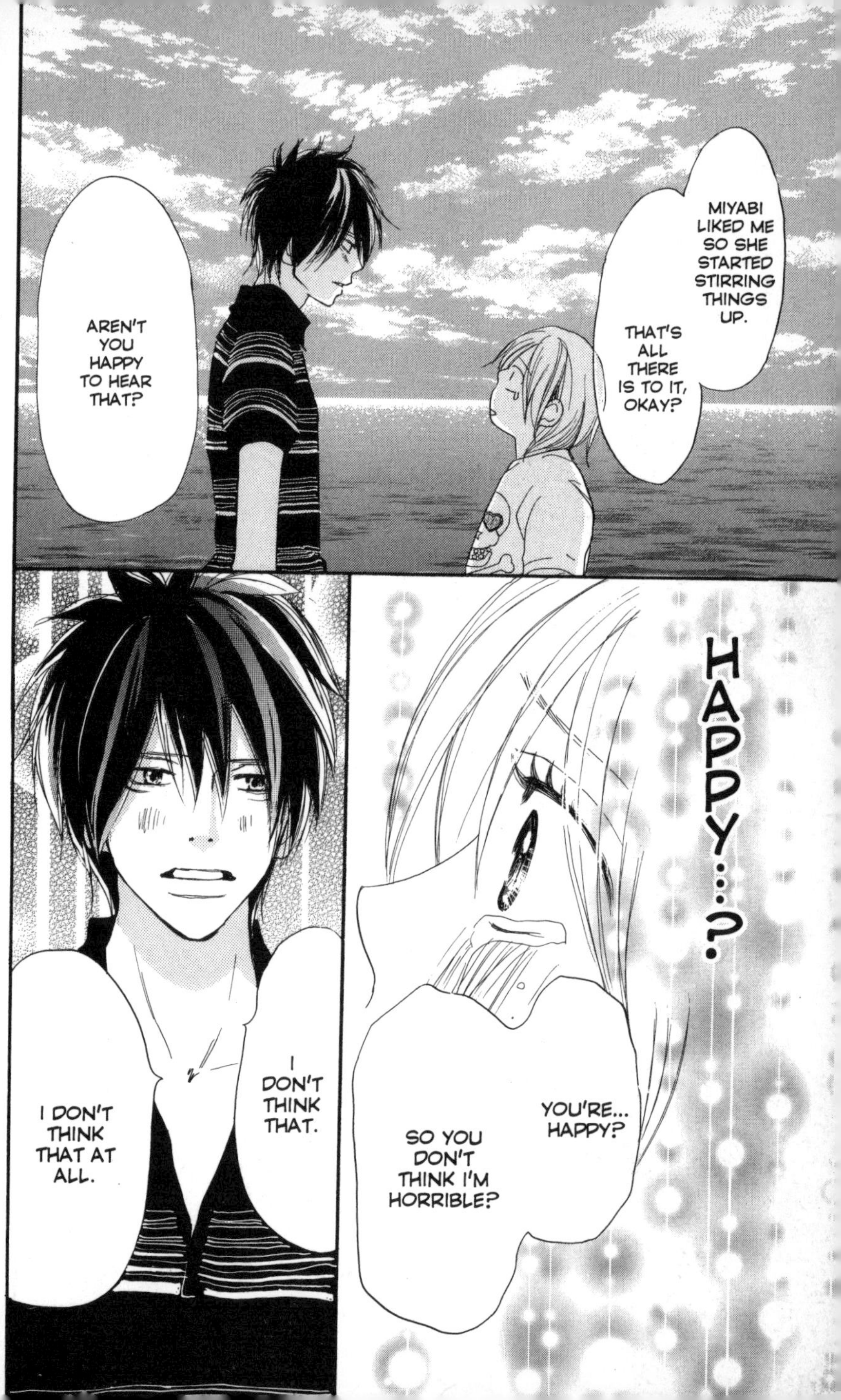
MIYABI LIKED ME SO SHE STARTED STIRRING THINGS UP.
THAT'S ALL THERE IS TO IT, OKAY?
AREN'T YOU HAPPY TO HEAR THAT?
HAPPY...?
YOU'RE... HAPPY?
SO YOU DON'T THINK I'M HORRIBLE?
I DON'T THINK THAT.
I DON'T THINK THAT AT ALL.

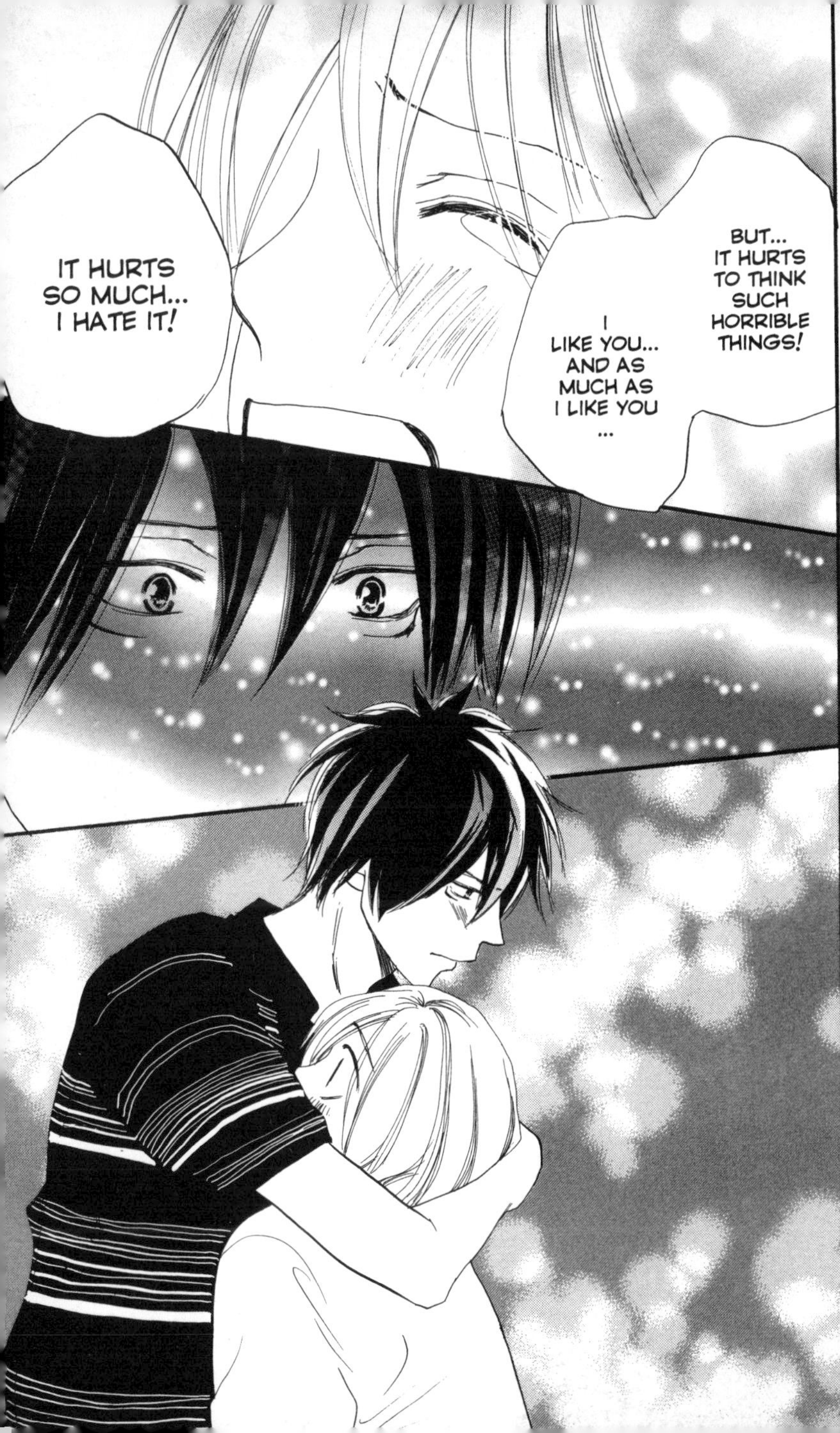
I LIKE YOU... AND AS MUCH AS I LIKE YOU ...
BUT... IT HURTS TO THINK SUCH HORRIBLE THINGS!
IT HURTS SO MUCH... I HATE IT!

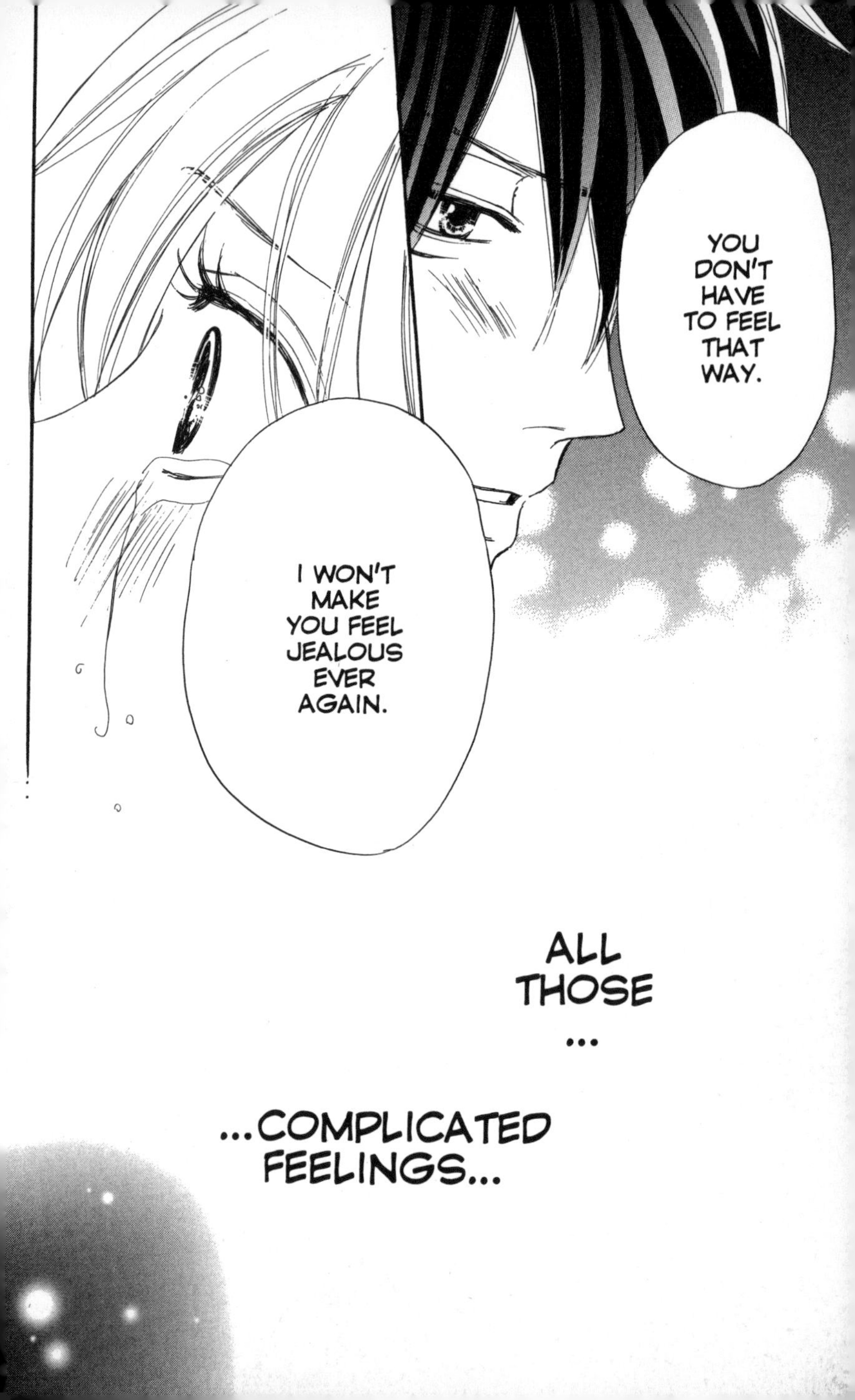
YOU DON'T HAVE TO FEEL THAT WAY.
I WON'T MAKE YOU FEEL JEALOUS EVER AGAIN.
ALL THOSE ...
...COMPLICATED FEELINGS...

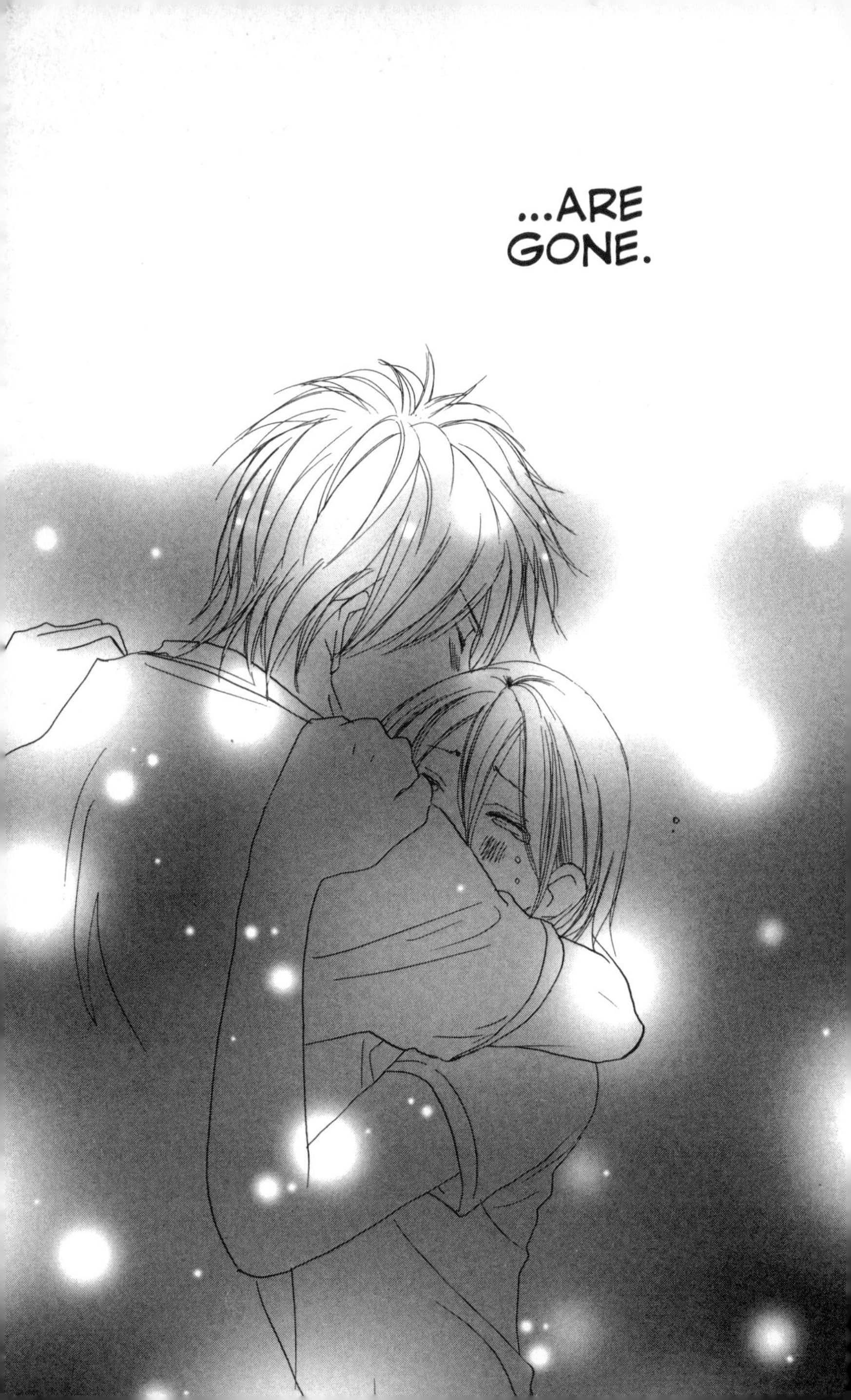
...ARE
GONE.

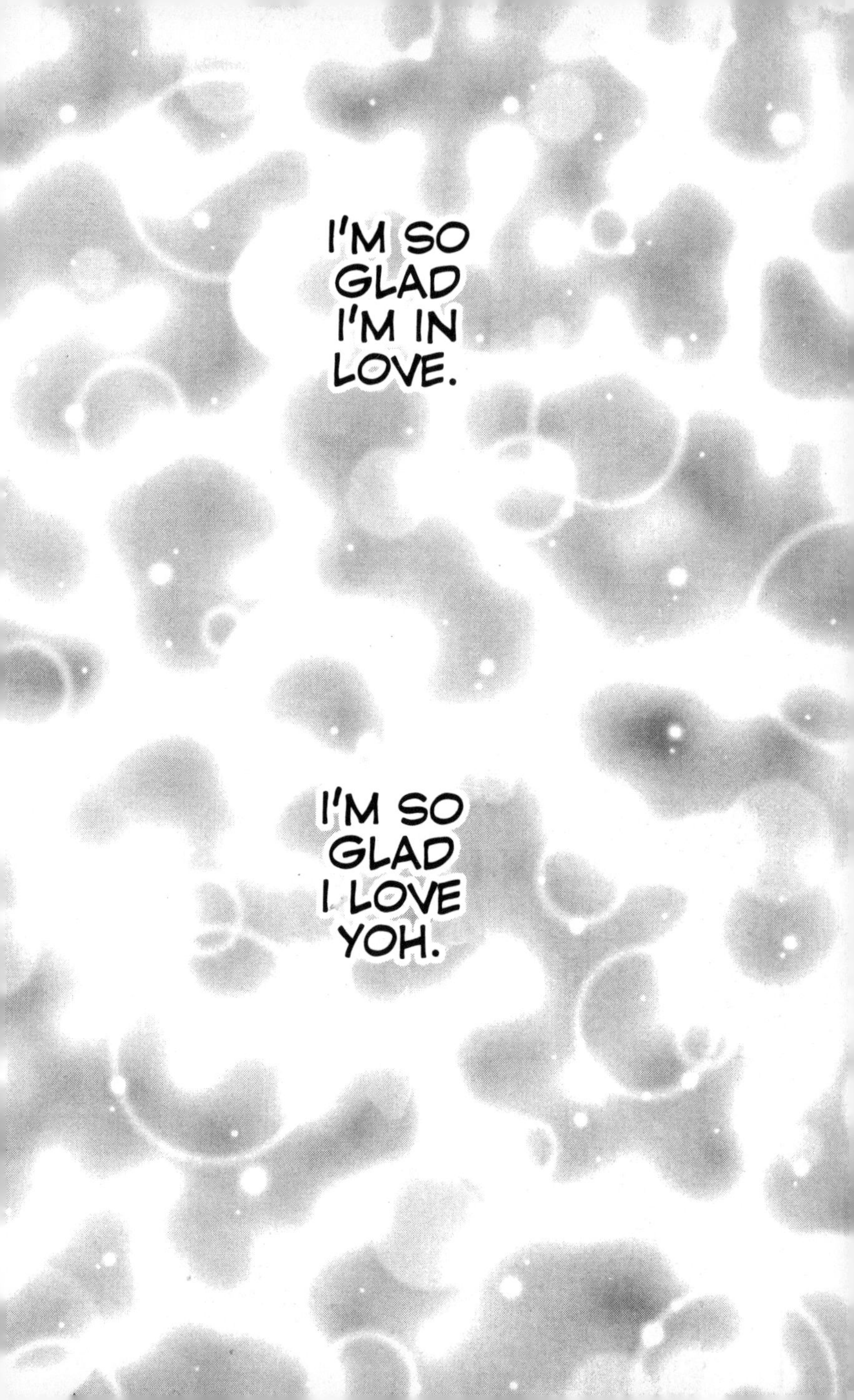
I'M SO GLAD I'M IN LOVE.
I'M SO GLAD I LOVE YOH.

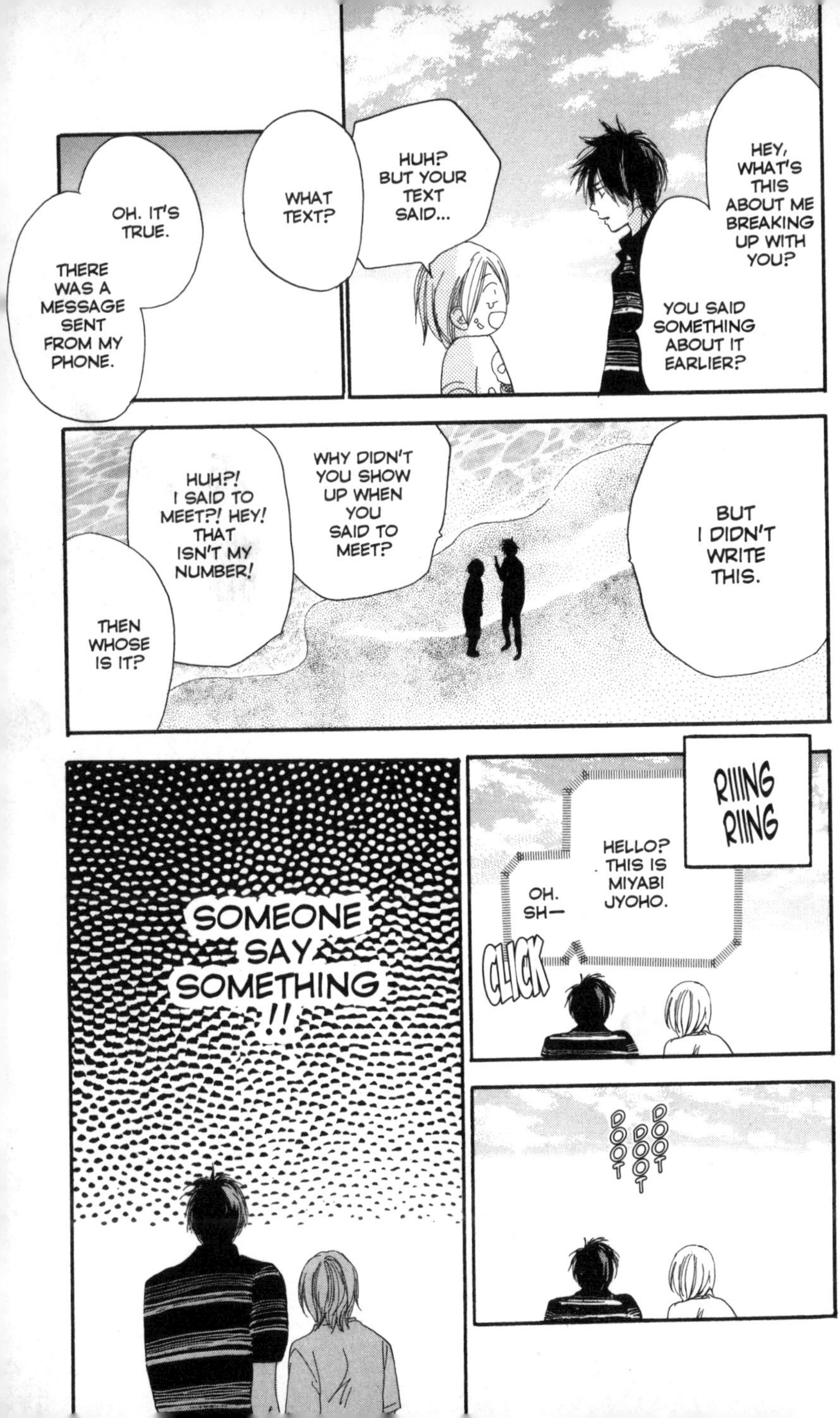
HEY, WHAT'S THIS ABOUT ME BREAKING UP WITH YOU?
YOU SAID SOMETHING ABOUT IT EARLIER?
HUH? BUT YOUR TEXT SAID...
WHAT TEXT?
OH. IT'S TRUE.
THERE WAS A MESSAGE SENT FROM MY PHONE.
BUT I DIDN'T WRITE THIS.
WHY DIDN'T YOU SHOW UP WHEN YOU SAID TO MEET?
HUH?! I SAID TO MEET?! HEY! THAT ISN'T MY NUMBER!
THEN WHOSE IS IT?
RIIING RIING
HELLO? THIS IS MIYABI JYOHO.
OH. SH—
CLICK
DOOT DOOT DOOT
SOMEONE SAY SOMETHING!!

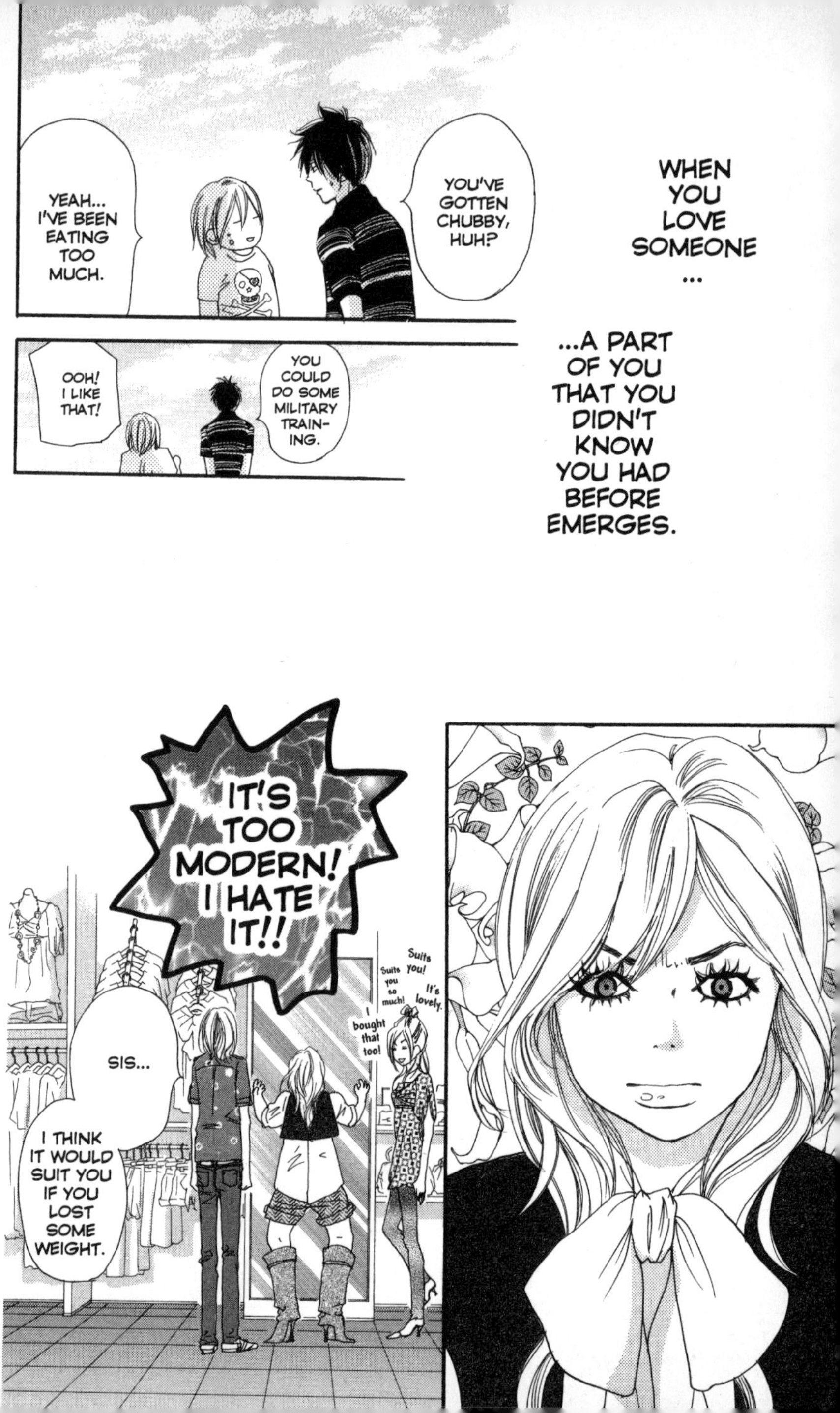
WHEN YOU LOVE SOMEONE ...
YOU'VE GOTTEN CHUBBY, HUH?
YEAH... I'VE BEEN EATING TOO MUCH.
YOU COULD DO SOME MILITARY TRAIN-ING.
OOH! I LIKE THAT!
...A PART OF YOU THAT YOU DIDN'T KNOW YOU HAD BEFORE EMERGES.
IT'S TOO MODERN! I HATE IT!!
Suits you!
It's lovely.
Suits you so much!
I bought that too!
SIS...
I THINK IT WOULD SUIT YOU IF YOU LOST SOME WEIGHT.

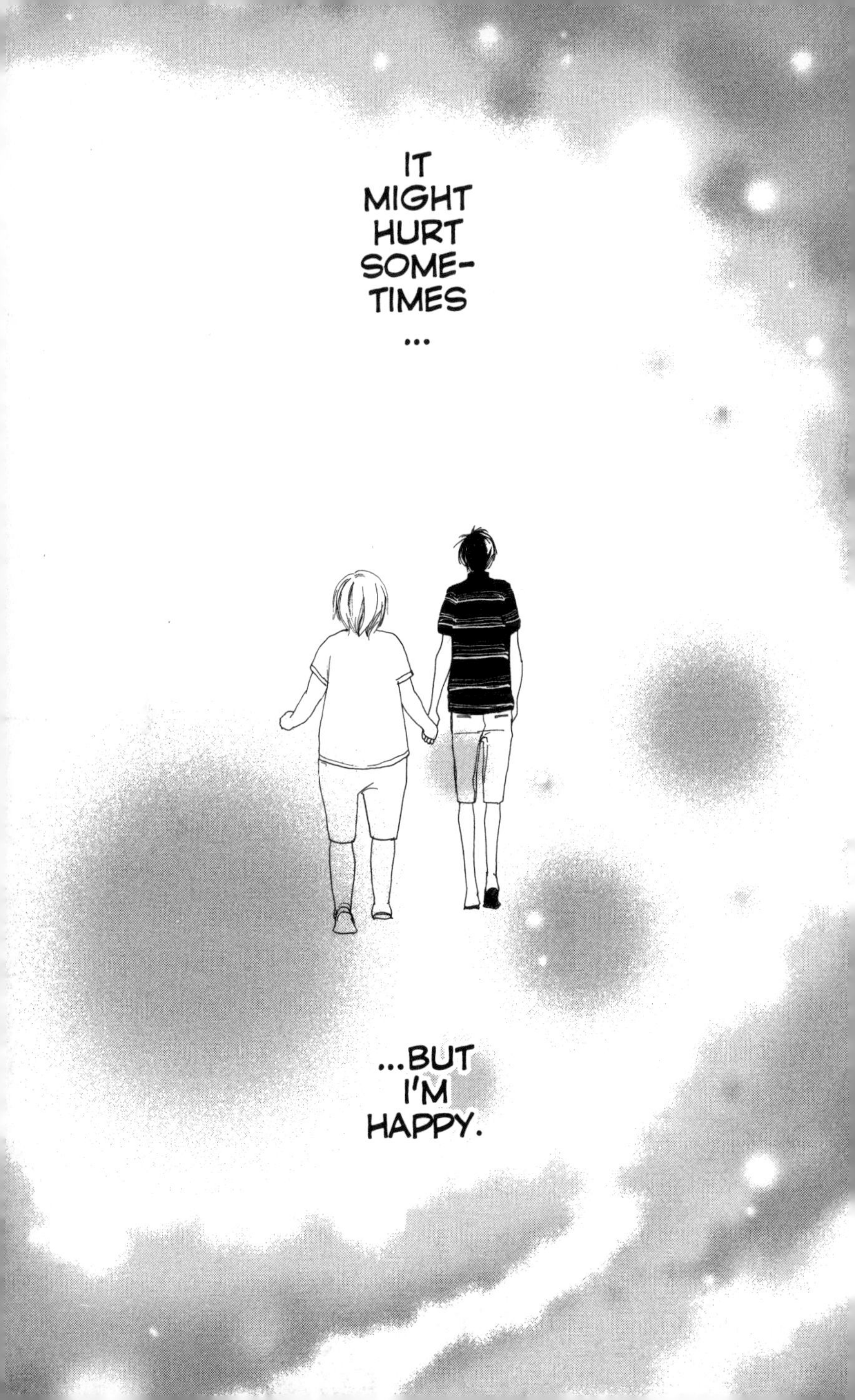
IT MIGHT HURT SOME-TIMES...
...BUT I'M HAPPY.

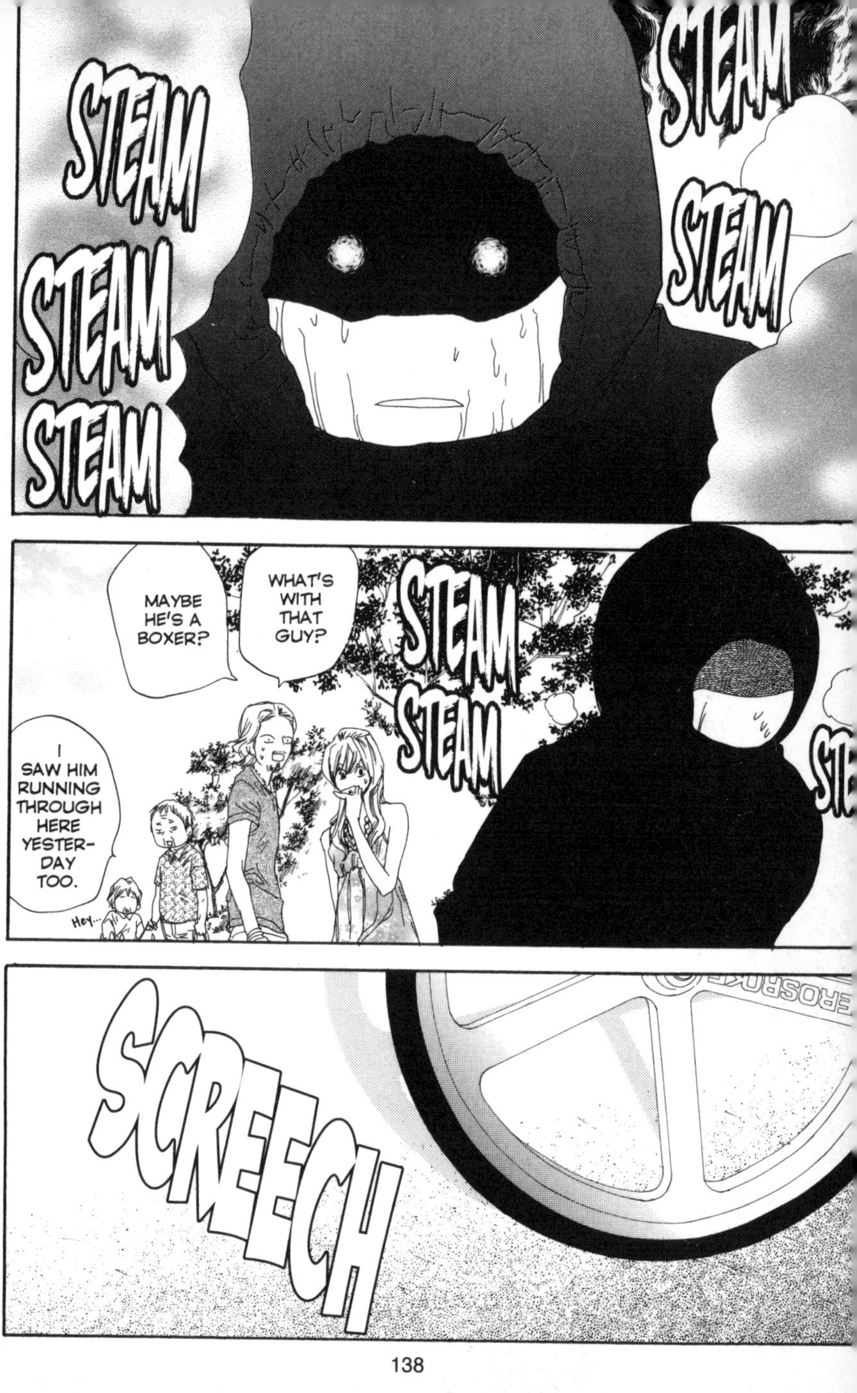
STEAM
STEAM
STEAM
STEAM
STEAM
STEAM
STEAM
WHAT'S WITH THAT GUY?
MAYBE HE'S A BOXER?
I SAW HIM RUNNING THROUGH HERE YESTER-DAY TOO.
Hey...
SCREECH

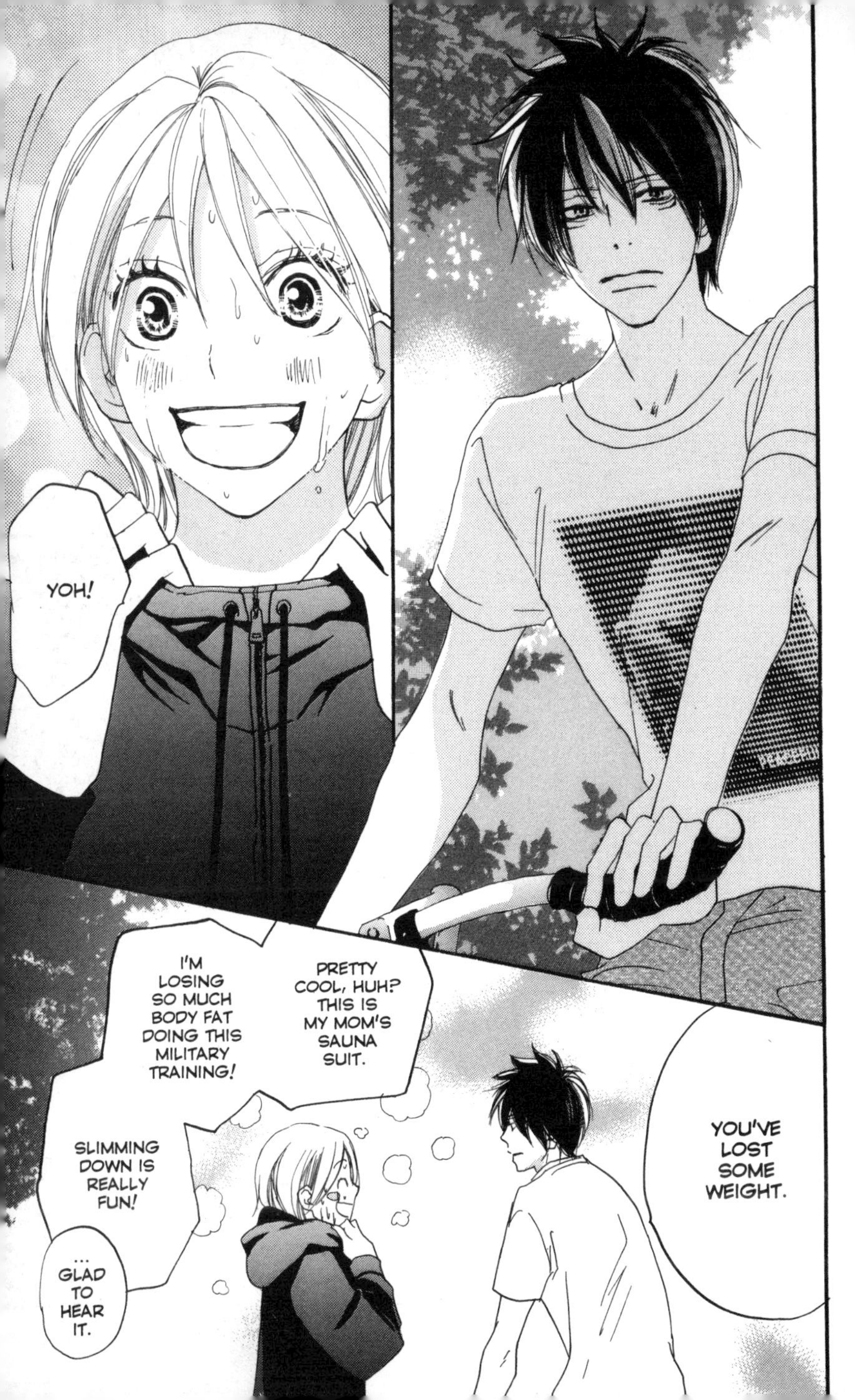
YOH!
YOU'VE LOST SOME WEIGHT.
PRETTY COOL, HUH? THIS IS MY MOM'S SAUNA SUIT.
I'M LOSING SO MUCH BODY FAT DOING THIS MILITARY TRAINING!
SLIMMING DOWN IS REALLY FUN!
... GLAD TO HEAR IT.

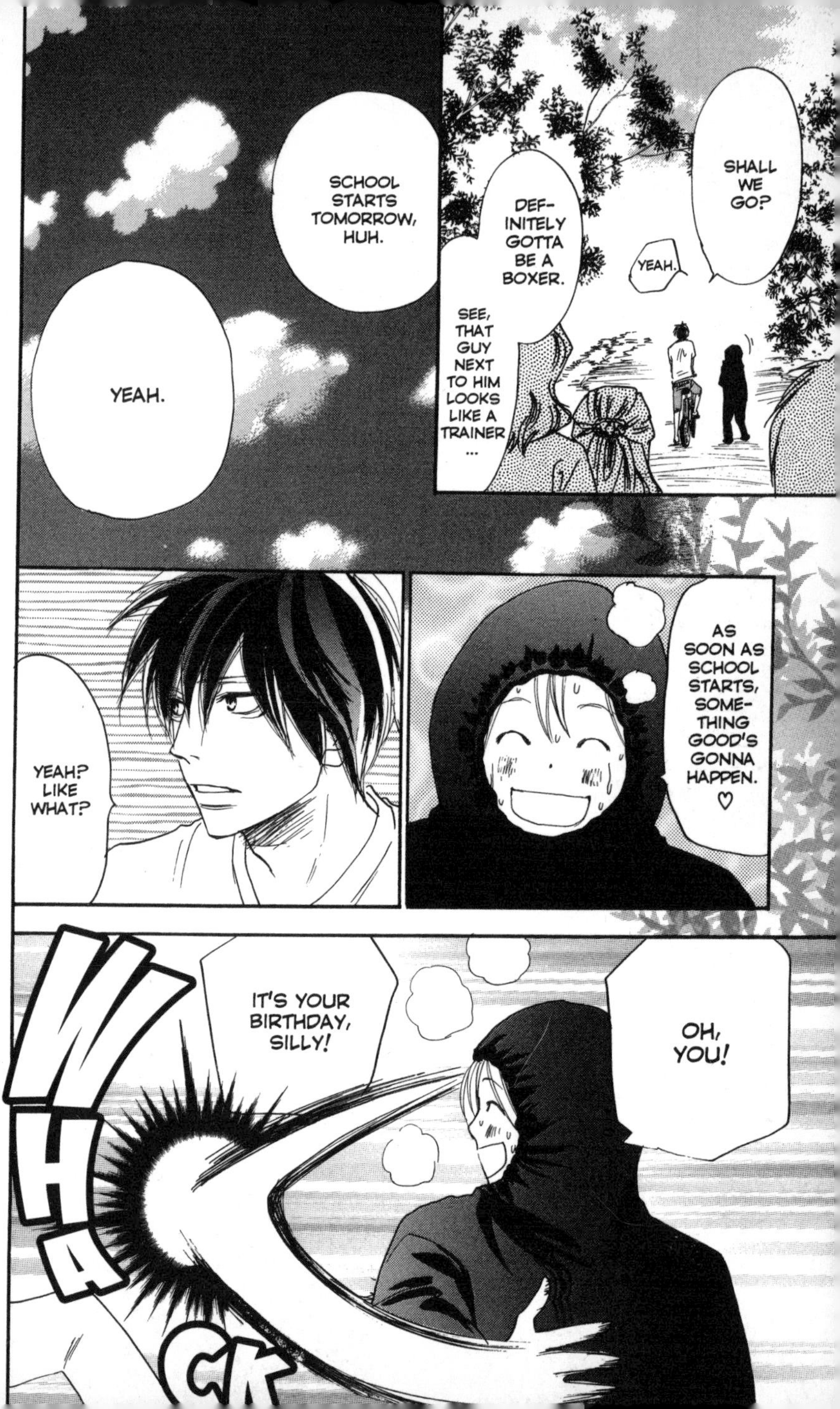
SHALL WE GO?
YEAH.
DEF-INITELY GOTTA BE A BOXER.
SEE, THAT GUY NEXT TO HIM LOOKS LIKE A TRAINER...
SCHOOL STARTS TOMORROW, HUH.
YEAH.
AS SOON AS SCHOOL STARTS, SOME-THING GOOD'S GONNA HAPPEN. ♡
YEAH? LIKE WHAT?
OH, YOU!
IT'S YOUR BIRTHDAY, SILLY!
WHACK

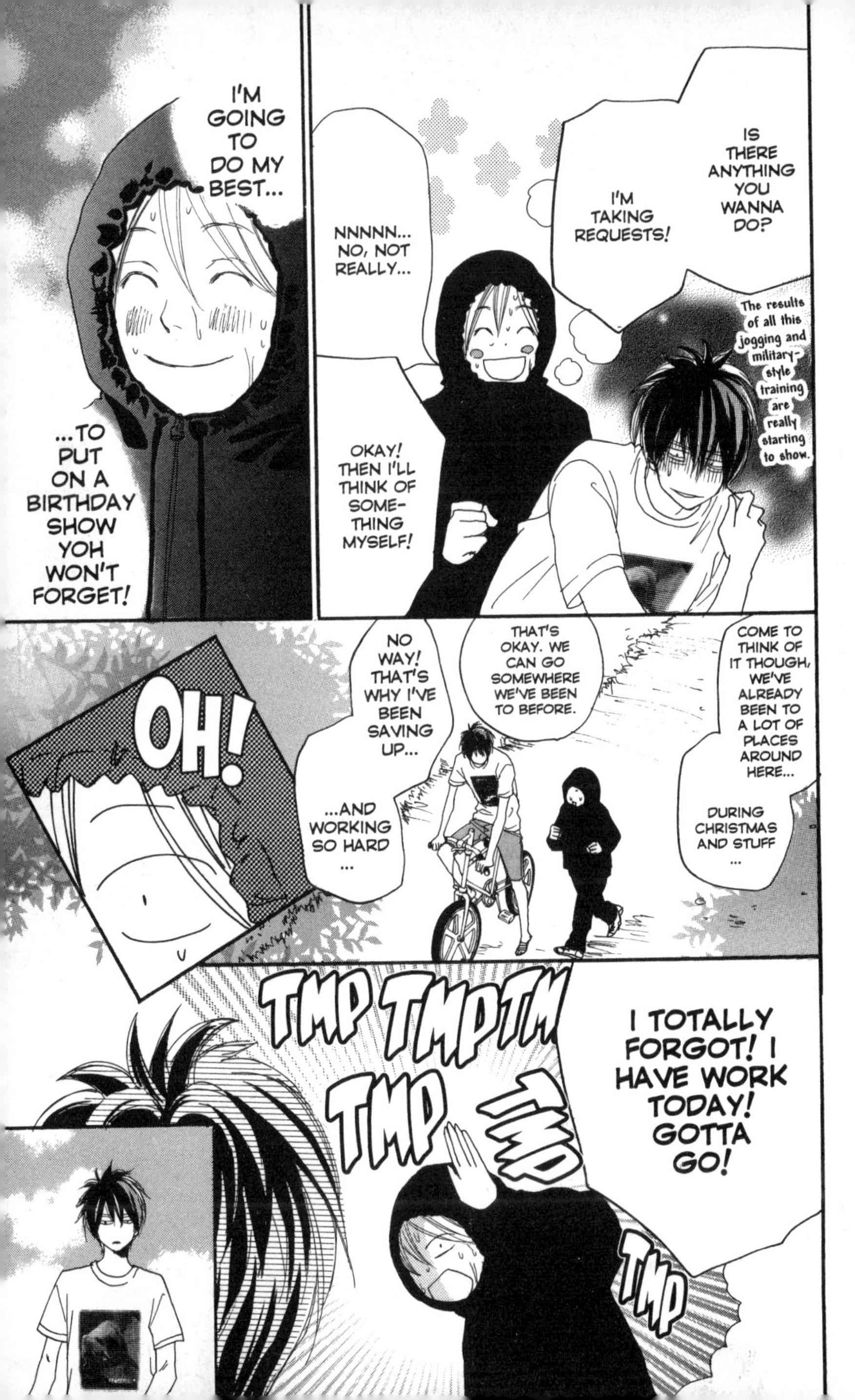
IS THERE ANYTHING YOU WANNA DO?
I'M TAKING REQUESTS!
The results of all this jogging and military-style training are really starting to show.
NNNNN... NO, NOT REALLY...
OKAY! THEN I'LL THINK OF SOMETHING MYSELF!
I'M GOING TO DO MY BEST...
...TO PUT ON A BIRTHDAY SHOW YOH WON'T FORGET!
COME TO THINK OF IT THOUGH, WE'VE ALREADY BEEN TO A LOT OF PLACES AROUND HERE...
DURING CHRISTMAS AND STUFF ...
THAT'S OKAY. WE CAN GO SOMEWHERE WE'VE BEEN TO BEFORE.
NO WAY! THAT'S WHY I'VE BEEN SAVING UP...
...AND WORKING SO HARD ...
OH!
I TOTALLY FORGOT! I HAVE WORK TODAY! GOTTA GO!
TMP TMPTM
TMP
TMP
TMP

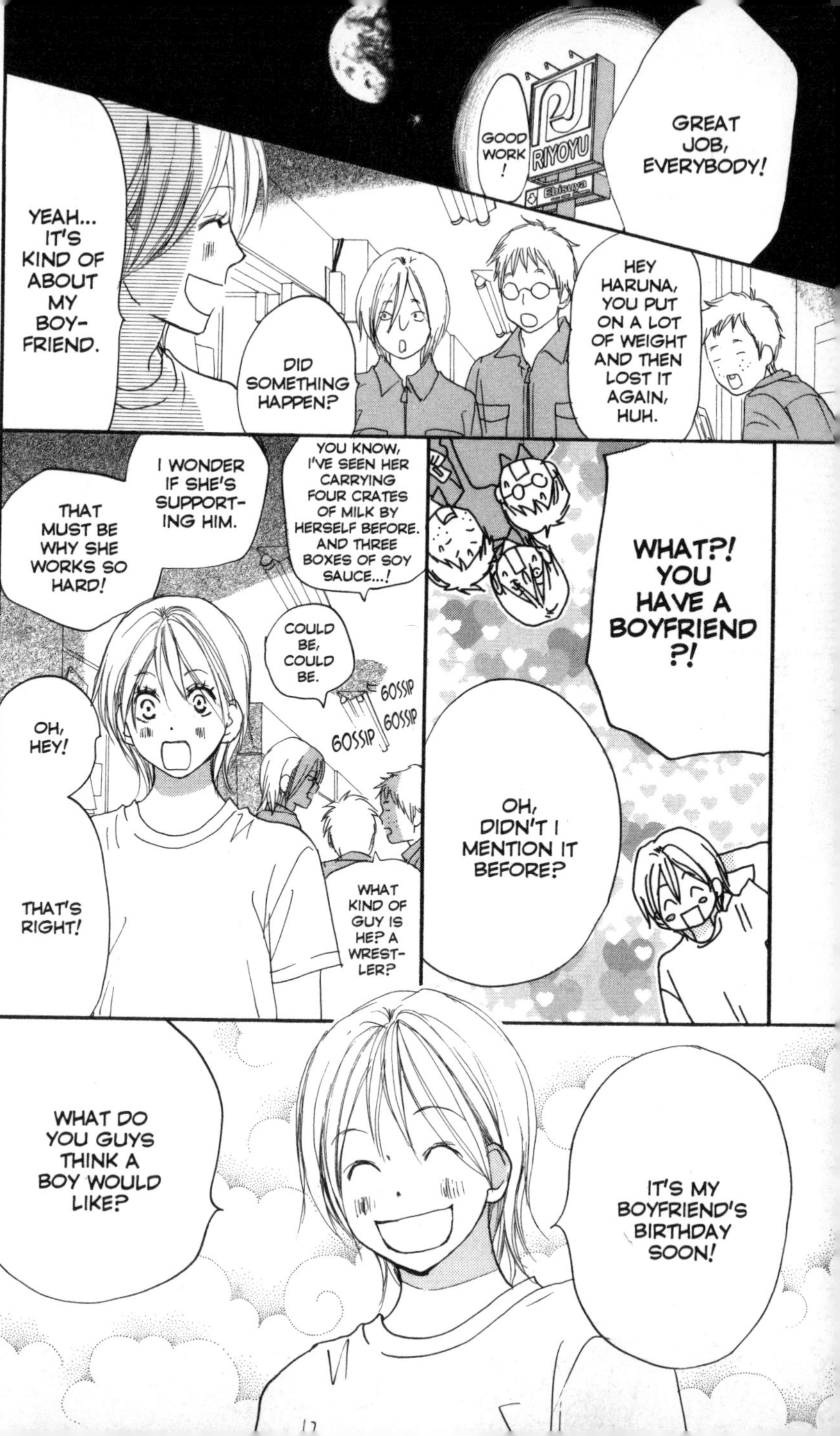
GREAT JOB, EVERYBODY!
GOOD WORK!
RIYOYU
Ebisuya
HEY HARUNA, YOU PUT ON A LOT OF WEIGHT AND THEN LOST IT AGAIN, HUH.
DID SOMETHING HAPPEN?
YEAH... IT'S KIND OF ABOUT MY BOY-FRIEND.
WHAT?! YOU HAVE A BOYFRIEND?!
OH, DIDN'T I MENTION IT BEFORE?
YOU KNOW, I'VE SEEN HER CARRYING FOUR CRATES OF MILK BY HERSELF BEFORE. AND THREE BOXES OF SOY SAUCE...!
I WONDER IF SHE'S SUPPORT-ING HIM.
THAT MUST BE WHY SHE WORKS SO HARD!
COULD BE, COULD BE.
GOSSIP
GOSSIP
GOSSIP
WHAT KIND OF GUY IS HE? A WREST-LER?
OH, HEY!
THAT'S RIGHT!
IT'S MY BOYFRIEND'S BIRTHDAY SOON!
WHAT DO YOU GUYS THINK A BOY WOULD LIKE?

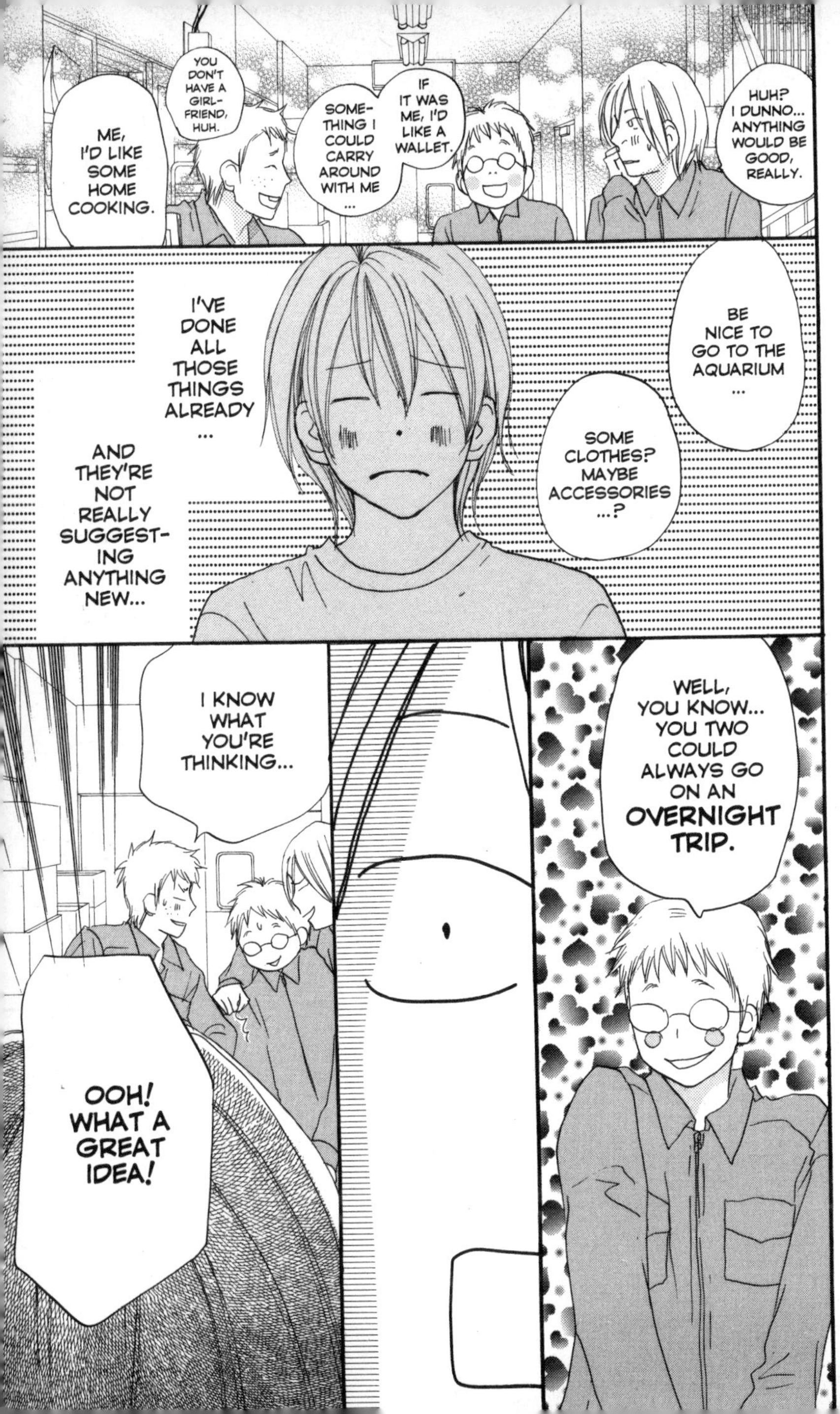
HUH? I DUNNO... ANYTHING WOULD BE GOOD, REALLY.
IF IT WAS ME, I'D LIKE A WALLET.
SOMETHING I COULD CARRY AROUND WITH ME...
YOU DON'T HAVE A GIRLFRIEND, HUH.
ME, I'D LIKE SOME HOME COOKING.
BE NICE TO GO TO THE AQUARIUM...
SOME CLOTHES? MAYBE ACCESSORIES...?
I'VE DONE ALL THOSE THINGS ALREADY...
AND THEY'RE NOT REALLY SUGGESTING ANYTHING NEW...
WELL, YOU KNOW... YOU TWO COULD ALWAYS GO ON AN OVERNIGHT TRIP.
I KNOW WHAT YOU'RE THINKING...
OOH! WHAT A GREAT IDEA!

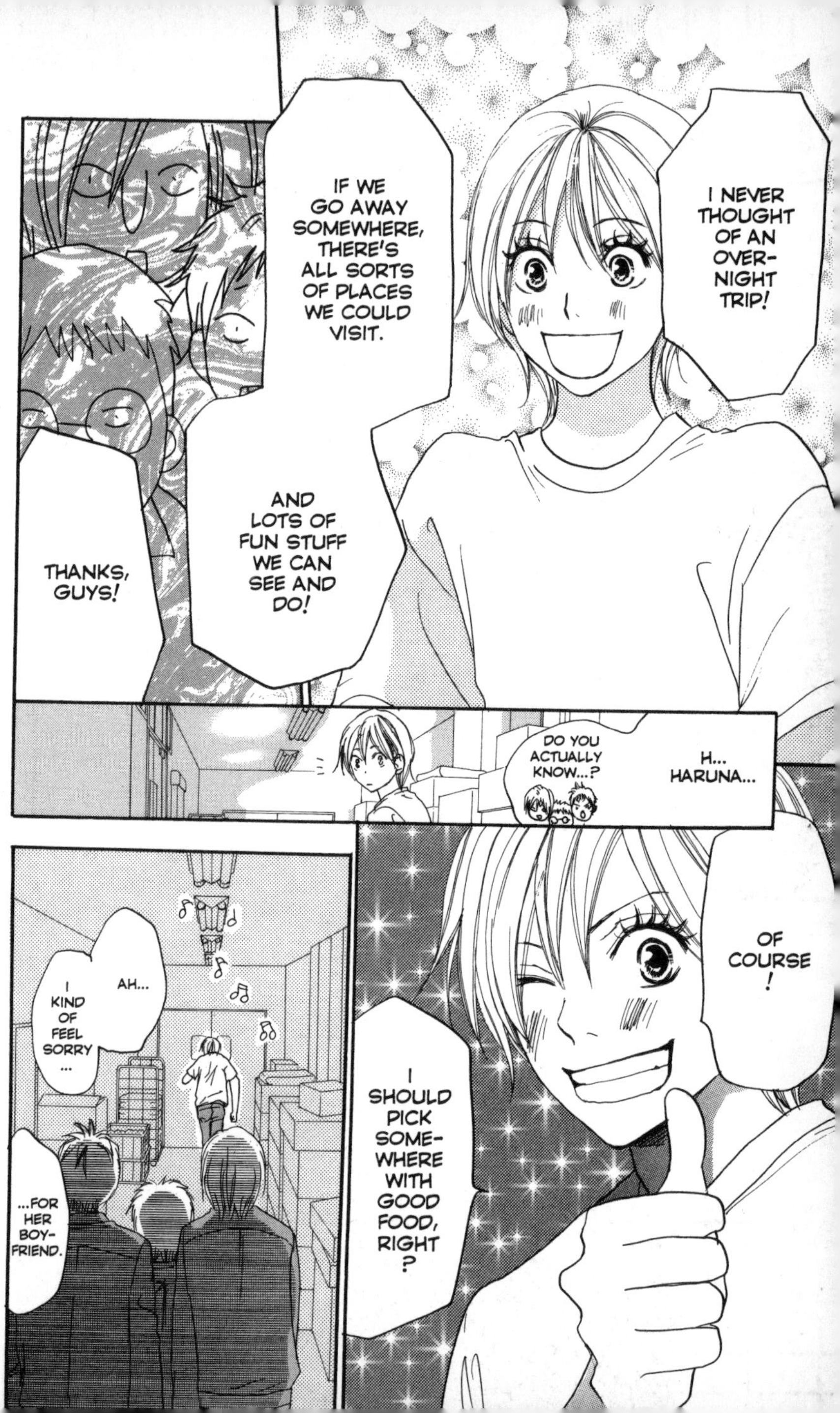
I NEVER THOUGHT OF AN OVER-NIGHT TRIP!
IF WE GO AWAY SOMEWHERE, THERE'S ALL SORTS OF PLACES WE COULD VISIT.
AND LOTS OF FUN STUFF WE CAN SEE AND DO!
THANKS, GUYS!
H... HARUNA...
DO YOU ACTUALLY KNOW...?
OF COURSE!
I SHOULD PICK SOME-WHERE WITH GOOD FOOD, RIGHT?
AH...
I KIND OF FEEL SORRY...
...FOR HER BOY-FRIEND.

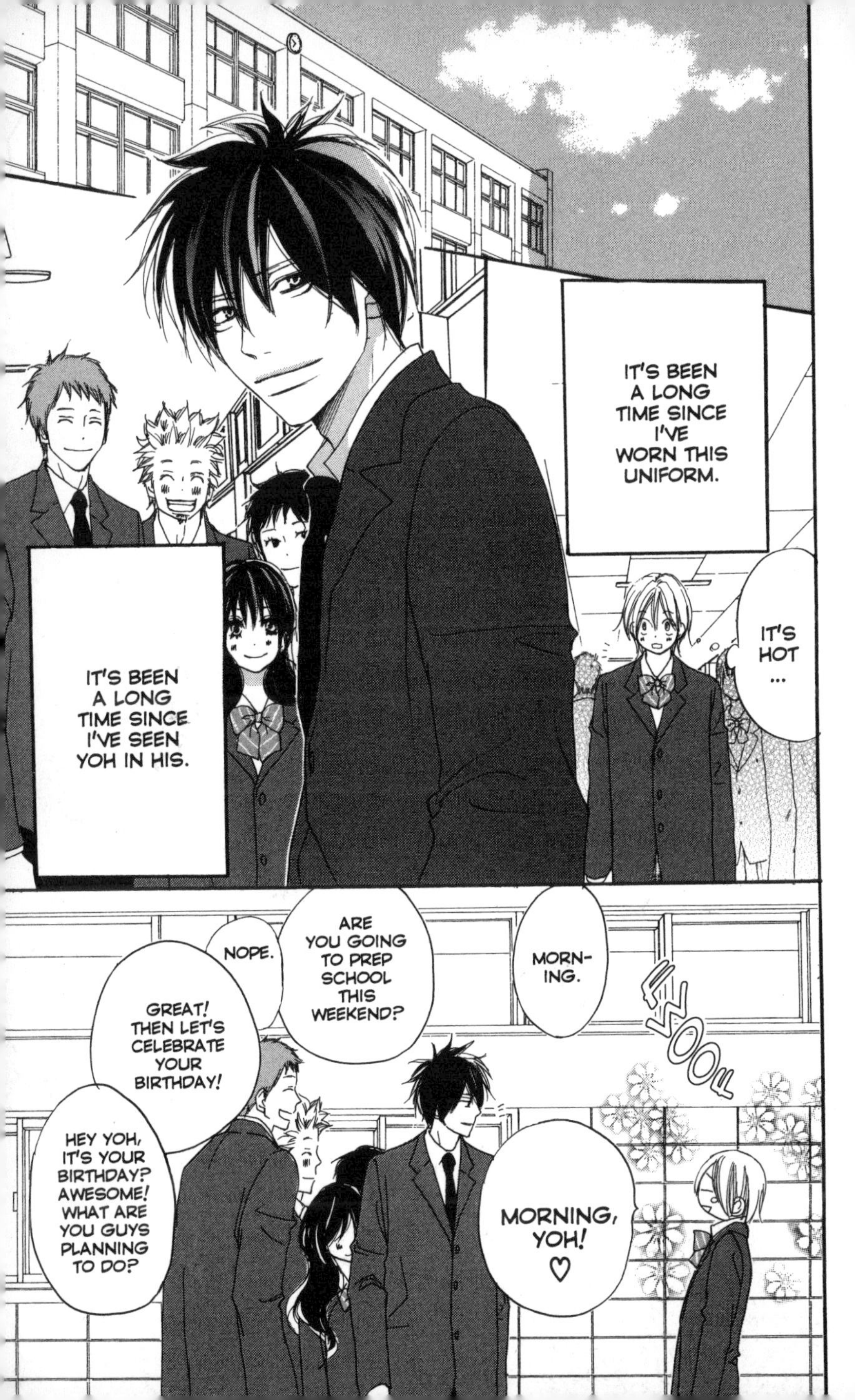
IT'S BEEN A LONG TIME SINCE I'VE WORN THIS UNIFORM.
IT'S HOT ...
IT'S BEEN A LONG TIME SINCE I'VE SEEN YOH IN HIS.
MORNING.
FWOOF
MORNING, YOH! ♡
ARE YOU GOING TO PREP SCHOOL THIS WEEKEND?
NOPE.
GREAT! THEN LET'S CELEBRATE YOUR BIRTHDAY!
HEY YOH, IT'S YOUR BIRTHDAY? AWESOME! WHAT ARE YOU GUYS PLANNING TO DO?

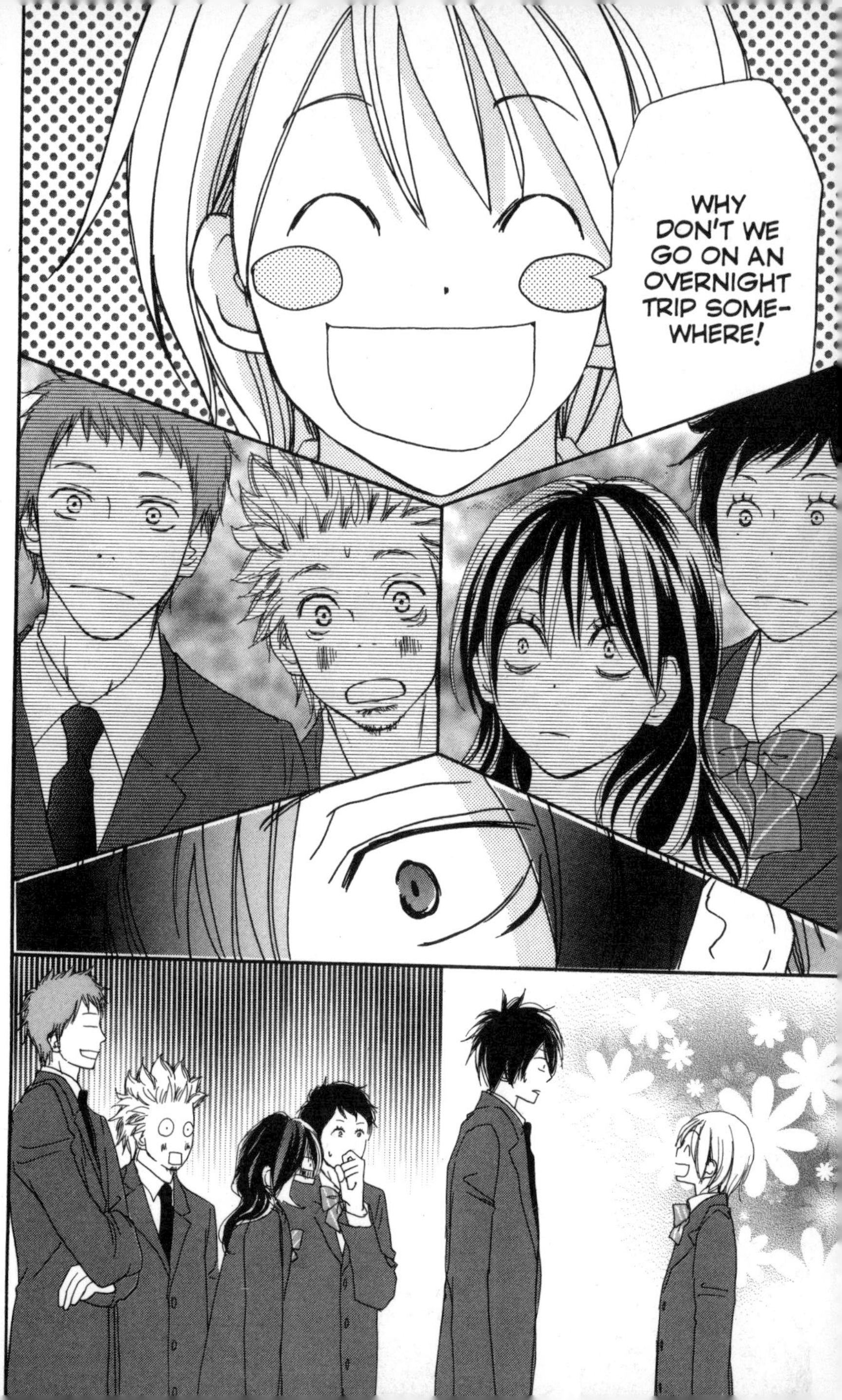
WHY DON'T WE GO ON AN OVERNIGHT TRIP SOME-WHERE!

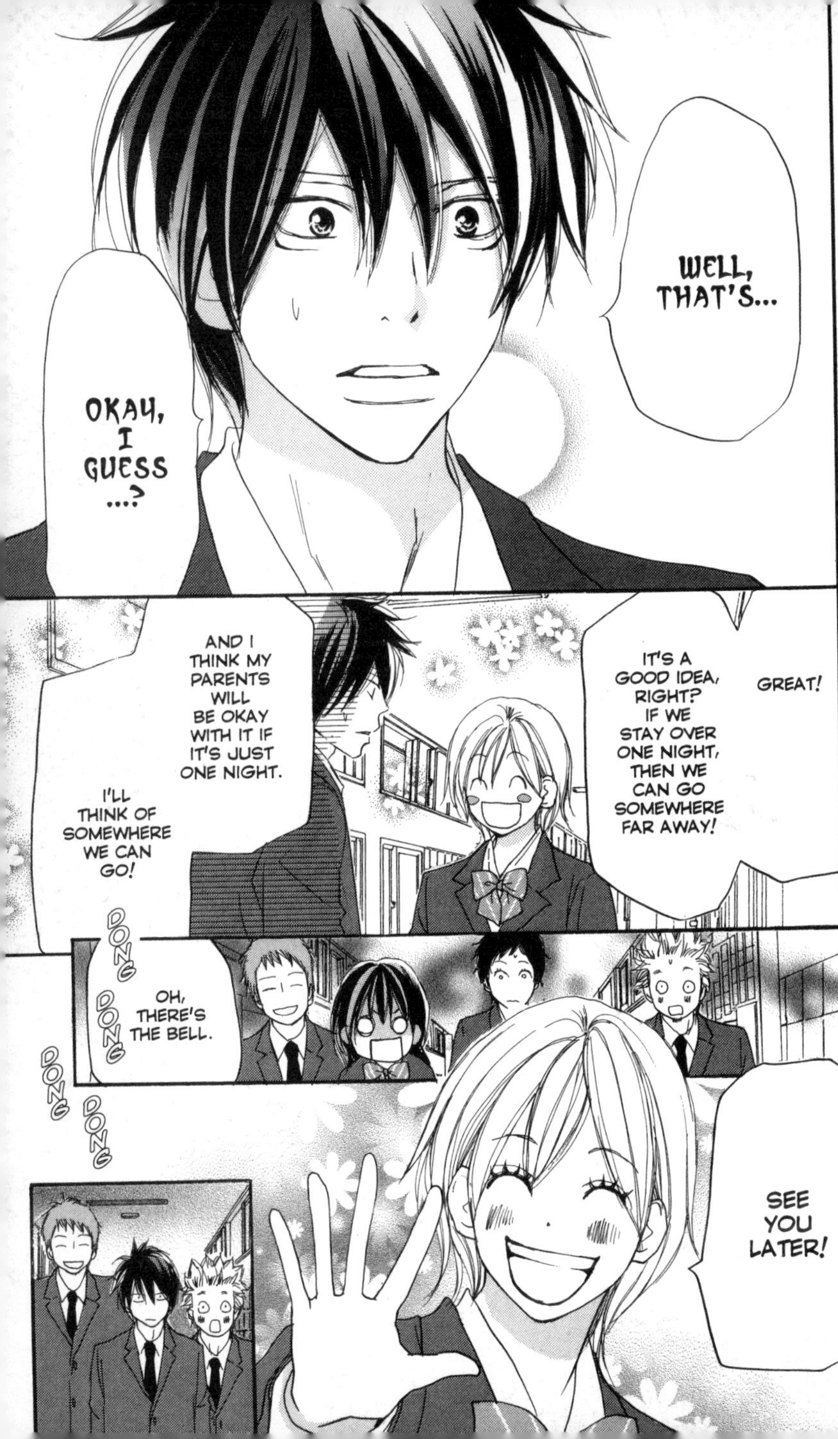
WELL, THAT'S...
OKAY, I GUESS...?
GREAT!
IT'S A GOOD IDEA, RIGHT? IF WE STAY OVER ONE NIGHT, THEN WE CAN GO SOMEWHERE FAR AWAY!
AND I THINK MY PARENTS WILL BE OKAY WITH IT IF IT'S JUST ONE NIGHT.
I'LL THINK OF SOMEWHERE WE CAN GO!
OH, THERE'S THE BELL.
DONG DONG
DONG DONG
DONG DONG
SEE YOU LATER!

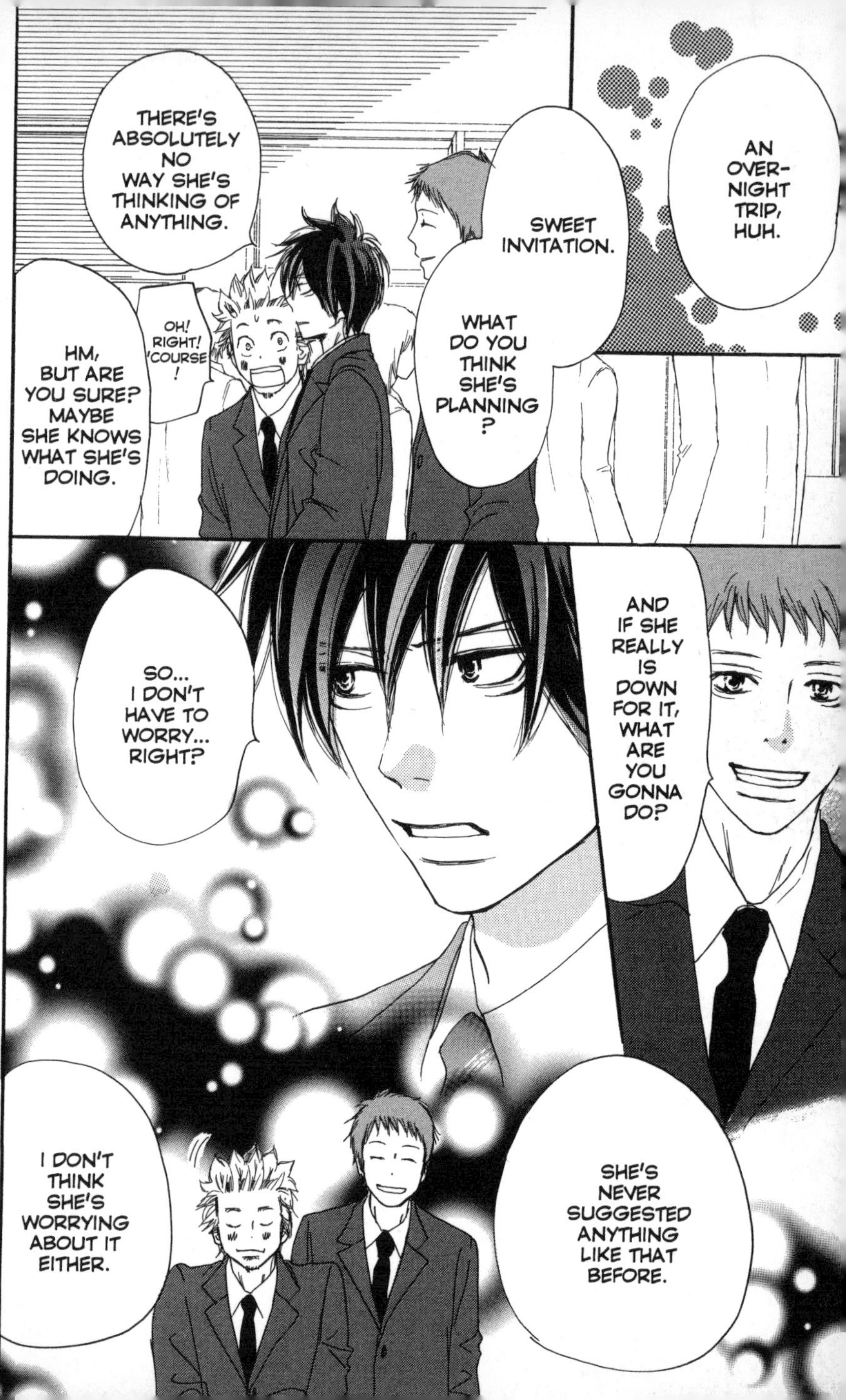
AN OVER-NIGHT TRIP, HUH.
SWEET INVITATION.
WHAT DO YOU THINK SHE'S PLANNING?
THERE'S ABSOLUTELY NO WAY SHE'S THINKING OF ANYTHING.
OH! RIGHT! 'COURSE!
HM, BUT ARE YOU SURE? MAYBE SHE KNOWS WHAT SHE'S DOING.
AND IF SHE REALLY IS DOWN FOR IT, WHAT ARE YOU GONNA DO?
SO... I DON'T HAVE TO WORRY... RIGHT?
SHE'S NEVER SUGGESTED ANYTHING LIKE THAT BEFORE.
I DON'T THINK SHE'S WORRYING ABOUT IT EITHER.

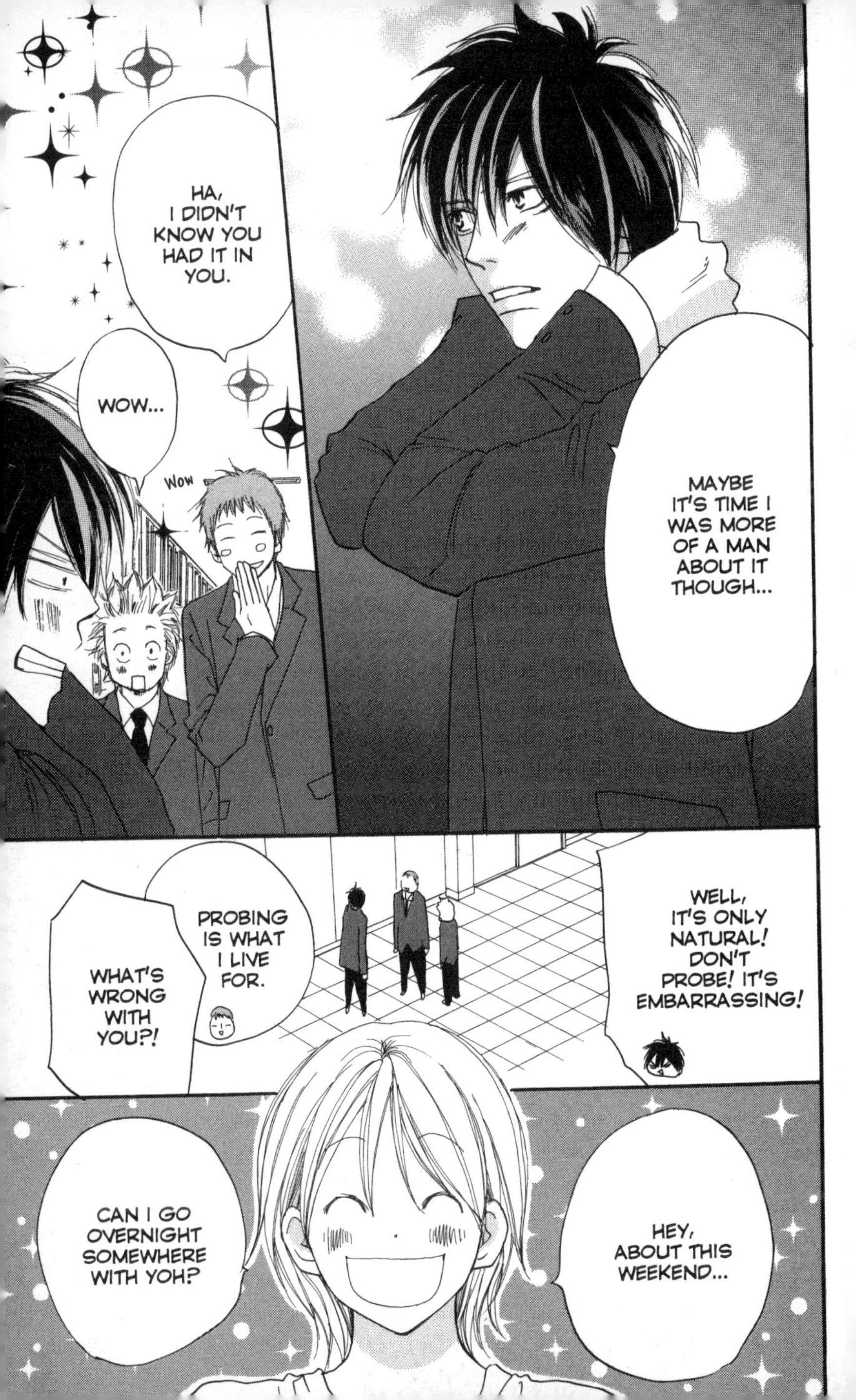
MAYBE IT'S TIME I WAS MORE OF A MAN ABOUT IT THOUGH...
HA, I DIDN'T KNOW YOU HAD IT IN YOU.
WOW...
WOW
WELL, IT'S ONLY NATURAL! DON'T PROBE! IT'S EMBARRASSING!
PROBING IS WHAT I LIVE FOR.
WHAT'S WRONG WITH YOU?!
HEY, ABOUT THIS WEEKEND...
CAN I GO OVERNIGHT SOMEWHERE WITH YOH?

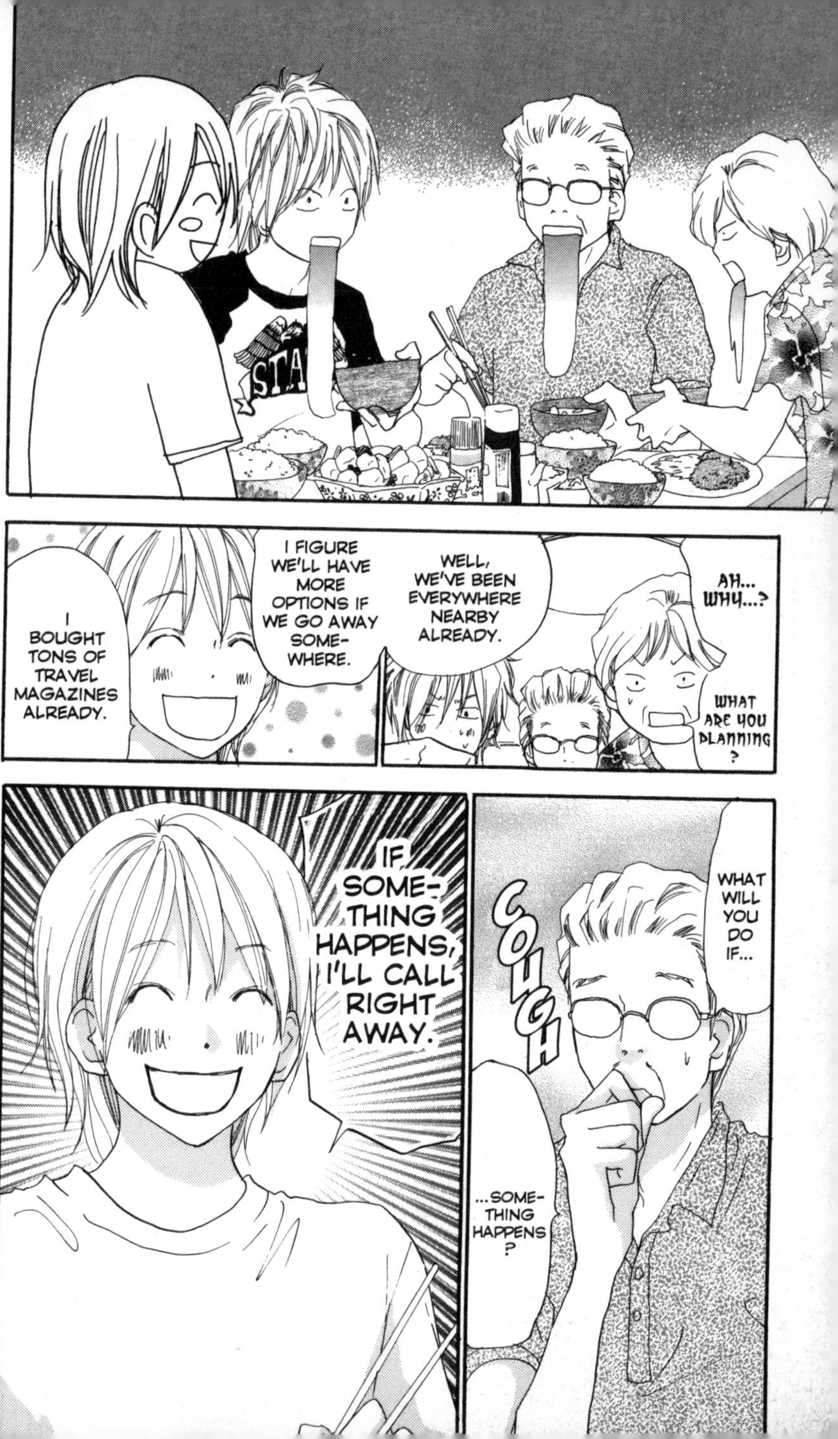
AH... WHY...?
WHAT ARE YOU PLANNING?
WELL, WE'VE BEEN EVERYWHERE NEARBY ALREADY.
I FIGURE WE'LL HAVE MORE OPTIONS IF WE GO AWAY SOME-WHERE.
I BOUGHT TONS OF TRAVEL MAGAZINES ALREADY.
WHAT WILL YOU DO IF...
COUGH
...SOME-THING HAPPENS?
IF SOME-THING HAPPENS, I'LL CALL RIGHT AWAY.

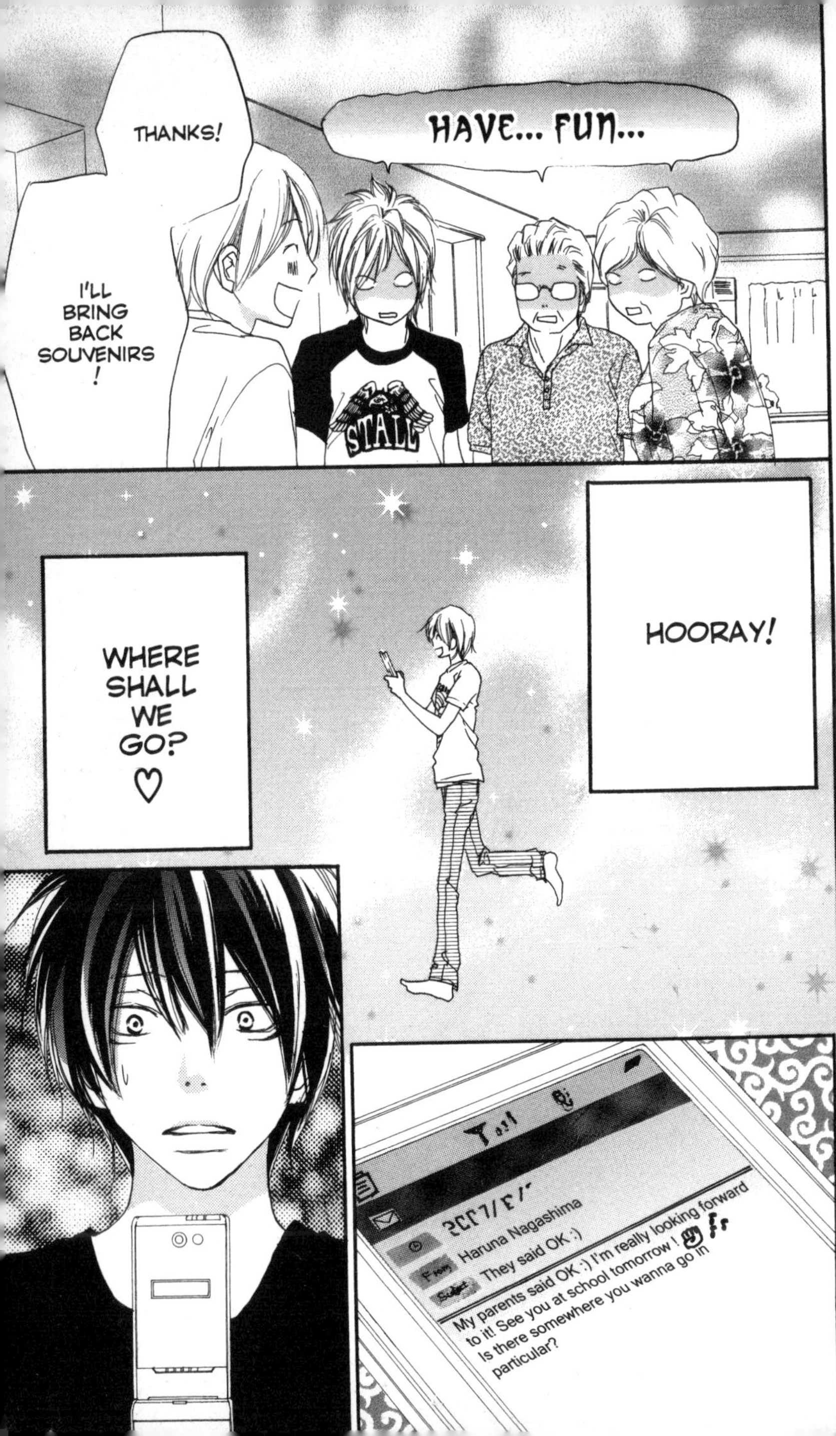
HAVE... FUN...
THANKS!
I'LL BRING BACK SOUVENIRS!
HOORAY!
WHERE SHALL WE GO? ♡
Haruna Nagashima
They said OK :)
My parents said OK :) I'm really looking forward to it! See you at school tomorrow! Is there somewhere you wanna go in particular?

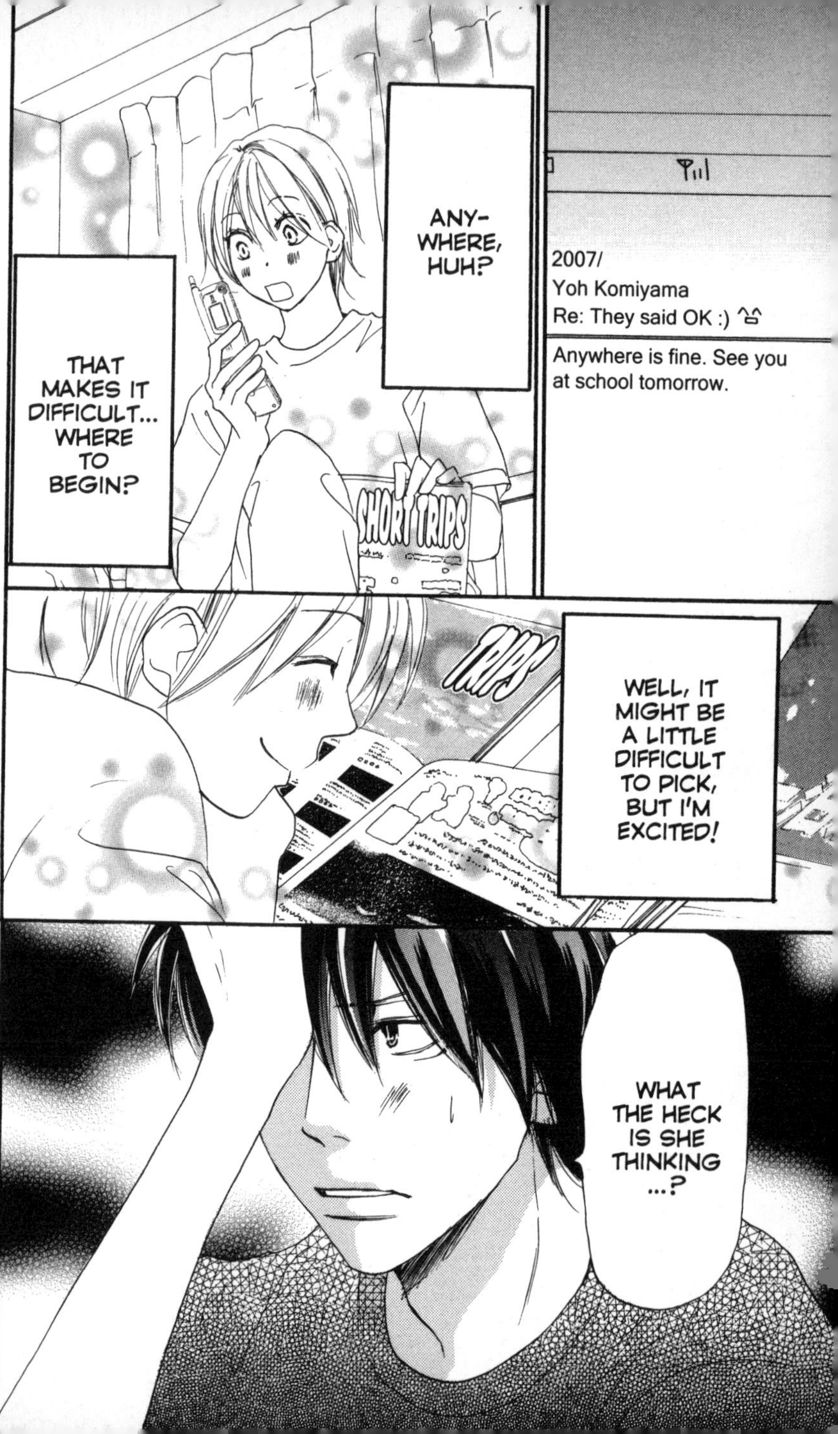

2007/
Yoh Komiyama
Re: They said OK :)
Anywhere is fine. See you at school tomorrow.
ANY-WHERE, HUH?
THAT MAKES IT DIFFICULT... WHERE TO BEGIN?
SHORT TRIPS
WELL, IT MIGHT BE A LITTLE DIFFICULT TO PICK, BUT I'M EXCITED!
TRIPS
WHAT THE HECK IS SHE THINKING ...?

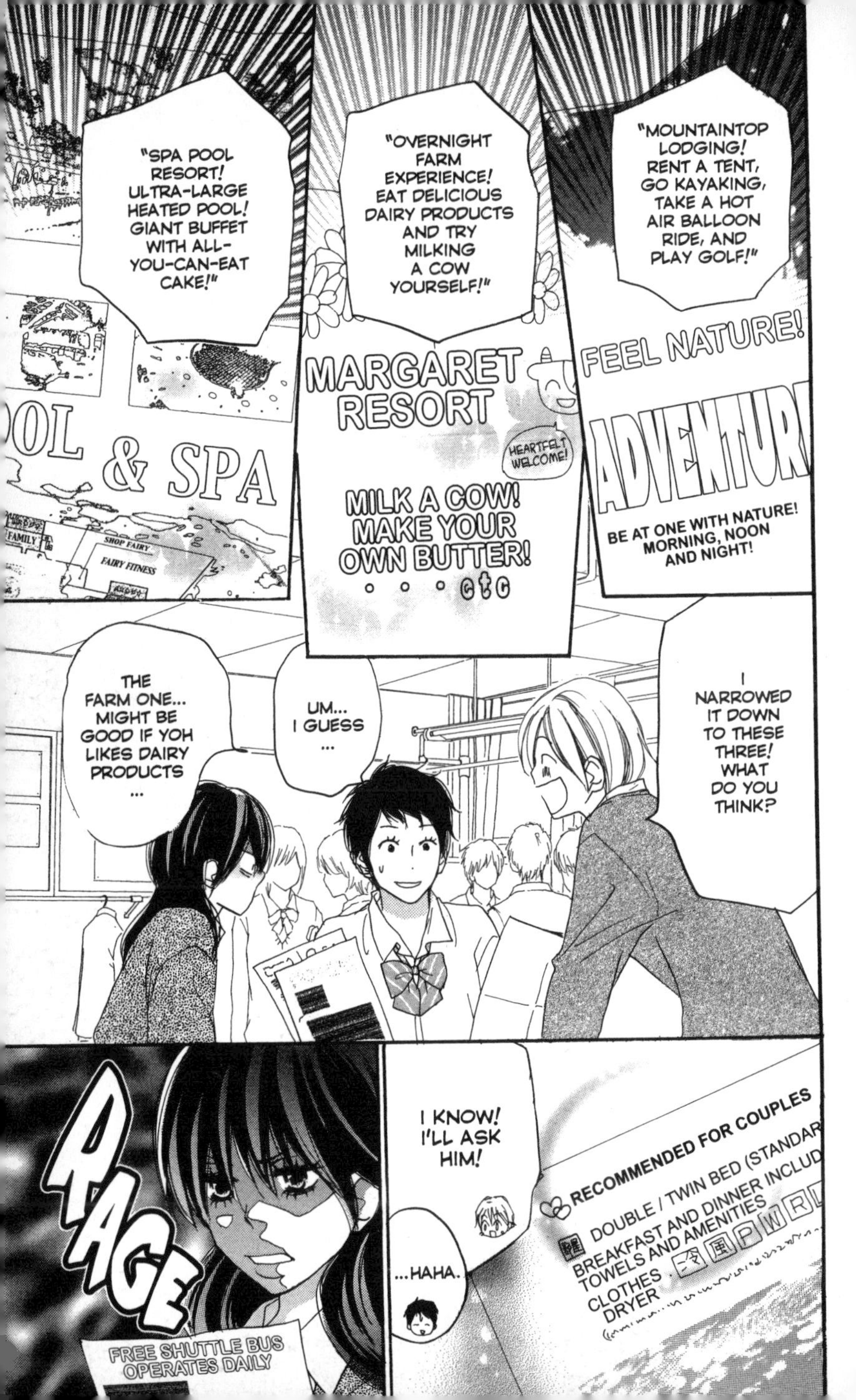
"MOUNTAINTOP LODGING! RENT A TENT, GO KAYAKING, TAKE A HOT AIR BALLOON RIDE, AND PLAY GOLF!"
FEEL NATURE!
ADVENTUR
BE AT ONE WITH NATURE! MORNING, NOON AND NIGHT!
"OVERNIGHT FARM EXPERIENCE! EAT DELICIOUS DAIRY PRODUCTS AND TRY MILKING A COW YOURSELF!"
MARGARET RESORT
HEARTFELT WELCOME!
MILK A COW! MAKE YOUR OWN BUTTER!
etc
"SPA POOL RESORT! ULTRA-LARGE HEATED POOL! GIANT BUFFET WITH ALL-YOU-CAN-EAT CAKE!"
OOL & SPA
FAMILY
SHOP FAIRY
FAIRY FITNESS
I NARROWED IT DOWN TO THESE THREE! WHAT DO YOU THINK?
UM... I GUESS...
THE FARM ONE... MIGHT BE GOOD IF YOH LIKES DAIRY PRODUCTS...
I KNOW! I'LL ASK HIM!
...HAHA.
RECOMMENDED FOR COUPLES
DOUBLE / TWIN BED (STANDAR
BREAKFAST AND DINNER INCLUD
TOWELS AND AMENITIES
CLOTHES DRYER
RAGE
FREE SHUTTLE BUS OPERATES DAILY

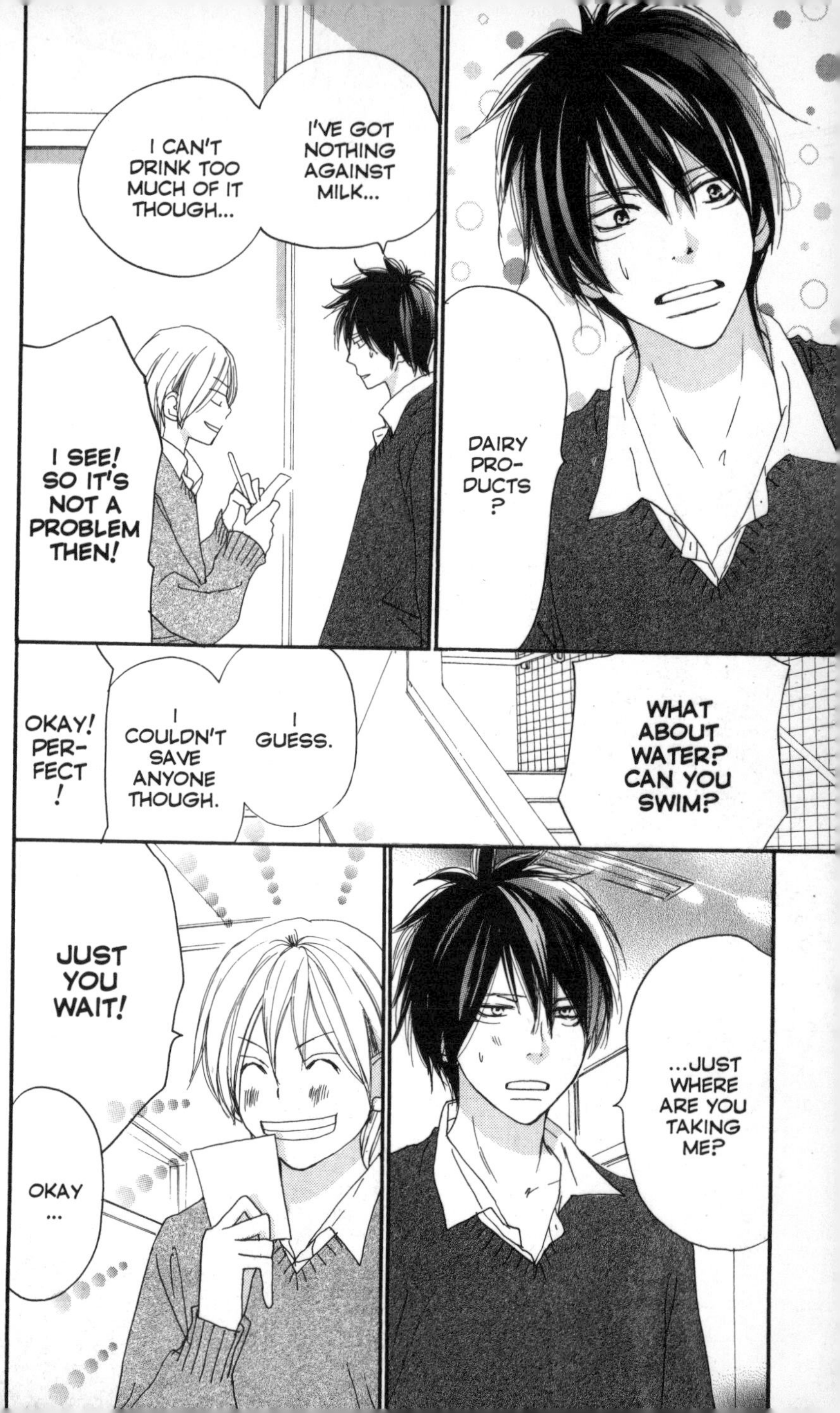
DAIRY PRODUCTS?
I'VE GOT NOTHING AGAINST MILK...
I CAN'T DRINK TOO MUCH OF IT THOUGH...
I SEE! SO IT'S NOT A PROBLEM THEN!
WHAT ABOUT WATER? CAN YOU SWIM?
I GUESS.
I COULDN'T SAVE ANYONE THOUGH.
OKAY! PERFECT!
...JUST WHERE ARE YOU TAKING ME?
JUST YOU WAIT!
OKAY...

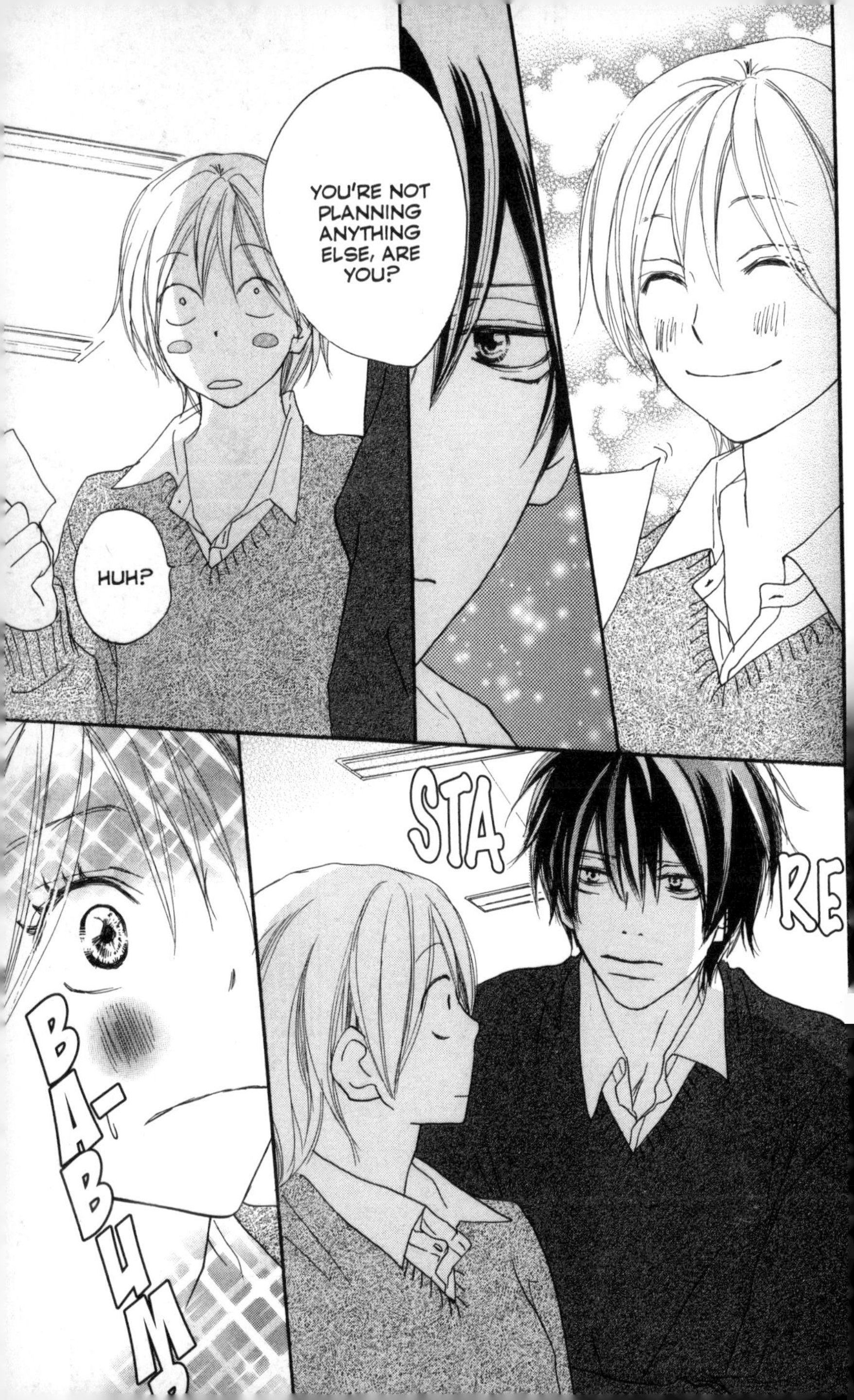
YOU'RE NOT PLANNING ANYTHING ELSE, ARE YOU?
HUH?
STA RE
BA-BUM

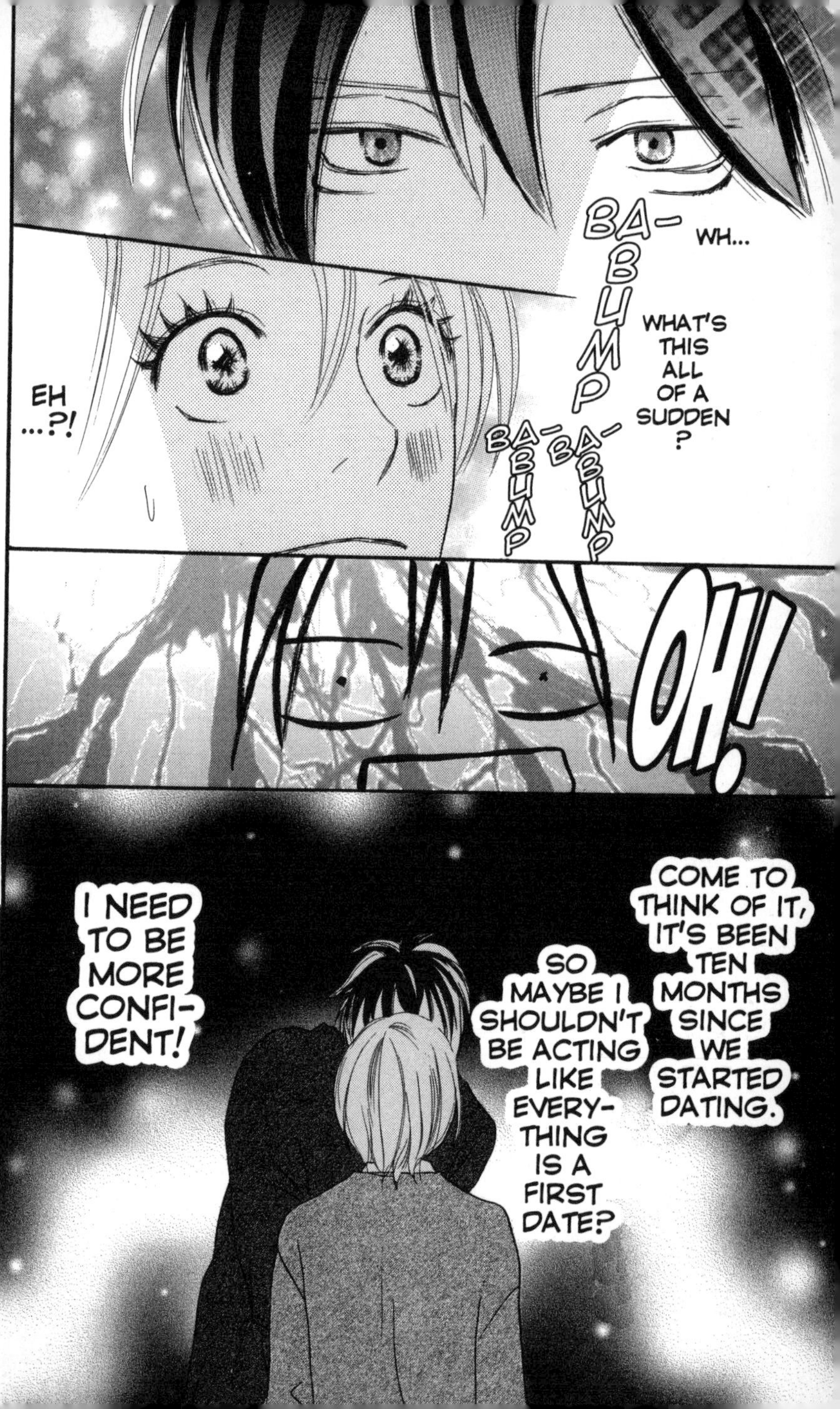
BA-BUMP
WH...
WHAT'S THIS ALL OF A SUDDEN?
BA-BUMP
BA-BUMP
EH ...?!
OH!
COME TO THINK OF IT, IT'S BEEN TEN MONTHS SINCE WE STARTED DATING.
SO MAYBE I SHOULDN'T BE ACTING LIKE EVERYTHING IS A FIRST DATE?
I NEED TO BE MORE CONFIDENT!

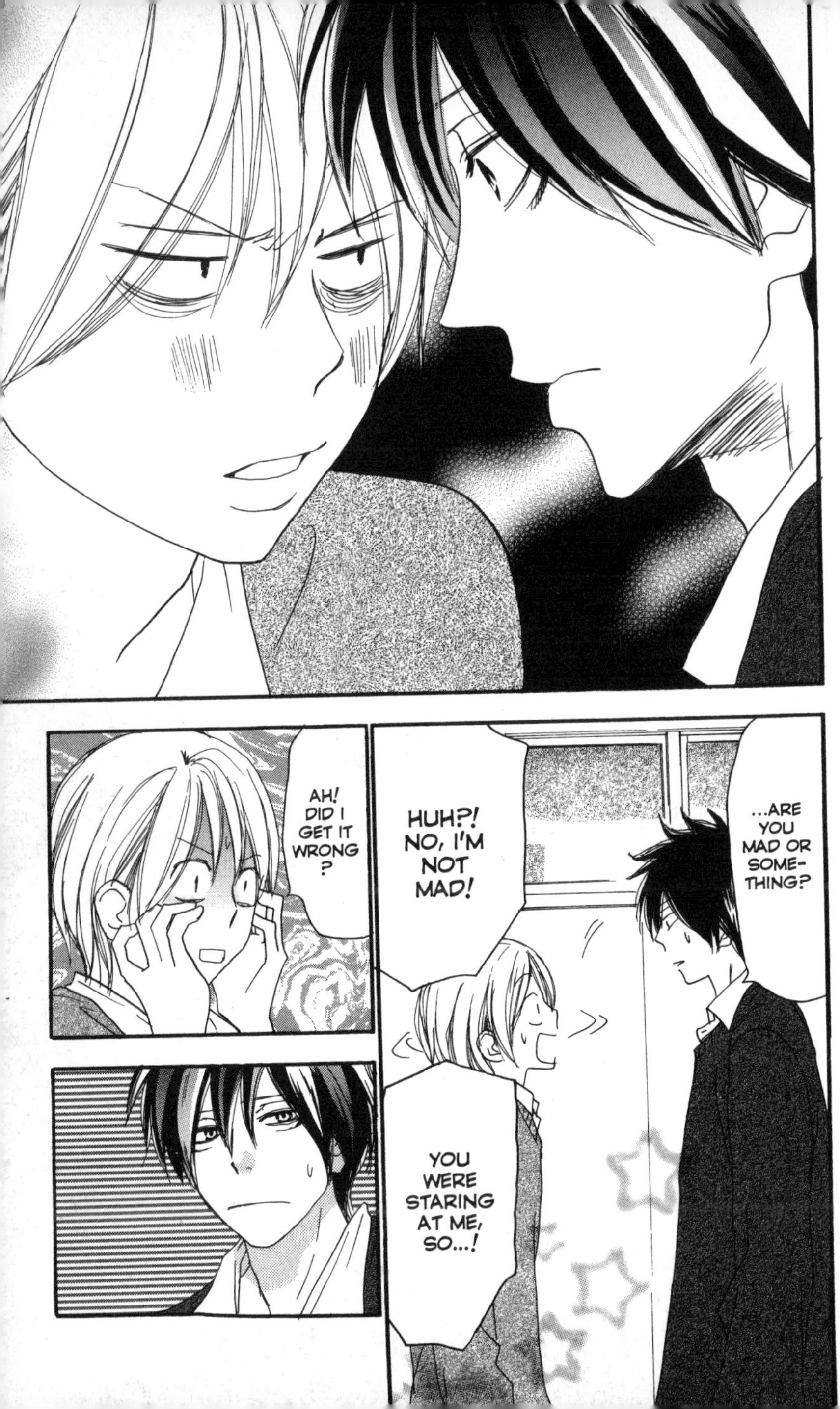
...ARE YOU MAD OR SOME-THING?
HUH?! NO, I'M NOT MAD!
YOU WERE STARING AT ME, SO...!
AH! DID I GET IT WRONG?

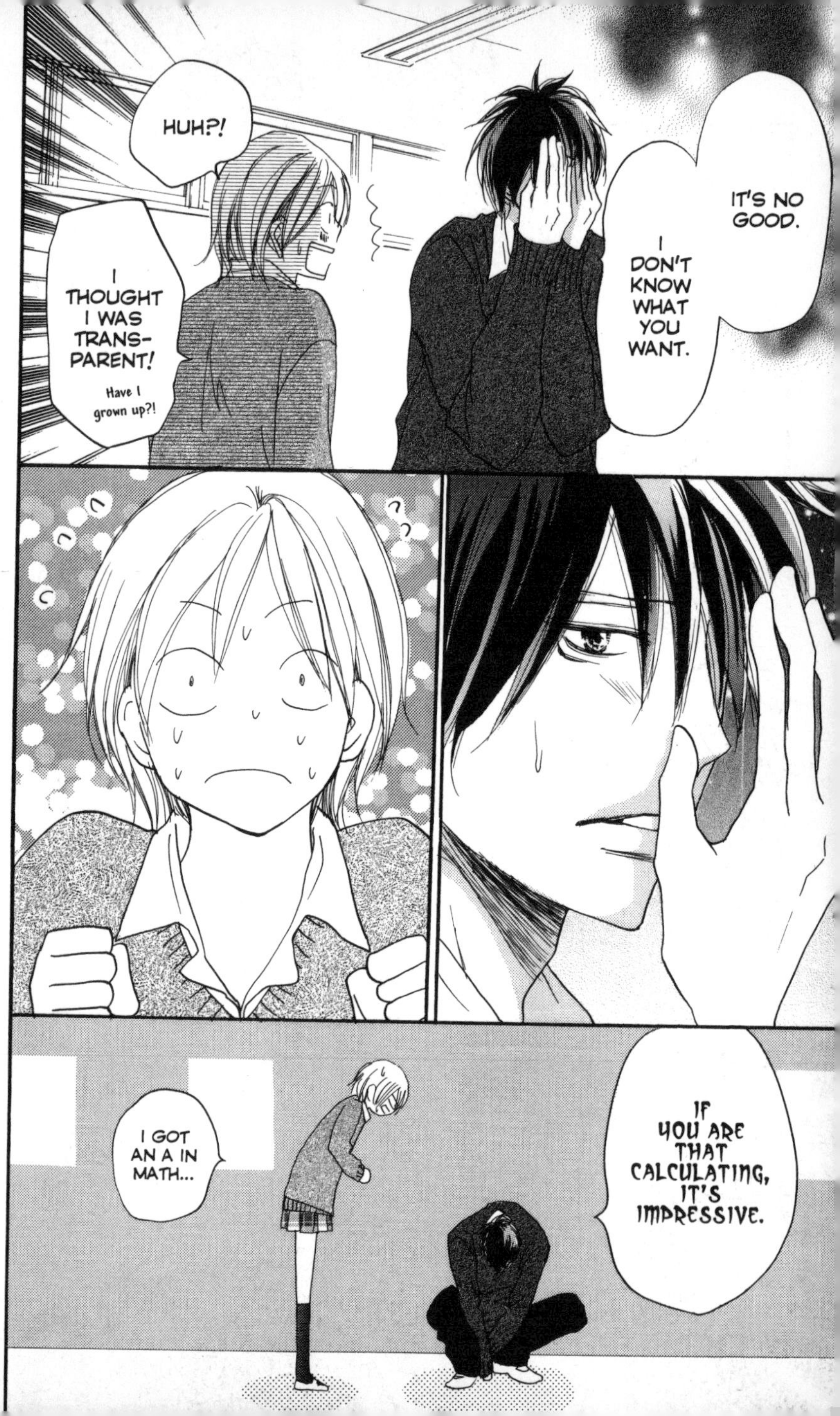

IT'S NO GOOD.
I DON'T KNOW WHAT YOU WANT.
HUH?!
I THOUGHT I WAS TRANS-PARENT!
Have I grown up?!
IF YOU ARE THAT CALCULATING, IT'S IMPRESSIVE.
I GOT AN A IN MATH...

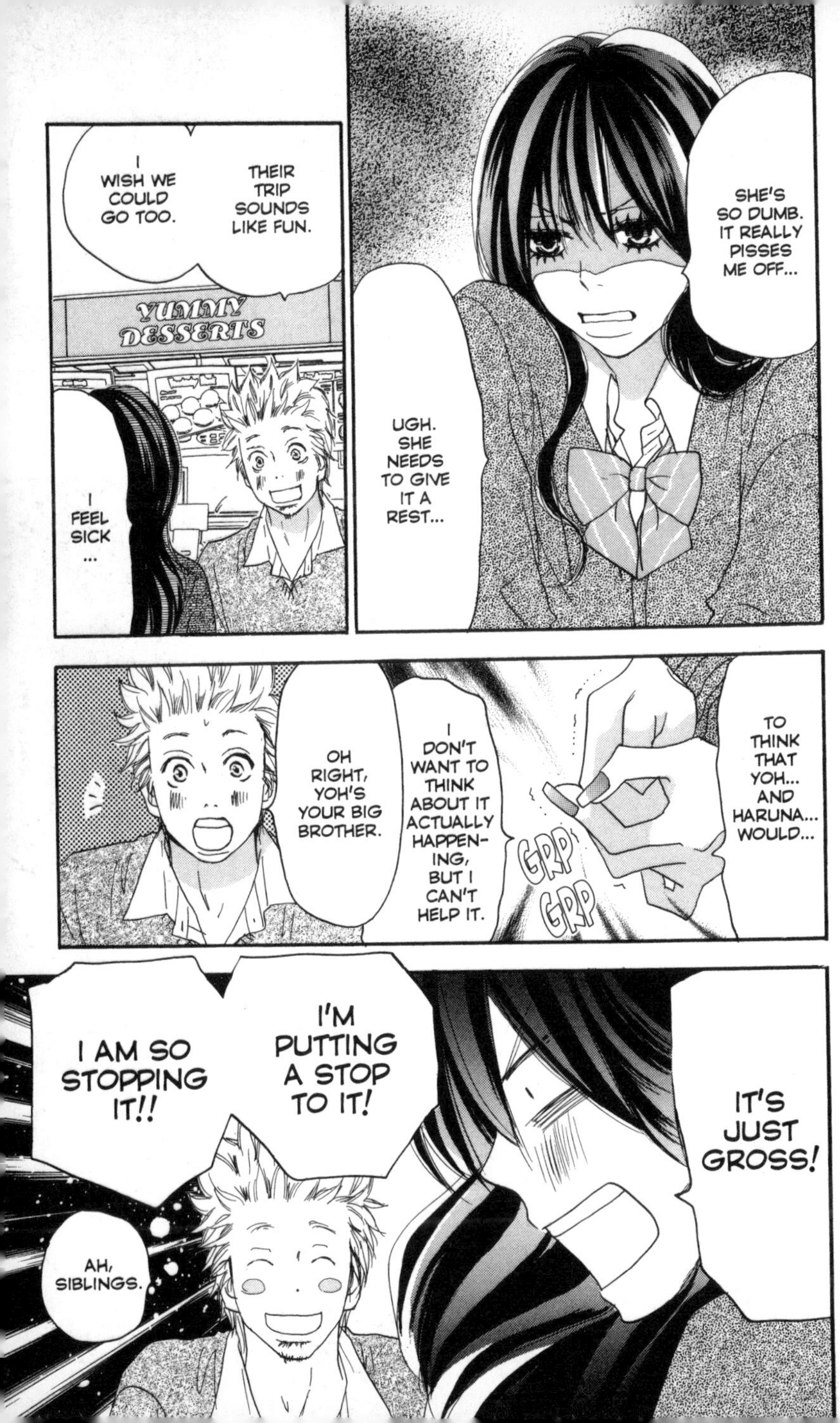
SHE'S SO DUMB. IT REALLY PISSES ME OFF...
UGH. SHE NEEDS TO GIVE IT A REST...
THEIR TRIP SOUNDS LIKE FUN.
I WISH WE COULD GO TOO.
YUMMY DESSERTS
I FEEL SICK...
TO THINK THAT YOH... AND HARUNA... WOULD...
GRP GRP
I DON'T WANT TO THINK ABOUT IT ACTUALLY HAPPEN-ING, BUT I CAN'T HELP IT.
OH RIGHT, YOH'S YOUR BIG BROTHER.
IT'S JUST GROSS!
I'M PUTTING A STOP TO IT!
I AM SO STOPPING IT!!
AH, SIBLINGS.

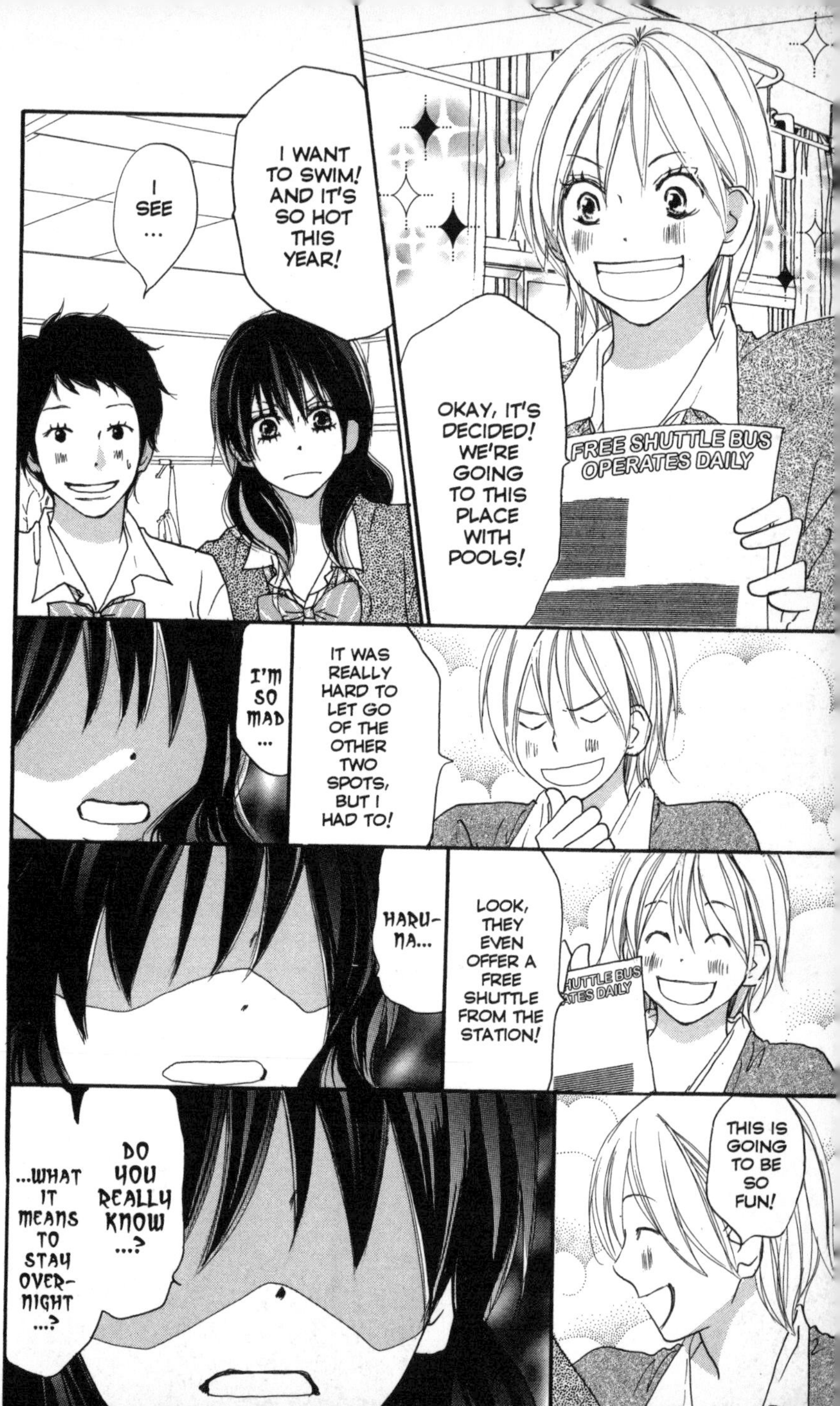
OKAY, IT'S DECIDED! WE'RE GOING TO THIS PLACE WITH POOLS!
FREE SHUTTLE BUS OPERATES DAILY
I WANT TO SWIM! AND IT'S SO HOT THIS YEAR!
I SEE...
IT WAS REALLY HARD TO LET GO OF THE OTHER TWO SPOTS, BUT I HAD TO!
I'M SO MAD...
LOOK, THEY EVEN OFFER A FREE SHUTTLE FROM THE STATION!
HARUNA...
THIS IS GOING TO BE SO FUN!
DO YOU REALLY KNOW...?
...WHAT IT MEANS TO STAY OVERNIGHT...?

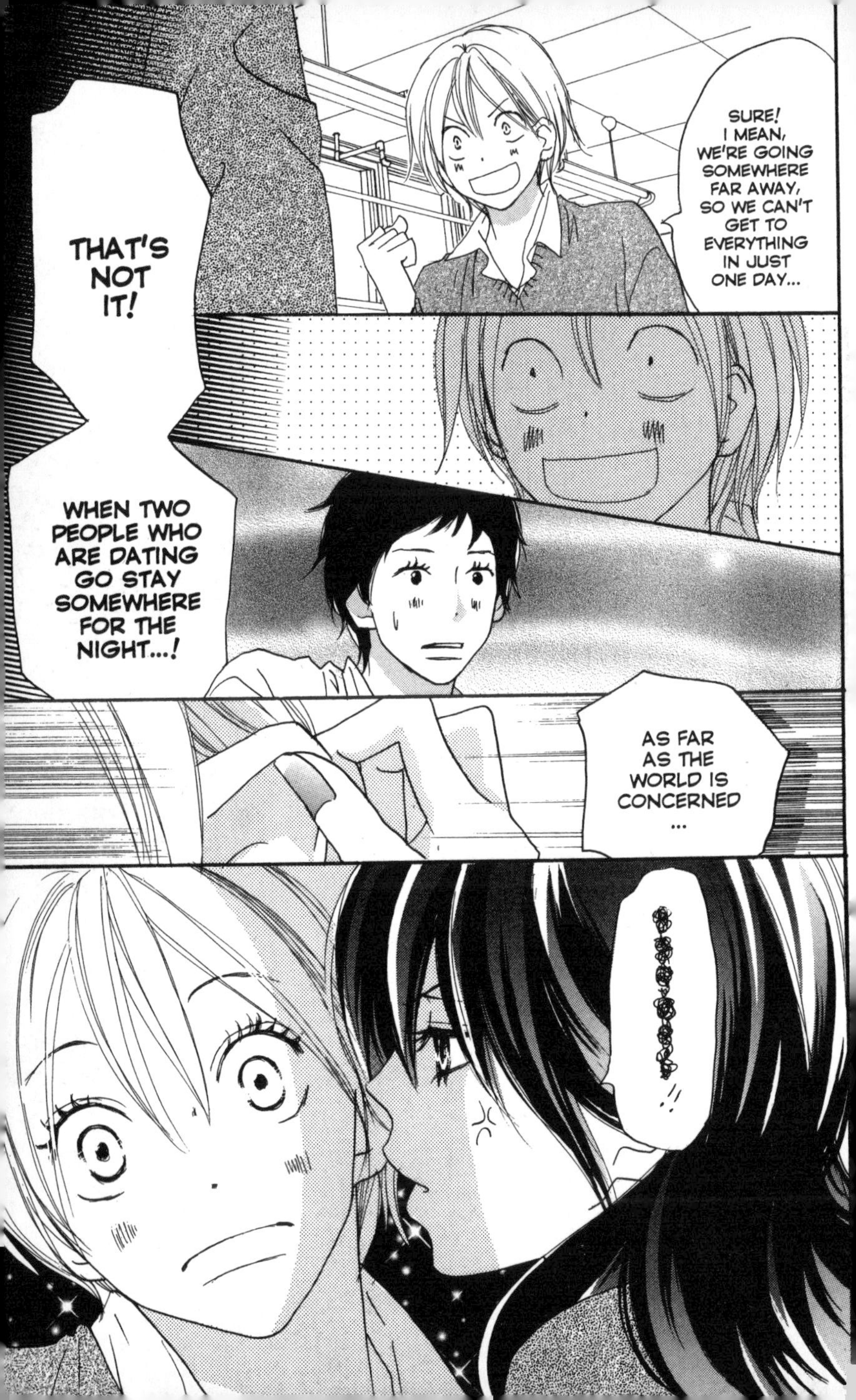
SURE! I MEAN, WE'RE GOING SOMEWHERE FAR AWAY, SO WE CAN'T GET TO EVERYTHING IN JUST ONE DAY...
THAT'S NOT IT!
WHEN TWO PEOPLE WHO ARE DATING GO STAY SOMEWHERE FOR THE NIGHT...!
AS FAR AS THE WORLD IS CONCERNED ...

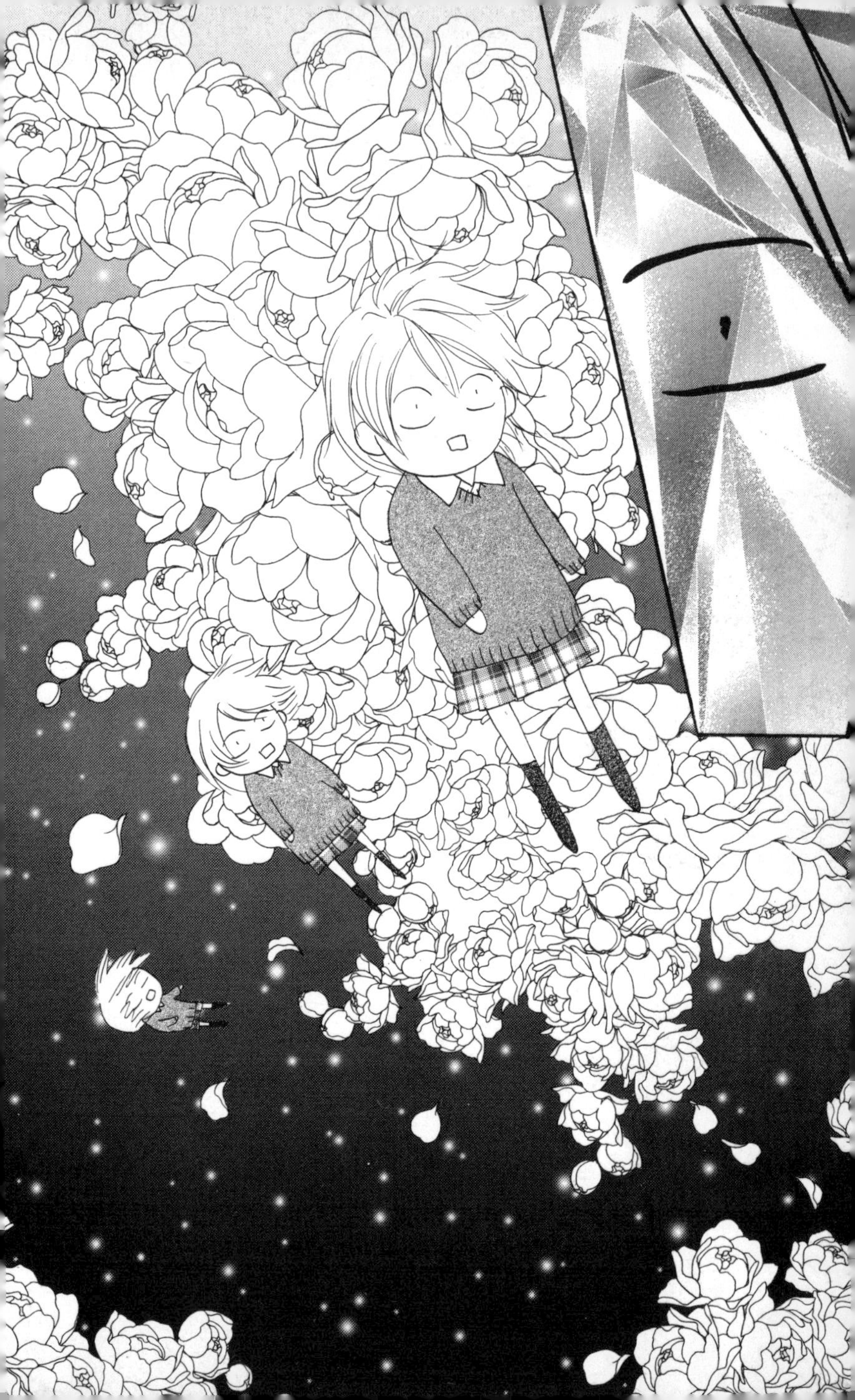

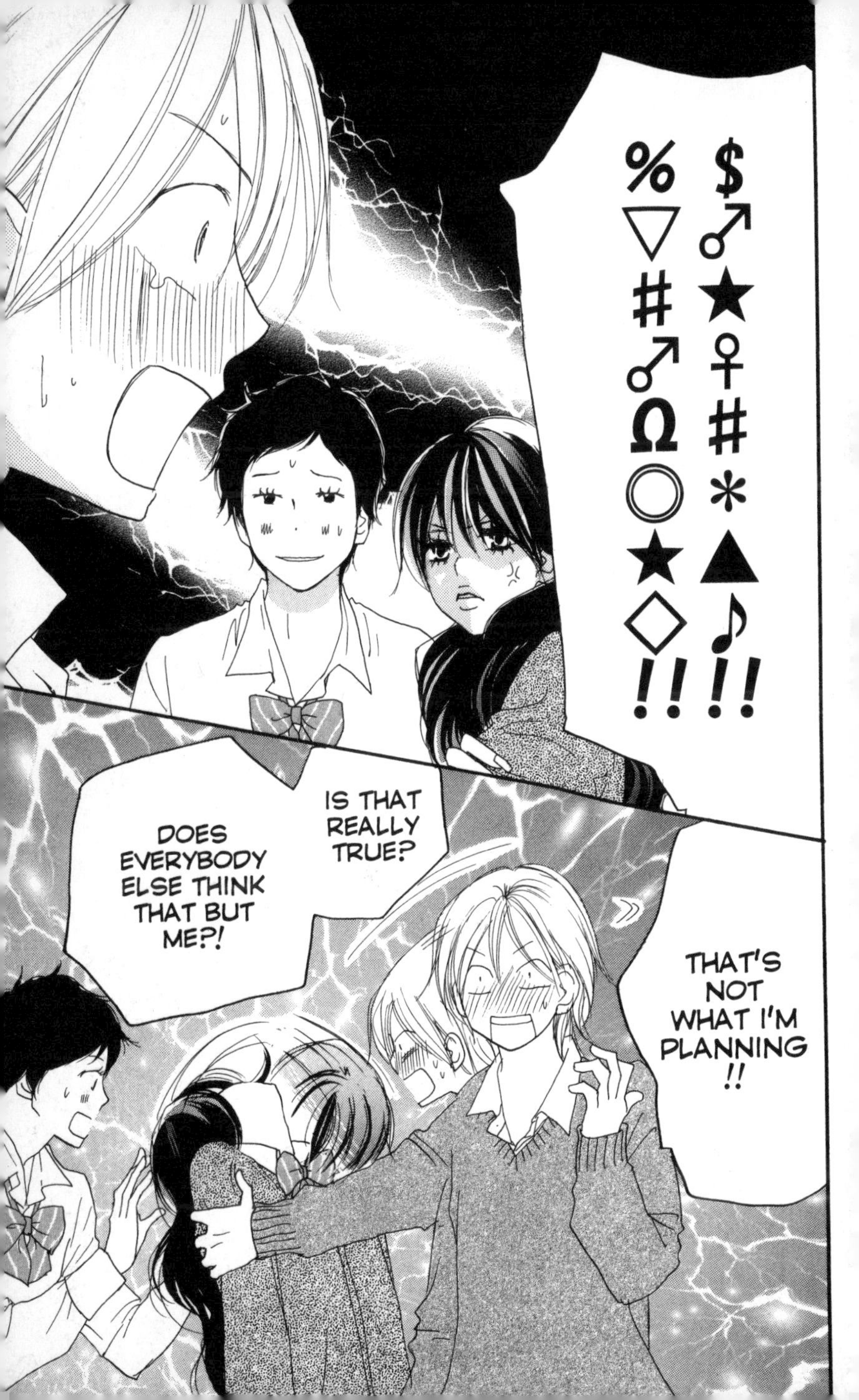
%$▽♂#★♂♀Ω#◎*★▲◇♪!!!!
THAT'S NOT WHAT I'M PLANNING!!
IS THAT REALLY TRUE?
DOES EVERYBODY ELSE THINK THAT BUT ME?!

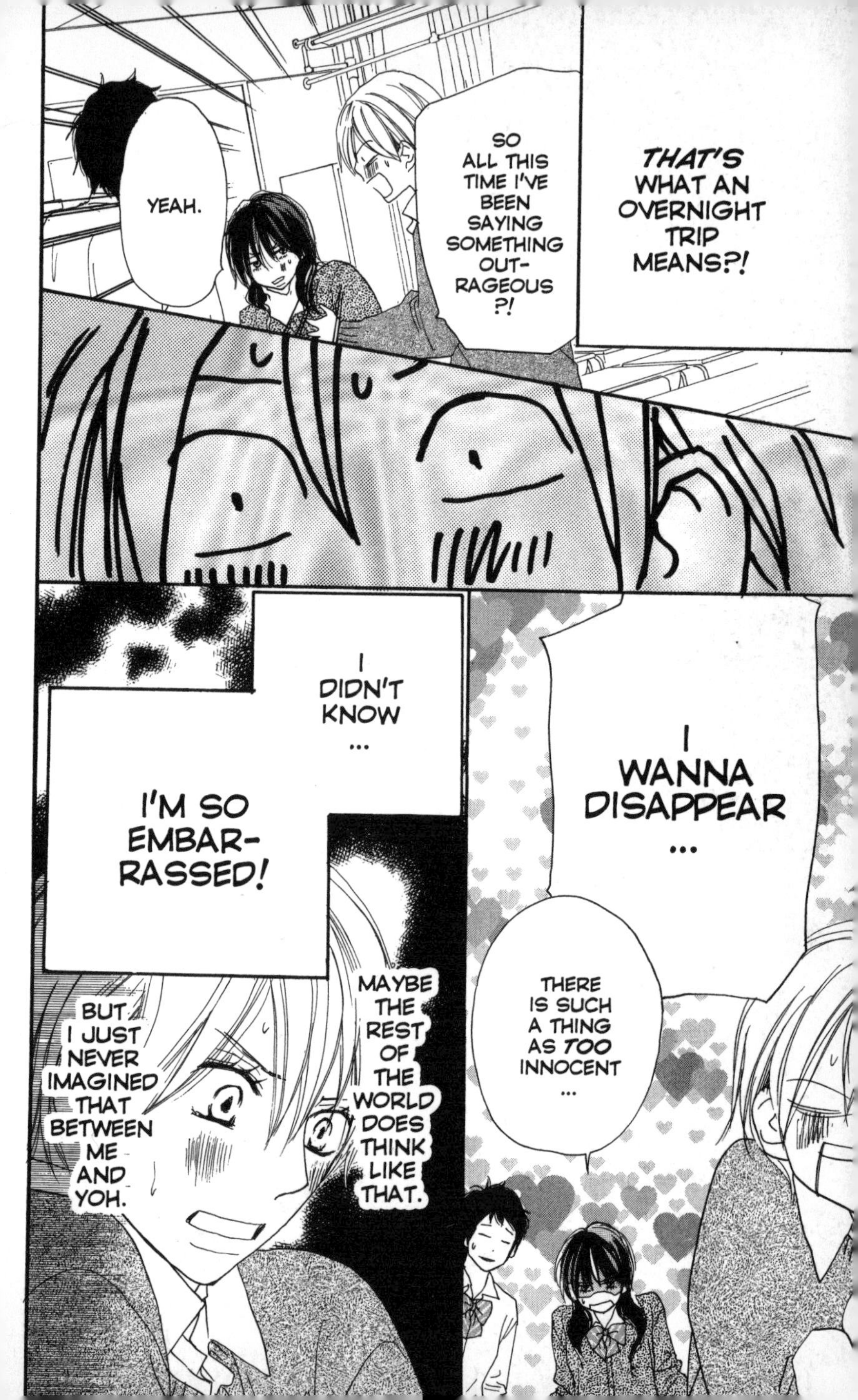
THAT'S WHAT AN OVERNIGHT TRIP MEANS?!
SO ALL THIS TIME I'VE BEEN SAYING SOMETHING OUT-RAGEOUS?!
YEAH.
I WANNA DISAPPEAR...
THERE IS SUCH A THING AS *TOO* INNOCENT...
I DIDN'T KNOW...
I'M SO EMBAR-RASSED!
MAYBE THE REST OF THE WORLD DOES THINK LIKE THAT.
BUT I JUST NEVER IMAGINED THAT BETWEEN ME AND YOH.

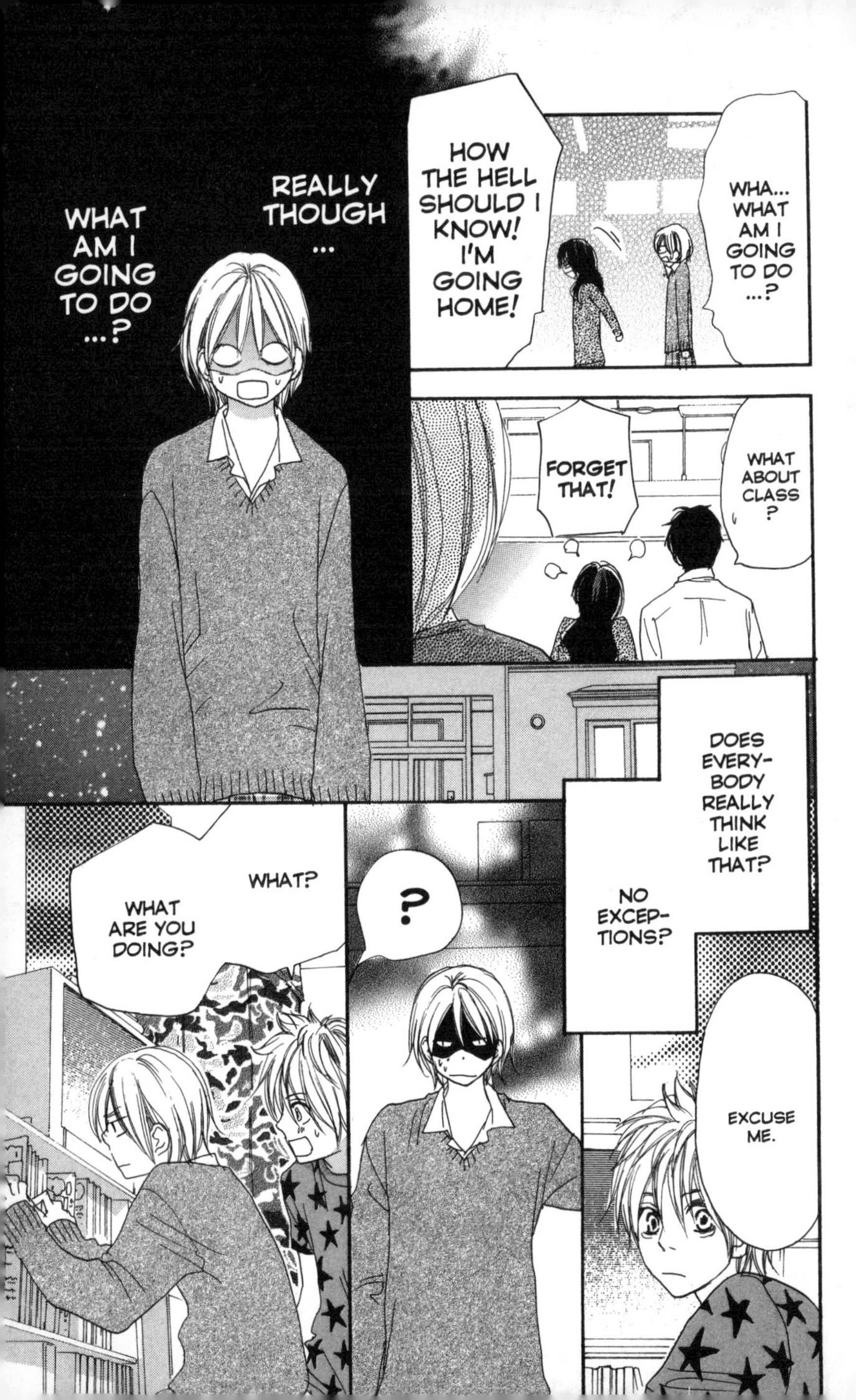
WHA... WHAT AM I GOING TO DO ...?
HOW THE HELL SHOULD I KNOW! I'M GOING HOME!
WHAT ABOUT CLASS?
FORGET THAT!
REALLY THOUGH ...
WHAT AM I GOING TO DO ...?
DOES EVERY-BODY REALLY THINK LIKE THAT?
NO EXCEP-TIONS?
EXCUSE ME.
?
WHAT?
WHAT ARE YOU DOING?

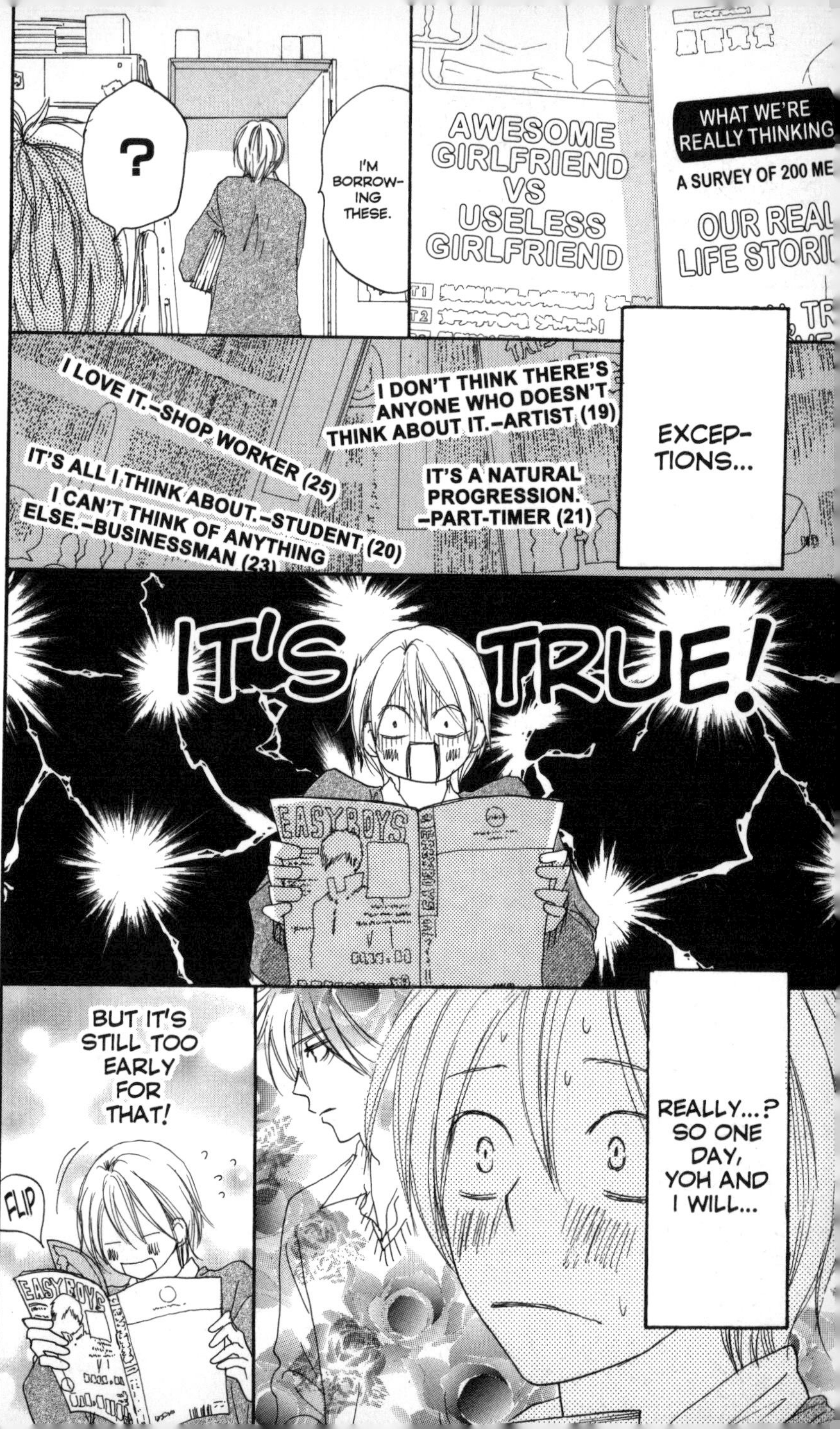
WHAT WE'RE REALLY THINKING
A SURVEY OF 200 ME
OUR REAL LIFE STORI
AWESOME GIRLFRIEND VS USELESS GIRLFRIEND
I'M BORROWING THESE.
?
EXCEPTIONS...
I DON'T THINK THERE'S ANYONE WHO DOESN'T THINK ABOUT IT.–ARTIST (19)
IT'S A NATURAL PROGRESSION. –PART-TIMER (21)
I LOVE IT.–SHOP WORKER (25)
IT'S ALL I THINK ABOUT.–STUDENT (20)
I CAN'T THINK OF ANYTHING ELSE.–BUSINESSMAN (23)
IT'S TRUE!
EASYBOYS
REALLY...? SO ONE DAY, YOH AND I WILL...
BUT IT'S STILL TOO EARLY FOR THAT!
FLIP
EASYBOYS

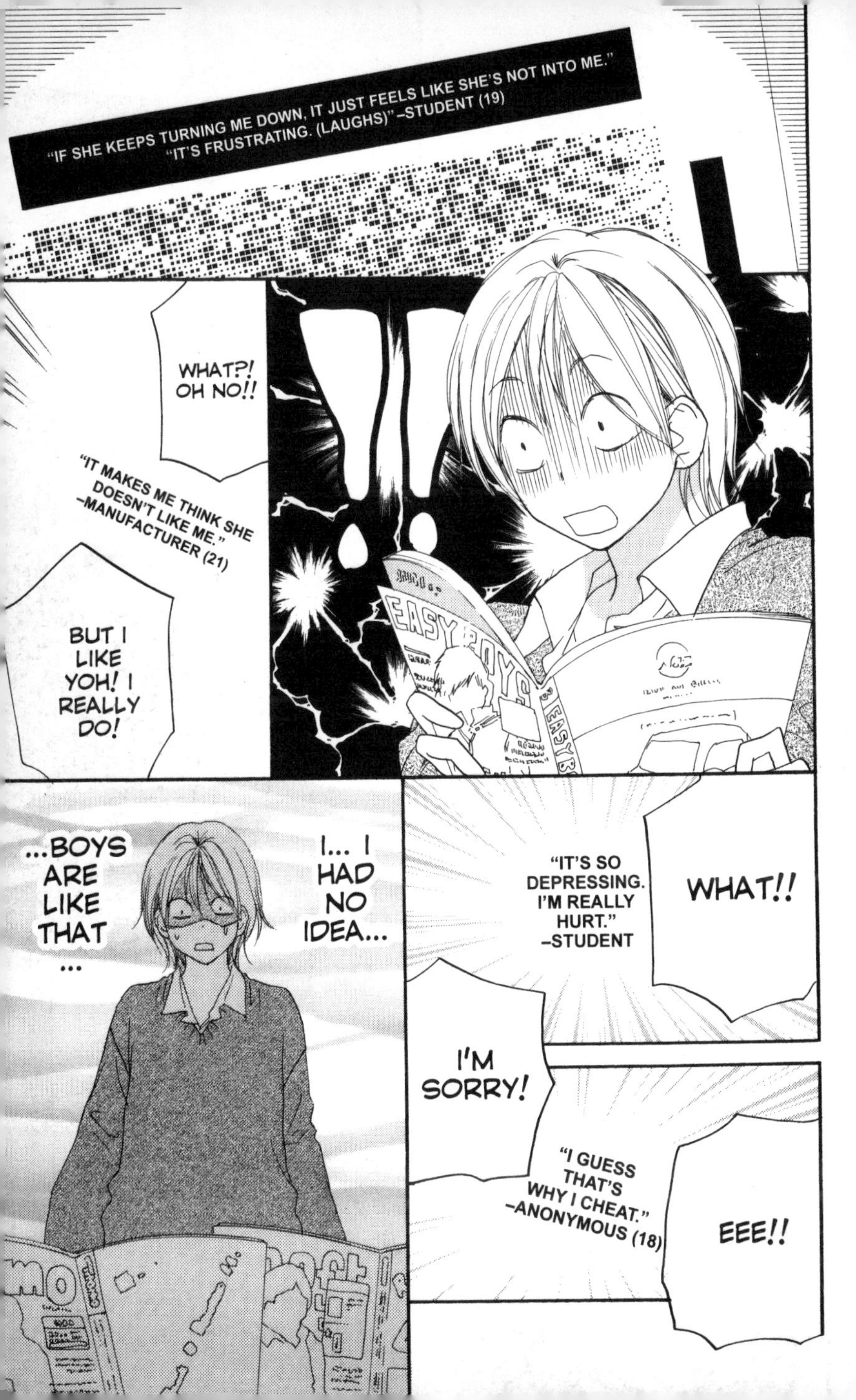

"IF SHE KEEPS TURNING ME DOWN, IT JUST FEELS LIKE SHE'S NOT INTO ME." "IT'S FRUSTRATING. (LAUGHS)" –STUDENT (19)
WHAT?! OH NO!!
"IT MAKES ME THINK SHE DOESN'T LIKE ME." –MANUFACTURER (21)
BUT I LIKE YOH! I REALLY DO!
EASY BOYS
WHAT!!
"IT'S SO DEPRESSING. I'M REALLY HURT." –STUDENT
I'M SORRY!
"I GUESS THAT'S WHY I CHEAT." –ANONYMOUS (18)
EEE!!
I... I HAD NO IDEA...
...BOYS ARE LIKE THAT...

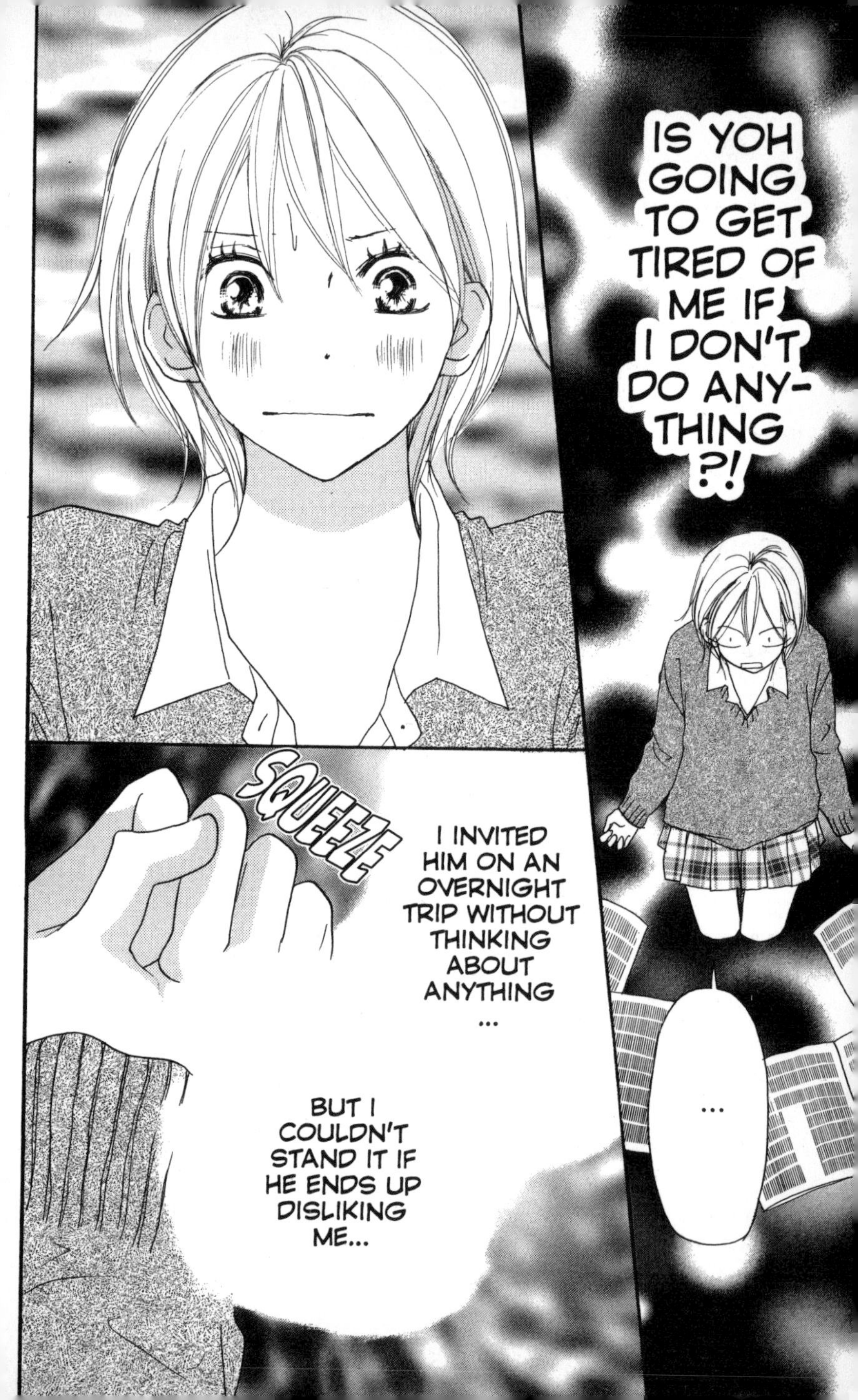
IS YOH GOING TO GET TIRED OF ME IF I DON'T DO ANYTHING ?!
...
SQUEEZE
I INVITED HIM ON AN OVERNIGHT TRIP WITHOUT THINKING ABOUT ANYTHING ...
BUT I COULDN'T STAND IT IF HE ENDS UP DISLIKING ME...

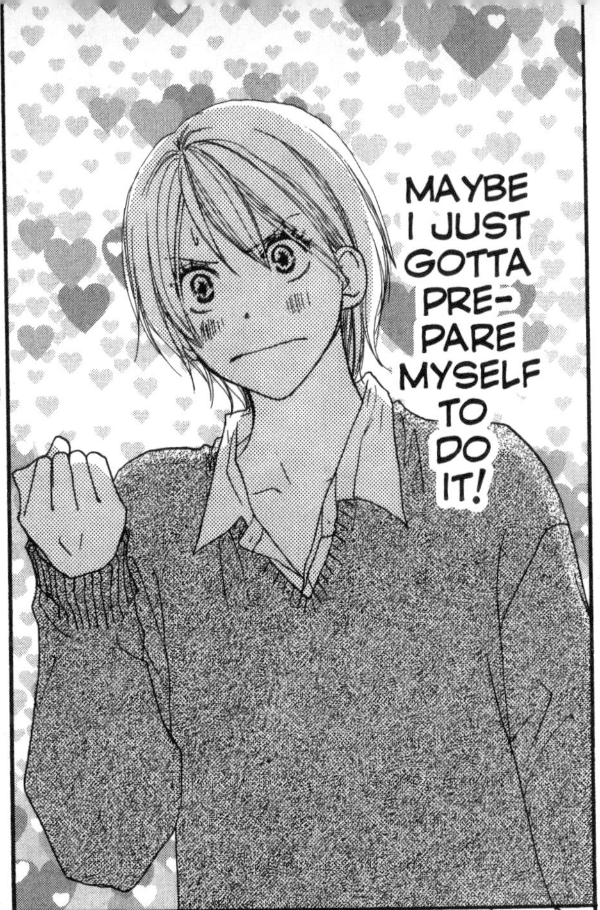
MAYBE I JUST GOTTA PRE-PARE MYSELF TO DO IT!

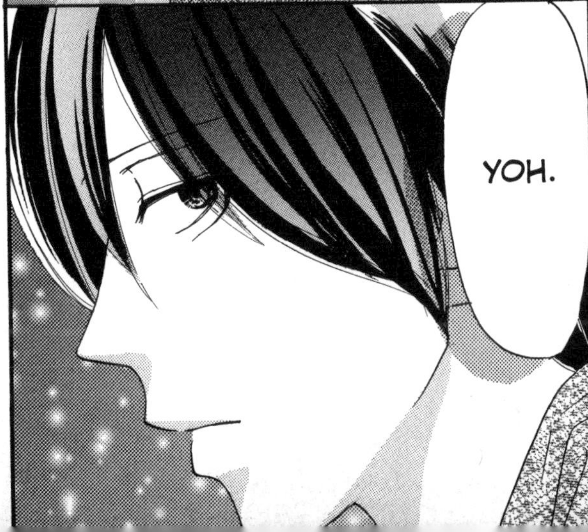
YOH.

3

This note is food-related again and actually involves English too.

I went to a burger joint and ordered orange juice, but what I got was cola. I mean... the whole reason I'm learning English is so this sort of thing doesn't happen! I can't really handle fizzy drinks...

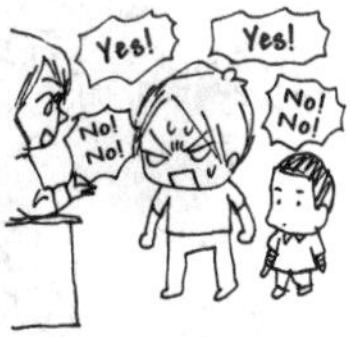
Yes!
Yes!
No! No!
No! No!

I'm getting better at listening, but I'm just answering with "yes" and "no" at the moment.

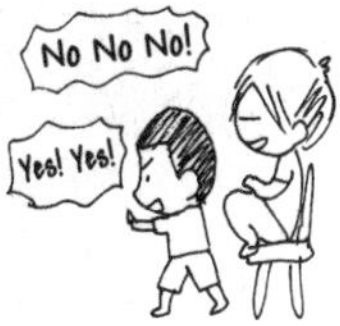
No No No!
Yes! Yes!

Anyway, that's how my son learned to say "yes" and "no" in English. Or maybe those are the only words he knows how to even say...

Hahaha...
I'm trying.
↑
Not very convincing, huh.

I'm trying!!

Well, in the next volume...
See you again ♡
↑
Did I get it right?

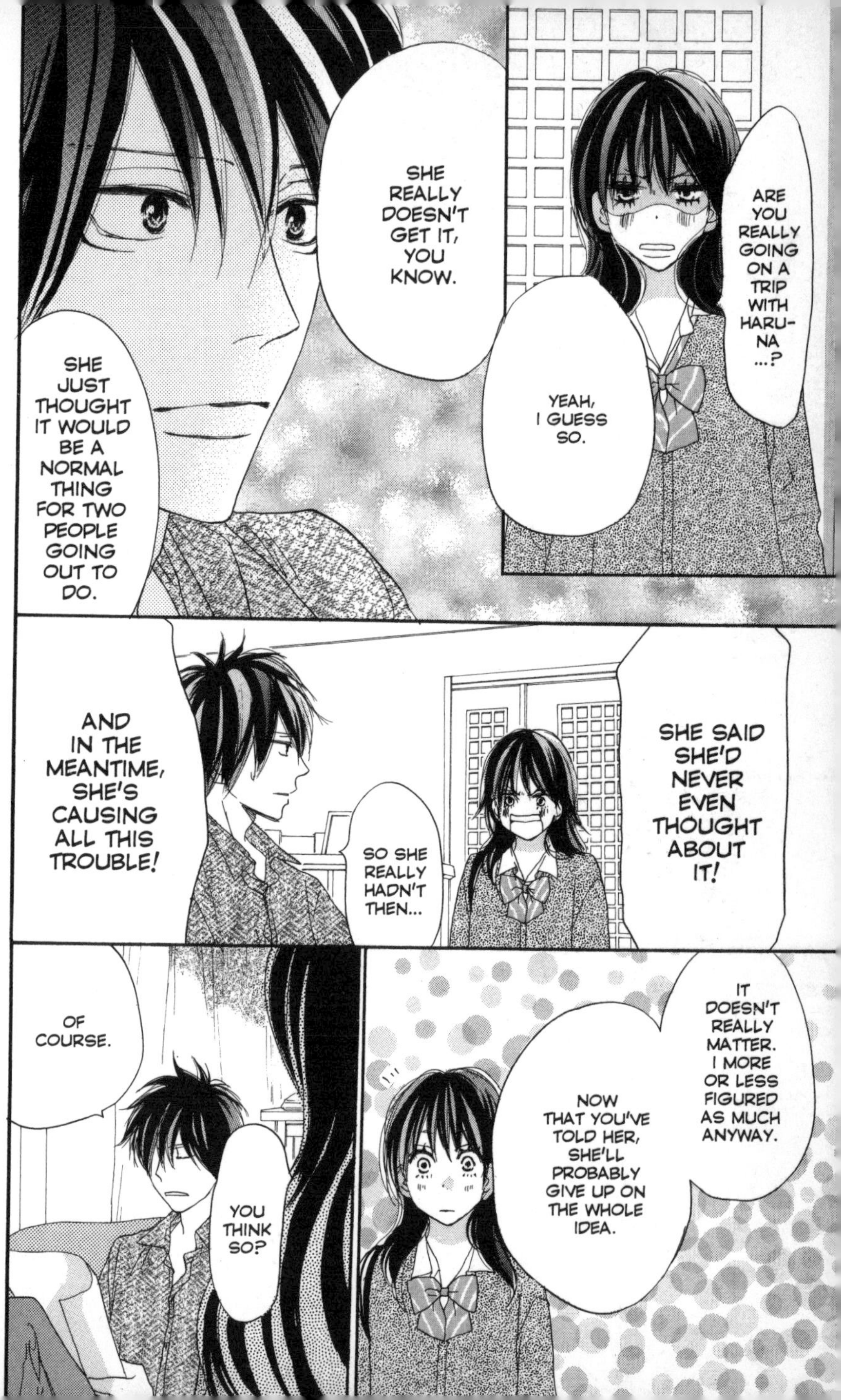
ARE YOU REALLY GOING ON A TRIP WITH HARU-NA...?
YEAH, I GUESS SO.
SHE REALLY DOESN'T GET IT, YOU KNOW.
SHE JUST THOUGHT IT WOULD BE A NORMAL THING FOR TWO PEOPLE GOING OUT TO DO.
SHE SAID SHE'D NEVER EVEN THOUGHT ABOUT IT!
SO SHE REALLY HADN'T THEN...
AND IN THE MEANTIME, SHE'S CAUSING ALL THIS TROUBLE!
IT DOESN'T REALLY MATTER. I MORE OR LESS FIGURED AS MUCH ANYWAY.
NOW THAT YOU'VE TOLD HER, SHE'LL PROBABLY GIVE UP ON THE WHOLE IDEA.
YOU THINK SO?
OF COURSE.

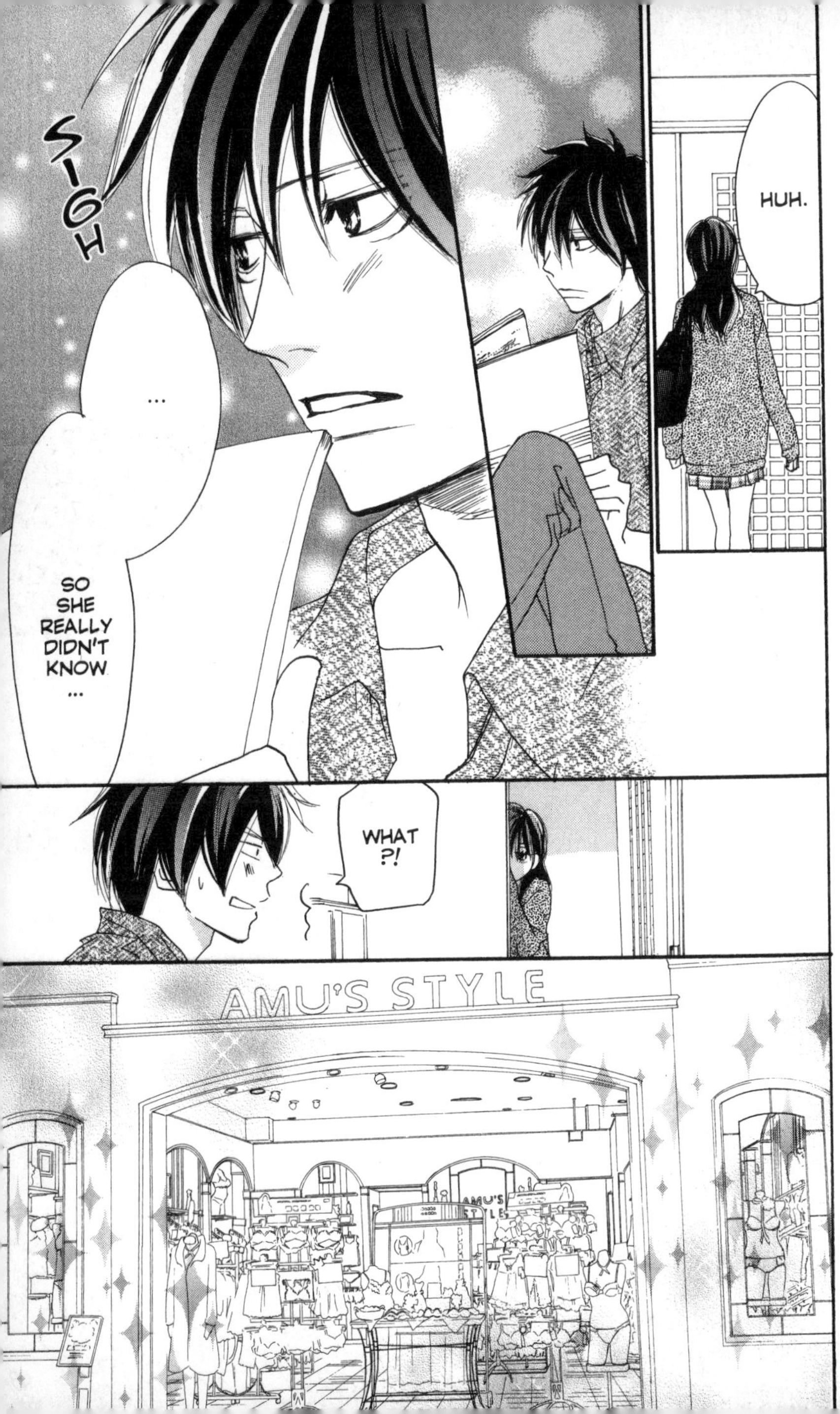

HUH.
SIGH
...
SO SHE REALLY DIDN'T KNOW...
WHAT?!
AMU'S STYLE

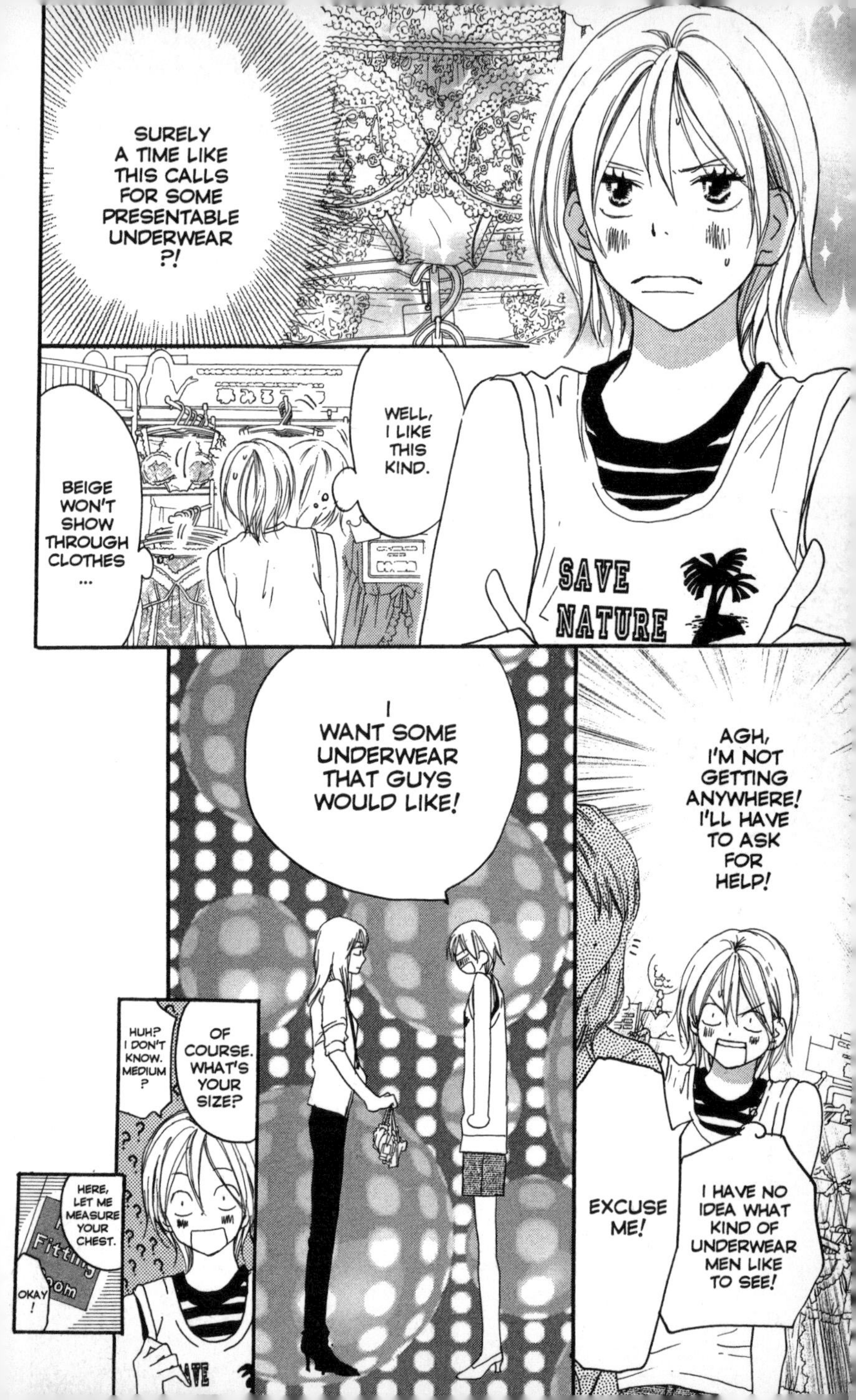
SAVE NATURE
SURELY A TIME LIKE THIS CALLS FOR SOME PRESENTABLE UNDERWEAR ?!
WELL, I LIKE THIS KIND.
BEIGE WON'T SHOW THROUGH CLOTHES ...
AGH, I'M NOT GETTING ANYWHERE! I'LL HAVE TO ASK FOR HELP!
I HAVE NO IDEA WHAT KIND OF UNDERWEAR MEN LIKE TO SEE!
EXCUSE ME!
I WANT SOME UNDERWEAR THAT GUYS WOULD LIKE!
OF COURSE. WHAT'S YOUR SIZE?
HUH? I DON'T KNOW. MEDIUM ?
HERE, LET ME MEASURE YOUR CHEST.
OKAY !

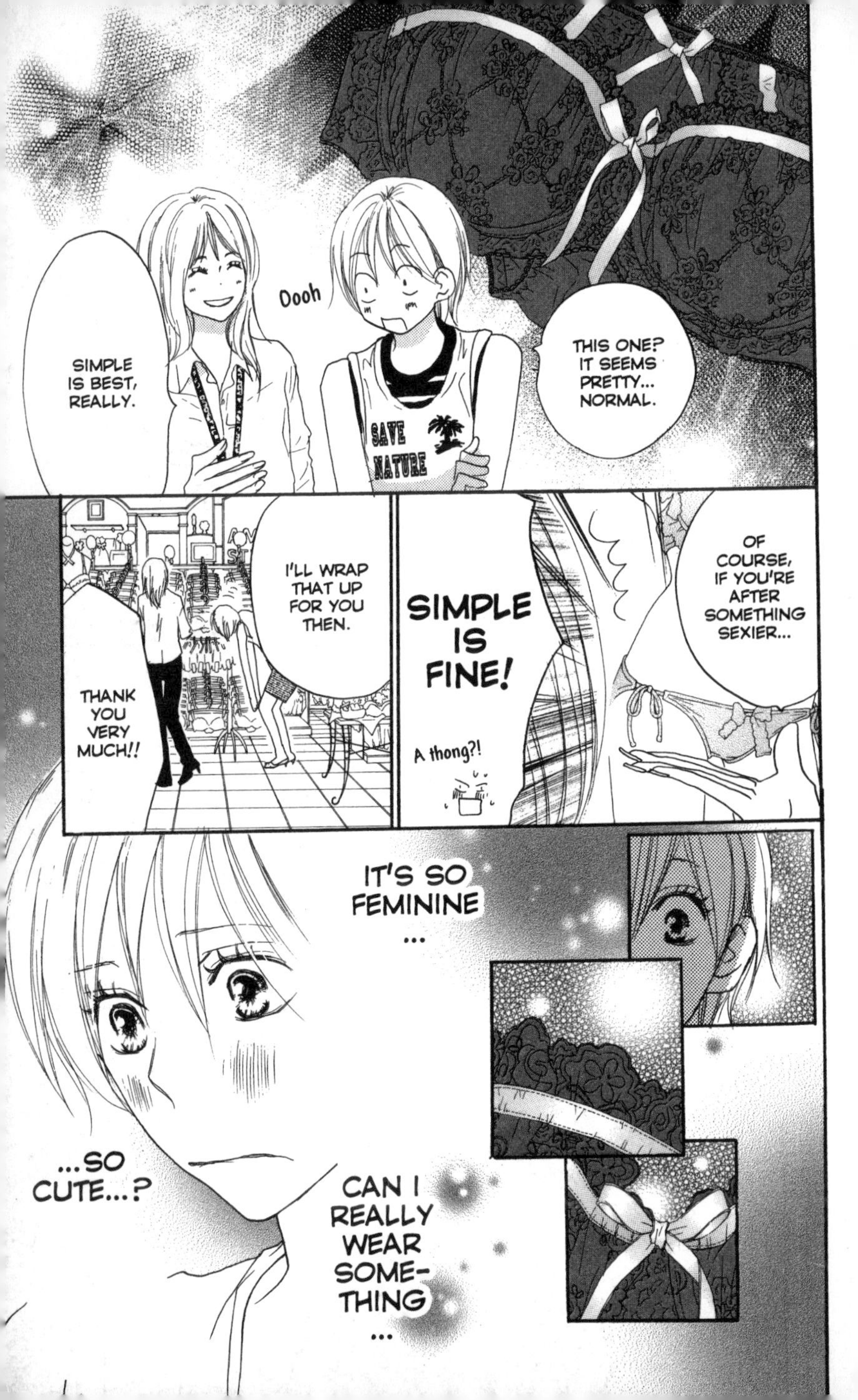
THIS ONE? IT SEEMS PRETTY... NORMAL.
Oooh
SAVE NATURE
SIMPLE IS BEST, REALLY.
OF COURSE, IF YOU'RE AFTER SOMETHING SEXIER...
A thong?!
SIMPLE IS FINE!
I'LL WRAP THAT UP FOR YOU THEN.
THANK YOU VERY MUCH!!
IT'S SO FEMININE ...
CAN I REALLY WEAR SOME-THING ...
...SO CUTE...?

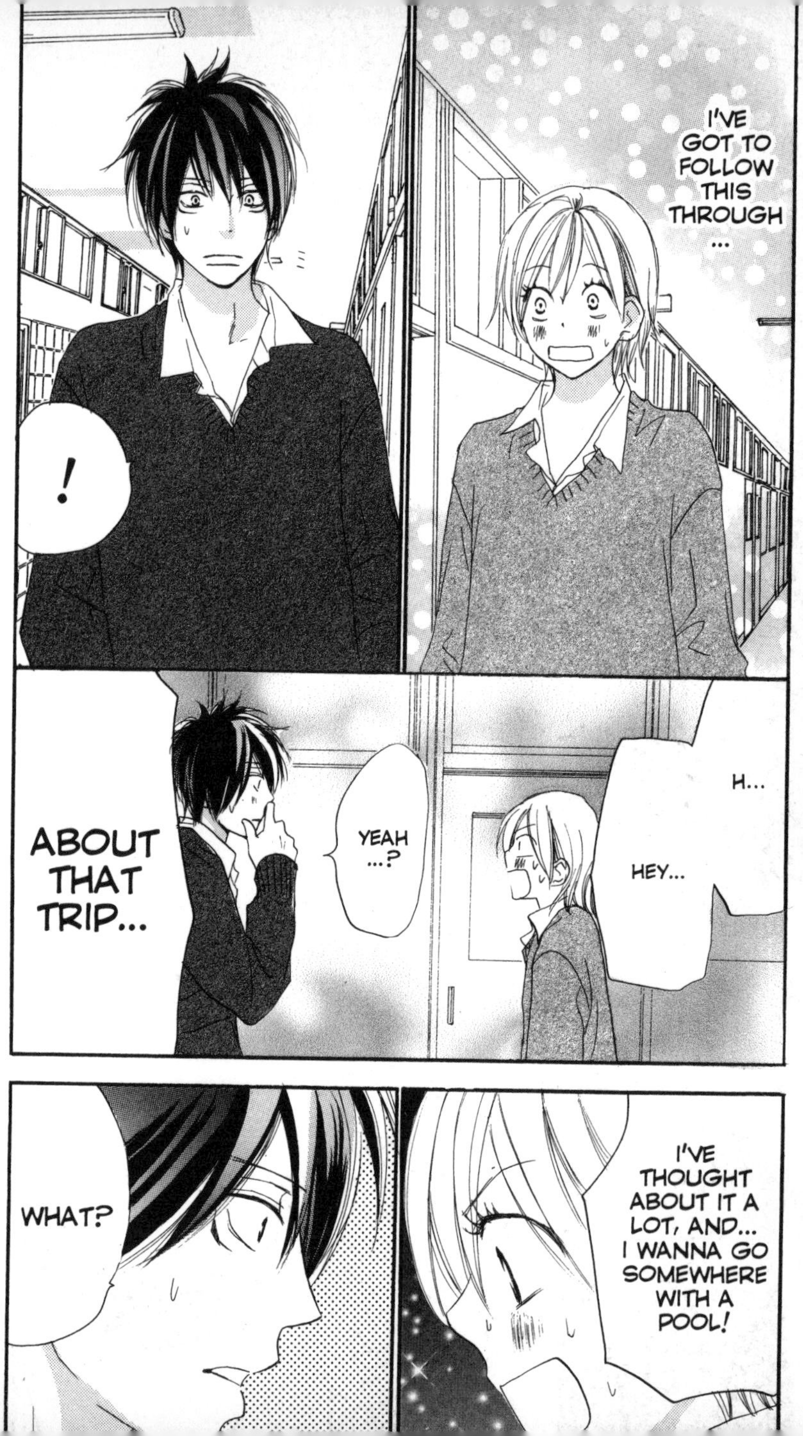
I'VE GOT TO FOLLOW THIS THROUGH...
!
H...
HEY...
YEAH ...?
ABOUT THAT TRIP...
I'VE THOUGHT ABOUT IT A LOT, AND... I WANNA GO SOMEWHERE WITH A POOL!
WHAT?

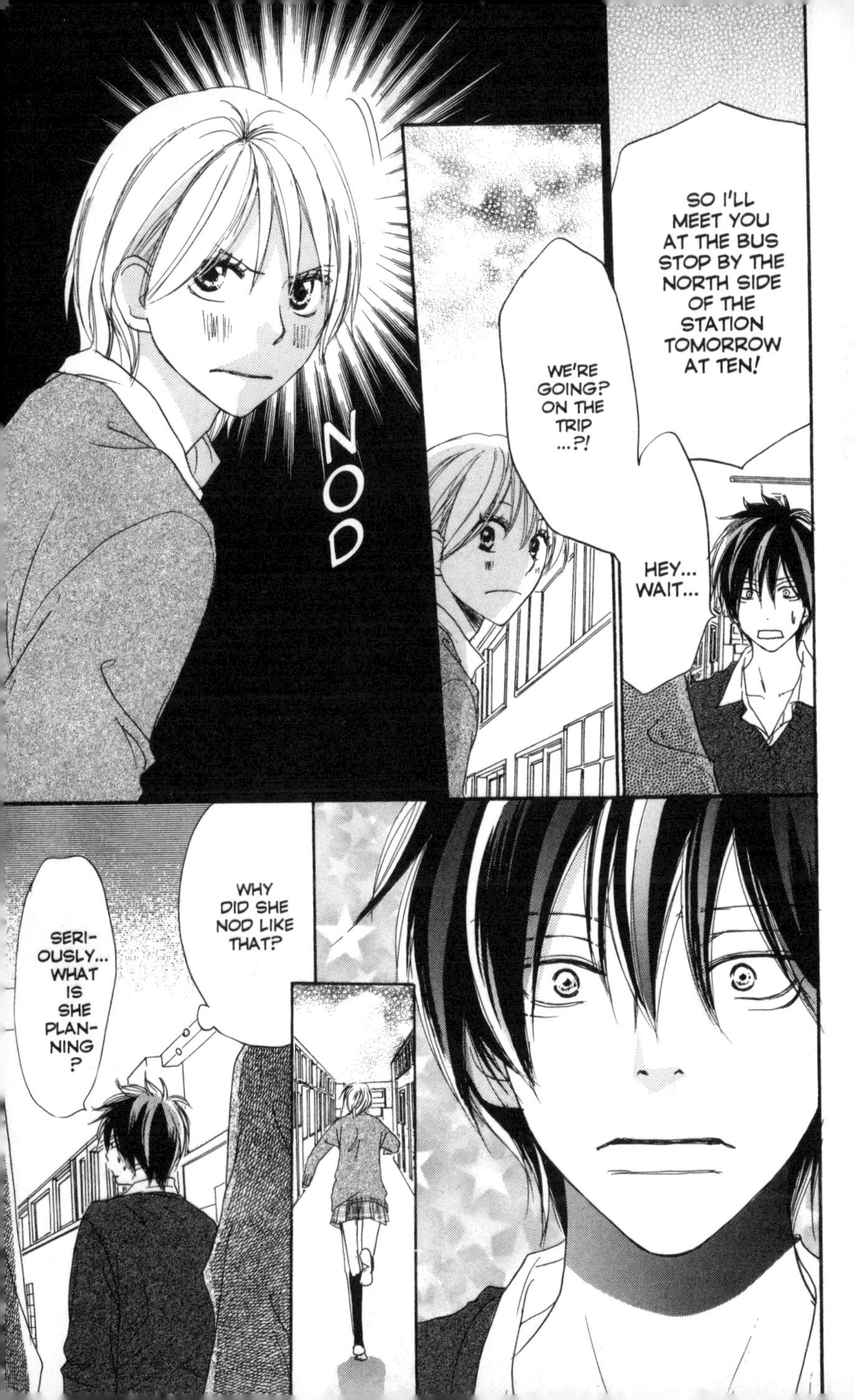
SO I'LL MEET YOU AT THE BUS STOP BY THE NORTH SIDE OF THE STATION TOMORROW AT TEN!
WE'RE GOING? ON THE TRIP ...?!
HEY... WAIT...
NOD
WHY DID SHE NOD LIKE THAT?
SERI-OUSLY... WHAT IS SHE PLAN-NING?

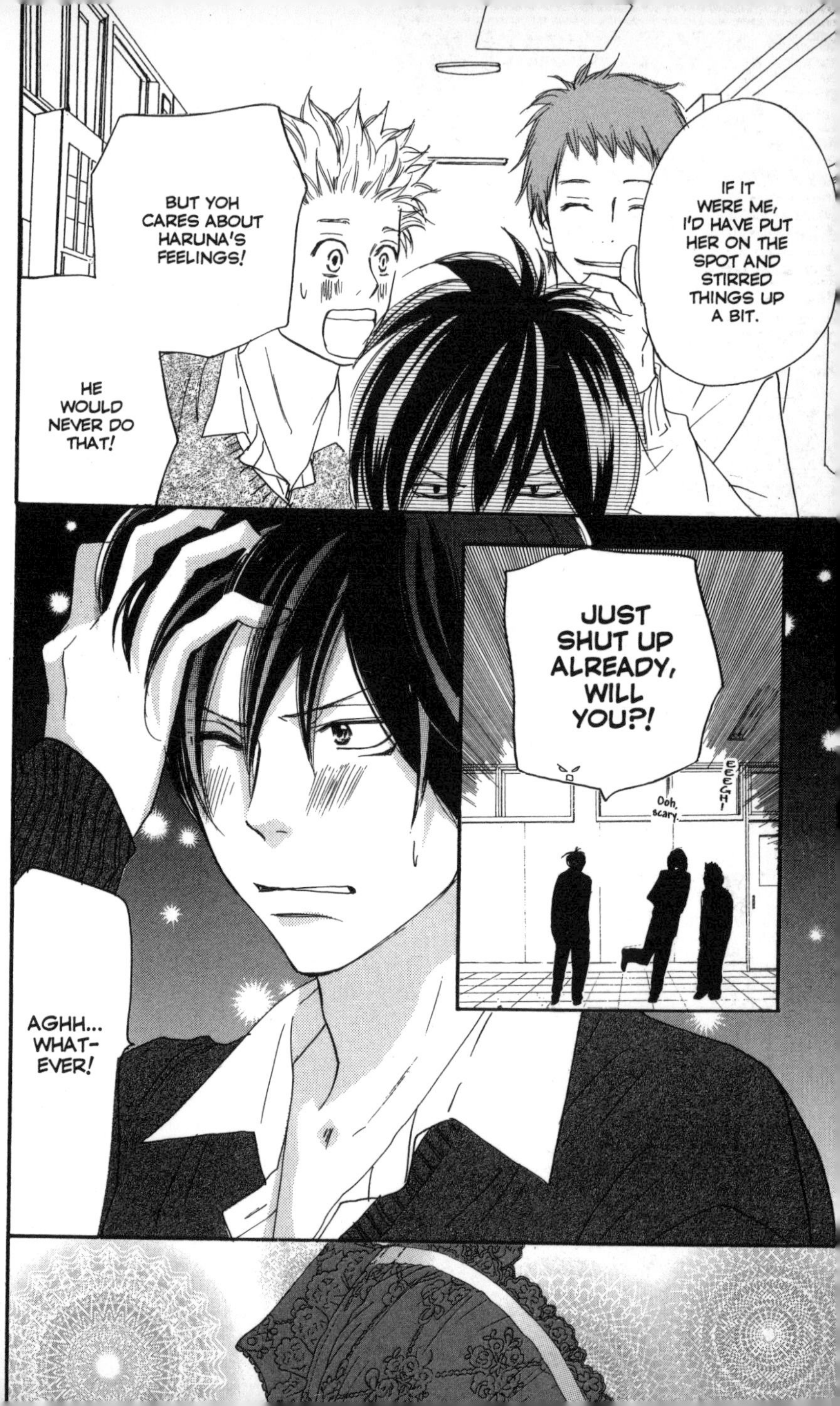
IF IT WERE ME, I'D HAVE PUT HER ON THE SPOT AND STIRRED THINGS UP A BIT.
BUT YOH CARES ABOUT HARUNA'S FEELINGS!
HE WOULD NEVER DO THAT!
JUST SHUT UP ALREADY, WILL YOU?!
EEEGH!
Ooh, scary.
AGHH... WHAT-EVER!

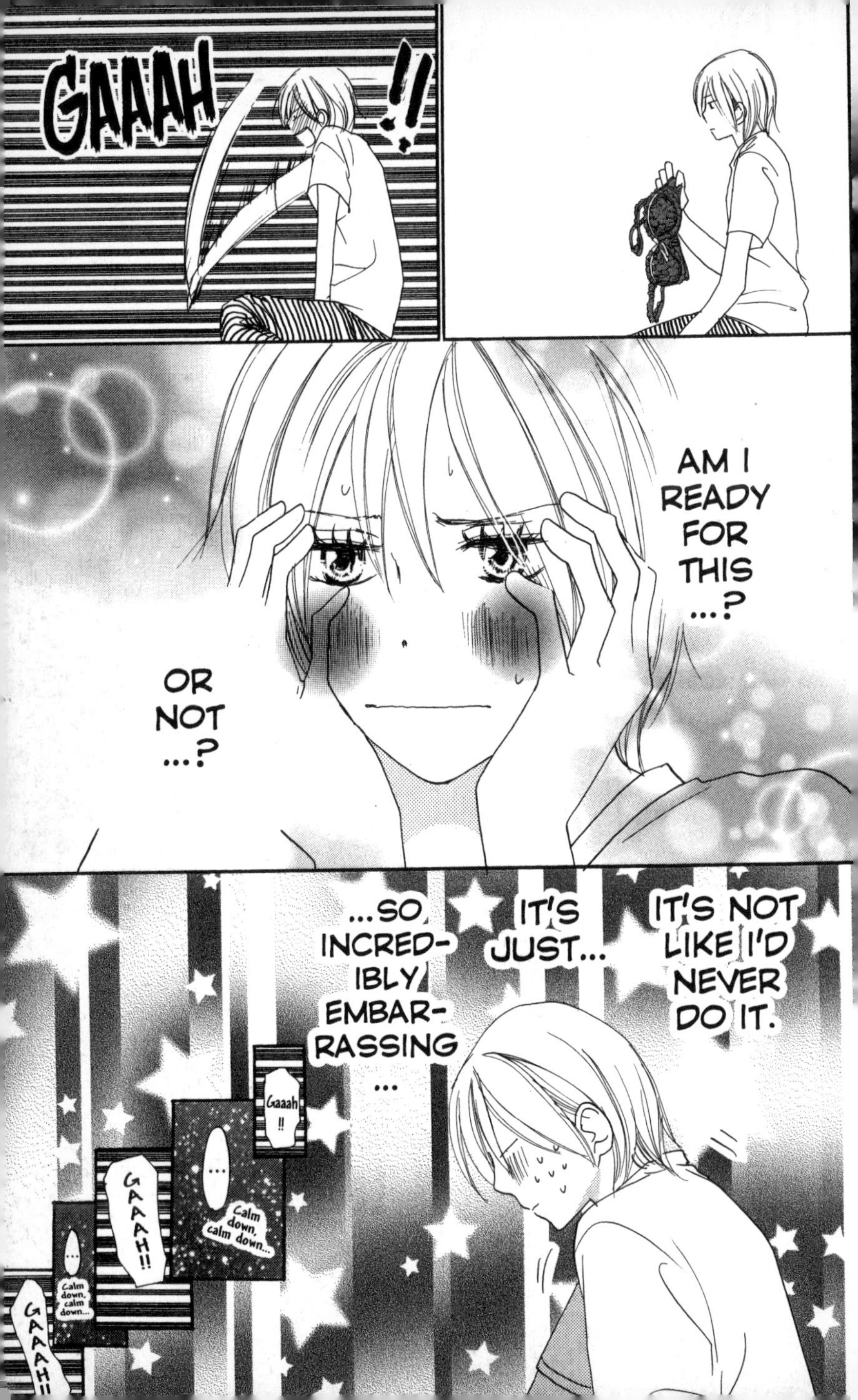
GAAAH!!
AM I READY FOR THIS...?
OR NOT...?
IT'S NOT LIKE I'D NEVER DO IT.
IT'S JUST...
...SO INCREDIBLY EMBARRASSING...
Gaaah!!
...
Calm down, calm down...
GAAAH!!
...
Calm down, calm down...
GAAAH!!

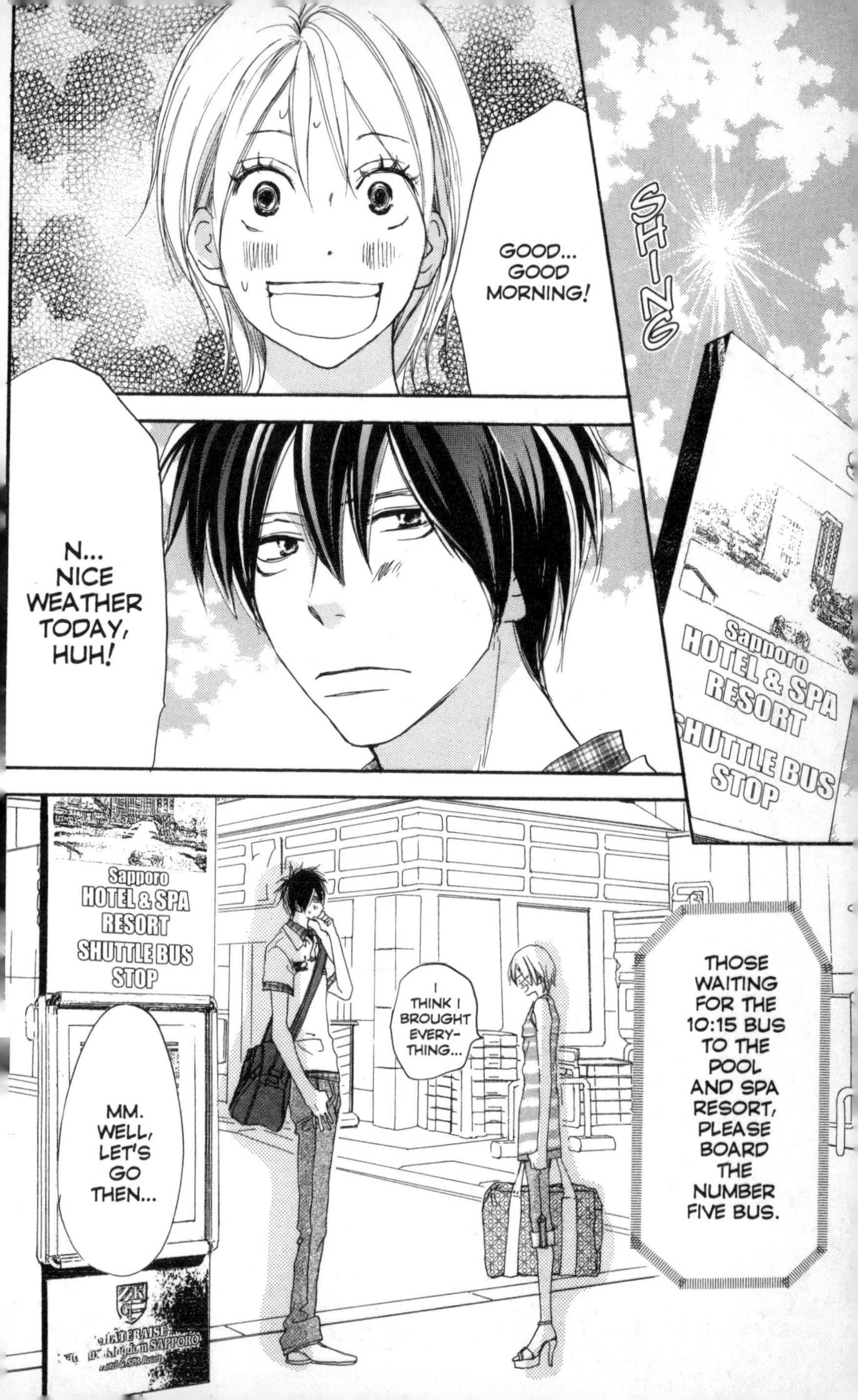
SHING
Sapporo HOTEL & SPA RESORT SHUTTLE BUS STOP
GOOD... GOOD MORNING!
N... NICE WEATHER TODAY, HUH!
THOSE WAITING FOR THE 10:15 BUS TO THE POOL AND SPA RESORT, PLEASE BOARD THE NUMBER FIVE BUS.
I THINK I BROUGHT EVERY-THING...
MM. WELL, LET'S GO THEN...
Sapporo HOTEL & SPA RESORT SHUTTLE BUS STOP

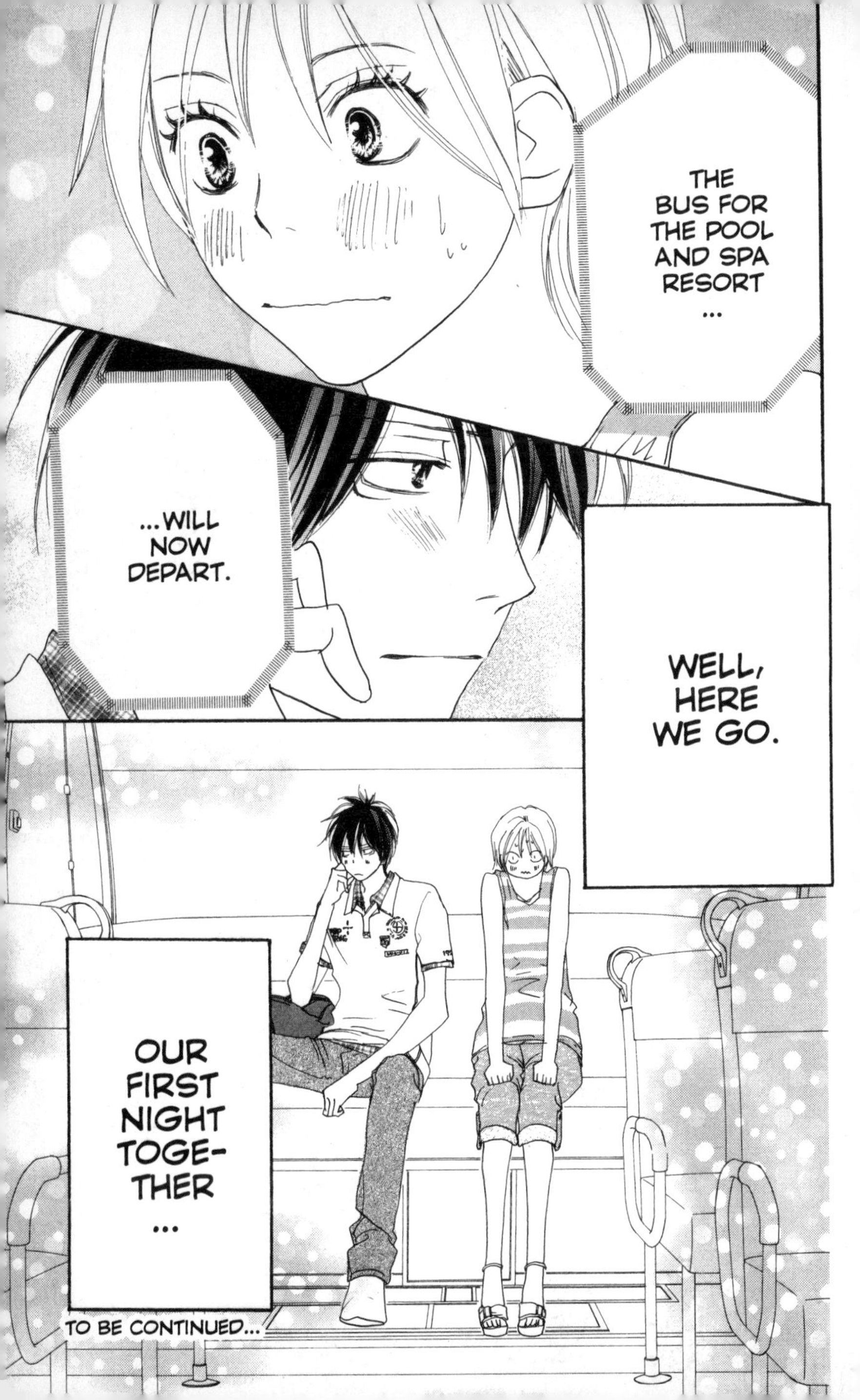
THE BUS FOR THE POOL AND SPA RESORT ...
...WILL NOW DEPART.
WELL, HERE WE GO.
OUR FIRST NIGHT TOGE-THER ...
TO BE CONTINUED...

I got a new computer, and it's so fast! I used to always carelessly press keys by accident, and it'd take ages to reboot. While I waited for it to reboot, I got so depressed... But now even when I mess up, I don't get depressed for long since my computer reboots quicker. I'm so happy that both my computer and I reboot faster!

– Kazune Kawahara

Kazune Kawahara is from Hokkaido Prefecture and was born on March 11th (a Pisces!). She made her manga debut at age 18 with *Kare no Ichiban Sukina Hito* (His Most Favorite Person). Her other works include *Sensei!*, serialized in *Bessatsu Margaret* magazine. Her hobby is interior redecorating.

HIGH SCHOOL DEBUT
VOL. 11
The Shojo Beat Manga Edition

STORY & ART BY
KAZUNE KAWAHARA

Translation & Adaptation/Gemma Collinge
Touch-up Art & Lettering/Rina Mapa
Cover Design/Courtney Utt
Interior Design/Amy Martin
Editor/Amy Yu

VP, Production/Alvin Lu
VP, Publishing Licensing/Rika Inouye
VP, Sales & Product Marketing/Gonzalo Ferreyra
VP, Creative/Linda Espinosa
Publisher/Hyoe Narita

Printed in the U.S.A.

Published by VIZ Media, LLC
P.O. Box 77010
San Francisco, CA 94107

Shojo Beat Manga Edition
10 9 8 7 6 5 4 3 2 1
First printing, September 2009

www.viz.com store.viz.com

Story and Art by Miki Aihara | Creator of *Honey Hunt* and *Tokyo Boys & Girls*

Three volumes of the original manga combined into a larger format with an exclusive cover design and bonus content

Full-length novel with an alternate ending and a bonus manga episode

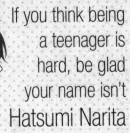

Hot Gimmick

If you think being a teenager is hard, be glad your name isn't Hatsumi Narita

With scandals that would make any gossip girl blush and more triangles than you can throw a geometry book at, this girl may never figure out the game of love!